W9-APX-757

EDITED BY THOMAS F. O'DEA
and JANET K. O'DEA

readings
on the
sociology
of religion

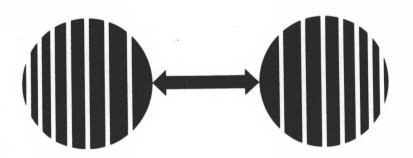

READINGS IN MODERN SOCIOLOGY SERIES

Alex Inkeles, editor

readings
on the
sociology
of religion

prentice-hall international, inc., London

prentice-hall of australia, pty. ltd., Sydney

prentice-hall of canada, ltd., Toronto

prentice-hall of india private limited, New Delhi

prentice-hall of japan, inc., Tokyo

BL60
027

readings
on the
sociology
of religion

Thomas F. O'Dea

Janet K. O'Dea
University of California
Santa Barbara

prentice-hall, inc. / englewood cliffs, new jersey

NOV 2 7 1973

178761

prentice-hall readings in modern sociology series
Alex Inkeles, Editor

© 1973 by
PRENTICE-HALL, INC., Englewood Cliffs, N.J.

All rights reserved. No part of this book may be reproduced in any form or by any means without permission in writing from the publisher.

ISBN: 0–13–761940–5

Library of Congress Catalog Card No.: 72–8593

Printed in the United States of America

10   9   8   7   6   5   4   3   2   1

contents

Preface

It is almost a cliché to observe that we live in troubled times, yet to understand the character of our age and the demands it makes upon us both as human beings and as citizens is not easy. No one can escape the limits of time and place; everyone is the product of his age and circumstances. But study and thought do make a difference. By trying to understand the dimensions of our situation, we are able to act more intelligently. Even partial light is better than total darkness.

In the past, religious life has provided men their most profound relationship to a higher ground of existence. In the context of religion they have responded to a reality conceived as in some way supramundane and supraempirical and have developed aims and aspirations that have infused their lives with meaning. Through religion they have found a fundamental sense of direction. An understanding of the character of religion, its historic relation to the struggle of mankind for significant existence, and its peculiar condition in a modern secularized world is fundamental to a comprehension of man's situation in the last quarter of the twentieth century and the opening decades of the twenty-first.

Immanuel Kant, reflecting upon the mystery of human existence and consciousness, asked three questions: What may I believe? What can I hope for? What ought I to do? He suggested that those three questions constituted the central problem of human existence: What is man? For man is a being problematic to himself. Studying religion, we probe suggested answers to these questions; studying the sociology of religion, we seek to comprehend how the concrete conditions of life have been related to such answers —how they affected the answers and were in turn affected by them.

Today American students pursue the academic study of religion not only because of an academic interest in the subject, important as that in itself may be. They are part of the contemporary crisis. They study religious life in its many manifestations as part of their personal search for a deeper authenticity, for an existentially justified sense of direction. The final answer to man's contemporary search, within or without the older religious traditions, cannot be given by social science. Final positions are based on commitments of faith. Yet serious men in all religious traditions have always seen a close and significant relationship between ultimate decisions and realistic and rational learning. Despite their many differences, both Eastern and Western religions have emphasized the role of intelligence in man's religious quest. It can therefore be suggested that the study of the sociology of religion can contribute to the larger interests of modern man. The intelligent conduct of the modern quest does not appear possible without the help of the sociological approach—as one among many—with its particular disciplined perspective and analytic procedure.

Men are conditioned by the concrete circumstances of their existence. Situational conditioning cannot be totally escaped even when men reach out for a relationship to transcendence. Yet men can achieve relative emancipation from such conditioning through understanding. They can consciously and rationally recognize the dimensions of their historical situation and the social forces that impinge upon them. An authentic enlargement of their self-consciousness and self-determination becomes possible. Hence, the study of the sociology of religion should be the concern not only of those interested in pursuing the study of sociology, but also of all who seek to understand the general intellectual, spiritual, and human concerns of our age. The knowledge of the human condition gained through that study can be a genuine though partial contribution to the modern quest of so many students today.

Religion itself is a vast and variegated field. Study of religion would be woefully incomplete did it not include the realistic setting and empirical circumstances that have provided the historical contexts for religious life. The sociology of religion, which is concerned with that circumstantial aspect of the religious life of mankind, is itself a large and growing field. Reflecting the many-sided character of religion as a whole, it also presents a great variety of approaches, methods, and focuses of interest. Although the field is relatively new, a vast array of theoretical, empirical, and interpretive materials already exists. This vastness and variety make it difficult to choose significant sample readings that will give the student an authentic introduction to the field and at the same time be representative of the work that has been done. Confronted by such a task, we had to establish explicit guidelines for selection.

This book is designed to be both a general reader on the sociology of religion and a companion volme to a text, *The Sociology of Religion*, written by Thomas F. O'Dea (Englewood Cliffs, N.J.: Prentice-Hall, Inc., 1966). We decided to follow the general organization of that text, varying it occasionally for proper presentation of the material. Because space is a central consideration in ventures of this kind, we decided not to include readings that are adequately condensed and paraphrased in the text itself, despite our recognition of the undoubted significance as classics in the field of many such works. It was also necessary to exclude other classics either because they were considered difficult to read or because any meaningful excerpt proved too long. Such considerations led us to depart occasionally from the order of the text, choosing some topics and omitting others. The result is a sampling of readings that should not only illustrate the presentation of the text, but also supplement and enlarge its scope.

We enlarged the range of the text in significant respects. Although the text deals mainly with Western religion, we felt that the general significance of the book would be emphasized by the inclusion of material dealing with Eastern religions. Since the relation of Eastern religion to socioeconomic development is particularly crucial today, we have included not only a classical selection by Max Weber on Hinduism and society, but also a contemporary and extremely suggestive selection by Gunnar Myrdal. Because we sought selections that would provide a larger and deeper relevance, while not departing from high scholarly standards, we have included not only the works of classical and contemporary sociologists, but the works of other authors as well when we found that their contributions illuminated essential elements of our presentation. We have devoted a full chapter to secularization, that complex and controversial phenomenon so significant to the social and religious experience of contemporary man. We have also noted the searching and protest of modern American young people, whose confusion and questing reflect our contemporary crisis and bear witness to the continuing presence of the religious element in human consciousness and its strategic centrality to the human predicament.

Part 1

religion
and society:
the functionalist
approach

Some of the earliest and most significant contributions to the sociology of religion were made by functionalists, whose chief concern was to analyze the role of religion within the context of the ongoing social system. They recognized that religion performed a strategic function within a society, shaping the meaning content of the culture and supporting social control and societal integration. They saw that in certain situations men were brought to the edge —and beyond—of human understanding and control. In such situations men reached out toward a transcendent dimension of their experience. In relation to this Beyond they found meaning, solace, and strength. Reaching beyond the empirical here-and-now, they derived the power to live within the difficult contexts of uncertainty, powerlessness, and finitude and to cope with the problems of scarcity inherent in the human condition.

The sociologist can delineate several positive functions in analyzing the relationship of religion to society.[1] First, religion provides support in the face of deprivation, frustration, and disappointment. The ritual framework of religion offers stability and order in a world of flux and disorder. By legitimating accepted norms and values and relating them to a more universal ethic and its transcendent basis, religion can affirm the established social order and contribute to the unity of society. Paradoxically, religion may also threaten social stability by offering a critique of the status quo in light of a transcendent norm. Religious prophecy rests on the freedom and capacity of the individual to judge society according to the demands of—and, indeed, as an agent of—a higher authority; it has often challenged established social structures. Such a challenge may have a negative effect on the society by raising impossible ideals, but it can also provide the basis and incentive for reforms that enable the society to continue under changing conditions and to meet more fully the needs of its members. Moreover, the prophet who arises in the context of an established religion often propounds ethical ideals whose significance extends far beyond his society and time, and thus becomes an influence of more universal significance.

Participation in a religious tradition offers man a way to self-understanding,

---

[1] See Thomas F. O'Dea, *The Sociology of Religion* (Englewood Cliffs, N. J., 1966), p. 14.

self-realization, and self-definition. Religious beliefs and practices provide the individual with roots in the historic past, even as they open for him a relationship to transcendence that involves an orientation toward the future. Both the experience of the Beyond and its expression within ritual and social forms of the religious community may provide the framework within which man can realize significant aspects of his self and come to a mature sense of his identity.

The readings in this section discuss some of the strategic functions of religions. The first selection, from *The Transformations of Man* by Lewis Mumford, is concerned with the basic role of religion in answering man's problem of meaning. Mumford uses a term used by Karl Jaspers, and speaks of an *axial period* between 800 and 200 B.C. during which crucial changes in human consciousness occurred in various parts of the world. New forms of religious consciousness, representing a kind of breakthrough to a new level of human self-awareness, developed in response to both the regimenting effects of the first forms of city life upon the individual and the disruption and disorder that were upsetting many traditional ways of life. The results were new insights into the meaning of man's existence and new communities founded upon those insights. Axial religions are characterized by emphasis upon the inner self and upon the nurture of an inner individuation. Their teachings distinguish between the objective world of the senses, seen as a source of ultimate disillusionment, and the world of the Spirit, which is eternal and true. Toward the Spirit man must orient his life, devoting his energies to self-cultivation in the light of ideals that transcend the here-and-now. Axial religious communities, based upon the experience of inward-turning and the consequent personal transformation, were open to all men who could share in that experience. Mumford's description of these communities and the conceptions upon which they were built is an excellent study of the function of religion in establishing a world view and providing an orientation for men in periods of enlarging human awareness.

Early functionalist thinkers stressed the social character of religion and the practical significance of religion for societal survival. Emile Durkheim held such a view and saw religion as the worship of society itself. He saw the sacred as the social and God as the projection of the greater whole of which man was a part and by which he was nurtured: society and its organizations. While this view was extreme, Durkheim saw accurately the importance of the social role of religion and how society continually legitimated and reinforced the normative structure that was its very core through the beliefs and rites of religion. The latent function of religion, according to Durkheim, is the continual reconstitution and reaffirmation of society. A brief selection from his *Elementary Forms of Religious Life,* in which he analyzed Australian aboriginal religion, is presented in this section.

The selection by Edward Conze, the great Buddhist scholar, demonstrates how religious beliefs can have political utility and how they can be manipulated for political purposes. Buddhist conceptions appealed greatly to monarchs who were interested in sacralizing their authority, expanding their empires, and justifying a hierarchy of social classes. The Conze reading shows both the functional value of religion for social control and its vulnerability to political exploitation.

On the other hand, the capacity of religion to disturb and disrupt the existing order is also evident in numerous historical examples. The great German sociologist Max Weber gave a classical description of the critical function of religion while discussing prophecy in his book *The Sociology of Religion*. We present here a selection from *Ancient Judaism* in which Weber discussed the apostolic prophet, the man who was convinced that he had been commissioned by Yahweh to bring the entire Hebrew nation back to the covenant traditions which they were violating. Weber depicts the social context in which the prophets spoke and the conflicts which their message aroused. It is evident from Weber's study that Hebrew prophecy is a model for the role of religion in opposing social consensus and behavior in the name of a transcendent ideal.

Generally, functionalists have tended to view religion as a collective matter and have emphasized its supportive value for society. However, the individual and the group must not be conceived of as an exaggerated dichotomy in religious or social life. Religious life always involves a give-and-take between the two. In his work *Young Man Luther,* the eminent psychoanalyst Erik H. Erikson shows how intimately the psychological, historical, and religious aspects of human existence are intertwined, through an analysis of the personal identity crisis of a great religious figure. As Erikson states,

Luther, so it seems, at one time was a rather endangered young man, beset with a syndrome of conflicts whose outline we have learned to recognize, and whose components to analyze. He found a spiritual solution, not without the well-timed help of a therapeutically clever superior in the Augustinian order. His solution roughly bridged a political and psychological vacuum which history had created in a significant portion of Western Christendom.

The clear relationship between theological development and psychological maturation in Luther's life offers a striking example of the connections between religion and individual growth.

religion and meaning

one

Axial Man

LEWIS MUMFORD

1

The terms axial period and axial religions have been used by the philosopher, Karl Jaspers, to describe a fact that various observers had intermittently noted during the last century: namely, that in Europe and Asia a profound change of a religious and moral nature took place, more or less within the span of the sixth century B.C. at widely separated points. At that time, the earliest universal religions, Buddhism and Zoroastrianism, came forth, while those that appeared later, Christianity, Mithraism, Manichaeism, Islam, continued the transformations begun then. With this a new kind of person and a new kind of community took form.

The word axial, as I myself used it independently in *The Conduct of Life,* presents a double meaning. It marks, first of all, a real turning point of human history; this change of direction was noted early in the pres-

From pp. 71–89 in *Transformation of Man* by Lewis Mumford. Copyright 1956 by Lewis Mumford. By permission of Harper & Row, Publishers, Inc.

ent century by J. Stuart Glennie. But axial has also another meaning, as in the discipline of axiology: it has to do with values; and one uses it to indicate the profound change in human values and goals that took place after the sixth century. Though this change was a decisive one, I would not separate it as arbitrarily as Jaspers has done from the earlier developments of religion and ethics. If the theological perceptions of Ikhnaton (Akh-enaton) had not been resisted and forcibly overthrown by the old Memphite priesthood, Egypt would probably have produced the first viable axial religion, centered in a naturalistic monotheism, appealing to all men, seven centuries or so before Zoroaster, Buddha, or Confucius.

The individual elements that went into the axial religions had already existed in embryonic forms, sometimes indeed in a well-developed state, in earlier religions. The most fundamental early contribution was the notion that temporal events, touching finite beings, had an eternal significance: that the brief life of man does not end at death, but is continued in another sphere; and that the quality of that longer existence is the subject of an ultimate judgment, which determines whether he who is judged is to participate fully in that afterlife or be deprived of its benefits, perhaps even punished.

That the cosmic forces themselves make for righteousness, that there is some close connection between man's assumed role and processes that lie outside his control, shaping his life for good or bad, were well-established principles in Chaldea and Egypt before even the correlated idea, of a single divine providence, came into existence. Religion's basic premises are the unity and meaningfulness of all life, indeed, of all existence. This reached its ultimate expression in the U-panishads: Brahman and Atman are one. One may interpret this to mean that the outer world and the inner self are in origin identical, or that they become one through a dynamic process of reciprocal creation.

Even before their axial prophets, Amos and Isaiah, had given a wider province to the religion of the Jews, the Israelites had transformed their tribal deity into the single unqualified creator and ruler of the universe: indeed, they had gone farther and attributed to him an existence so different in every dimension from man's that, though intercourse was under certain conditions possible, God remained at best without name or describable attributes: the inscrutable power Moses and Job confronted, whose ways defy reasoned explanation and override human judgment. If we now see in Moses' monotheism a continuation of Ikhnaton's vision, we must call these religions protoaxial, for they were based on similar intuitions and pointed in the same direction.

The axial tendency to picture life itself as a constant battle between the forces of good and evil, between Ahriman and Ormuzd, as the followers of Zoroaster put it, goes back to an earlier dawn of ethical consciousness among the Egyptians. With them, the gods, who at first exacted only obedience, in time imposed honesty and justice, mercy and forbearance, in all human relations; and they applied their own cosmic time scale to all petty human operations, rescuing them from that pettiness. To exercise watchful care, not only in the rituals and sacrifices to the gods, but in one's relations to one's fellows, became a mark of civilized man's waxing religious sense. If he were violent, deceitful, unjust, brutal, reckless of consequences, he would offend the gods no less than if he neglected to pay respect to their image or give offerings to the priesthood.

Even the tendency to cultivate the inner life at the expense of the outer life, and to make a complete separation between the natural and the ideal is far from a novel contribution: that in fact is the whole duty of the priesthood, forever dividing the sacred from the secular. By the time of Isaiah, a new type of person, meek, silent, unassertive—introverted, as we would now say—was beginning to replace the proud energetic hero as an ideal type. In what respects, then, do the axial religions make a radical departure?

2

The central change brought in by axial religion is the redefinition—in fact the recasting—of the human personality. In that act, values that emerge only in the personality replace those that belonged to institutions and institutional roles. The new feelings, emotional attachments, sentiments are now incarnated in a living image, that of the prophet. The life that he lives, the values he expresses, become a visible pattern for other men to follow. The Son of Man is man in his proper person—raised to his highest power—not a supernatural being to fear and obey, but a true man, to love and follow. The godlike images that preaxial man had projected were indeed remote and awful; but when examined more closely, they only magnified human or subhuman dispositions that were all too accessible to the mean sensual man. One might envy the gods their supernatural powers; but men who lived in communities could not imitate the gods without running into trouble: on the human level these qualities expressed paranoia and produced crime.

The axial prophet both remakes the concept of God and remints the human image. The personal takes precedence over the social. In the case of Buddhism, Buddha's original presentation of the cosmic process divested it of all organic images, animal or human. Though his analysis denied the reality of "self," his own self became, ironically, a pattern for his followers to imitate. He could not by rational means do away with the deepest source of his own appeal. Even where, as in most of the other axial religions, God is attached not only to process and power, but to love and fulfillment, the emphasis falls on the great mediator, seemingly almost God himself in human form, who initiates the axial change: a Confucius, a Jesus, a Mahomet, or their successors who, in their own persons, renew the original image through their faithful reincarnation. Was there not some singular power in a Buddha who could create generation upon generation of Buddhists, transforming the idea into flesh? Upon the organic tissue and social skin of man, the axial prophet superimposes a new self, an impalpable envelope, the platonic form of axial man.

What is this new self? In the first place it is a self that is purified, as those conceived in the image of older deities were not, from too close attachment to man's animal nature. The ritual of the baptismal bath, threading through the axial religions, gives a symbolic emphasis to this inner cleansing. It is not merely that the prophet rejects the animal role of eating and sleeping and feeding and mating as a sufficient occupation for men: he seeks to subdue every kind of animal craving and desire, to loosen all the bonds that tie him too closely to bare survival, to turn all organic and social activities into mere preparations for an existence of greater significance and beatitude. To live in the highest sense is to be released from the pressure to survive.

This curbing of man's biological nature imposes a whole regimen of self-denial and bodily starvation: the eye must not be tempted by beautiful images; the palate must not be delighted with tastes nor the skin with sleek clothing nor the body bedizened with ornament; nor yet must the muscles be encouraged by dances or gymnastic exercises. In short, every sort of bodily activity must be repressed or starved; and above all, the sexual impulses. The ideal life for the axial prophet—there are exceptions like Confucius and Mahomet—is one released from sexual excitation and domestic responsibility: chaste, self-contained, subdued, conducted as far as possible away from the temptations that the mere presence of a member of the other sex may arouse. By all these means, the soul is to be quickened, and freed from the sordid cares and delusive pleasures that lower its powers.

With this emancipation from man's bodily appetites and cravings goes another kind of emancipation, almost equally hard to achieve: an emancipation from social attachment. The goods of civilization, too, are rejected or treated as threats to the soul's integrity. As Socrates, most influential of the Western axial philosophers, said: "All I do is go round and persuade young and old among you not to give so much attention to your bodies and your money as to the perfection of your souls." In preferring bachelorhood to wedlock, the prophet may, like Buddha, Jesus, and Mani, turn his back on the family: the obligations of the household become obstacles to self-perfection; for he who strives to please his wife forgets to please God, as Paul of Tarsus observed. As far as possible this new self is detached, too, from the responsibilities of an organized community: its law, government, military obligations, economic operations, social duties, sacred rituals and symbols seem both hateful and harmful to the new self. What are they but a mass of vain repetitions and empty observances that, in the very act of ensuring a society's existence, hamper the soul's development?

By rejection of tribal and civilized institutions the believer dismantles a great part of the apparatus of civilized life. In this new attitude toward one's fellow, in this emphasis on personal values that challenge the customs of society, the prophet seeks indeed to bring about a new kind of community: the community of the "saved." Herein lies the great appeal of these axial religions to those who are disoriented or depressed by the hollowness of civilization's achievements. In forfeiting the goods of this world those who have found "salvation" seek to gain dominion over death itself: in giving up the goods of life they hope to achieve a greater good in eternity.

This image of a new man does not at first seek to impose itself by force or command: it relies upon the persuasiveness, or say rather the infectiousness, of the prophet's example. And the fact that men rally about him and seek in astonishing numbers to understand his precepts, to follow his way, and to refashion themselves in his very image shows that he represents a part of the human self that had not hitherto been adequately represented either by archaic or civilized society. In some measure, he makes them conscious of their secret aspirations, as he reinforces their dissatisfaction with animal complacency, technical proficiency, social routine, in short, with what William James called the Bitch Goddess, Success. The wonders and miracles that the prophet works awaken them truly to the undisclosed inner resources of life. As once the hero had stirred his fellows to conscious collective deeds that transformed the external world, so the saint rouses them to spiritual efforts that had heretofore been equally unimaginable. These new spiritual attributes often prove evanescent, like those products of nuclear fission that have but a brief half life; but, like them, they show potentialities that go far beyond the familiar organic and social stabilities.

This heightening of the human potential may itself indicate from within something about the nature of the universe. An underlying urge to self-transformation possibly lies at the basis of all existence, finding expression in the process of growth, development, renewal, directed change, perfection. This impulse to self-transformation may be structured in the whole organic world; in fact, it may have its origins in the whole self-constituting cosmic process that built up the elements; for the farther back one pushes the tendency toward self-transformation, the more basic it seems—and the more utterly unexplainable, except in mythical terms that derive from conscious human purpose.

Living forms transcended the limited possibilities of "matter" by arriving, through the complex protein molecule, at a succession of unstable combinations that were self-sustaining —transient but capable of development. The process of self-transformation, finding wider scope in living organisms, resulted in one species after another, in a staggering diversity of forms, moving slowly upward toward mind, consciousness, widened opportunities for expression and self-direction. When the energy of this formative movement was exhausted, each species showed a tendency to level off at its own grade and remain there indefinitely, until either external pressure or some irresistible internal impulse resulted in a further transformation. This has its parallels in man's own self-transformation.

Archaic man had gone so far and had halted: civilized man had gone so far and had halted again. Now axial man came forward to attempt by faith and watchful discipline a further transformation, lessening his bodily needs, his physical apparatus, his institutional supports, in order to concentrate upon inner growth. He demanded a great change in the human form: but in a more restricted area, for his province is the individual soul. At the beginning of Egyptian civilization, only the Pharaoh dared to lay claim to a soul. With the axial religions, the democratization of heaven, which had already begun in Babylonia and Egypt, became universal. At this point the soul seems to "step forth" from the body, to use a term known to the Dionysiac cult.

Through axial man there rise to consciousness perceptions, feelings, and aspirations of a transcendent order, probably long buried in the unconscious. These stirrings now become objects of meditation and deliberate search. To achieve his new self, axial man at first forgoes the whole man, and is indifferent to the natural question as to what would happen if the new principles of his religion, with their detachment and disembodiment, were widely adopted. Would not the birth rate be perilously lowered if the prophet's followers took his injunctions seriously? Would the axial religion itself not be overwhelmed by numbers, if not by force, on the part of nonbelievers? The fact that these vexatious questions did not keep the axial religions from spreading widely shows that other pressures were powerfully at work.

3

With axial religion came a new challenge and a new possibility. Unlike earlier cults, the axial religions were not confined to a territory or society; their members did not enter them by birth. One inherited the gods of Egypt or Babylonia, just as one inherited the other elements of their culture; but one did not, in their formative period, inherit the axial God or his prophet: one rather embraced them by a conscious act of choice, by an expression of faith that accompanied an effort at inner transformation. The new self was to be achieved, not primarily by indoctrination and habituation, though that would come later, but by conversion: an act of grace. This universal self was, fundamentally, the product of a revulsion against the accepted forms of life, fortified by a sense of unfathomed possibilities that remained to be explored.

The axial religions often took form during a period of social distintegration, when the normal satisfactions and the normal securities of civilized life no longer seemed possible: they sought to give a positive content to these negative moments. But a time of troubles does not inevitably lead to this particular remedy: if it did, it would be hard to explain the absorption in worldly enterprise after the disruptions of the fourteenth century, when Europe experienced the most catastrophic loss of population it had known since the sixth century A.D. Similarly, but in reverse, the first appearance of the mystery religions came in the sixth century B.C. before the full flowering of Hellenic culture, and antedated by more than a century the wars and devastations that followed. Probably it would be closer to truth to say that the heat of events often hastened a slow process of inner ripening, which was going on under widely different , circumstances, to produce the same ultimate fruit.

Through the axial religions, a new kind of society was formed which overpassed all existing boundaries: a society of believers, united by a supernatural faith and a vision of perfection. The axial religions broke down the ancient isolation of tribe and village, city, state and even of empire: they marched across frontiers and summoned all men to a new life. The dividing lines between the in-group and the out-group, between Jew and Gentile, between Greek and barbarian, between neighbor and foreigner, were effaced. All men could become part of this new society, no matter what their social rank, their economic status, their political obligations, their color or their sex: they were children of one god, brothers and sisters in a single family.

This fact gave to each of the axial religions a far wider potential territory than the greatest of empires had ever achieved by force of arms.

In that widening of the area of communication and co-operation they carried further the great advance made by civilization. True: no axial religion has up to now ever achieved anything like effective world-wide distribution; and that limitation should awaken pertinent questions. But the belief in universality was part of this new orientation; for the soul came from God and all men were subject equally to his providence, and had a share in the heavenly promise.

In this respect, no less than in its sense of the unplumbed resources of the inner life, when freed from external compulsions, axial religion was in the line of growth: it projected a destination far beyond that of archaic or civilized man, and conceived a new kind of person, capable of imagining and preparing for a universal community, if not capable on its own one-sided terms of achieving such a society. While this capacity for ignoring boundaries was one of the distinguishing marks of the axial religions, they broke down another great division equally characteristic of civilized man: they broke down, at least in relation to God and eternity, the division between classes. In times when the cult of arbitrary power and luxurious indulgence had increased the oppressions of the rich and powerful and aroused the resentments of the poor, the axial religions intervened with a temporary solution. In the sight of God, even the rich and poor were brothers. That again was not a new perception: one finds it already in the Egyptian texts. But it now became a principle of organization within a new institution: the church, or congregation of believers. To be saved was to be accepted as a member of this new community, in an unfettered fellowship that transcended all other ties, even that of the family.

From this time on the human personality can be formally divided into three parts, lately detected and described by Sigmund Freud, but always more or less acknowledged since the time of Aristotle. First: a basic biological self (the Old Adam), connected with man's animal past, stable, durable, requiring tens of thousands of years to produce any fundamental organic changes. This primeval self is the seat of all the vital processes: it holds, in its organs and tissues, the ultimate potentialities of mind and spirit; but it is to the more developed self as the quarry is to the carved statue. Second: a derivative social self, shaped by man's transmitted culture, by nurture, discipline, education, externalized in institutions and structures that create a common recognizable form for all its members. This self shows the beginnings of a differentiated ego; but it is largely a creature of habit and tradition; and in civilized regimes it splits up into an occupational self, a domestic self, a political self, as various situations impose their appropriate roles and dramas. In its most inclusive form it becomes the corporate "national self," on its way to a common human goal, but unable on its own terms to reach it. These civilized fragments are the relatively uniform blocks of stone, far removed from the quarry, but still to be shaped into individualized statues.

Finally, there is an ideal self, the superego, the latest layer of the self, though dimly visible from the moment of man's emergence: the most frail, the most unstable, the most easily overthrown part of the human psyche, perhaps also the most subject to debasement. Yet this ideal self seeks a position of dominance, for it represents the path of continued growth and development.

One is born *with* the first self, the biological substratum or id: one is born *into* the second self, the social self, which makes the animal over into a modified human image, and directs its purely animal propensities into useful social channels, carved by a particular group. But one must be reborn if one is to achieve the third self. In that rebirth, the latest part of the self, assuming leadership, projects a destination that neither man's animal nature nor his social achievements have so far more than faintly indicated. In this detachment lies the promise of further growth.

The belief in the possibility of this rebirth is one of the identifying marks of the axial religions, indeed their chief contribution to the human condition. But in the act of defining these new possibilities for development, they failed, to their eventual embarrassment, to allow for the natural history of man. In the hope of speeding conversion, they rejected the lower elements and broke up the unity of the living organism, instead of putting man's vitalities more fully at the service of the higher self.

the preservation
of the social order

two

Origin of the Idea of the Totemic Principle or Mana

EMILE DURKHEIM

The proposition established in the preceding chapter determines the terms in which the problem of the origins of totemism should be posed. Since totemism is everywhere dominated by the idea of a quasi-divine principle, immanent in certain categories of men and things and thought of under the form of an animal or vegetable, the explanation of this religion is essentially the explanation of this belief; to arrive at this, we must seek to learn how men have been led to construct this idea and out of what materials they have constructed it.

I

It is obviously not out of the sensations which the things serving as totems are able to arouse in the mind; we have shown that these things are frequently insignificant. The lizard, the caterpillar, the rat, the ant, the

Reprinted with permission of The Macmillan Company and Allen & Unwin, Ltd. from *The Elementary Forms of Religious Life* by Emile Durkheim, translated by Joseph W. Swain. Copyright by Allen & Unwin, Ltd. Firs Free Press Paperback.

frog, the turkey, the bream-fish, the plum-tree, the cockatoo, etc., to cite only those names which appear frequently in the lists of Australian totems, are not of a nature to produce upon men these great and strong impressions which in a way resemble religious emotions and which impress a sacred character upon the objects they create. It is true that this is not the case with the stars and the great atmospheric phenomena, which have, on the contrary, all that is necessary to strike the imagination forcibly; but as a matter of fact, these serve only very exceptionally as totems. It is even probable that they were very slow in taking this office. So it is not the intrinsic nature of the thing whose name the clan bears that marked it out to become the object of a cult. Also, if the sentiments which it inspired were really the determining cause of the totemic rites and beliefs, it would be the pre-eminently sacred thing; the animals or plants employed as totems would play an eminent part in the religious life. But we know that the centre of the cult is actually elsewhere. It is the figurative representations of this plant or animal and the totemic emblems and symbols of every sort, which have the greatest sanctity; so it is in them that is found the source of that religious nature, of which the real objects represented by these emblems receive only a reflection.

Thus the totem is before all a symbol, a material expression of something else.[1] But of what?

From the analysis to which we have been giving our attention, it is evident that it expresses and symbolizes two different sorts of things. In the first place, it is the outward and visible form of what we have called the totemic principle or god. But it is also the symbol of the determined society called the clan. It is its flag; it is the sign by which each clan distinguishes itself from the others, the visible mark of its personality, a mark borne by everything which is a part of the clan under any title whatsoever, men, beasts or things. So if it is at once the symbol of the god and of the society, is that not because the god and the society are only one? How could the emblem of the group have been able to become the figure of this quasi-divinity, if the group and the divinity were two distinct realities? The god of the clan, the totemic principle, can therefore be nothing else than the clan itself, personified and represented to the imagination under the visible form of the animal or vegetable which serves as totem.

But how has this apotheosis been possible, and how did it happen to take place in this fashion?

II

In a general way, it is unquestionable that a society has all that is

necessary to arouse the sensation of the divine in minds, merely by the power that it has over them; for to its members it is what a god is to his worshippers. In fact, a god is, first of all, a being whom men think of as superior to themselves, and upon whom they feel that they depend. Whether it be a conscious personality, such as Zeus or Jahveh, or merely abstract forces such as those in play in totemism, the worshipper, in the one case as in the other, believes himself held to certain manners of acting which are imposed upon him by the nature of the sacred principle with which he feels that he is in communion. Now society also gives us the sensation of a perpetual dependence. Since it has a nature which is peculiar to itself and different from our individual nature, it pursues ends which are likewise special to it; but, as it cannot attain them except through our intermediacy, it imperiously demands our aid. It requires that, forgetful of our own interests, we make ourselves its servitors, and it submits us to every sort of inconvenience, privation and sacrifice, without which social life would be impossible. It is because of this that at every instant we are obliged to submit ourselves to rules of conduct and of thought which we have neither made nor desired, and which are sometimes even contrary to our most fundamental inclinations and instincts.

Even if society were unable to obtain these concessions and sacrifices from us except by a material constraint, it might awaken in us only the idea of a physical force to which we must give way of necessity, instead of that of a moral power such as religions adore. But as a matter of fact, the empire which it holds over consciences is due much less to the physical supremacy of which it has the privilege than to the moral

---

1 Pickler, in *Der Ursprung des Totemismus: Ein Beitrag zur Materialistirchen Geschichtstheorie* (Berlin), had already expressed, in a slightly dialectical manner, the sentiment that this is what the totem essentially is.

authority with which it is invested. If we yield to its orders, it is not merely because it is strong enough to triumph over our resistance; it is primarily because it is the object of a venerable respect.

We say that an object, whether individual or collective, inspires respect when the representation expressing it in the mind is gifted with such a force that it automatically causes or inhibits actions, *without regard for any consideration relative to their useful or injurious effects.* When we obey somebody because of the moral authority which we recognize in him, we follow out his opinions, not because they seem wise, but because a certain sort of physical energy is immanent in the idea that we form of this person, which conquers our will and inclines it in the indicated direction. Respect is the emotion which we experience when we feel this interior and wholly spiritual pressure operating upon us. Then we are not determined by the advantages or inconveniences of the attitude which is prescribed or recommended to us; it is by the way in which we represent to ourselves the person recommending or prescribing it. This is why commands generally take a short, peremptory form leaving no place for hesitation; it is because, in so far as it is a command and goes by its own force, it excludes all idea of deliberation or calculation; it gets its efficacy from the intensity of the mental state in which it is placed. It is this intensity which creates what is called a moral ascendancy.

Now the ways of action to which society is strongly enough attached to impose them upon its members, are, by that very fact, marked with a distinctive sign provocative of respect. Since they are elaborated in common, the vigour with which they have been thought of by each particular mind is retained in all the other minds, and reciprocally. The representations which express them within each of us have an intensity which no purely private states of consciousness could ever attain; for they have the strength of the innumerable individual representations which have served to form each of them. It is society who speaks through the mouths of those who affirm them in our presence; it is society whom we hear in hearing them; and the voice of all has an accent which that of one alone could never have.[2] The very violence with which society reacts, by way of blame or material suppression, against every attempted dissidence, contributes to strengthening its empire by manifesting the common conviction through this burst of ardour.[3] In a word, when something is the object of such a state of opinion, the representation which each individual has of it gains a power of action from its origins and the conditions in which it was born, which even those feel who do not submit themselves to it. It tends to repel the representations which contradict it, and it keeps them at a distance; on the other hand, it commands those acts which will realize it, and it does so, not by a material coercion or by the perspective of something of this sort, but by the simple radiation of the mental energy which it contains. It has an efficacy coming solely from its psychical properties, and it is by just this sign that moral authority is recognized. So opinion, primarily a social thing, is a source of authority, and it might even be asked whether all authority is not the daughter of opinion.[4] It may be ob-

---

[2] See our *Division du travail social,* 3rd ed., pp. 64 ff.

[3] *Ibid.,* p. 76.

[4] This is the case at least with all moral authority recognized as such by the group as a whole.

jected that science is often the antagonist of opinion, whose errors it combats and rectifies. But it cannot succeed in this task if it does not have sufficient authority, and it can obtain this authority only from opinion itself. If a people did not have faith in science, all the scientific demonstrations in the world would be without any influence whatsoever over their minds. Even to-day, if science happened to resist a very strong current of public opinion, it would risk losing its credit there.[5]

Since it is in spiritual ways that social pressure exercises itself, it could

---

[5] We hope that this analysis and those which follow will put an end to an inexact interpretation of our thought, from which more than one misunderstanding has resulted. Since we have made constraint the *outward sign* by which social facts can be the most easily recognized and distinguished from the facts of individual psychology, it has been assumed that according to our opinion, physical constraint is the essential thing for social life. As a matter of fact, we have never considered it more than the material and apparent expression of an interior and profound fact which is wholly idea: this is *moral authority*. The problem of sociology—if we can speak of *a* sociological problem—consists in seeking, among the different forms of external constraint, the different sorts of moral authority corresponding to them and in discovering the causes which have determined these latter. The particular question which we are treating in this present work has as its principal object, the discovery of the form under which that particular variety of moral authority which is inherent in all that is religious has been born, and out of what elements it is made. It will be seen presently that even if we do make social pressure one of the distinctive characteristics of sociological phenomena, we do not mean to say that it is the only one. We shall show another aspect of the collective life, nearly opposite to the preceding one, but none the less real.

not fail to give men the idea that outside themselves there exist one or several powers, both moral and, at the same time, efficacious, upon which they depend. They must think of these powers, at least in part, as outside themselves, for these address them in a tone of command and sometimes even order them to do violence to their most natural inclinations. It is undoubtedly true that if they were able to see that these influences which they feel emanate from society, then the mythological system of interpretations would never be born. But social action follows ways that are too circuitous and obscure, and employs psychical mechanisms that are too complex to allow the ordinary observer to see whence it comes. As long as scientific analysis does not come to teach it to them, men know well that they are acted upon, but they do not know by whom. So they must invent by themselves the idea of these powers with which they feel themselves in connection, and from that, we are able to catch a glimpse of the way by which they were led to represent them under forms that are really foreign to their nature and to transfigure them by thought.

But a god is not merely an authority upon whom we depend; it is a force upon which our strength relies. The man who has obeyed his god and who, for this reason, believes the god is with him, approaches the world with confidence and with the feeling of an increased energy. Likewise, scoial action does not confine itself to demanding sacrifices, privations and efforts from us. For the collective force is not entirely outside of us; it does not act upon us wholly from without; but rather, since society cannot exist except in and through individual consciousnesses,[6] this force must also penetrate us and organize itself within us; it thus becomes an integral part of our being and by that very fact this is elevated and magnified.

There are occasions when this strengthening and vivfying action of society is especially apparent. In the midst of an assembly animated by a common passion, we become susceptible of acts and sentiments of which we are incapable when reduced to our own forces; and when the assembly is dissolved and when, finding ourselves alone again, we fall back to our ordinary level, we are then able to measure the height to which we have been raised above ourselves. History abounds in examples of this sort. It is enough to think of the night of the Fourth of August, 1789, when an assembly was suddenly led to an act of sacrifice and abnegation which each of its members had refused the day before, and at which they were all surprised the day after.[7] This is why all parties, political, economic or confessional, are careful to have periodical reunions where their members may revivify their common faith by manifesting it in common. To strengthen those sentiments which,

if left to themselves, would soon weaken, it is sufficient to bring those who hold them together and to put them into closer and more active relations with one another. This is the explanation of the particular attitude of a man speaking to a crowd, at least if he has succeeded in entering into communion with it. His language has a grandiloquence that would be ridiculous in ordinary circumstances; his gestures show a certain domination; his very thought is impatient of all rules, and easily falls into all sorts of excesses. It is because he feels within him an abnormal over-supply of force which overflows and tries to burst out from him; sometimes he even has the feeling that he is dominated by a moral force which is greater than he and of which he is only the interpreter. It is by this trait that we are able to recognize what has often been called the demon of oratorical inspiration. Now this exceptional increase of force is something very real; it comes to him from the very group which he addresses. The sentiments provoked by his words come back to him, but enlarged and amplified, and to this degree they strengthen his own sentiment. The passionate energies he arouses re-echo within him and quicken his vital tone. It is no longer a simple individual who speaks; it is a group incarnate and personified.

Beside these passing and intermittent states, there are other more durable ones, where this strengthening influence of society makes itself felt with greater consequences and frequently even with greater brilliancy. There are periods in history when, under the influence of some great collective shock, social interactions have become much more frequent and active. Men look for each other and assemble together more than ever.

---

6 Of course this does not mean to say that the collective consciousness does not have distinctive characteristics of its own (on this point, see *Rreprésentations individuelles et représentations collectives,* in *Revue de Métaphysique et de Morale,* 1898, pp. 273 ff.).

7 This is proved by the length and passionate character of the debates where a legal form was given to the resolutions made in a moment of collective enthusiasm. In the clergy as in the nobility, more than one person called this celebrated night the dupe's night, or, with Rivarol, the St. Bartholomew of the estates (see Stoll, *Suggestion und Hypnotismus in der Völkerpsychologie,* 2nd ed., p. 618, n. 2).

That general effervescence results which is characteristic of revolutionary or creative epochs. Now this greater activity results in a general stimulation of individual forces. Men see more and differently now than in normal times. Changes are not merely of shades and degrees; men become different. The passions moving them are of such an intensity that they cannot be satisfied except by violent and unrestrained actions, actions of superhuman heroism or of bloody barbarism. This is what explains the Crusades,[8] for example, or many of the scenes, either sublime or savage, of the French Revolution.[9] Under the influence of the general exaltation, we see the most mediocre and inoffensive bourgeois become either a hero or a butcher.[10] And so clearly are all these mental processes the ones that are also at the root of religion that the individuals themselves have often pictured the pressure before which they thus gave way in a distinctly religious form. The Crusaders believed that they felt God present in the midst of them, enjoining them to go to the conquest of the Holy Land; Joan of Arc believed that she obeyed celestial voices.[11]

But it is not only in exceptional circumstances that this stimulating action of society makes itself felt; there is not, so to speak, a moment in our lives when some current of energy does not come to us from without. The man who has done his duty finds, in the manifestations of every sort expressing the sympathy, esteem or affection which his fellows have for him, a feeling of comfort, of which he does not ordinarily take account, but which sustains him, none the less. The sentiments which society has for him raise the sentiments which he has for himself. Because he is in moral harmony with his comrades, he has more confidence, courage and boldness in action, just like the believer who thinks that he feels the regard of his god turned graciously towards him. It thus produces, as it were, a perpetual sustenance for our moral nature. Since this varies with a multitude of external circumstances, as our relations with the groups about us are more or less active and as these groups themselves vary, we cannot fail to feel that this moral support depends upon an external cause; but we do not perceive where this cause is nor what it is. So we ordinarily think of it under the form of a moral power which, though immanent in us, represents within us something not ourselves: this is the moral conscience, of which, by the way, men have never made even a slightly distinct representation except by the aid of religious symbols.

In addition to these free forces which are constantly coming to renew our own, there are others which are fixed in the methods and traditions which we employ. We speak a language that we did not make; we use instruments that we did not invent; we invoke rights that we did not found; a treasury of knowledge is transmitted to each generation that it did not gather itself, etc. It is to society that we owe these varied benefits of civilization, and if we do not ordinarily see the source from which we get them, we at least know that they are not our own work. Now it is these things that give man his own place among things; a man is a man only because he is civilized. So he

---

8 See Stoll, *Suggestion und Hypnotismus*, pp. 353 ff.

9 *Ibid.,* pp. 619, 635.

10 *Ibid.,* pp. 622 ff.

11 The emotions of fear and sorrow are able to develop similarly and to become intensified under these same conditions. They correspond to quite another aspect of the religious life.

could not escape the feeling that outside of him there are active causes from which he gets the characteristic attributes of his nature and which, as benevolent powers, assist him, protect him and assure him of a privileged fate. And of course he must attribute to these powers a dignity corresponding to the great value of the good things he attributes to them.[12]

Thus the environment in which we live seems to us to be peopled with forces that are at once imperious and helpful, august and gracious, and with which we have relations. Since they exercise over us a pressure of which we are conscious, we are forced to localize them outside ourselves, just as we do for the objective causes of our sensations. But the sentiments which they inspire in us differ in nature from those which we have for simple visible objects. As long as these latter are reduced to their empirical characteristics as shown in ordinary experience, and as long as the religious imagination has not metamorphosed them, we entertain for them no feeling which resembles respect, and they contain within them nothing that is able to raise us outside ourselves. Therefore, the representations which express them appear to us to be very different from those aroused in us by collective influences. The two form two distinct and separate mental states in our consciousness, just as do the two forms of life to which they correspond. Consequently, we get the impression that we are in relations with two distinct sorts of reality and that a sharply drawn line of demarcation separates them from each other: on the one hand is the world of profane things, on the other, that of sacred things.

Also, in the present day just as much as in the past, we see society constantly creating sacred things out of ordinary ones. If it happens to fall in love with a man and if it thinks it has found in him the principal aspirations that move it, as well as the means of satisfying them, this man will be raised above the others and, as it were, deified. Opinion will invest him with a majesty exactly analogous to that protecting the gods. This is what has happened to so many sovereigns in whom their age had faith: if they were not made gods, they were at least regarded as direct representatives of the deity. And the fact that it is society alone which is the author of these varieties of apotheosis, is evident since it frequently chances to consecrate men thus who have no right to it from their own merit. The simple deference inspired by men invested with high social functions is not different in nature from religious respect. It is expressed by the same movements: a man keeps at a distance from a high personage; he approaches him only with precautions; in conversing with him, he uses other gestures and language than those used with ordinary mortals. The sentiment felt on these occasions is so closely related to the religious sentiment that many peoples have confounded the two. In order to explain the consideration accorded to princes, nobles and political chiefs, a sacred character has been attributed to them. In Melanesia and Polynesia, for example, it is said that an influential

---

12 This is the other aspect of society which, while being imperative, appears at the same time to be good and gracious. It dominates us and assists us. If we have defined the social fact by the first of these characteristics rather than the second, it is because it is more readily observable, for it is translated into outward and visible signs; but we have never thought of denying the second (see our *Règles de la Méthode Sociologique,* preface to the second edition, p. xx, n. 1).

man has *mana,* and that his influence is due to this *mana.*[13] However, it is evident that his situation is due solely to the importance attributed to him by public opinion. Thus the moral power conferred by opinion and that with which sacred beings are invested are at bottom of a single origin and made up of the same elements. That is why a single word is able to designate the two.

In addition to men, society also consecrates things, especially ideas. If a belief is unanimously shared by a

___
[13] Codrington, *The Melanesians,* pp. 50, 103, 120. It is also generally thought that in the Polynesian languages, the word *mana* primitively had the sense of authority (see Tregear, *Maori Comparative Dictionary,* s.v.).

people, then, for the reason which we pointed out above, it is forbidden to touch it, that is to say, to deny it or to contest it. Now the prohibition of criticism is an interdiction like the others and proves the presence of something sacred. Even to-day, howsoever great may be the liberty which we accord to others, a man who should totally deny progress or ridicule the human ideal to which modern societies are attached, would produce the effect of a sacrilege. There is at least one principle which those the most devoted to the free examination of everything tend to place above discussion and to regard as untouchable, that is to say, as sacred: this is the very principle of free examination.

Buddhism and the Temporal Power

EDWARD CONZE

Without the support of kings and emperors, the triumphant spread of the Dharma throughout Asia would have been impossible. It was one of the greatest rulers of India, King Asoka (274–236 B.C.), who first made Buddhism into a world-religion, spread it through the length and breadth of India, brought it to Ceylon, Kashmir and Gandhara, and even sent missions to the Greek princes of his time—Antiochos II of Syria, Ptolemy Philadelphos and Antigonos Gonatas of Macedonia. After Asoka, the Buddhists were favoured by another great conqueror, the Scyth Kanishka (78–103 A.D.), who ruled

From *Buddhism: Its Essence and Development,* by Edward Conze. Reprinted by permission of Bruno Cassirer (Publishers) Ltd.

over the North of India, by Harshavardhana (606–647), and by the Pala dynasty (750–1150) which ruled over Bengal. Outside India, Chinese emperors and empresses were often converted to Buddhism, so were Mongol Khans, so in Japan a statesman of the calibre of Shotoku Taishi (572–621). In Further India, we find an abundance of Buddhist dynasties at various times.

Only very few of the monarchs just mentioned were Buddhists to the exclusion of other religious leanings. The Palas and the rulers of Ceylon and Burma were the exceptions. Buddhism does not require the exclusive allegiance of its adherents. Kadphises I—a Kuchana king (25–60 A.D.)—calls himself *constant adept of the true Dharma.* The money which he issues shows, on the one side, a seated Buddha, on the other the Zeus of the city of Kāpisa. Kanishka adorned his money with Gods from Iran—Verethraghna, Ardokhcho, Pharso—with the Hindu Shiva, and with the Buddha—shown either standing or in the lotus seat, with his name in Greek characters as Boddo, or Boudo. Gupta kings favoured both Vishnuism and Buddhism, the kings of Valabhī (490 onwards), though "devotees of Shiva," protected Buddhism, Harshavardhana combined Buddhist piety with a cult of the Sun, etc., etc. Similarly, outside India. The great Khan Mongka (ca. 1250) favoured Nestorians, Buddhists and Taoists, in the belief that, as he said to the Franciscan William of Rubrouck, *"all religions are like the fingers of one hand,"*—although to the Buddhists he said that Buddhism was like the palm of the hand, the other religions being the fingers. Kublai Khan combined leanings towards Buddhism with a partiality for Nestorianism.

Since it is the purpose of rulers to rule, it is unlikely that their conviction of the spiritual value of the Buddhist doctrine would be the only, or even the chief, motive for the protection which they extended to the Buddhist religion. In what manner, then, could the seemingly other worldly and anarchic doctrine of Buddhism increase the security of a ruler's power over his people? It does not only bring peace of mind to the otherworldly, but it also hands over the world to those who wish to grab it. In addition, the belief that this world is ineradicably bad and that no true happiness can be found in it, would tend to stifle criticism of the government. Oppression by government officials would appear partly as a necessary concomitant of this world of birth-and-death, and partly as a punishment for one's own past sins. The stress which Buddhism lays on non-violence would tend to pacify a country and to make the position of its rulers more secure. In addition, if the people regard this world as none too important, their cheerfulness will not be impaired by lack of possessions, and it is preferable to rule over a cheerful rather than a sullen people. In Buddhist society, a simple life would be held most in keeping with the religious doctrine, and people would want to be 'poor' in the sense in which Burmans were poor. M. Collis (*Trials in Burma*, p. 214) makes the following apt comment on the British contempt for the Burmans on account of their poverty:

A Burman who had, as many of the villagers had, his own house and his own farmland, a wife, and lots of children, a pony and a favourite actress, a bottle of wine and a book of verse, racing bullocks, and a carved teak-cart, a set of chess, and a set of dice, felt himself at the summit of felicity, and ignored the English view that he was a poor man because his cash income was about ten pounds a year.

Buddhism would everywhere discourage the accumulation of material wealth in the hands of individuals, and encourage people rather to give away any material wealth, and to invest it in works of piety, as has been the case in Burma and Tibet for so many centuries. If we consider that the encouragement of a desire for material possessions and for a higher 'standard of living' among the European masses has not only destroyed all despotic forms of government, but has undermined all steady and permanent governmental authority in Europe, we can understand why Buddhism should appear as a blessing to the habitually despotic rulers of Asia.

Ever since the Neolithic Age, rulers, particularly where they had to cope with large and heterogeneous empires, were to some extent deified. This idea of the divinity of Kings is quite familiar from Egypt, China and Japan. It played its rôle in Rome and Byzantium, has been superseded by democratic ideas only quite recently, and still shows a surprising vigour in the attitude which a number of Germans adopted to Hitler, or in some of the pronouncements made about Josef Stalin in the Soviet Union. In India the divinity of the Rajahs, however small their domain, has always been a commonplace of popular belief. The moral authority of a king would grow immensely if and when his will could appear as the will of God. It was particularly among the great conquerors that Buddhism found favour. The Buddhists actively increased the prestige of such a monarch by their theory of the *Wheelturning King,* in Sanscrit *Cakravartin.* The Scriptures give a somewhat idealised portrait of such a ruler. Here is the description from the Divyavadana (548–9) :

He is victorious at the head of his troops, just (dhārmiko = dikaios); a king of dharma, endowed with the 7 treasures, i.e. a chariot, an elephant, a horse, a jewel, a wife, a minister and a general. He will have 100 sons, brave and beautiful heroes, destroyers of the enemies' armies. He shall conquer the whole wide earth to the limits of the ocean, and then he will remove from it all the causes of tyranny and misery. He will rule without punishing, without using the sword, through Dharma and peacefulness.

It has been a fiction among Buddhists that the rulers who favoured them lived more or less up to this ideal conception. When later on the Mahayana elaborated a new pantheon of deities, Buddhist kings received some of the reflected glory. Rulers in Java, Cambodia and also in Ceylon in the 10th century, were regarded as Bodhisattvas. In Cambodia, at the end of the 12th century, Jayavarman VII consecrated a statue of his mother as Prajñāpāramitā, *Mother of Buddha.* In the 20th century, the King of Siam is still *The Holy Master Buddha* (PHRA PHUTTICCHAO). In an Uigur inscription of 1326, Chengis Khan is called a *Bodhisattva in his last birth.* Kublai Khan became in Mongol tradition, a *Cakravartin,* a sage and a saint (*Hutuktu*). Travellers often refer to the rulers of Mongolia and Tibet as 'living Buddhas.' This is a misnomer and does not express the sense in which the Dalai Lama is regarded as an incarnation of the Bodhisattva Avalokitesvara, or the Hutuktu of Urga as a manifestation of Amitāyus. The Buddhist idea is that the Buddhas and the Bodhisattvas conjure up phantom bodies which they send to different parts of the world, and that those dignitaries are such phantom bodies. Whatever the exact connotation, the prestige value of such suggestions is obvious. It will not only increase the docility of the population, but it will also induce the monks to act as spiritual policemen for the government. It is one of the curiosities of history that, outside India, under Buddhist influence, real theocracies on the Egyptian model were built up, in Indo-China, in Java, in Tibet.

In all pre-industrial societies one believed that the prosperity and welfare of the state depended on the harmony with the invisible and celestial forces which were the true rulers of the Universe. At every step in the Odyssey the fate of Odysseus is decided by a decision made on Olympus. By being friendly with the Buddhist monks a ruler would try to keep on good terms with the invisible forces, and a monk who could claim particular familiarity with them might rise to high office as a responsible adviser. So we read in Wei Shou's (c. 550 A.D.) account of Buddhism in China of a Kashmirean monk of c. 400 A.D., who was *"clever in fortune-telling, in preventive magic, and spoke in detail of the fortunes of other states, much of which came true. Mêng-Hsün often consulted him on affairs of state."*

The motives which we have explained so far would, of course, induce rulers to support not only Buddhism, but any other religion which would support their authority. There were, however, two factors which favoured Buddhism in particular. In many cases it was not Buddhism alone which was introduced into countries like Japan or Tibet, but the new religion was coupled with many advantages of a superior civilisation. In the case of Japan, for instance, the entire apparatus of Chinese civilisation was carried across the sea at the time when Shotoku Taishi decided to adopt the Buddhist faith. The Tibetans, together with the Buddhist dharma, also took over the secular sciences of India—such as grammar, medicine, astronomy and astrology. Secondly, there is something cosmopolitan and international about Buddhism, which would recommend it to monarchs who wished to unify large areas. There is nothing, or almost nothing, in the Buddhist interpretation of spiritual truth which ties it to any soil or any climate, to any race or tribe. Hinduism as compared with it is full of tribal taboos. In Buddhism there is nothing which cannot easily be transported from one part of the world to another. It can adapt itself as easily to the snowy heights of the Himalayas as to the parched plains of India, to the tropical climate of Java, the moderate warmth of apan and the bleak cold of outer Mongolia. Indians, Mongols, and the blue-eyed Nordics of Central Asia could all adjust it to their own needs. Although it is essentially hostile to industrialism, in Japan it managed during the last 40 years, to adjust itself even to the highly uncongenial industrial conditions. A creed as flexible and adaptable as that would be valuable to men who have to rule vast empires, because it would help to unify heterogeneous populations through giving them common beliefs and practices, and through the mutual contact which monks of different regions would cultivate. As far as the spread of Buddhism from Indian to non-Indian countries was concerned, merchants and traders played a prominent part. The strict caste rules of Hinduism made it difficult for orthodox Hindus to leave the country; special sea-voyages were frowned upon and held to pollute so that travellers on their return had to be purified. In consequence, a great deal of the external trade of India during the Middle Ages was in the hands of Buddhists who carried their religion wherever they went.

Having considered the problem of the services Buddhism rendered to the temporal power, we can now ask what it did for the masses and its lay followers.

religion and individual growth

three

from Young Man Luther

ERIK H. ERIKSON

2

Let us consider, then, what we may call the metabolism of generations.

Each human life begins at a given evolutionary stage and level of tradition, bringing to its environment a capital of patterns and energies; these are used to grow on, and to grow into the social process with, and also as contributions to this process. Each new being is received into a style of life prepared by tradition and held together by tradition, and at the same time disintegrating because of the very nature of tradition. We say that tradition "molds" the individual, "channels" his drives. But the social process does not mold a new being merely to housebreak him; it molds generations in order to be remolded, to be reinvigorated, by them. Therefore, society can never afford merely to suppress drives or to guide their sublimation. It must also support the primary function of every individual

Reprinted from *Young Man Luther* by Erik H. Erikson. By permission of W. W. Norton & Company, Inc. Copyright © 1958, 1962 by Erik H. Erikson.

ego, which is to transform instinctual energy into patterns of action, into character, into style—in short, into an identity with a core of integrity which is to be derived from and also contributed to the tradition. There is an optimum ego synthesis to which the individual aspires; and there is an optimum societal metabolism for which societies and cultures strive. In describing the interdependence of individual aspiration and of societal striving, we describe something indispensable to human life.

In an earlier book, I indicated a program of studies which might account for the dovetailing of the stages of individual life and of basic human institutions. The present book circumscribes for only one of these stages—the identity crisis—its intrinsic relation to the process of ideological rejuvenation in a period of history when organized religion dominated ideologies.

In discussing the identity crisis, we have, at least implicitly presented some of the attributes of any psychosocial crisis. At a given age, a human being, by dint of his physical, intellectual and emotional growth, becomes ready and eager to face a new life task, that is, a set of choices and tests which are in some traditional way prescribed and prepared for him by his society's structure. A new life task presents a *crisis* whose outcome can be a successful graduation, or alternatively, an impairment of the life cycle which will aggravate future crises. Each crisis prepares the next, as one step leads to another; and each crisis also lays one more cornerstone for the adult personality. I will enumerate all these crises (more thoroughly treated elsewhere) to remind us, in summary, of certain issues in Luther's life; and also to suggest a developmental root for the basic human values of faith, will, conscience, and reason—all necessary in rudimentary form for the identity which crowns childhood.

The first crisis is the one of early infancy. How this crisis is met decides whether a man's innermost mood will be determined more by basic trust or by basic mistrust. The outcome of this crisis—apart from accidents of heredity, gestation, and birth—depends largely on the quality of maternal care, that is, on the consistency and mutuality which guide the mother's ministrations and give a certain predictability and hopefulness to the baby's original cosmos of urgent and bewildering body feelings. The ratio and relation of basic trust to basic mistrust established during early infancy determines much of the individual's capacity for simple faith, and consequently also determines his future contribution to his society's store of faith—which, in turn, will feed into a future mother's ability to trust the world in which she teaches trust to newcomers. In this first stage we can assume that a historical process is already at work; history writing should therefore chart the influence of historical events on growing generations to be able to judge the quality of their future contribution to

history. As for little Martin, I have drawn conclusions about that earliest time when his mother could still claim the baby, and when he was still all hers, inferring that she must have provided him with a font of basic trust on which he was able to draw in his fight for a primary faith present before all will, conscience, and reason, a faith which is "the soul's virginity."

The first crisis corresponds roughly to what Freud has described as orality; the second corresponds to anality. An awareness of these correspondences is essential for a true understanding of the dynamics involved.

The second crisis, that of infancy, develops the infantile sources of what later becomes a human being's will, in its variations of willpower and wilfulness. The resolution of this crisis will determine whether an individual is apt to be dominated by a sense of autonomy, or by a sense of shame and doubt. The social limitations imposed on intensified wilfulness inevitably create doubt about the justice governing the relations of growth and growing people. The way this doubt is met by the grown-ups determines much of a man's future ability to combine an unimpaired will with ready self-discipline, rebellion with responsibility.

The interpretation is plausible that Martin was driven early out of the trust stage, out from "under his mother's skirts," by a jealously ambitious father who tried to make him precociously independent from women, and sober and reliable in his work. Hans succeeded, but not without storing in the boy violent doubts of the father's justification and sincerity; a lifelong shame over the persisting gap between his own precocious conscience and his actual inner state; and a deep nostalgia for a situation of infantile trust. His theological solution—spiritual return to a faith which is there before all doubt, combined with a political submission to those who by necessity must wield the sword of secular law—seems to fit perfectly his personal need for compromise. While this analysis does not explain either the ideological power or the theological consistency of his solution, it does illustrate that ontogenetic experience is an indispensable link and transformer between one stage of history and the next. This link is a psychological one, and the energy transformed and the process of transformation are both charted by the psychoanalytic method.

Freud formulated these matters in dynamic terms. Few men before him gave more genuine expression to those experiences which are on the borderline between the psychological and the theological than Luther, who gleaned from these experiences a religious gain formulated in theological terms. Luther described states of badness which in many forms pervade human existence from childhood. For instance, his description of shame, an emotion first experienced when the infant stands naked in space and feels belittled: "He is put to sin and shame before God...this shame is now a thousand times greater, that a man must blush in the presence of God. For this means that there is no corner or hole in the whole of creation into which a man might creep, not even in hell, but he must let himself be exposed to the gaze of the whole creation, and stand in the open with all his shame, as a bad conscience feels when it is really struck...."[1] Or

his description of doubt, an emotion first experienced when the child feels singled out by demands whose rationale he does not comprehend: "When he is tormented in *Anfechtung* it seems to him that he is alone: God is angry only with him, and irreconcilably angry against him: then he alone is a sinner and all the others are in the right, and they work against him at God's orders. There is nothing left for him but this unspeakable sighing through which, without knowing it, he is supported by the Spirit and cries 'Why does God pick on me alone?' "[2]

Luther was a man who would not settle for an easy appeasement of these feelings on any level, from childhood through youth to his manhood, or in any segment of life. His often impulsive and intuitive formulations transparently display the infantile struggle at the bottom of the lifelong emotional issue.

His basic contribution was a living reformulation of faith. This marks him as a theologian of the first order; it also indicates his struggle with the ontogenetically earliest and most basic problems of life. He saw as his life's work a new delineation of faith and will, of religion and the law: for it is clear that organized religiosity, in circumstances where faith in a world order is monopolized by religion, is the institution which tries to give dogmatic permanence to a reaffirmation of that basic trust—and a renewed victory over that basic mistrust—with which each human being emerges from early infancy. In this way organized religion cements the faith which will support future generations. Established law tries to formulate obligations and privileges,

---

[1] Martin Luther, *Werke* (Weimar: Weimarer Ausgabe, 1883), Vol. XIX, pp. 216–17. Translated in Gordon Rupp, *The Righteousness of God* (London: Hodder and Stoughton, 1953), Chap. VIII, p. 108.

[2] *Ibid.*, Vol. V, p. 79; translated in Rupp, *The Righteousness of God*, p. 107.

restraints and freedoms, in such a way that man can submit to law and order with a minimum of doubt and with little loss of face, and as an autonomous agent of order can teach the rudiments of discipline to his young. The relation of faith and law, of course, is an eternal human problem, whether it appears in questions of church and state, mysticism and daily morality, or existential aloneness and political commitment.

The third crisis, that of initiative versus guilt, is part of what Freud described as the central complex of the family, namely, the Oedipus complex. It involves a lasting unconscious association of sensual freedom with the body of the mother and the administrations received from her hand; a lasting association of cruel prohibition with the interference of the dangerous father; and the consequences of these associations for love and hate in reality and in phantasy. (I will not discuss here the cultural relativity of Freud's observations nor the dated origin of his term; but I assume that those who do wish to quibble about all this will feel the obligation to advance systematic propositions about family, childhood, and society which come closer to the core, rather than go back to the periphery, of the riddle which Freud was the first to penetrate.) We have reviewed the strong indications of an especially heavy interference by Hans Luder with Martin's attachment to his mother, who, it is suggested, secretly provided for him what Goethe openly acknowledged as his mother's gift—*"Die Frohnatur, die Lust zu fabulieren":* gaiety and the pleasure of confabulation. We have indicated how this gift, which later emerged in Luther's poetry, became guilt-laden and was broken to harness by an education designed to make a precocious student of the boy. We have

also traced its relationship to Luther's lifelong burden of excessive guilt. Here is one of Luther's descriptions of that guilt: "And this is the worst of all these ills, that the conscience cannot run away from itself, but it is always present to itself and knows all the terrors of the creature which such things bring even in this present life, because the ungoldly man is like a raging sea. The third and greatest of all these horrors and the worst of all ills is to have a judge."[3] He also said, "For this is the nature of a guilty conscience, to fly and to be terrified, even when all is safe and prosperous, to convert all into peril and death."[4]

The stage of initiative, associated with Freud's phallic stage of psychosexuality, ties man's budding will to phantasy, play, games, and early work, and thus to the mutual delineation of unlimited imagination and aspiration and limiting, threatening conscience. As far as society is concerned, this is vitally related to the occupational and technological ideals perceived by the child; for the child can manage the fact that there is no return to the mother as a mother and no competition with the father as a father only to the degree to which a future career outside of the narrower family can at least be envisaged in ideal future occupations: these he learns to imitate in play, and to anticipate in school. We can surmise that for little Martin the father's own occupation was early precluded from anticipatory phantasy, and that a life of scholarly duty was obediently and sadly envisaged instead. This precocious severity of obedience later made it impossible for young Martin to anticipate any career but that of unlimited study for its own sake, as

---

3 *Ibid.,* Vol. XLIV, p. 504.
4 *Ibid.,* Vol. IV, p. 602; translated in Rupp, *The Righteousness of God,* p. 109.

we have seen in following his path of obedience—in disobedience.

In the fourth stage, the child becomes able and eager to learn systematically, and to collaborate with others. The resolution of this stage decides much of the ratio between a sense of industry or work completion, and a sense of tool-inferiority, and prepares a man for the essential ingredients of the ethos as well as the rationale of his technology. He wants to know the *reason* for things, and is provided, at least, with rationalizations. He learns to use whatever simplest techniques and tools will prepare him most generally for the tasks of his culture. In Martin's case, the tool was literacy, Latin literacy, and we saw how he was molded by it—and how later he remolded, with the help of printing, his nation's literary habits. With a vengeance he could claim to have taught German even to his enemies.

But he achieved this only after a protracted identity crisis which is the main subject of this book. Whoever is hard put to feel identical with one set of people and ideas must that much more violently repudiate another set; and whenever an identity, once established, meets further crises, the danger of irrational repudiation of otherness and temporarily even of one's own identity increases.

I have already briefly mentioned the three crises which follow the crisis of identity; they concern problems of intimacy, generativity, and integrity. The crisis of intimacy in a monk is naturally distorted in its heterosexual core. What identity diffusion is to identity—its alternative and danger—isolation is to intimacy. In a monk this too is subject to particular rules, since a monk seeks intentional and organized isolation, and submits all intimacy to prayer and confession.

Luther's intimacy crisis seems to have been fully experienced and resolved only on the Wartburg; that is, after his lectures had established him as a lecturer, and his speech at Worms as an orator of universal stamp. On the Wartburg he wrote *De Votis Monasticis,* obviously determined to take care of his sexual needs as soon as a dignified solution could be found. But the intimacy crisis is by no means only a sexual, or for that matter, a heterosexual, one: Luther, once free, wrote to men friends about his emotional life, including his sexuality, with a frankness clearly denoting a need to share intimacies with them. The most famous example, perhaps, is a letter written at a time when the tragicomedy of these priests' belated marriages to runaway nuns was in full swing. Luther had made a match between Spalatin and an ex-nun, a relative of Staupitz. In the letter, he wished Spalatin luck for the wedding night, and promised to think of him during a parallel performance to be arranged in his own marital bed.[5]

Also on the Wartburg, Luther developed, with his translation of the Bible, a supreme ability to reach into the homes of his nation; as a preacher and a table talker he demonstrated his ability and his need to be intimate for the rest of his life. One could write a book about Luther on this theme alone; and perhaps in such a book all but the most wrathful utterances would be found to be communications exquisitely tuned to the recipient.

Owing to his prolonged identity crisis, and also to delayed sexual intimacy, intimacy and generativity were fused in Luther's life. We have

[5] E. L. Enders, *Martin Luthers Briefwechsel* (Frankfurt, 1894–1907), Vol. V, pp. 278–79.

given an account of the time when his generativity reached its crisis, namely, when within a short period he became both a father, and a leader of a wide following which began to disperse his teachings in any number of avaricious, rebellious, and mystical directions. Luther then tasted fully the danger of this stage, which paradoxically is felt by creative people more deeply than by others, namely, a sense of *stagnation,* experienced by him in manic-depressive form. As he recovered, he proceeded with the building of the edifice of his theology; yet he responded to the needs of his parishioners and students, including his princes, to the very end. Only his occasional outbursts expressed that fury of repudiation which was mental hygiene to him, but which set a lasting bad example to his people.

3

We now come to the last, the integrity crisis which again leads man to the portals of nothingness, or at any rate to the station of *having been.* I have described it thus:

Only he who in some way has taken care of things and people and has adapted himself to the triumphs and disappointments adherent to being, by necessity, the originator of others and the generator of things and ideas—only he may gradually grow the fruit of these seven stages. I know no better word for it than ego integrity. Lacking a clear definition, I shall point to a few constituents of this state of mind. It is the ego's accrued assurance of its proclivity for order and meaning. It is a post-narcissistic love of the human ego—not of the self—as an experience which conveys some world order and some spiritual sense, no matter how dearly paid for. It is the acceptance of one's one and only life cycle as something that had to be and that, by necessity, permitted of no substitutions: It thus

means a new, a different, love of one's parents. It is a comradeship with the ordering ways of distant times and different pursuits, as expressed in the simple products and sayings of such times and pursuits. Although aware of the relativity of all the various life styles which have given meaning to human striving, the possessor of integrity is ready to defend the dignity of his own life style against all physical and economic threats. For he knows that an individual life is the accidental coincidence of but one life cycle with but one segment of history; and that for him all human integrity stands or falls with the one style of integrity of which he partakes. The style of integrity developed by his culture or civilization thus becomes the "patrimony of his soul," the seal of his moral paternity of himself ("...*pero el honor/Es patrimonio del alma*": Calderon). Before this final solution, death loses its sting.[6]

This integrity crisis, last in the lives of ordinary men, is a life-long and chronic crisis in a *homo religiosus.* He is always older, or in early years suddenly becomes older, than his playmates or even his parents and teachers, and focuses in a precocious way on what it takes others a lifetime to gain a mere inkling of: the questions of how to escape corruption in living and how in death to give meaning to life. Because he experiences a breakthrough to the last problems so early in his life maybe such a man had better become a martyr and seal his message with an early death; or else become a hermit in a solitude which anticipates the Beyond. We know little of Jesus of Nazareth as a young man, but we certainly cannot even begin to imagine him as middle-aged.

This short cut between the youthful crisis of identity and the mature

---

6 E. H. Erikson, "Integrity," in *Childhood and Society* (New York: W. W. Norton & Company, Inc., 1950).

one of integrity makes the religionist's problem of individual identity the same as the problem of existential identity. To some extent this problem is only an exaggeration of an abortive trait not uncommon in late adolescence. One may say that the religious leader becomes a professional in dealing with the kind of scruples which prove transitory in many all-too-serious postadolescents who later grow out of it, go to pieces over it, or find an intellectual or artistic medium which can stand between them and nothingness.

The late adolescent crisis, in addition to anticipating the more mature crises, can at the same time hark back to the very earliest crisis of life —trust or mistrust toward existence as such. This concentration in the cataclysm of the adolescent identity crisis of both first and last crises in the human life may well explain why religiously and artistically creative men often seem to be suffering from a barely compensated psychosis, and yet later prove superhumanly gifted in conveying a total meaning for man's life; while malignant disturbances in late adolescence often display precocious wisdom and usurped integrity. The chosen young man extends the problem of his identity to the borders of existence in the known universe; other human beings bend all their efforts to adopt and fulfill the departmentalized identities which they find prepared in their communities. He can permit himself to face as permanent the trust problem which drives others in whom it remains or becomes dominant into denial, despair, and psychosis. He acts as if mankind were starting all over with his own beginning as an individual, conscious of his singularity as well as his humanity; others hide in the folds of whatever tradition they are part of because of membership, occupation, or special interests. To him, history ends as well as starts with him; others must look to their memories, to legends, or to books to find models for the present and the future in what their predecessors have said and done. No wonder that he is something of an old man (a *philosophus,* and a sad one) when his age-mates are young, or that he remains something of a child when they age with finality. The name Lao-tse, I understand, means just that.

The danger of a reformer of the first order, however, lies in the nature of his influence on the masses. In our own day we have seen this in the life and influence of Gandhi. He, too, believed in the power of prayer; when he fasted and prayed, the masses and even the English held their breath. Because prayer gave them the power to say what would be heard by the lowliest and the highest, both Gandhi and Luther believed that they could count on the restraining as well as the arousing power of the Word. In such hope great religionists are supported—one could say they are seduced—by the fact that all people, because of their common undercurrent of existential anxiety, at cyclic intervals and during crises feel an intense need for a rejuvenation of trust which will give new meaning to their limited and perverted exercise of will, conscience, reason, and identity. But the best of them will fall asleep at Gethsemane; and the worst will accept the new faith only as a sanction for anarchic destructiveness or political guile. If faith can move mountains, let it move obstacles out of *their* way. But maybe the masses also sense he who aspires to spiritual power, even though he speaks of renunciation, has an account to settle with an inner authority. He may disavow their rebellion, but he is a rebel. He may say in the deepest humility, as Luther said, that "his mouth is Christ's mouth"; his nerve is still the nerve of a usurper. So for a while the world may be worse for having had a vision of being better. From the oldest Zen poem to the most recent psychological formulation, it is clear that "the conflict between right and wrong is the sickness of the mind."[7]

The great human question is to what extent early child training must or must not exploit man's early helplessness and moral sensitivity to the degree that a deep sense of evil and of guilt become unavoidable; for such in the end can only result in clandestine commitment to evil in the name of higher values. Religionists, of course, assume that because a . sense of evil dominated them even as they combated it, it belongs not only to man's "nature," but is God's plan, even God's gift to him. The answer to this assumption is that not only do child training systems differ in their exploitation of basic mistrust, shame,

doubt, and guilt—so do religions. The trouble comes, first, from the mortal fear that instinctual forces would run wild if they were not dominated by a negative conscience; and second, from trying to formulate man's optimum as negative morality, to be reinforced by rigid institutions. In this formulation all man's erstwhile fears of the forces and demons of nature are reprojected onto his inner forces, and onto the child, whose dormant energies are alternatively vilified as potentially criminal, or romanticized as altogether angelic. Because man needs a disciplined conscience, he thinks he must have a bad one; and he assumes that he has a good conscience when, at times, he has an easy one. The answer to all this does not lie in attempts to avoid or to deny one or the other sense of badness in children altogether; the denial of the unavoidable can only deepen a sense of secret, unmanageable evil. The answer lies in man's capacity to create order which will give his children a disciplined as well as a tolerant conscience, and a world within which to act affirmatively.

---

[7] Seng-ta'an, Hsin-hsin, Ming. Alan Watts, *The Way of Zen* (New York: Pantheon Books, Inc., 1957).

the prophetic function

four

from Ancient Judaism

MAX WEBER

Social Context of the Prophetic Message

One important principle united the prophets as a status group: the gratuitous character of their oracles. This separated them from the prophets of the king, whom they cursed as destroyers of the land. And it distinguished the prophets from all groups that made an industry of prophecy in the manner of the old seers or dream-interpreters whom they despised and rejected. The complete inner independence of the prophets was not so much a result as a most important cause of their practice. In the main they prophesied disaster and no one could be sure whether on request, like King Zedekiah, he might not receive a prediction of doom and therewith an evil omen. One does not pay for evil omens nor expose oneself to them. Primarily unbidden and spontaneously impelled, rarely on request, the prophets hurled their frequently

Reprinted with permission of The Macmillan Company from *Ancient Judaism* by Max Weber, trans. and ed. by Hans Gerth and Don Martindale. Copyright 1952 by The Free Press.

frightful oracles against their audience.

However, as a status principle this gratuitous practice is, indeed, characteristic of a stratum of genteel intellectuals. The borrowing of this principle, later, by the plebeian intellectual strata of the rabbis and, from them, by the Christian apostles form exceptions of great importance for the sociology of religion. Moreover, the prophets did not by any means find their "community," so far as that term applies (of which more later) either solely or primarily in the demos. On the contrary, if they had any personal support at all, it was from distinguished, individual, pious houses in Jerusalem. Sometimes for several generations such served as their patrons. Jeremiah was supported by the same sib which also took part in the "finding" of Deuteronomy. Most sympathetic supporters were found among the *zekenim* as the guardians of the pious tradition and, particularly, the traditional respect for prophecy. Such was the case for Jeremiah in his capital trial; it was also true of Ezekiel, whom the elders consulted in Exile.

The prophets never obtained support from the peasants. Indeed, all prophets preached against debt slavery, the pawning of clothes, against all violation of the charity commandments, which benefited the little man. In Jeremiah's last prophecy, peasants and shepherds were the champions of piety. However, this form of prophecy was true only for Jeremiah. The peasants belonged as little to his following as the rural squirearchy; in fact, the 'am ha-aretz were among the more important opponents of the prophets, especially of Jeremiah who was opposed by his own sib. Because they were strict Yahwists, the prophets declaimed against the rural orgiasticism of the fertility cults and the most tainted rural places of worship. Above all the prophets declaimed against the shrines of Baal, which meant much to the rural population for economic as well as ideal reasons.

The prophets never received support from the king. For the prophets were champions of the Yahwistic tradition opposing kingship which was compromised by politically necessary concessions to foreign cults, intemperate drinking, and by the innovations of the Solomonic corvée state. Solomon was not of the slightest importance for any of the prophets. When a king is mentioned at all, it is David who is the pious ruler. Hosea viewed the kings of the Northern realm as illegitimate, because they had usurped the throne without the will of Yahwe. Amos mentioned the Nazarites and Nebiim among the institutions of Yahwe, but not the kings. Indeed, none of the prophets denied the legitimacy of the Davidians. However, respect even for this dynasty, such as it was, was only conditional. Isaiah's Immanuel-prophecy, after all, may well be considered as the prediction of a God-sent usurper. Yet it was for Isaiah that David's age represented the climax of national history. Relent-

less attacks against the conduct of the respective contemporary kings grew in intensity. Such raging outbursts of wrath and scorn as those of Jeremiah against Joiakim are rarely to be found. Joiakim shall go to earth like an ass (22:19) and the queen mother who apparently participated in the Astarte-cult, shall have her skirt pulled over her head that all might see her shame (13:18 ff.). But even Isaiah called his woe down on the land the king of which "is a child and is led by women" and he stood up boldly to the grown-up king in a personal encounter.

With obvious intent the prophetic tradition preserved the account of Elijah's conflicts with Ahab. The kings returned these antipathies in kind. They tolerated the prophets only in uncertain times, but, whenever they felt sure of themselves, they had recourse, like Manasseh, to bloody persecution. Beside the politically conditioned worship of foreign deities or incorrect cults, the wrath of the prophets against the kings was, above all, directed at world politics *per se*, the means and presuppositions of which were unholy. This applied particularly to the alliance with Egypt. Although fugitive Yahwe prophets, such as Uria, sought refuge in Egypt, and although Egyptian rule was lenient and certainly religiously non-propagandistic, the prophets rebelled with especial bitterness against this alliance. The reason is made obvious in Isaiah (28:18).

Dealings with Egypt are an "agreement with Sheol," that is to say with the chthonian gods of the realm of the dead which they loathed.[1] Obviously in this the prophets rest their

---

[1] It is a conjecture of Duhm that, at another place, it is Osiris presumably who is named among the deities whom Yahwe will destroy.

political attitudes solidly on the priestly tradition; their political stand is throughout religiously conditioned. As against the king, so the prophets declaimed against the mighty, particularly the *sarim* and *gibborim*. Along with the injustice of their courts, the prophets cursed, above all, their impious way of life and debauchery. But obviously the opposition of the prophets was independent of such single vices. The king and political-military circles could make no use whatever of the purely utopian exhortations and counsels of the prophets.

The Hellenic states of the sixth and fifth centuries regularly consulted oracles but in the end and precisely in the days of decision, as, for example, during the Persian war, they failed to honor the advice of their oracles even though they were politically oriented. As a rule, it was politically impossible for the kings of Judah to heed the advice of the prophets. And the knightly sense of dignity which here as elsewhere is aloof from prophetic belief, necessarily made them reject as beneath them Jeremiah's advice with respect to Babylon. They disdained these screaming ecstatics of the streets.

On the other side, the popular opposition against the distinguished knights and patricians of the time of the kings which the intellectual strata had nourished played its part in the attitude of the prophets. Avarice is the preeminent vice, that is to say, usurious oppression of the poor. The prophets are not interested in the royal army. Their future kingdom is a kingdom of peace. In this they did not by any means represent something like "Little Judah" pacifists. Amos promised to Judah dominion over Edom and over those people which are called by Yahwe's name (9:12). The old popular hope of world domination recurred repeatedly. Increasingly, however, the idea gained currency that the political aspirations of Israel would only be realized through a miracle of God, as once at the Red Sea, but not through autonomous military power, and, least of all, through political alliances. Ever anew the wrath of the prophets turned against such alliances. The basis of the opposition was again religious. It was not simply because of the danger of strange cults that such antipathy was felt. Rather, Israel stood in the *berith* with Yahwe. Nothing must enter competition with the *berith*, especially not trust in human help, which would bespeak of godless disbelief and evoke Yahwe's wrath. As Jeremiah saw the matter, if Yahwe had ordained the conquest of the people by Nebuchadnezzar, one must accept the fact.

Defensive alliances against the great kings were offenses against God so long as the great kings were executors of his will. If they were not and if He wished to help Israel, He would do so alone, Isaiah taught. Probably he was the first for this reason to preach indefatigably against all and every attempt to work out an alliance. Clearly, the whole attitude toward internal as well as foreign affairs was purely religious in motivation, nothing bespeaks of political expediencies. The relationship to the priests also was religiously conditioned.

No prophet before Ezekiel spoke favorably of the priests. Amos recognized, as noted, only the Nazarites and Nebiim as Yahwe's tools, but he failed to mention the priests. The very existence of their type of free prophecy was, from the time of its appearance, a clear symptom of the weakness of priestly power. Had the place of the priest been like that in Egypt, or even in Babylon, or in Jerusalem after the Exile, free prophecy would doubtlessly have been suppressed as dangerous competition. Since originally, in the confederate time, there was no central shrine and no official sacrifice, this was impossible. Meanwhile the prestige of the old royal prophets and seers then of Elijah and the Elisha-school was firmly established. Powerful sibs of pious laity backed the prophets. Therefore, the priests had to tolerate them despite frequent and sharp antagonisms. But, they were by no means always antagonistic to the priests. Isaiah had close relations with the priests of Jerusalem and Ezekiel was throughout priestly in outlook. On the other hand, we find the sharpest conceivable personal conflicts with the cult priests, first with Amos in Beth-el and last with Jeremiah in Jerusalem. The latter's trial (Jer. 26) suggests almost a prologue to what was to happen in the same place six hundred years later. Tradition of the events possibly exerted some actual influence later.

Jeremiah was charged with a capital crime because he had prophesied for the Temple the fate of the shrine in Shiloh which the Philistines once had destroyed. He was dragged before the court of officials and elders, and the priests and prophets of salvation acted as his accusers. However the difference of the times is evident in the result. Jeremiah was acquitted on advice of the elders, in spite of the complaint of the priests, on the ground that there existed the precedent of Micah's case. Micah, they said, had prophesied under Hezekiah similar events.[2] The occurrence indicates that prophecies against the Temple itself were rare. Above all such oracles in the last analysis implied no

doubt in the Temple's legitimacy. Later, to be sure, Jeremiah readily comforted himself and others for the loss of the Ark of the Covenant under Nebuchadnezzar. His prophecy, nevertheless, deals with the destruction of the Temple as a grievous misfortune which was only conditionally held out as a punishment for sins in case of failing conversion (26:13).

In fact, no prophet attacked the Temple proper. Amos called the sacrifice in Beth-el and Gilgal transgressions (4:4; 5:5) presumably meaning by this only the cult practices of the peasants. Such cult practices were deeply hated by all representatives of shepherd piety. The people should not frequent these places, but "seek Yahwe" (ibid.). Amos knew Zion as the seat of Yahwe in the same manner as Hosea acknowledged Judah as the one undefiled seat of Yahwe. Isaiah's trust in the invincibility of Jerusalem in his late oracles doubtlessly rested on the presence there of the Temple. It was in a temple vision during his youth that he had seen the heavenly court. For Micah, despite his oracle of doom, Mount Zion remained the future place of the pure Torah and prophecy of Yahwe. The prophets preached only against the impurities of the cult practiced there, particularly against defilement by sacred courtesans. In the case of Hosea almost the whole strength of the prophet was absorbed by the fight against the worship of Baal, a fight which runs through pre-exilic prophecy. But they never preached for the correct priestly cult.

Jeremiah has evidently at first welcomed Deuteronomy and thus the centralization of the cult in the Temple of Jerusalem (2:3), but later (8:8) he terms it the product of the lying "pen of the scribes" because its authors held fast to false worship (8:5) and rejected the prophetic

---

[2] The present version of text, Micah 1:55, is not entirely correct in this.

word (8:9). The implications of this are clarified elsewhere (7:4; 11 ff.), namely, the Temple in itself is useless and will suffer the fate of Shiloh unless the decision is made to change conduct. What is particularly stressed here, alongside single social ethical wrongs, is trust in "unprofitable lying words" (of Zion priests) (7:8). This was the one decisive thing, the failure of the priests to heed those divine imperatives which the prophet announced as directly inspired by Yahwe. Besides the prophet criticized their personal sinfulness.

Thus, in characteristic fashion, the bearer of personal charisma refused to recognize office charisma as a qualification to teach if the priestly teacher is personally unworthy. For, the prophet who did not participate in the cult naturally considered the teaching of God's word (*dabar*) as he received it as religiously all important, hence also in priestcraft the teaching (*torah*) not the cult (Jer. 8:6; 18:18). This held also for Jerusalem (Micah 4:2). Likewise the prophet naturally considered as important for the people only obedience to the *debarim* and the *torah* and not the sacrifice nor ritualistic prescriptions like observance of the Sabbath and circumcision which later in the Exile obtained such decisive significance. Even with Amos, a shepherd, Yahwe is impatient of the Sabbath of the disobedient people,[3] and Jeremiah opposes to external circumcision the "circumcision of the foreskin of the heart" (9:24 ff.) as the only truly important fact.

This does not necessarily imply a denial but, rather, a strong devaluation of all ritual. The prophets, here too, have accepted the intellectual's conceptions which grew out of the *torah*. Yahwe, at least according to the postulate, was a god of just ethical compensation and they considered the mundane fortune of individuals—of which Isaiah speaks (3:10)—just as much as the direct "fruit of their doings," as that of the people. The older prophets at least juxtaposed this massive ethical righteousness of deeds to the equally massive ritualism of the priests. The opposition to the priestly evaluation of the sacrifice increased until, with Amos and Jeremiah, it was completely depreciated. Sacrifice is not commanded by Yahwe and therefore it is useless (Jer. 6:20, 7:21). Even Amos (5:25) argued that no sacrifice was offered in the desert. If the people are rebellious and their hands bloody, then, according to Isaiah (1:11 f.) their sacrifices and fasts are an abomination to Yahwe. Considering Isaiah's relationship to the priesthood and his esteem for the fortress-Temple, it is safe to assume that such words imply no unconditional rejection of cult and sacrifice. The same may well be true of the other prophets. Nevertheless the attitude toward sacrifice in the oracles is cold to the point of enmity.

Through all prophecy sounded the echoes of the "nomadic ideal" as the tradition of the literati idealized the kingless past. To be sure, the shepherd Amos who promised Judah riches in wine (9:13) was as little a Rechabite as Jeremiah. And Jeremiah was the one prophet who entered into personal relationship with the order and upheld its piety as exemplary for Israel. But in his old age, Jeremiah bought an acre of land. Compared to the luxurious and therefore haughty present which was disobedient to Yahwe, the desert times remained to the prophets the truly pious epoch. In the end, Israel will

---

[3] It has generally been assumed, and rightly, that Jeremiah is not the author of Jer. 17:19f.

again be reduced to a desert and the Messiah king as well as the survivors will eat the nourishment of the steppes: honey and cream.

The total attitude of the prophets has often been described as "culture hostility." This should not be understood to mean their personal lack of culture. The prophets are conceivable only on the great sounding board of the world-political stage of their times. Similarly, they are conceivable only in connection with extensive cultural sophistication and a strong cultured stratum, though, for the reasons previously discussed, only in the frame of a small state somewhat similar to Zwingli in a single canton. They were all literate and on the whole obviously well informed as to the peculiarities of Egyptian and Mesopotamian culture, especially, also, in astronomy. The manner in which the prophets used sacred numbers, for example Jeremiah's use of the number "70" may well permit us to infer that they had more than a hazy knowledge of Babylonian astronomy. In any case, tradition records no trait that would permit the inference of any attempts at flight from the world or the denial of culture in the Indian sense.

In addition to the *torah*, the prophets knew also the *chokma* or *'ezah* (Jer. 18:18) of the teachers of prudent living (*chakamim*). However, the educational level of the prophets may well have been more comparable to that of the Orphics and folk prophets of Hellas than to that of the genteel sages as represented by Thales. Not only all aesthetic and all values of genteel living in general, but, also, all worldly wisdom was viewed by them with quite alien eyes. These attitudes were sustained by the antichrematistic tradition of the puritanically pious in their environment who were suspicious of the court, the *gibborim* and the priests. In its inner structure, however, these attitudes of the prophets were purely religiously conditioned by the manner in which they elaborated their experiences.

Part 2

the religious experience

Social forms arise from human experience and interaction; religious forms arise from religious experience and the interaction of people concerned with such experience. Religious experience, the personal subjective relationship of man with the Beyond, is at the very heart of religious life. Religious experience engenders the religious forms and organizations which offer to those who participate in a religious tradition modes of relationship to the Beyond and a social framework for human brotherhood and fellowship. The relationship of the individual to the Beyond is the substance of personal faith. The distinction made by W. C. Smith between faith and "cumulative tradition" is helpful to us in describing the religious experience:

By faith I mean personal faith ... an inner religious experience or involvement of a particular person; the impingement upon him of the transcendent, putative or real. By "cumulative tradition" I mean the entire mass of overt objective data that constitute the historical deposit, as it were, of the past religious life of the community in question: temples, scriptures, theological systems, dance patterns, legal and other social institutions, conventions, moral codes, myths, and so on; anything that can be and is transmitted from one person, one generation, to another, and that the historian can observe.[1]

The student of religion must seek to understand both the subjective aspects of experience and attitude—to understand the faith of men—and the objective forms, created by religious life, that provide its context. He must approach the former through the latter and develop special sensitivity, empathy, and vicarious insight into the experience of *Homo religiosus*.

Many anthropologists, sociologists, and historians of religion have contributed to our understanding of the religious experience. The first selection in this section is a brief passage from the work of Van der Leeuw, the well-known Dutch phenomenologist, describing the experience of the sacred as the encounter with power. Van der Leeuw's work reflects much of the research of earlier scholars, for example, Rudolf Otto's treatment of the holy. Our passage focuses upon men's attitudes toward the sacred object and upon the subsequent translation of these attitudes into established observances, forms,

---

[1] W. C. Smith, *The Meaning and End of Religion* (New York: New American Library, Inc., 1962), p. 141.

and traditions which provide the substance of cumulative traditions and the context for subjective faith.

The classic definition of faith as ultimate concern, posited by the great theologian Paul Tillich, points to the unique and profound character of religious experience. Men during all ages and in every part of the world have exhibited an openness to the Beyond; they have been touched by the ultimate and have related to it in many ways. Biblical men responded to the transcendent God in terms of an I–Thou relation. In archaic and primitive societies and, indeed, in the context of popular religion in the great civilizations of history, men have regarded all nature as sacred and living and have responded to it in ways similar to the I–Thou relation of Western religious man to God. Men related to the imposing presence of dynamic sacred powers within natural forms and processes. We present in this section a simple ancient Mesopotamian poem on salt and grain, quoted and commented upon by the important student of the ancient Middle East, Thorkild Jacobsen. The selection reveals archaic man's religious relation to nature.

The sociologist is not asked to make an ontological judgment about the truth of the religious experience. He seeks to understand man in society, a goal that demands some understanding of man's religious dimension. On this level it is possible to delineate fundamental characteristics of the religious experience which together approximate a definition of it. Joachim Wach, an eminent sociologist of religion, suggests four formal criteria for the identification and definition of religious experience:

1. Religious experience is a response to what is experienced as ultimate reality; that is, in religious experience we react not to any single or finite phenomenon, material or otherwise, but to what we realize as undergirding and conditioning all that constitutes our world of experiences. . . . 2. Religious experience is a total response of the total being to what is apprehended as ultimate reality. That is, we are involved not exclusively with our mind, our affections, or our will, but as integral persons. 3. Religious experience is the most intense experience of which man is capable. That is not to say that all expression of religious experience testifies to this intensity but that, potentially, genuine religious experience is of this nature, as is instanced in conflicts between different basic drives and motivations. Religious loyalty, if it is religious loyalty, wins over all other loyalties. The modern term "existential" designates the profound concern and the utter seriousness of this experience. 4. Religious experience is practical, that is to say it involves an imperative, a commitment which impels man to act. This activistic note distinguishes it from aesthetic experience, of which it shares the intensity, and joins it with moral experience. Moral judgment, however, does not necessarily represent a reaction to ultimate reality.[2]

---

[2] Joachim Wach, "Universals in Religion," in Wach, *Types of Religious Experience* (Chicago: The University of Chicago Press, 1951), pp. 32–33.

the experience of the sacred

five

from Religion in Essence and Manifestation

G. VAN DER LEEUW

Power

1. That which those sciences concerned with Religion regard as the *Object* of Religion is, for Religion itself, the active and primary Agent in the situation or, in this sense of the term, the *Subject*. In other words, the religious man perceives that with which his religion deals as primal, as originative or causal; and only to reflective thought does this become the Object of the experience that is contemplated. For Religion, then, God is the active Agent in relation to man, while the sciences in question can concern themselves only with the activity of man in his relation to God; of the acts of God Himself they can give no account whatever.

2. But when we say that *God* is the Object of religious experience, we must realize that "God" is frequently an extremely indefinite concept which

From *Religion in Essence and Manifestation* by G. Van der Leeuw, published by George Allen & Unwin Ltd. By permission of Allen & Unwin, Ltd. and Peter Smith Publisher, Inc.

does not completely coincide with what we ourselves usually understand by it. Religious experience, in other terms, is concerned with a "Somewhat." But this assertion often means no more than that this "Somewhat" is merely a vague "something"; and in order that man may be able to make more significant statements about this "Somewhat," it must force itself upon him, must oppose itself to him as being Something *Other*. Thus the first affirmation we can make about the Object of Religion is that it is a *highly exceptional* and *extremely impressive* "*Other*." Subjectively, again, the initial state of man's mind is amazement; and as Söderblom has remarked, this is true not only for philosophy but equally for religion. As yet, it must further be observed, we are in no way concerned with the supernatural or the transcendent: we can speak of "God" in a merely figurative sense; but there arises and persists an experience which connects or unites itself to the "Other" that thus obtrudes. Theory, and even the slightest degree of generalization, are still far remote; man remains quite content with the purely practical recognition that this Object is a departure from all that is usual and familiar; and this again is the consequence of the *Power* it generates. The most primitive belief, then, is absolutely empirical; as regards primitive religious experience, therefore, and even a large proportion of that of antiquity, we must in this respect accustom ourselves to interpret the supernatural element in the conception of God by the simple notion of an "Other," of something foreign and highly unusual, and at the same time the consciousness of absolute dependence, so well known to ourselves, by an indefinite and generalized feeling of remoteness.

3. In a letter written by the missionary R. H. Codrington, and published by Max Müller in 1878, the idea of *mana* was referred to for the first time, and naturally in the style of those days, as a "Melanesian name for the Infinite," this description of course being due to Müller;[1] while Codrington himself gave, both in his letter and his own book of 1891, a much more characteristic definition: "It is a power or influence, not physical, and in a way supernatural; but it shows itself in physical force, or in any kind of power or excellence which a man possesses. This Mana is not fixed in anything, and can be conveyed in almost anything; but spirits...have it and can impart it. ...All Melanesian religion consists, in fact in getting this Mana for one's self, or getting it used for one's benefit."[2] Taken generally, this description has completely justified itself. In the South Sea Islands *mana* always means a Power; but the islanders include in this term, together with its derivatives and compounds, such various substantival, adjectival and verbal ideas as Influence, Strength, Fame, Majesty, Intelligence, Authority, Deity, Capability, extraordinary Power: whatever is successful, strong, plenteous: to reverence, be capable, to adore and to prophesy. It is quite obvious, however, that the supernatural, in our sense of this term, cannot here be intended; Lehmann even reproached Codrington for referring to the supernatural at all, and proposed to retain the simple meaning of "successful, capable." Now *mana* actually has this significance; the warrior's *mana,* for instance, is demonstrated by his continuous success in combat, while repeated defeat shows that his *mana* has deserted him. But Lehmann, on his part, sets up a false antithesis between the ideas of "the supernormal" and "the amazing" on the one hand, and on the other the primitive ideas of "the powerful" and "the mighty" in general. It is precisely a characteristic of the earliest thinking that it does not exactly distinguish the magical, and all that borders on the supernatural, from the powerful;[3] to the primitive mind, in fact, all marked "efficiency" is *per se* magical, and "sorcery" *eo ipso* mighty; and Codrington's own phrase, "in a way supernatural," appears to have expressed the accurate implication. Here we must certainly clearly distinguish such ideas from what we ourselves regard as supernatural. Power is authenticated (or verified) empirically: in all cases whenever anything unusual or great, effective or successful is manifested, people speak of *mana.* There is, at the same time, a complete absence

---

[1] *The Origin and Growth of Religion,* 53.

[2] *The Melanesians,* 118, Note 1.

[3] *Cf.* here Rudolf Otto, *Das Gefühl des Überweltlichen (Sensus numinus),* 1932, 55: "What is comprehended as 'Power' is also comprehended as *tremendum.* It renders its objects *tabu*"; *cf.* E. Arbmann, *Seele und Mana, AR.* 29, 1931, 332.

of theoretical interest. What is "natural" in the sense of what may ordinarily be expected never arouses the recognition of *mana;* "a thing is *mana* when it is strikingly effective; it is not *mana* unless it is so," asserts a Hocart Islander. It is just as unmistakably authenticated by a dexterous plunge into the sea as by the conduct of the tribal chieftain. It indicates equally good luck (*veine*) as potency, and there is no antithesis whatever between secular acts and sacred; every extraordinary action generates the experience of Power, and the belief in Power is in the fullest sense practical; "originally therefore the conception of magical power and that of capacity in general are most probably identical."[4] Power may be employed in magic, while the magical character pertains to every unusual action; yet it would be quite erroneous to designate potency in general as magical power, and Dynamism as the theory of magic. Magic is certainly manifested by power; to employ power, however, is not in itself to act magically, although every extraordinary action of primitive man possesses a tinge of the magical.[5] The creation of the earth is the effect of the divine *mana,* but so is all capacity; the chief's power, the happiness of the country, depend on *mana:* similarly the beam of the latrine has its own mode, probably because excreta, like all parts of the body, function as receptacles of power. That any reference to magic in the technical sense is superfluous is clear from the statement that "the foreigners were after all victorious, and now the Maori are completely subjected to the *mana* of the English."[6] Yet to the primitive mind the alien authority is no such perfectly reasonable a power as it is to ourselves; again Codrington has described the situation correctly by his "in a way supernatural." Characteristic also is the manner in which the indigenes explain the power of the Christian mass:[7] "If you go to the priest and ask him to pray so that I may die, and he consents, then he celebrates mass, so that I shall die. I die suddenly, and the people say that the priest's mass is *mana,* because a youth has perished."

It is inevitable, still further, that since Power is in no degree systematically understood,, it is never homogeneous nor uniform. One may possess either great or limited *mana;* two magicians may attack each other by employing two sorts of *mana.* Power enjoys no moral value whatever. *Mana* resides alike in the poisoned arrow and in European remedies, while with the Iroquois *orenda*[8] one both blesses and curses. It is simply a matter of Power, alike for good or evil.

4. Codrington's discovery was followed by others in the most diverse parts of the world. The *orenda* of the Iroquois has just been referred to; "it appears that they interpreted the activities of Nature as the ceaseless strife between one *orenda* and another."[9] The Sioux Indians again, be-

---

4 Preuss, *AR.* IX, 1906.
5 "To seek to derive numinous power from magical is altogether to invert the situation, since long before the magician could appropriate and manipulate it, it had been 'apperceived as numinous' in plant and animal, in natural processes and objects, in the horror of the skeleton, and also independently of all these." Otto, *Gefühl des Überweltlichen,* 56.

6 Lehmann, *Mana,* 24.
7 *Ibid.,* 58 (Wallis Island).
8 *Cf.* below.
9 Hewitt, "Orenda and a Definition of Religion," *Amer. Anthropologist,* N.S. IV, 1902.

lieve in *wakanda,* at one time a god of the type of an originator,[10] at another an impersonal Power which acquires empirical verification whenever something extraordinary is manifested. Sun and moon, a horse (a *wakanda*-dog!), cult implements, places with striking features: all alike are regarded as *wakan* or *wakanda,* and once again its significance must be expressed by widely different terms:—powerful, holy, ancient, great, *etc.* In this instance also the theoretical problem of the universality of *wakanda* is not raised; the mind still remains at the standpoint of empirically substantiating the manifestation Power.

In contrast with *mana,* however, and together with some other ideas of Power, *wakanda* represents one specific type, since it is capable of transformation into the conception of a more or less personal god. This is also the case with the *manitu* of the Algonquins of North-West America, which is a power that confers their capacity on either harmful or beneficent objects, and gives to European missionaries their superiority over native medicine-men. Animals are *manido* whenever they possess supernatural power;[11] but *manitu* is also employed in a personal sense for spirit, and *kitshi* manitu is the Great Spirit, the Originator. The Dyaks of Borneo, similarly, recognize the power of *petara,* which is something, but also someone, while in Madagascar the *hasina*-power confers upon the king, on foreigners and whites their striking and supernormal qualities.

Among the ancient Germans, too, the idea of Power was dominant. The power of life, luck (*hamingja*), was a quantitative potency. Men fought by inciting their luck against somebody (Old Nordic: *etia hamingju*), and were defeated because they possessed too little "luck."[12] The Swedish peasant senses "power" in bread, in the horse, *etc.,* while in Nordic folklore the woman whose child has been stolen by a troll is unable to pursue her because she "has been robbed of her power."

Finally, Power may be assigned to some definite bearer or possessor from whom it emanates. Such a power is the Arabian *baraka,*[13] which is regarded as an emanation from holy men and closely connected with their graves; it is acquired by pilgrimage, and to be cured of some disease a king's wife seeks the *baraka* of a saint. This beneficent power also is confined to specific localities; thus the place in which to study is not indifferent so far as its results are concerned, and in Mecca "the attainment of knowledge is facilitated by the *baraka* of the spot."[14]

5. But even when Power is not expressly assigned a name the idea of Power often forms the basis of religion, as we shall be able to observe almost continually in the sequel. Among extensive divisions of primitive peoples, as also those of antiquity, the Power in the Universe was almost invariably an impersonal Power. Thus we may speak of Dynamism—of the interpretation of the Universe in terms of Power; I prefer this expression to both Animatism and Pre-

---

10 *Cf.* Chap. 18.

11 *Cf.* an animal fairy tale of the Algonquins: "The elks, which were *manido,* knew in advance what the hunter would do"; and they were able, "since they were *manido,* at any time to return to life." W. Krickeberg, *Indianermärchen aus Nord-Amerika,* 1924, 69.

12 V. Grönbech, *Vor Folkeaet i Oldtiden,* I, 1909, 189 *f.*

13 Derived from the root *brk,* to bless.

14 O. Rescher, *Studien über den Inhalt von* 1001 *Nacht, Islam* 9, 1918, 24 *f.*

Animism:—to the former because "Universal Animation" smacks too much of theory. The primitive mind never halts before the distinction between inorganic, and organic, Nature; what it is always concerned with is not Life, which appears to explain itself, but Power, authenticated purely empirically by one occurrence after another; thus the Winnebago (Sioux) offers tobacco to any unusual object because it is *wakan*. From the term "Pre-Animism," however, it would be inferred that, chronologically, priority is due to the idea of Power as contrasted with other conceptions such as the animistic.[15]

Potency. Awe. *Tabu*

1. The experience of the potency of things or persons may occur at any time; it is by no means confined to specific seasons and occasions. Powerfulness always reveals itself in some wholly unexpected manner; and life is therefore a dangerous affair, full of critical moments. If then one examines them more closely, even the most ordinary events, the customary associations with one's neighbours, or similarly one's long familiar tasks, prove to be replete with "mystic" interconnections. We may say indeed (as *e.g.* Marett maintains) that the explanation of any fact, however natural it may appear, is ultimately always "mystic." But we should probably express ourselves in more

primitive fashion if we completely ignored our own scheme of explanation in terms of single causes, and in place of this interpreted life as a broad current of mighty powers whose existence we do not specifically observe, but which occasionally makes itself conspicuous by either the damming or the flooding of its waters. If, for instance, one of the Toradja tribes in Celebes is preparing for an expedition and an earthen pot is broken, then they remain at home, saying that it is *measa*.[16] This may be translated as "a sign": only not in any rationalistic sense as indicating some future misfortune, but that the current of life has been interrupted: If then one thing has been broken, why not more? Similarly, when an Ewe tribesman finds refuge from his enemies on a white ant hill he ascribes his escape to the power residing there.[17] Thus the place, the action, the person in which the power reveals itself receive a specific character. Bearers of *mana,* for example, are sharply distinguished from the rest of the world: they are self-sufficient. By the Greeks, similarly, a body struck by lightning was regarded as holy, ἱερὄς, because powerfulness was manifested in it.[18]

Objects, persons, times, places or actions charged with Power are called *tabu* (*tapu*), a word from the same cultural domain as *mana*. It indicates "what is expressly named," "exceptional," while the verb *tapui* means "to make holy."[19] *Tabu* is thus a

15 Lehmann (*Mana,* 83) criticizes Marett for abandoning his conception of Pre-Animism as a stage "logically but also in some sense chronologically prior to animism" (*The Threshold of Religion,* 11), because "only the genetic method of approach can lead to the solution of our problem." But this method can in no case attain *our* goal, which is the comprehension of the phenomena in accord with their spiritual content.

16 A. C. Kruyt, "Measa," *Bydr. Taal-, Land- en Volkenkunde Ned. Indie,* 74–76, 1918–1920.
17 K. Th. Preuss, *Glauben und Mystik im Schatten des höchsten Wesens,* 1926, 25.
18 *Cf.* Euripides, *The Suppliant Women,* 934 *ff.*
19 Söderblom, *Das Werden des Gottesglaubens,* 31 *f.*

sort of warning: "Danger! High voltage!" Power has been stored up, and we must be on our guard. The *tabu* is the expressly authenticated condition of being replete with power, and man's reaction to it should rest on a clear recognition of this potent fullness, should maintain the proper distance and secure protection.

The *tabu* is observed in different ways and with regard to highly contrasted objects. To the Greek the *king* and the *foreigner* or *stranger* appeared as objects of *aidos,* of awe, to be duly respected by keeping one's distance.[20] Almost everywhere the king is looked upon as powerful, so that he should be approached only with the greatest caution, while the foreigner, bearer of a power unknown and therefore to be doubly feared, stands on an equal footing with an enemy; *hostis* is both stranger or foreigner, and enemy. One may either kill the alien, if one is in a position so to do, or bid him welcome; but in no case are his coming and going to be regarded with indifference. *Greeting* is therefore a religious act, intended to intercept the first onset of the power, and into which the name of God is introduced or to which an appeasing influence is attached (*e.g.* the Semitic peace greeting: *adieu*: *Grüssgott*). *Hospitality,* therefore, as well as *war,* is a religious act, intended either to repel the alien power or to neutralize it. *Sex life* is also full of potency, *woman* being distinguished from man by mysterious peculiarities; thus the *veil* served as a defence even before it became a symbol of bashfulness.[21] Everything concerned with the sexual is

"exceptional": when one is sexually impure one must be careful, and not *e.g.* undertake any important matter such as war. Nor should one approach a menstruating woman, who is often excluded from a cult for this very reason:—her potent influence would antagonize the power to be acquired by means of the cult; hence the formula: *hostis vinctus mulier virgo exesto*—"Let every stranger, bound person, woman or virgin stand aside" —associated with certain Roman sacrifices. Similarly as regards Cato's warning in connection with the "vow for the cattle: a woman may not take part in this offering nor see how it is performed."[22] Some one day, again, or series of days, is regarded as being more potent than others. Sabbath, Sunday, Christmas Day and their primitive and heathen equivalents are sacred: no work is done, or at least no important affairs undertaken. Thus the battle of Thermopylae was lost because the "holy days" (ἱερομηνία) imposed on the Spartans a cessation of hostilities; and for the same reason they arrived at Marathon too late. On very sacred days even the slightest labour was forbidden; for critical times must never be allowed to pass unnoticed but must be met by some relevant exceptional behaviour on man's own part, such as fasting. *Tabu,* then, is the avoidance of deed and of word, springing from awe in the presence of Power. Words concerning critical affairs like hunting, war, sex intercourse, should not be uttered, but rather be replaced by a specially elaborated *tabu* language, remnants of which we still retain in our sportsmen's slang and thieves' jargon. Even a peculiar women's terminology occurs side by side with the men's.

---

20 Cf. *Theol. Wörterbuch zum N.T.,* Αἰδώς.

21 *De Agri Cultura,* 83; *votum pro bubus: mulier ad eam rem divinam ne adsit neve videat quo modo fiat.*

---

22 *Cf.* I *Cor.* xi. 5 *ff.*

But the mere avoidance, as such, of potency cannot suffice. Among the Kaian of Central Borneo, for example, neither man nor woman may touch slaughtered fowl during the woman's pregnancy, nor may the man pound the soil, *etc.*;[23] to our minds the connection and the purpose here are obscure. The *tabu,* however, is anything but a measure of utility: Power has revealed itself, either as cessation or as superfluity. It is therefore not only a question of avoiding it, but also of thinking of some defence against it. Sometimes the mode of protection is intelligible to us, as with veil or some sort of ritual or discipline such as fasting; often, however, we cannot fathom it at all. Associations then appear which we moderns quite fail to understand, and feelings to which we are wholly insusceptible. But even when we do succeed, what we regard as a causative connection does not emerge, just as little as there arises an emotional reaction in the sense of our reverence or devotion, though both these may be incorporated in the primitive attitude. The *tabu,* further, may be decreed; some power bearer, a king or priest, can endow an object with his own power and proclaim a season of potency; in Polynesia the king's messenger thus announces the *tabu:*

Tabu—no one may leave his house!
Tabu—no dog may bark!
Tabu—no cock may crow!
Tabu—no pig may grunt!
Sleep—sleep, till the *tabu* is past![24]

In Manipur, in Assam, the village priest ordains a similar communal *tabu* called *genna*; the gates of the village are closed; the friend outside must stay there, and the stranger who may chance to be within remains; the men cook their own food and eat it without the women. All the food *tabus* are carefully observed; trading and catching fish, hunting, mowing grass and felling trees are forbidden. Thus an intentionally evoked interruption of life occurs: the moment is critical, one holds one's breath! At particularly sacred times, in fact, holiday-making still retains a ritual air even in some European rural districts. In Dutch Gelderland on Christmas Eve fifty years ago, for example, everything indoors was carefully arranged; neither plough nor harrow might be left outside, all implements being brought into the barns and the gates leading to the fields closed. Everything must be locked up and under cover in its right place, "otherwise *'Derk met den beer'* (the wild huntsmen) would take it with them."[25]

Violation of the *tabu* brought in its train not punishment, but an automatic reaction of Power; it was quite unnecessary to inflict any penalties when Power assailed one spontaneously. With the best intentions, for instance, Uzzah wished to support the ark of the covenant; the touch of the sacred object, however, entailed death.[26] But it was no divine arbitrariness, and still less divine justice, that struck him down: it was the purely dynamic anger of the Lord.[27] Even a comic sidelight is instructive

---

[23] A. W. Nieuwenhuis, *Quer durch Borneo,* II, 1907, 101.

[24] P. Hambruch, *Südseemärchen,* 1921, No. 66; *cf.* also Frazer, *The Belief in Immortality,* II, 389; no fire may be kept alight, no canoe launched, no swimming enjoyed. The dogs' and pigs' mouths are tied up so that they cannot bark nor grunt.

[25] H. W. Heuvel, *Oud-achterhoeksch boerenleven,* 1927, 471.

[26] 2 *Sam.* vi.

[27] Actually, not the wrath of Jahveh, but simply "wrath"; "it was not difficult for 'primitive man' to speak of wrath that was not the wrath of *anyone* whatever." Otto, *Gef. des Überwelt.* 55.

here:—In Thuringia every form of work was most strictly prohibited on "Golden (Trinity) Sunday"; and a lad who, in spite of this, had sewn a button on his trousers on the holy day could only with the utmost difficulty save himself from death by a lightning stroke the next day, by sacrificing the garment concerned and allowing it to slip into the water, when it was promptly carried off by Nemesis.[28] From our viewpoint, of course, only the lad was guilty and not his trousers! But Power questions not as to guilt or innocence; it reacts, exactly as the electric current shocks anyone who carelessly touches the wire. In Central Celebes death is the penalty for incest, not, however, as a punishment, but merely as a means of limiting the evil results of the outrage to the delinquents; that the latter should die was regarded as a matter of course.[29] Death by being cast from the *Saxum Tarpeium,* which the Romans inflicted upon traitors, was likewise not punishment but a reaction of the Power; the *tribuni plebis,* who were sacrosanct, that is, the bearers of a most formidable potency, appear as the executioners, while whoever fell, without dying as the result, saved his life; "it is a matter less of an execution than of an intentional accident."[30]

Naturally the effectiveness of the *tabu* was believed in without any reservations whatever. A Maori would die of hunger rather than light a fire with the lighting utensils of a chief,[31] and Howitt heard of a Kurnai boy who had stolen some opossum meat and eaten this before the food

tabus permitted. The tribal elders persuaded him that he would never be a man; he lay down, and in three weeks was dead.[32] Similar examples might be multiplied indefinitely.

2. We characterize the distance between the potent and the relatively powerless as the relationship between *sacred* and *profane,* or secular. The "sacred" is what has been placed within boundaries, the exceptional (Latin *sanctus*); its powerfulness creates for it a place of its own. "Sacred" therefore means neither completely moral nor, without further qualification, even desirable or praiseworthy. On the contrary, sacredness and even impurity may be identical: in any event the potent is dangerous. The Roman *tribunus plebis,* just referred to, was so sacred, *sacrosanctus,* that merely to meet him on the street made one impure.[33] Among the Maori also *tapu* means "polluted" just as much as "holy"; but in any case it carries a prohibition with it, and therefore prescribes keeping one's proper distance. It is, then, scarcely correct to regard the contrast between sacred and secular as developing out of the distinction between threatening danger and what is not perilous.[34] Power has its own specific quality which forcibly impresses men as dangerous. Yet the perilous is not sacred, but rather the sacred dangerous. In a quite classical way Söderblom has presented the contrast between holy and profane as the

---

[28] O. von Reinsberg-Düringsfeld, *Das festliche Jahr,*[2] 1898, 24.

[29] Kruyt, "Measa."

[30] A. Piganiol, *Essai sur les Origines de Rome,* 1917, 149.

[31] Frazer, *op. cit.,* 44.

[32] Elsie C. Parsons, "Links between Morality and Religion in Early Culture," *Amer. Anthrop.,* 17, 1915, 46.

[33] Plutarch, *Quaestiones romanae,* 81. This passage seems not quite clear, but in any case impurity, involved by the sacredness of the tribune, is implied.

[34] As B. Ankermann does in Chantepie, 152; *cf.* GENERAL, LITERATURE, p. 19 *ante.*

primal and governing antithesis in all religion, and has shown how the old viewpoint, that Wonder, Θαυμάζειν, is the beginning of Philosophy, can be applied with yet greater justice to Religion. For whoever is confronted with potency clearly realizes that he is in the presence of some quality with which in his previous experience he was never familiar, and which cannot be evoked from something else but which, *sui generis* and *sui juris,* can be designated only by religious terms such as "sacred" and "numinous." All these terms have a common relationship in that they indicate a firm conviction, but at the same time no definite conception, of the completely different, the absolutely distinct. The first impulse aroused by all this is avoidance, but also seeking: man should avoid Power, but he should also seek it. No longer can there be a "why" or "wherefore" here; and Söderblom is undeniably correct when, in this connection, he defines the essence of all religion by saying that it is mystery.[35] Of that aspect there was already a deep subjective assurance even when no god was invoked. For to religion "god" is a late comer.

3. In the human soul, then, Power awakens a profound feeling of awe which manifests itself both as fear and as being attracted. There is no religion whatever without terror, but equally none without love, or that *nuance* of being attracted which corresponds to the prevailing ethical level. For the simplest form of religious feeling Marett has suggested the fine word *Awe,* and Otto the term *Scheu,* which is somewhat less com-prehensive; the Greek *aidos* too is most pertinent.[36] The expression adopted must be a very general one, since it is a question of establishing an attitude which includes the whole personality at all its levels and in countless *nuances.* Physical shuddering, ghostly horror, fear, sudden terror, reverence, humility, adoration, profound apprehension, enthusiasm—all these lie *in nuce* within the awe experienced in the presence of Power. And because these attitudes show two main tendencies, one away from Power and the other towards it, we speak of the *ambivalent* nature of awe.

Of course *tabu* means a prohibition, and Power reveals itself first of all always as something to be avoided. Everywhere, too, the prohibition announces itself earlier than the command; but Freud has very ably shown how the former always implies the latter.[37] Man is fully conscious only of the prohibition, while the command usually remains unrecognized. What we hate we love, and what we truly love we could, at the same time hate. "For each man kills the thing he loves" said Oscar Wilde, and this is far more than a brilliant phrase. In the presence of the something different which we recognize as "Wholly Other," our conduct is always ambivalent. Love may be described as an attempt to force oneself into the place of the other; hate, as the fear of love.

But whether the sacred releases feelings of hate and fear, or those of love and reverence, it always confronts man with some absolute task. The *tabu* has therefore, and not without justification, been described as

---

35 Very well expressed in the Essay: "Points of Contact for Missionary Work," *Int. Review of Missions,* 1919.

36 *Cf.* Murray, *The Rise of the Greek Epic.*

37 *Totem and Taboo,* 31 *f.,* 41 *f.*

the oldest form of the categorical imperative.[38] Of course we must not think of Kant's argument in this connection. Nevertheless *tabu* and categorical imperative have in common the character of complete irrationality as well as absoluteness. "Thou shalt" —what one should do is a secondary issue; why one should do it is not a question at all. Confronted with Power, which he experiences as being of completely contrasted nature, man apprehends its absolute demand. An irruption occurs in his life, and he is drawn in two directions: he is seized with dread, and yet he loves his dread.

4. Having once established itself, awe develops into *observance;* and we can trace this advance in the Roman concept *religio,* which originally signified nothing more than *tabu.* In the description of an eerie place, in *Virgil,* the primal awe still glimmers: the sacred grove of the Capitol has a "dread awe" (*religio dira*).[39] But the ancient shudder lives also in custom: a sudden death is a *portentum* —a sign of potency that enters *in religionem populo,*[40] or as we should say, "renders the people impure." It was, then, preferable to put up with a ceremonial repetition of the consular election, rather than permit a *tabu* to remain in force over the people.[41] Again, an illness is thus exorcised: *hanc religionem evoco educo excanto*

de istis membris . . .[42] "I call out, I draw out, I sing out, this pollution from these limbs." Thus we can comprehend the definition given by Masurius Sabinus: "*religiosum* is that which because of some sacred quality is removed and withdrawn from us."[43] This is, precisely, the sacred; and constant regard to it is the chief element in the relationship between man and all that is extraordinary. The most probable derivation of the word is from *relegere*—to observe or pay attention; *homo religiosus,* therefore, is the antithesis to *homo negligens.*[44]

We can now understand, still further, how it is that awe, in the long run, must become pure observance, and intense dread mere formalism. In this respect Freud's conclusions are wholly justified: primeval prohibitions "descend, like a hereditary disease."[45] Nevertheless Freud has forgotten that no matter how much man's practical religious conduct may thus be governed by transmissible *tabus,* still profound awe and "aweful" potency must have subsisted to begin with. Observance, then, is just benumbed awe which, at any moment, can be revived. Even in our own country people's "ancient custom," in Indonesian *adat* and in court and university ceremonial, there still lives something of the awe of contact with Power. At the court of Philip IV of Spain, who died in 1665,

---

[38] Freud, *ibid.* Preface, rather than 114 *f.,* on the equivalence with conscience. So far as I am aware, the first writer to whom the resemblance suggested itself was J. E. Harrison, *Epilegomena to the Study of Greek Religion,* 11.

[39] *Aeneid,* VIII, 347.

[40] Cicero, *De Deorum Natura,* II, 4, 10.

[41] *Ibid.* 11; *quam haerere in re publica religionem.*

[42] G. Appel, *De Romanorum precationibus,* 1909, 43.

[43] Gellius, IV, ix, 8; *religiosum est, quod propter sanctitatem aliquam remotum ac sepositum a nobis est.*

[44] *Cf.* W. F. Otto, *Religio und Superstitio, AR.* 12, 1909; 14, 1911. Felix Hartmann, *Glotta,* 4, 1913, 368 *f.* Max Kobbert, *De verborum religio et religiosus usu apud Romanos quaestiones selectae,* 1910.

[45] *Faust,* Part I.

an officer who freed the queen from the stirrup of her runaway horse had to go into exile; an incident in which it is obvious how the touch *tabu* had developed into court etiquette.

Even when vivid awe has been lost, observance continues to serve highly practical purposes. In Indonesia and Polynesia, for instance, the *tabu* is a means of asserting unquestionable right of possession to a piece of ground; some sign indicates the prohibition of stealing it or trespassing on it.[46] We should none the less be quite mistaken in concluding that the *tabu* came into being by virtue of these purely utilitarian considerations, or even that it was invented by the great ones of the earth for their own profit and benefit. Frequently it may certainly be mere routine practice, but it always has intense awe as its presupposition. The "sign," again, resembles our warning notices so closely that it may readily be confused with them; but the punishment threatened by the police is omitted, although it will doubtless appear of its own accord: on Amboina the trespasser is smitten with leprosy; and further, the prohibition itself is not rationally grounded; on the same island a rough sketch of a female sex organ—that is, something particularly "potent"—replaces the legal notification.[47] "Property" in its primitive sense, then, is something quite different from what it is with us—it is a "mystical" relation between owner and owned; the possessor is not the *beatus possidens,* but the depositary of a power that is superior to himself.

Once the belief in *tabu* has completely become mere observance, an empty shell, then man breaks his fetters. In the Euripidean *Herakles* neither Nature nor pure humanity can be defiled by the *tabu* of death; Herakles need only take off the veil and show his head to the light:

> Eternal is the element:
> Mortal, thou canst not pollute the
> heavens.

again:

> No haunting curse can pass from friend
> to friend.[48]

This is essentially the "modern" feeling, which opposes power in nature and personality.

---

[46] Here *Mark* vii. 11 *f.* may be referred to, where the duty of children to maintain their parents is rendered futile by an alleged *tabu* of such support as a sacrifice (*korban*).

---

[47] J. G. Riedel, *De Sluik- en kroesharige rassen tusschen Selebes en Papoea,* 1886, 62.

[48] *Herakles,* 1232 *ff.* (Way).

the dimension of ultimacy

six

What Faith Is

Faith as Ultimate Concern

Faith is the state of being ultimately concerned: the dynamics of faith are the dynamics of man's ultimate concern. Man, like every living being, is concerned about many things, above all about those which condition his very existence, such as food and shelter. But man, in contrast to other living beings, has spiritual concerns—cognitive, aesthetic, social, political. Some of them are urgent, often extremely urgent, and each of them as well as the vital concerns can claim ultimacy for a human life or the life of a social group. If it claims ultimacy it demands the total surrender of him who accepts this claim, and it promises total fulfillment even if all other claims have to be subjected to it or rejected in its name. If a national group makes the life and growth of the nation its ultimate concern, it demands that all other concerns, economic well-being, health and life, family, aesthetic and cognitive

From pp. 1–4 in *Dynamics of Faith* by Paul Tillich. Copyright © 1957 by Paul Tillich. By permission of Harper & Row, Publishers, Inc.

truth, justice and humanity, be sacrificed. The extreme nationalisms of our century are laboratories for the study of what ultimate concern means in all aspects of human existence, including the smallest concern of one's daily life. Everything is centered in the only god, the nation—a god who certainly proves to be a demon, but who shows clearly the unconditional character of an ultimate concern.

But it is not only the unconditional demand made by that which is one's ultimate concern, it is also the promise of ultimate fulfillment which is accepted in the act of faith. The content of this promise is not necessarily defined. It can be expressed in indefinite symbols or in concrete symbols which cannot be taken literally, like the "greatness" of one's nation in which one participates even if one has died for it, or the conquest of mankind by the "saving race," etc. In each of these cases it is "ultimate fulfillment" that is promised, and it is exclusion from such fulfillment which is threatened if the unconditional demand is not obeyed.

An example—and more than an example—is the faith manifest in the religion of the Old Testament. It also

50 the religious experience

has the character of ultimate concern in demand, threat and promise. The content of this concern is not the nation—although Jewish nationalism has sometimes tried to distort in into that—but the content is the God of justice, who, because he represents justice for everybody and every nation, is called the universal God, the God of the universe. He is the ultimate concern of every pious Jew, and therefore in his name the great commandment is given: "You shall love the Lord your God with all your heart, and with all your soul, and with all your might" (Deut 6:5). This is what ultimate concern means and from these words the term "ultimate concern" is derived. They state unambiguously the character of genuine faith, the demand of total surrender to the subject of ultimate concern. The Old Testament is full of commands which make the nature of this surrender concrete, and it is full of promises and threats in relation to it. Here also are the promises of symbolic indefiniteness, although they center around fulfillment of the national and individual life, and the threat is the exclusion from such fulfillment through national extinction and individual catastrophe. Faith, for the men of the Old Testament, is the state of being ultimately and uncondi-tionally concerned about Jahweh and about what he represents in demand, threat and promise.

Another example—almost a counter-example, yet nevertheless equally revealing—is the ultimate concern with "success' and with social standing and economic power. It is the god of many people in the highly competitive Western culture and it does what every ultimate concern must do: it demands unconditional surrender to its laws even if the price is the sacrifice of genuine human relations, personal conviction, and creative *eros*. Its threat is social and economic defeat, and its promise—indefinite as all such promises—the fulfillment of one's being. It is the breakdown of this kind of faith which characterizes and makes religiously important most contemporary literature. Not false calculations but a misplaced faith is revealed in novels like *Point of No Return*. When fulfilled, the promise of this faith proves to be empty.

Faith is the state of being ultimately concerned. The content matters infinitely for the life of the believer, but it does not matter for the formal definition of faith. And this is the first step we have to make in order to understand the dynamics of faith.

religion and relationship

seven

The Mesopotamian Attitude Toward the Phenomena of Nature

THORKILD JACOBSEN

Assuming...that the Mesopotamian view of the universe was as old as Mesopotamian civilization itself, we must next ask how it could be at all possible to take such a view. Certainly for us it has no meaning whatever to speak of the universe as a state—of stones and stars, winds and waters, as citizens and as members of legislative assemblies. Our universe is made up largely of things, of dead matter with neither life nor will. This leads us to the question of what the Mesopotamian saw in the phenomena which surrounded him, the world in which he lived.

...The world appears to primitive man neither inanimate nor empty but redundant with life. It was said of primitive man that 'any phenomenon may at any time face him not as "It" but as "Thou." In this confrontation "Thou" reveals individuality, qualities, will.' Out of the repeated experience of the 'I–Thou' relationship a fairly consistent personalistic view may develop. Objects and phenomena in man's environment become personified in varying degrees. They are somehow alive; they have wills of their own; each is a definite personality. We then have what the late Andrew Lang disapprovingly described as 'that inextricable confusion in which men, beasts, plants, stones, stars are all on one level of personality and animated existence.'[1]

A few examples may show that Lang's words well describe the Mesopotamian's approach to the phenomena around him. Ordinary kitchen salt is to us an inanimate substance, a mineral. To the Mesopotamian it was a fellow-being whose help might be sought if one had fallen victim to sorcery and witchcraft. The sufferer would then address it as follows:

O Salt, created in a clean place,
For food of gods did Enlil destine thee.
Without thee no meal is set out in Ekur,
Without thee god, king, lord, and prince
    do not smell incense.
I am so-and-so, the son of so-and-so,

From *Before Philosophy* by Henri Frankfurt et al., pp. 142–48, first published by The University of Chicago Press, 1946. Reprinted by permission of The University of Chicago Press.

---

[1] "Mythology," in the *Encyclopaedia Britannica* (11th ed.), Vol. XIX, p. 134.

Held captive by enchantment,
Held in fever by bewitchment.
O Salt, break my enchantment! Loose my spell!
Take from me the bewitchment!—And as my Creator
I shall extol thee.[2]

As Salt, a fellow-creature with special powers, can be approached directly, so can Grain. When a man offered up flour to conciliate an angry deity, he might say to it:

I will send thee to my angry god, my angry goddess,
Whose heart is filled with furious rage against me.
Do thou reconcile my angry god, my angry goddess.

Both Salt and Grain are thus not the inanimate substances for which we know them. They are alive, have personality and a will of their own. So had any phenomenon in the Mesopotamian world whenever it was approached in a spirit other than that of humdrum, practical, everyday pursuits: in magic, in religion, in speculative thought. In such a world it obviously gives better sense than it does in our world to speak of the relations between phenomena of nature as social relations, of the order in which they function as an order of wills, as a state.

By saying that the phenomena of the world were alive for the Mesopotamian, that they were personified, we have made things simpler than they actually are. We have glossed over a potential distinction which was felt by the Mesopotamian. It is not correct to say that each phenomenon was a person; we must say that there was a will and a personality in each phenomenon—in it and yet somehow behind it, for the single concrete phenomenon did not completely circumscribe and exhaust the will and personality associated with it. For instance, a particular lump of flint had a clearly recognizable personality and will. Dark, heavy, and hard, it would show a curious willingness to flake under the craftsman's tool though that tool was only of horn softer than the stone against which it was pressed. Now, this characteristic personality which confronts one here, in this particular lump of flint, may meet one also over there, in another lump of flint, which seems to say: 'Here I am again—dark, heavy, hard, willing to flake, I, Flint!' Wherever one met it, its name was 'Flint,' and it would suffer itself to flake easily. That was because it has once fought the god Ninurta, and Ninurta had imposed flaking on it as a punishment.[3]

We may consider another example —the reeds which grew in the Mesopotamian marshes. It is quite clear from our texts that, in themselves, they were never divine. Any individual reed counted merely as a plant, a thing, and so did all reeds. The concrete individual reed, however, had wonderful qualities which inspired awe. There was a mysterious power to grow luxuriantly in the marshes. A reed was capable of amazing things, such as the music which would come out of a shepherd's pipe, or the meaningful signs which would take form under the scribe's reed stylus and make a story or a poem. These powers, which were to be found in every reed and were always the same, combined for the Mesopotamian into a divine personality—that of the goddess Nidaba. It was Nidaba who made the reeds thrive in the marshes; if she were not near, the shepherd could not soothe the heart

---

[2] *Maqlû,* Tablet VI, 111–19.

[3] Verdict on Flint in *Lugal-e.*

with music from his reed pipe. To her would the scribe give praise when a difficult piece of writing had come out from under his stylus and he saw it to be good. The goddess was thus the power in all reeds; she made them what they were, lent them her mysterious qualities. She was one with every reed in the sense that she permeated it as an animating and characterizing agent; but she did not lose her identity in that of the concrete phenomenon and was not limited by any or even all existing reeds.[4] In a crude but quite effective manner the Mesopotamian artists suggested this relationship when they depicted the reed-goddess. She is shown in human form as a venerable matron. But the reeds also are there: they sprout from her shoulders—are bodily one with her and seem to derive directly from her.

In a great many individual phenomena, such as individual lumps of flint or individual reeds, the Mesopotamian thus felt that he was confronted by a single self. He sensed, as it were, a common power-centre which was charged with a particular personality and was itself personal. This personal power-centre pervaded the individual phenomena and gave them the character which they are seen to have: 'Flint' all lumps of flint, Nidaba all reeds, etc.

Even more curious than this, however, is the fact that one such self might infuse itself into other different selves and, in a relation of partial identity, lend them of its character. We may illustrate by quoting a Mesopotamian incantation by which a man sought to become identical with Heaven and Earth:

I am Heaven, you cannot touch me,
I am Earth, you cannot bewitch me![5]

The man is trying to ward off sorcery from his body, and his attention is centred on a single quality of Heaven and Earth, their sacred inviolability. When he has made himself identical with them, this quality will flow into him and merge with his being, so that he will be secure from attacks by witchcraft.

Very similar is another incantation in which a man endeavours to drench every part of his body in immunity by such identification with gods and sacred emblems. It reads:

Enlil is my head, my face is the day;
Urash, the peerless god, is the protecting spirit leading my way.
My neck is the necklace of the goddess Ninlil,
My two arms are the sickle of the western moon,
My fingers tamarisk, bone of the gods of heaven;
They ward off the embrace of sorcery from my body;
The gods Lugal-edinna and Latarak are my breast and knees;
Muhra my ever-wandering feet.[6]

Here again the identity sought is only partial. Qualities of these gods and sacred emblems are to infuse the man's members and make him inviolable.

As it was thought possible for a man to achieve partial identity with various gods, so could one god enjoy partial identity with other gods and thus share in their natures and abilities. We are told, for instance, that the face of the god Ninurta is Shamash, the sun-god; that one of Ninurta's ears is the god of wisdom, Ea—and so on through all of Ninurta's members.[7] These curious statements may be taken to mean that Ninurta's face derived its dazzling radiance from, and thus shared in,

---

4 Cf. the Nidaba hymn, *OECT I*, 36–39.
5 *Maqlû*, Tablet III, 151–52.

6 *Ibid.*, VI, 1–8.
7 *KAR* 102.

that brilliance which is characteristically the sun-god's and concentrates itself in him. In similar manner, his ear—for the Mesopotamians believed the ear, not the brain, to be the seat of intelligence—shares in that supreme intelligence which is the outstanding characteristic of the god Ea.

Sometimes such statements of partial identity take a slightly different form. We are told, for instance, that the god Marduk is the god Enlil when there is question of ruling and taking counsel, but that he is Sîn, the moon-god, when he acts as illuminer of the night, etc.[8] This apparently means that the god Marduk, when he rules and makes decisions, partakes of the personality, qualities, and abilities of the divine executive par excellence, the god Enlil. When, on the other hand, Marduk, as the planet Jupiter, shines in the nightly skies, he shares in those special powers which characterize the moon-god and have their centre in him.

Any phenomenon which the Mesopotamian met in the world around him was thus alive, had its own personality and will, its distinct self. But the self which revealed itself, for example, in a particular lump of flint, was not limited by that particular lump; it was in it and yet behind it; it permeated it and gave it character as it did lumps of flint. And as one such 'self' could permeate many individual phenomena, so it might also permeate other selves and thereby give to them of its specific character to add to the qualities which they had in their own right.

To understand nature, the many and varied phenomena around man, was thus to understand the personalities in these phenomena, to know

their characters, the direction of their wills, and also the range of their powers. It was a task not different from that of understanding other men, knowing their characters, their wills, the extent of their power and influence. And intuitively the Mesopotamian applied to nature the experience he had of his own human society, interpreting it in social terms. A particularly suggestive example will illustrate this. Under our eyes, as it were, objective reality assumes the form of a social type.

According to Mesopotamian beliefs, a man who had been bewitched could destroy the enemies who had bewitched him by burning images of them. The characteristic self of the enemy stared up at him from the image. He could get at it and harm it there, as well as in the person. And so he consigned the images to the fire while addressing it as follows:

Scorching Fire, warlike son of Heaven,
Thou, the fiercest of thy brethren,
Who like Moon and Sun decidest
    lawsuits—
Judge thou my case, hand down the
    verdict.
Burn the man and woman who bewitched
    me;
Burn, O Fire, the man and woman who
    bewitched me;
Scorch, O Fire, the man and woman who
    bewitched me;
Burn them, O Fire;
Scorch them, O Fire;
Take hold of them, O Fire;
Consume them, O Fire;
Destroy them, O Fire.[9]

It is quite clear that the man approaches the fire for the destructive power he knows to be in it. But the fire has a will of its own; it will burn the images—and in them his enemies —only if it so chooses. And in decid-

[8] *CT* XXIV, 50, No. 47406 obv. 6 and 8.

[9] *Maqlû,* Tablet II, 104–15.

ing whether to burn the images or not, the fire becomes a judge between the man and his enemies: the situation becomes a lawsuit in which the man pleads his cause and asks the fire to vindicate him. The power which is in fire has taken definite form, has been interpreted in social terms; it is a judge.

As the fire here becomes a judge, other powers take form in similar pregnant situations. The thunderstorm was a warrior; he flung deadly lightning, and one could hear the roar emitted by the wheels of his war chariot. The earth was a woman, a mother; she gave birth each year to the new vegetation. In such cases the Mesopotamians did only what other people have done throughout the ages. 'Men,' as Aristotle says, 'imagine not only the forms of the gods but their ways of life to be like their own.'[10]

If we were to try to single out a typically Mesopotamian feature, we should perhaps point to the degree to which this people found and emphasized organized relationships of the powers they recognized. While all the people tend to humanize non-human

powers and frequently visualize them as social types, Mesopotamian speculative thought seems to have brought out and systematized to an unusual degree the implications of social and political function latent in such typifying and to have elaborated them into clear-cut institutions. This particular emphasis would seem to be closely bound up with the nature of the society in which the Mesopotamian lived and from which he derived his terms and his evaluation.

When the universe was taking form for the Mesopotamian, he lived, we have argued, in a Primitive Democracy. All great undertakings, all important decisions, originated in a general assembly of all the citizens; they were not the affair of any single individual. It is accordingly natural that, in trying to understand how the great cosmic events were brought about, he should be especially intent upon the ways in which the individual forces of the cosmos co-operated to run the universe. Cosmic institutions would naturally come to loom important in his view of the universe, and the structure of the universe would stand out clearly as the structure of a state.

---

[10] *Politics,* 1252b.

Part 3

the institutionalization
of religion

A primary focus of the sociologist's interest in religion is the institutions established to give formal expression to the basic religious experience and to preserve it. The first and major institution is that of worship, of cult. The complex system of rituals found in every religion evolves as a response to the sacred realm and expresses man's inner need to act out his relation to the sacred in concrete actions and gestures and to draw close to its life-giving power. Through song, dance, prayer, sacrifice, and symbols, which embody and represent the divine, man expresses religious attitudes and communicates his religious feelings to others. Ritual provides an externalized emotional patterning of act and relation that becomes particularly important in times of personal or communal crisis, when such practices provide a structured mode of expression and response that supports individual morale and group solidarity.

Functionalists like Malinowski and Durkheim have stressed the positive role of ritual in strengthening group cohesion. However, it is important to note that although ceremonial acts have this effect, they are not performed for this purpose. The intent of the participants in cultic activity is to establish contact with the sacred, and the value of the cult to social solidarity and individual identity is secondary and derivative. The central meaning of the cult is described brilliantly by Hartley Burr Alexander, philosopher, poet, and anthropologist, in *The World's Rim*, his interpretation of the ceremonies and symbolism of the North American Indians. Our selection from his work describes the act of smoking the Pipe of Peace and explicates its central significance.

In the end the rite of the calumet is the Indian's profound gesture to the World, whose physical figure and inward being and powers he images and addresses in the ceremonial smoke. To bring his life, outward and inward, into harmony with that of all nature is in essence the meaning of the sacred fume which arises from the pipe whose bowl is an altar and whose stem is the breath's passage...the whole meaning of human existence is bound up with the ritual of the calumet.[1]

Alexander's analysis of this specific ritual helps us comprehend the deep universal significance of ritual in the life of religious man.

---

[1] Hartley Burr Alexander, *The World's Rim* (Lincoln, Neb.: University of Nebraska Press, 1967), p. 4.

Intimately related to the cult as an expression of man's relationship to the sacred is myth. Ritual is a formalized pattern of word, act, and gesture; myth is the assertion in words of one's relation to the sacred. Like ritual, of which it is often a part, myth involves emotional participation. In the course of mythic narration men recount, represent, and dramatically take part in holy events. Tellers and listeners affirm the actuality of the sacred realm in experiencing it and emotionally verify for themselves the truth of the sacred tales, while relating interiorly to their content. The profound significance of myth in religious life is analyzed in the selection by Mircea Eliade.

Every experience must be objectified in some way if its meaning and impact are to be preserved and transmitted from one man to another and from one generation to the next. A social organization must be established within whose framework the original experience and the traditions built upon it can be shared, taught, and communicated. Ritual is a group affair. Tradition is the property of a community; trained specialists are necessary for its transmission. Religious symbols and meaning are developed and transmitted by leaders who possess special spiritual gifts and who are endowed with special authority. Whether the bearer of the religious tradition be a natural group such as a family, tribe, or nation, or a specifically religious organization such as a church or monastic group, an ordered organization is a necessary institutional form.

All the problems and conflicts of secular human organizations exist within religious groups. Indeed, they are often exacerbated because the religious orientation to ultimacy and the sacred heightens and deepens human experience. The sociologist of religion, whose chief concern with religion is precisely on this institutional level, must examine the internal structure of the religious organization as well as its relationship to the general society. The third selection deals with the character of the specifically religious organization; later selections examine the relation of religion to society.

Religious life in its earliest observed forms is fully integrated into the folk society. Fustel de Coulanges, W. Robertson Smith, and the early anthropologists have emphasized that preliterate and archaic societies are permeated with religious values. Under these conditions religion's function of reaffirming and strengthening group solidarity is most evident. However, as Robert Lowie, the well-known anthropologist, has pointed out in his study of primitive religion, religious individualism is not absent even in early times or among contemporary preliterates. When societies become larger and more differentiated, individuals find themselves participating in various subgroups, which are often not closely or meaningfully related to each other. Religious groups develop as distinct entities; they may conflict with other groups in society and with the general society itself. Specifically religious organizations are based not on ties of blood or ethnic relatedness, but on the sharing of a religious experience and tradition. Joachim Wach has described the evolution from natural groups as the bearers of religious traditions to specifically religious organizations.[2] This development is based on both a growing complication of

---

[2] Joachim Wach, *The Sociology of Religion* (Chicago: The University of Chicago Press, 1951).

social life and new religious experience and conceptions. Universal notions about the nature of man and the Deity emerge as men transcend the geographical and biological limits of folk society. The relationship between structural and intellectual development in religion has been traced by Gustav Mensching. Our brief selection from his work focuses on the internal organization of religious groups and the difference between folk and universal religion.

cult

eight

The Pipe of Peace

HARTLEY BURR ALEXANDER

I

No symbol native to the peoples of America has more profoundly stirred the imagination of the immigrant white race than that of the ceremonial pipe of the Indian—the hobowaken, the calumet, the pipe of peace, as it has variously been called. Hardly a trait of the Indian cultures, and certainly no ritual trait, was more widely disseminated among the tribes and nations of the red man before the era of the discovery than was the use of tobacco—its smoking and its symbolism. No gift of the New World found such ready and wide acceptance by mankind generally; it early entered every continent and archipelago, and its use rapidly spread beyond the outposts of European civilization, further than its nearest New World competitor, maize, or Indian corn. But maize, too, speedily found its way into remote lands. Africans and Asiatics of today are astonished to learn that it is to America and the

Reprinted from *The World's Rim* by Hartley Burr Alexander by permission of University of Nebraska Press. Copyright © 1953 by University of Nebraska Press.

American Indian that they owe both the food and the narcotic.

It was not, however, as a ritual act that tobacco smoking was adopted and carried by the Old World races. In the Old World smoking was what it has remained, an individual habit or a social convention; appetite, not idea, governed its expansion. For the Indian, on the other hand, and probably from the very beginning, the use of tobacco was primarily ritual, and the plant itself in some degree sanctified. It is true that the Indian also knew the appetitive and social employments of the "weed"—for chewing and for snuff as well as for the fume of pipe, cigar and cigarette; but all this was, and is still, secondary to the first and essential meaning of the smoked or breathed tobacco— a ritual offering or a supplication. In the ritual smoking of the pipe it is not easy to say whether the fume that goes forth is a gift of incense or a breath of prayer: something of each is clearly present.

In any case, for the Indian peoples the whole complex that goes with tobacco and its use is instilled with sanctions. The field in which the plant is cultivated, the cured leaves, the decorated pouch which contains tobacco and pipe, and above all the ceremonial pipe itself—all share in that hallowing which makes of them the most potent and universal matter of Indian "medicine." It may well be that tobacco first came into use as *materia medica* in the European sense; for it was and is used for the healing of bodily as well as of physical ills, and this might plausibly be associated with its original function. But whatever truth may be attached to this notion, it is to a far broader significance that the full ritual of the pipe became developed. In the end the rite of the calumet is the Indian's profound gesture to the World, whose physical figure and inward being and powers he images and addresses in the ceremonial smoke. To bring his life, outward and inward, into harmony with that of all nature is in essence the meaning of the sacred fume which arises from the pipe whose bowl is an altar and whose stem is the breath's passage. That the instrument employed has been called "the Pipe of Peace" is due, no doubt, to the fact that every Indian council in which men sought to resolve their differences and every rite in which they endeavored to put themselves into tranquil accord with the powers which participate with man in the life of nature, was inaugurated with the ceremonial smoking. The whole meaning of human existence is bound up with the ritual of the calumet.

II

In his account of the Iroquois, Lewis Morgan, historian of the Five Nations, gives this description of the opening of their councils:[1] "The master of ceremonies, rising to his feet, filled and lighted the pipe of peace from his own fire. Drawing three whiffs, one after the other, he blew the first toward the zenith, the second toward the ground, and the third toward the sun. By the first act he returned thanks to the Great Spirit for the preservation of his life during the past year, and for being permitted to be present at this council. By the second he returned thanks to his Mother, the Earth, for her various productions which had ministered to his sustenance. And by the third, he returned thanks to the Sun for his never-failing light, ever shining upon all." Père De Smet, one of the most wide-wandering of the Jesuit missionaries in North America, makes repeated allusions to the ritual use of the pipe.[2] "On all great occasions," he says, "in their religious and political ceremonies, and at their great feasts, the calumet presides; the savage sends its first fruits, or its first puffs, to the Great Waconda, or Master of Life, to the Sun which gives them light, and to the Earth and Water by which they are nourished; then they direct a puff to each point of the compass, begging of Heaven all the elements and favorable winds." Elsewhere De Smet remarks:[3] "It was really a touching spectacle to see the calumet, the Indian emblem of peace, raised heavenward by the hand of a savage, presenting it to the Master of Life, imploring his pity on all his children on earth and begging him to confirm the good resolutions which they had made."

[1] Lewis H. Morgan, *League of the Ho-Dé-No-Sau-Ness or Iroquois* (New York: Dodd, Mead & Co., 1901), Vol. II, Appendix B, Sec. 62, p. 232.

[2] Hiram M. Chittenden and Alfred T. Richardson, *Life, Letters, and Travels of Father Pierre-Jean De Smet, S.J.* (New York: Francis P. Harper, 1905), Vol. III, p. 1008.

[3] *Ibid.*, Vol. II, pp. 681–82.

An earlier and still more famous Jesuit explorer was Marquette, and few passages touching the significance of the calumet are more important than his account of its use among the Illinois, with whom, he says,[4]

there is nothing more mysterious nor more remarkable. So much honor is not rendered to the crowns and sceptres of kings as they render to the calumet. It seems to be the god of peace and war, the arbiter of life and death. It is enough to carry it with one and to show it in order to journey with assurance in the midst of enemies, who, in the height of combat, lower their arms when it is displayed. It is for this that the Illinois gave me one to serve as safeguard among all the nations by whom I must pass in my travel. There is a calumet for peace and another for war, which are only distinguished by the color of the plumage with which they are adorned. The red is the mark of war: they employ it only to end their differences, to confirm their alliances, and to speak with strangers. It is composed of two pieces, of a red stone polished like marble and pierced in such a fashion that one end serves to receive the tobacco while the other engages in the stem, which is a baton two feet long, as large as an ordinary cane, and pierced through the center. It is embellished with the head and neck of various birds of handsome plumage; and they add thereto great plumes, red green, or of other colors, in fans and pendants. They make particular state of this, because they regard it as the calumet of the sun; and in fact they present it to the sun to smoke when they wish to obtain calm or rain or fair weather. They are scrupulous not to bathe themselves at the beginning of the summer or to partake of the new fruits until after they have danced the calumet.

Marquette goes on to describe the

dance of the calumets which, he states, they perform for making peace or war, for public rejoicings, or for the honoring of another nation or of important personages. The ceremony begins with songs, and when all are assembled the Manitou is saluted

by waving the calumet and throwing smoke from its mouth as if they were presenting incense. It was customary first respectfully to take the calumet, and supporting it with the two hands to cause it to dance in cadence, following the air of the songs. They caused it to make differing figures: now they made it to be seen of the whole assembly, turning it from one side to the other; now they presented it to the sun, as if they wished to cause it to smoke; now they directed it toward the earth; now they extended its wings as if for flight; again it was brought to the mouth of the assistants that they might smoke,—and all in cadence.

A second act, as described by Marquette, is still more interesting from the point of view of the symbolism of the pipe. In this, to the beating of a drum a combat was simulated in which one of the actors was armed with bow and arrow and tomahawk, while his opponent carried only a calumet, which nevertheless dramatically prevailed over the warlike armament. "The act could pass for a very pretty *entrée de ballet* in France," comments Marquette, "and the festival terminates, as usually among the Indians, with recountings of feats of arms by the warriors, and once more by the action of smoking, after which the chief presented the calumet to the nation which had been invited to this ceremony, as mark of the lasting peace which would hold between the two nations."

Probably the most instructive native account of the meaning of a ceremonial smoke-offering is that given by Sword, a Dakota shaman. According to this teacher, before a

———
4 Journal of the first journey of Marquette, section vi: "Du naturel des Ilinois, de leurs moeurs et de leurs coustumes. De l'estime qu'ils ont pour le calumet ou pipe à prendre du tabac, et de la danse qu'ils font en son honneur."

shaman can perform a cermony in which deities participate, he must fill and light a pipe and say:[5] "Friends of Wakinyan, I pass the pipe to you first. Circling I pass to you who dwell with the Father. Circling pass to beginning day. Circling pass to the beautiful one. Circling I complete the four quarters and the time. I pass the pipe to the Father with the Sky. I smoke with the Great Spirit. Let us have a blue day."

Beginning with the West the mouthpiece is pointed to the four directions, or rather to the Winds of these quarters. Wakinyan, in the Siouan tetralogies,[6] is the Winged One, associated with the Rock, which is the deity of the West, and the Winged are the strong ones of the West. Next in turn the pipe is offered to the North Wind, the East Wind, and the South Wind. The North Wind is the companion of Wazi, the Wizard, "beginning day" designates the lodge of the East Wind, while the "beautiful one" is the feminine deity who is companion of the South Wind and who dwells in his lodge "under the Sun at midday." "It pleases the South Wind to be addressed through his companion rather than directly," said Sword. The Four Winds are the messengers of the gods, and for this reason should be first addressed. The shaman explained the meaning of the rite as follows:

When the offering has been made to the South Wind the Shaman should move the pipe in the same manner until the mouthpiece again points toward the west, and say, "Circling I complete the four

quarters and the time." He should do this because the Four Winds are the four quarters of the circle and mankind knows not where they may be or whence they may come and the pipe should be offered directly toward them. The four quarters embrace all that are on the world and all that are in the sky. Therefore, by circling the pipe, the offering is made to all the gods. The circle is the symbol of time, for the daytime, the night time, and the moon time are circles above the world, and the year time is a circle around the border of the world. Therefore, the lighted pipe moved in a complete circle is an offering to all the times.

When the Shaman has completed the four quarters and the time he should point the mouthpiece of the pipe toward the sky and say, "I pass the pipe to the father with the sky." This is an offering to the Wind, for when the Four Winds left the lodge of their father, the Wind, he went from it, and dwells with the sky. He controls the seasons and the weather, and he should be propitiated when good weather is desired.

Then the Shaman should smoke the pipe and while doing. so, should say, "I smoke with the Great Spirit. Let us have a blue day."

To smoke with the Great Spirit means that the one smoking is in communion with the Great Spirit. Then he may make a prayer. The prayer here is for a blue day. Ordinarily, a blue day means a cloudless or successful day. When a Shaman formally prays for a blue day, it means an enjoyable day and an effective performance of a ceremony.

Chief Standing Bear is a fellow tribesman of Sword. Reared in early life in the thought and customs of his people and later passing through the schools of the white man, he understands the ideals of the two peoples as few of either race can. It is from him that we have these words:[7]

[5] See J. R. Walker, "The Sun Dance and Other Ceremonies of the Oglala Division of the Teton Dakota," *American Museum of Natural History, Anthropological Papers*, Vol. XVI, Part II (New York, 1917), p. 157.

[6] *Ibid.*, p. 80 and pp. 157–58.

[7] Chief Standing Bear, *Land of the Spotted Eagle* (Boston: Houghton Mifflin Company, 1933), pp. 201–2.

The pipe was a tangible, visible link that joined man to Wakan Tanka and every puff of smoke that ascended in prayer unfailingly reached His presence. With it faith was upheld, ceremony sanctified, and the being consecrated. All the meanings of moral duty, ethics, religious and spiritual conceptions were symbolized in the pipe. It signified brotherhood, peace, and the perfection of Wakan Tanka, and to the Lakota[8] the pipe stood for that which the Bible, Church, State, and Flag, all combined, represented in the mind of the white man. Without the pipe no altar was complete and no ceremony effective. . . . Smoking was the Indian Angelus, and whenever its smoke ascended, men, women, and children acknowledged the sacred presence of their Big Holy.

III

Descriptions such as those just quoted indicate the essential ritual form and the significance attached to the ceremonial smoking of the calumet. In practice the rite varies from tribe to tribe and ceremony to ceremony, and indeed from individual to individual. But there are universal features which indicate the primary symbolism and lead us into certain matters of human understanding and of the mind's radical metaphors which should enlighten us not only in the field of American Indian thought but also in the ideas and symbols of all mankind.

In the ceremonial gesture of the smoke offering, the several puffs may be directed to three, four, five, six, or seven points; but in every case these points belong to the one general system which in full is defined only by all seven. The smoke may be directed to the Above, the Below, and the Here; it may be directed to the four cardinals of the compass—East, South, West, and North, for it usually

moves sunwise in sequence; it may be offered to the Quarters of the Earth and to the Above or to the Here, and this would yield a five-puff rite; or again to the Quarters, the Sky and the Earth, and this would yield six; and finally, in the full form, smoke will be blown to the six points which define the plane of earth's horizon and the zenith and nadir of its axis, and to that Middle Place where the axis cuts the plane to form the site of the ceremony and the ritual center of the World. Conceptually these seven points define man's primary projection of the universe, his World Frame, or cosmic abode, within which is to be placed all the furniture of creation. For it is only necessary to connect the four cardinals with a line marking the circle of the visible horizon, and, following the courses of the sun and stars, to draw the line of the wheel of day, circumvolent from sunrise to zenith, from setting to nadir and again downward and onward to returning dawn, in order to complete the great circles drawn upon the face of the abyss which yield us the terrestrial and the celestial spheres. It is clear that the Indian, after the manner of our compass, not only organized the plane of the earth with respect to the radical four of the cardinal points, but that he also subdivided the Above and the Below into zones and latitudes. First it is important to perceive that the red man's projection of his universe, incipiently at least, is a circumscribing sphere with axis and equator, longitudes and latitudes, and that the ritual of the pipe is schematically a recognition of the points from which the great lines of the sphere are generated.

This primary projection of the physical world is of course not uniquely a product of American Indian thought. The quaternity of the cardinal directions and the trinity of

---

8 "Lakota" is a variant of "Dakota," the native name of the Sioux peoples.

heaven, earth and hell belong to many lands and peoples. It is a mathematical construction, but it is one developed not from chance but from a reason universal to mankind, and that reason is to be found in the human skeleton itself. Man is upright, erect, in his active habit, and he is four-square in his frame, and these two facts give him his image of a physical world circumscribing his bodily life. In the Indo-European and in many other languages of the Old World and the New the primitive orientation of man is indicated by those root-names for the directions which are, in meaning, for the east, "the before," for the west "the behind," for the south "the right hand," and for the north "the left hand." That the heavens are figured as the crown and front, earth's middle as the navel and the bowels, and earth's base as the footing of creation is symbolized in the image of that Titan who adorns the symbolic art of many peoples. The axial dimension of the universe is thus deduced from the standing position of a man. So standing, there at the middle, the human skeleton yields a world-frame with its four quarters and its three bodily divisions. Certainly it is no matter of merely idle imagination to note that the intellectual feat which our conception of a "world" implies is profoundly associated with just those physical traits which most mark off man from his fellow mammalians; for had we remained quadrupeds, with horse and elephant, ox and dog, it is only to be assumed that (had any world been possible) our cardinal points must have been six and not four. Heaven could never have been so high nor hell so low for creatures whose mouth gives the main source of tactile definition. Geometry is the most human of sciences, clearly derivative from that bodily frame and

carriage from which we formulate the dimensions of the world and the structures of that space which we are willing to call the real space.

In this connection it is notable that as for the Greek, so for the American Indian, numbers possess strongly a geometrical signifiance. They are symbols of order, and especially of the order of space, rather than indicators of class or quantity; and to certain of them there attaches also the glamor of fortune or fate, as reflected alike in tale and ritual. In the main, it is the number *four* that to the red man carried the notion of luck or charm which the European associates more readily with three; and this luckiness of four is perhaps because this most geometrical of all the numbers—symbol of the plane of Earth—accords with the vividly spatial and visual form which Nature takes on for the Indian's eyes. Four-part and cruciform emblems, crosses of every style and quartered designs are extremely common in Indian art, giving expression to the quaternities of his thought, and in his metaphysical moments the whole realm of distinguishable things is apt to be organized in fours or in multiples of fours. The kinds of living things, animals, birds, insects, plants are organized into fours; so are the meteorologicals, the winds and the stars and the heavenly bodies; so the hills and waters; and so also the storeys or regions of the world above and the world below, which for many of the native peoples are four. But perhaps the most significant and individual symbolism of all is that of color. Here again a fourfold order is established, each cardinal direction having its own color (not invariable for all tribes or societies), while the above is the realm of the union of the radical colors and the below the realm of their deprivation. Such primarily symbolic colors are associated with the living kinds of plants and animals, with beads and with minerals, and intricately with ceremony and costume; they even form a sound language, songs not less than powers and "medicines" having their color values. One may say that for the Indian more than for any other human race colors are the elements of the whole phantasm of Nature and are, with number, the teachers of its innermost wisdom.[9] It is not a little odd that on another level of speculation our physical science likewise rests its claim to understanding upon formulary numbers and the spectra of radiant energy.

. . .

IV

But it is not only as a definition of the dimensions of cosmic space and time, as a projection of the world and its years, that the symbolism of the calumet is significant. The regions which circumscribe the Here are, after all, only the projected environment fitted about the body and life of the Central Man, much as a mollusc's shell is given shape and order by its bodily life. *Cosmos*, order, is essentially physiological, or at most psychophysical, in its logic. The meters with which the world is diagrammed and so made comfortable to the mind (for order is such comfort) are derived from man's bones and muscles and organs, his senses, desires and intuitions—in brief from his conscious life. The world of understanding is anthropomorphic, which is but

___
9 See H. B. Alexander, *Mythology of All Races* (Boston: Marshall Jones Company, 1916), Vol. X, pp. 286–87, note 31, and the passages there cited. See also "Handbook of the American Indians," *Bur. of Am. Ethnol., Bul. 30,* Part I (Washington, D.C., 1907), "Color Symbolism."

another way of saying that man is at its center and is himself the principle of its structural being. One of the most curious and interesting types of Mediaeval-learned illustration is that of the schematic man, each organ and part emblematically reduplicated in a structure of nature, which in turn is no more than the counterpart of his organism—the world itself being conceived as a vaster man-being. Not even the heavens are remote from their especial and complementary relations to his organs and functions; the zodiacal signs betoken celestial influences upon his organs as well as vital forms projected into the starfield; and all astrology is only a more complex disquisition upon this impulsive sense that the world is somehow a figure conformed to man's own, like a vaster chart of his anatomy. Indeed, in subtler modes we have not yet escaped this sense of a man-centered cosmos; for the measures of our physics and astrophysics are themselves, at their cores, imaginary numbers derived from our bodily life: man bonelengths meter space, man paces yield us linear miles and motions, man work gives meaning to energy, man purpose to cause, and the whole cycle of our vital activities creates for us the intelligibilities of day and year and lifetime. Projected mathematically, by the numberings first counted out from our digits, all these give us our science-construed cosmos.

Indian thinking symbolizes this human centrality of man, no less than has European. This is true in both the social and the individual senses; for while it is evident that the Indian, like men of other continents than his, draws his spatial and temporal tokens from the body and life of a type-forming anatomical individual, there is also, with him as with other men, a social symbolism, intrinsic in his cosmos. Man is at the center of the world not only individually, as a form of flesh and bone, but socially; and one may say that in most Indian ritual thinking the individual *is,* vicariously, his human group—whether it be clan or tribe or ceremonial federation. This may be represented diagramatically, as it is in the way the encampment of a prairie people is set up on the occasion of festal celebration. There is the outer circle of the horizon, which defines "the place wherein the people dwell"; there is the great tribal camp circle, with its sky and earth divisions into which are assorted the living clans; and in the center there is the Medicine Lodge, usually circular, the site of the mystery and the Here-place of the world, with respect to which all else is oriented. The social form thus shapes itself after the pattern of the world whole, circumscribed by physical nature and circumscribing that central symbolic man-being of which it is in turn the reality.[10]

In his striking analysis of the symbolic man of the Osage tribe Francis La Flesche called attention to this triplicate relation as centrally symbolized by the ceremonial pipe. In the ritual devoted to this pipe upon the occasion of entering war, the pipe is offered by its tribal keeper to the men who represent the two great divisions of the tribe, the Sky-people and the Earth-people. In the chant the several parts of the pipe are spoken of as if they were the parts of the body of a man. This man,

symbolized by the pipe, is for each warrior his own body, but he is also the tribe socially, which in its several parts is likewise thought of as a man, and as reflecting that world of sky and earth by which man is surrounded. The idea is probably quite akin to that which still impels nations to adopt some such anthropomorphic symbolism of their social life—in an Uncle Sam, a John Bull—just as in antiquity peoples deified their national existences in man-form gods or goddesses. When about to set forth upon a national venture, the Osage adds to such symbolism only his own form of ceremonial communion, that of the pipe and its smoking—American substitute for the sacrifice at the high altar of the Classical nations, or perhaps for the celebrant Mass of Christian nations. The words of the Osage chant, as abridged by La Flesche, are the vivid paraphrase of the symbol:[11]

Behold, this pipe. Verily a man!
Within it I have placed my being.
Place within it your own being, also,
Then free shall you be from all that
  brings death.

Behold, the neck of the pipe!
Within it I have placed my own neck.
Place within it your neck, also,
Then free shall you be from all that
  brings death, O, Honga!

Behold, the mouth of the pipe!
Within it I have placed my own mouth.
Place within it your mouth, also,
Then free shall you be from all that
  brings death, O, Honga!

Behold, the right side of the pipe!
Within it I have placed the right side of
  my own body.
Place within it the right side of your own
  body, also,

---

10 See James Hastings, ed., *Encyclopedia of Religion and Ethics,* "Philosophy: Primitive," and authorities cited there. For details as to camp circles, consult especially James Dorsey, "Siouan Sociology," *Bur. of Am. Ethnology, Fifteenth Annual Report* (1897), pp. 20ff., and Francis La Flesche, "The Osage Tribe," *Thirty-sixth Annual Report* (1921).

---

11 La Flesche, "The Symbolic Man of the Osage Tribe," *Art and Archaeology,* Vol. IX, No. 2 (1920), pp. 68–72.

Then free shall you be from all that
brings death, O, Honga!

Behold, the spine of the pipe!
Within it I have placed my own spine.
Place within it your own spine, also,
Then free shall you be from all that
brings death, O, Honga!

Behold, the left side of the pipe!
Within it I have placed the left side of
my own body, O, Honga!
Place within it the left side of your own
body,
Then shall you be free from all that
brings death, O, Honga!

Behold, the hollow of the pipe!
Within it I have placed the hollow of my
own body.
Place within it the hollow of your own
body, also,
Then shall you be free from all that
brings death, O, Honga!

Behold, the thong that holds together the
bowl and the stem!
Within it I have placed my breathing-
tube.
Place within it your own breathing-tube,
also,
Then shall you be free from all that
.brings death, O, Honga!

When you turn from the rising sun to the
setting sun to go against your enemies,
This pipe shall you use when you go forth
to invoke aid from Wakonda,
Then shall your prayers be speedily
granted, O, Honga!
Yea even before the sun shall o'er-top the
walls of your dwelling,
Your prayers shall surely be granted, O,
Honga!

This ritual prayer is clearly a half-
magical spell, intended to ensure life-
preservation to the men going into
peril. In this sense it is individual. But
it is also for the tribe, whose safety is
likewise at stake, and which is personified in the Symbolic Man. The
line "when you turn from the rising
sun to the setting sun to go against
your enemies" makes this clear. For
on the occasion of war the whole symbolism of Osage ritual life was re-

versed. In times of peace the Osage
camp-circle faced the east, with the
Earth-people to the south and the
Sky-people to the north. In wartime
this image was transposed: the
Honga, symbolizing the vital energies
of Earth, encamped to the north, the
Tsizhu, the Sky-people, to the south;
while the tribal man, symbolizing all
and symbolized in the pipe, now faced
the west. There are such changes in
symbolism in other tribes, where the
shift from peace to war is felt to shift
the whole cosmic plan: the colors
shift their quarters and into nature
Discordia enters with Bellona.

VII

In the Osage ritual just described
the pipe is in the charge of a leader
who, while he is in a sense actual
chieftain of the war-party, yet does
none of the fighting. It is his function
to appoint the man who is to conduct the attack, but it is his more essential rôle to guard the sacred pipe
and employ it in supplications for
success: the pipe is, in brief, of the
nature of a palladium, or at least of a
sacred vessel such as the Hebrew Ark,
and its keeper is a man who holds
himself apart from actual bloodshed,
even while his enterprise is that of
war.

This is only one among many cases
in which the calumet is not a Pipe of
Peace but a Pipe of War. The Kiowa,
for example, employed a red pipe as
symbol for enlistment in a war-party:
the organizer of the expedition sent
this pipe to the several war societies,
and while no man need accept it, to
take and smoke it was the pledge of
participation. Pipes of war and peace
are mentioned from early times onward, so that it is clearly in part a
misunderstanding to name the ceremonial pipe the "pipe of peace." In
many uses it was so, and it is possible

that this was its first and widest employment; but the mere fact that the pipe and its smoking, and in the main the cultivation of tobacco, were in the hands of men and warriors, with the women excluded, indicates that it was from early times much more than a symbol of peaceful pledges or intentions.

Its fuller symbolism is very clearly that of a sacred, or "medicine" emblem, to be employed wherever the issue was serious or fateful. This might be a purely social occasion, and every society appears to have had in its ceremonial bundle its own sacred pipe or pipes; the giving of a pipe to a group was, like a coronation, the token of the transmission to them of social rights; and in myth and in the ritual commemoration of myth the pipe is an accompaniment of the reception of a culture gift. In the Dakota legend of the gift of maize from the White Buffalo Cow, represented as a beautiful Woman-from-Heaven, a Brulé version tells how the divine giver appeared to two young men, and with kernels of maize of the four colors, she presented them with a pipe, saying:[12] "This pipe is related to the heavens, and you shall live with it. . . . Clouds of many colors may come up from the south, but look at the pipe and the blue sky and know that the clouds will soon pass away and all will become blue and clear again. . . . When it shall be blue in the west, know that it is closely related to you through the pipe and

the blue heavens, and by that you shall grow rich. . . . I am the White Buffalo Cow; my milk is of four kinds; I spill it upon the earth that you may live by it." It is clear that the symbolism underlying the ritual gift is here more than social and more than a mere gesture to the structure of Nature: the pipe is itself, in some deeply indefinable sense, a mystic token of man's union with nature, and like the Christian cross, of his temporal and spiritual salvation.

No less than for the group this symbolism holds also for the individual. When the watcher goes forth to keep his vigil for the Sun Dance, he bears with him as first essential the pipe which is his offering, and the pipe itself may constitute a man's prayer. In her account of the Omaha attitude toward Wakonda, the Great Spirit or Mystery of the Siouan peoples, Alice Fletcher speaks in this fashion of personal prayers:[13] "A man would take a pipe and go alone to the hills; there he would silently offer smoke and utter the call, *Wakanda ho!*, while the moving cause, or purport of his prayer, would remain unexpressed in words. If his stress of feeling was great, he would have the pipe on the ground where his appeal had been made. This form of prayer (made only by men) was called. . . 'addressing with the pipe.' "

No symbol could more specifically summarize the last and most intrinsic symbolism of the pipe. Central in the universe is man; central in man is his mind's thought and his heart's aspiration. The pipe of peace was the emblem of each.

[12] Garrick Mallery, "Picture Writing of the American Indians," *Bur. of Am. Ethnology, Tenth Annual Report* (1893), p. 290. Further details regarding this important Dakota myth are to be found in Chap. V of Hartley Burr Alexander, *The World's Rim.*

[13] Fletcher and La Flesche, "The Omaha Tribe," *Bur. of Am. Ethnol., Twenty-seventh Annual Report* (1911), p. 599.

myth

nine

from Myth and Reality

MIRCEA ELIADE

Attempt at a Definition of Myth

It would be hard to find a definition of myth that would be acceptable to all scholars and at the same time intelligible to nonspecialists. Then, too, is it even possible to find *one* definition that will cover all the types and functions of myths in all traditional and archaic societies? Myth is an extremely complex cultural reality, which can be approached and interpreted from various and complementary viewpoints.

Speaking for myself, the definition that seems least inadequate because most embracing is this: Myth narrates a sacred history; it relates an event that took place in primordial Time, the fabled time of the "beginnings." In other words, myth tells how, through the deeds of Supernatural Beings, a reality came into existence, be it the whole of reality, the Cosmos, or only a fragment of reality

—an island, a species of plant, a particular kind of human behavior, an institution. Myth, then, is always an account of a "creation"; it relates how something was produced, began to *be*. Myth tells only of that which *really* happened, which manifested itself completely. The actors in myths are Supernatural Beings. They are known primarily by what they did in the transcendent times of the "beginnings." Hence myths disclose their creative activity and reveal the sacredness (or simply the "supernaturalness") of their works. In short, myths describe the various and sometimes dramatic breakthroughs of the sacred (or the "supernatural") into the World. It is this sudden breakthrough of the sacred that really *establishes* the World and makes it what it is today. Furthermore, it is as a result of the intervention of Supernatural Beings that man himself is what he is today, a mortal, sexed, and cultural being.

We shall later have occasion to enlarge upon and refine these few preliminary indications, but at this point it is necessary to emphasize a fact that we consider essential: the myth is regarded as a sacred story,

From pp. 3–20 in *Myth and Reality* by Mircea Eliade. Copyright © 1963 by Harper & Row, Publishers, Inc. By permission of Harper & Row, Publishers, Inc.

and hence a "true history," because it always deals with *realities*. The cosmogonic myth is "true" because the existence of the World is there to prove it; the myth of the origin of death is equally true because man's mortality proves it, and so on.

Because myth relates the *gesta* of Supernatural Beings and the manifestation of their sacred powers, it becomes the exemplary model for all significant human activities. When the missionary and ethnologist C. Strehlow asked the Australian Arunta why they performed certain ceremonies, the answer was always: "Because the ancestors so commanded it."[1] The Kai of New Guinea refused to change their way of living and working, and they explained: "It was thus that the Nemu (the Mythical Ancestors) did, and we do likewise."[2] Asked the reason for a particular detail in a ceremony, a Navaho chanter answered: "Because the Holy People did it that way in the first place."[3] We find exactly the same justification in the prayer that accompanies a primitive Tibetan ritual: "As it has been handed down from the beginning of earth's creation, so must we sacrifice. . . . As our ancestors in ancient times did—so do we now."[4]

The same justification is alleged by the Hindu theologians and ritualists. "We must do what the gods did in the beginning" (*Satapatha Brāhmana,* VII, 2, 1, 4). "Thus the gods did; thus men do" (*Taittiriya Brāhmana,* I, 5, 9, 4).[5]

As we have shown elsewhere,[6] even the profane behavior and activities of man have their models in the deeds of the Supernatural Beings. Among the Navahos "women are required to sit with their legs under them and to one side, men with their legs crossed in front of them, because it is said that in the beginning Changing Woman and the Monster Slayer sat in these positions."[7] According to the mythical traditions of an Australian tribe, the Karadjeri, all their customs, and indeed all their behavior, were established in the "Dream Time" by two Supernatural Beings, the Bagadjimbiri (for example, the way to cook a certain cereal or to hunt an animal with a stick, the particular position to be taken when urinating, and so on).[8]

There is no need to add further examples. As we showed in *The Myth of the Eternal Return,* and as will become still clearer later, the foremost function of myth is to reveal the exemplary models for all human rites and all significant human activities— diet or marriage, work or education, art or wisdom. This idea is of no little importance for understanding the man of archaic and traditional

[1] C. Strehlow, *Die Aranda-und-Loritja-Stämme in Zentral-Australien,* vol. III, p. i; cf. Lucien Lévy-Bruhl, *La mythologie primitive* (Paris, 1935), p. 123. See also T. G. H. Strehlow, *Aranda Traditions* (Melbourne University Press, 1947), p. 6.

[2] C. Keysser, quoted by Richard Thurnwald, *Die Eingeborenen Australiens und der Südseeinseln* (=Religionsgeschichtliches Lesebuch, 8, Tübingen, 1927), p. 28.

[3] Clyde Kluckhohn, "Myths and Rituals: A General Theory," *Harvard Theological Review,* vol. 35 (1942), p. 66. Cf. *ibid.* for other examples.

[4] Matthias Hermanns, *The Indo-Tibetans* (Bombay, 1954), pp. 66 ff.

[5] See M. Eliade, *The Myth of the Eternal Return* (New York, 1954), pp. 21 ff.

[6] *Ibid.,* pp. 27 f.

[7] Clyde Kluckhohn, "Myths and Rituals," quoting W. W. Hill, *The Agricultural and Hunting Methods of the Navaho Indians* (New York, 1938), p. 179.

[8] Cf. M. Eliade, *Myths, Dreams and Mysteries* (New York, 1960), pp. 191 ff.

societies, and we shall return to it later.

"True Stories" and "False Stories"

We may add that in societies where myth is still alive the natives carefully distinguish myths—"true stories"—from fables of tales, which they call "false stories." The Pawnee "differentiate 'true stories' from 'false stories,' and include among the 'true' stories in the first place all those which deal with the beginning of the world; in these the actors are divine beings, supernatural, heavenly, or astral. Next come those tales which relate the marvellous adventure of the national hero, a youth of humble birth who became the saviour of his people, freeing them from monsters, delivering them from famine and other disasters, and performing other noble and beneficent deeds. Last come the stories which have to do with the world of the medicine-men and explain how such-and-such a sorcerer got his superhuman powers, how such-and-such an association of shamans originated, and so on. The 'false' stories are those which tell of the far from edifying adventures and exploits of Coyote, the prairie-wolf. Thus in the 'true' stories we have to deal with the holy and the supernatural, while the 'false' ones on the other hand are of profane content, for Coyote is extremely popular in this and other North American mythologies in the character of a trickster, deceiver, sleight-of-hand expert and accomplished rogue."[9]

Similarly, the Cherokee distinguish between sacred myths (cosmogony, creation of the stars, origin of death) and profane stories, which explain, for example, certain anatomical or physiological peculiarities of animals. The same distinction is found in Africa. The Herero consider the stories that relate the beginnings of the different groups of the tribe "true" because they report facts that *really* took place, while the more or less humorous tales have no foundation. As for the natives of Togo, they look on their origin myths as "absolutely real."[10]

This is why myths cannot be related without regard to circumstances. Among many tribes they are not recited before women or children, that is, before the uninitiated. Usually the old teachers communicate the myths to the neophytes during their period of isolation in the bush, and this forms part of their initiation. R. Piddington says of the Karadjeri: "the sacred myths that women may not know are concerned principally with the cosmogony and especially with the institution of the initiation ceremonies."[11]

Whereas "false stories" can be told anywhere and at any time, myths must not be recited except *during a period of sacred time* (usually in autumn or winter, and only at night).[12] This custom has survived even among peoples who have passed beyond the Turco-Mongols and the Tibetans the epic songs of the Gesar cycle can be recited only at night and in winter. "The recitation is assimilated to a powerful charm. It helps to obtain

9 R. Pettazzoni, *Essays on the History of Religions* (Leiden, 1954), pp. 11–12. Cf. also Werner Müller, *Die Religionen der Waldlandindianer Nordamerikas* (Berlin, 1956), p. 42.

10 R. Pettazzoni, *Essays on the History of Religions* p. 13.

11 R. Piddington, quoted by L. Lévy-Bruhl, p. 115. On initiation ceremonies, cf. Eliade, *Birth and Rebirth* (New York, 1958).

12 See examples in R. Pettazzoni, *Essays on the History of Religions* p. 14, n. 15.

all sorts of advantages, particularly success in hunting and war. . . . Before the recitation begins, a space is prepared by being powdered with roasted barley flour. The audience sit around it. The bard recites the epic for several days. They say that in former times the hoofprints of Gesar's horse appeared in the prepared space. Hence the recitation brought the real presence of the hero."[13]

What Myths Reveal

This distinction made by natives between "true stories" and "false stories" is significant. Both categories of narratives present "histories," that is, relate a series of events that took place in a distant and fabulous past. Although the actors in myths are usually Gods and Supernatural Beings, while those in tales are heroes or miraculous animals, all the actors share the common trait that they do not belong to the everyday world. Nevertheless, the natives have felt that the two kinds of "stories" are basically different. For everything that the myths relate *concerns them directly,* while the tales and fables refer to events that, even when they have caused changes in the World (cf. the anatomical or physiological peculiarities of certain animals), have not altered the human condition as such.[14]

Myths, that is, narrate not only the origin of the World, of animals, of plants, and of man, but also all the primordial events in consequence of which man became what he is today—mortal, sexed, organized in a society, obliged to work in order to live, and working in accordance with certain rules. If the World *exists,* if man *exists,* it is because Supernatural Beings exercised creative powers in the "beginning." But after the cosmogony and the creation of man other events occurred, and man *as he is today* is the direct result of those mythical events, *he is constituted by those events.* He is mortal because something happened *in illo tempore.* If that thing had not happened, man would not be mortal—he would have gone on existing indefinitely, like rocks; or he might have changed his skin periodically like snakes, and hence would have been able to renew his life, that is, begin it over again indefinitely. But the myth of the origin of death narrates what happened *in illo tempore,* and, in telling the incident, explains *why* man is mortal.

Similarly, a certain tribe live by fishing—because in mythical times a Supernatural Being taught their ancestors to catch and cook fish. The myth tells the story of the first fishery, and, in so doing, at once reveals a superhuman act, teaches men how to perform it, and, finally, explains why this particular tribe must procure their food in this way.

It would be easy to multiply examples. But those already given show why, for archaic man, myth is a matter of primary importance, while tales and fables are not. Myth teaches him the primordial "stories" that have constituted him existentially; and everything connected with his existence and his legitimate mode of existence in the Cosmos concerns him directly.

We shall presently see what conse-

---

[13] R. A. Stein, *Recherches sur l'épopée et le barde au Tibet* (Paris, 1959), pp. 318–19.

[14] Of course, what is considered a "true story" in one tribe can become a "false story" in a neighboring tribe. "Demythicization" is a process that is already documented in the archaic stages of culture. What is important is the fact that "primitives" are always aware of the difference between myths ("true stories") and tales or legends ("false stories"). Cf. Appendix I ("Myths and Fairly Tales").

quences this peculiar conception had for the behavior of archaic man. We may note that, just as modern man considers himself to be constituted by History, the man of the archaic societies declares that he is the result of a certain number of mythical events. Neither regards himself as "given," "made" once and for all, as, for example, a tool is made once and for all. A modern man might reason as follows: I am what I am today because a certain number of things have happened to me, but those things were possible only because agriculture was discovered some eight to nine thousand years ago and because urban civilizations developed in the ancient Near East, because Alexander the Great conquered Asia and Augustus founded the Roman Empire, because Galileo and Newton revolutionized the conception of the universe, thus opening the way to scientific discoveries and laying the groundwork for the rise of industrial civilization, because the French Revolution occurred and the ideas of freedom, democracy, and social justice shook the Western world to its foundations after the Napoleonic wars—and so on.

Similarly, a "primitive" could say: I am what I am today because a series of events occurred before I existed. But he would at once have to add: events that took place *in mythical times* and therefore make up a *sacred history* because the actors in the drama are not men but Supernatural Beings. In addition, while a modern man, though regarding himself as the result of the course of Universal History, does not feel obliged to know the whole of it, the man of the archaic societies is not only obliged to remember mythical history but also to *re-enact* a large part of it periodically. It is here that we find the greatest difference between the man of the archaic societies and modern man:

the irreversibility of events, which is the characteristic trait of History for the latter, is not a fact to the former.

Constantinople was conquered by the Turks in 1453 and the Bastille fell on July 14, 1789. Those events are irreversible. To be sure, July 14th having become the national holiday of the French Republic, the taking of the Bastille is commemorated annually, but the historical event itself is not re-enacted.[15] For the man of the archaic societies, on the contrary, what happened *ab origine* can be repeated by the power of rites. For him, then, the essential thing is to know the myths. It is essential not only because the myths provide him with an explanation of the World and his own mode of being in the World, but above all because, by re-collecting the myths, by re-enacting them, he is able to repeat what the Gods, the Heroes, or the Ancestors did *ab origine*. To know the myths is to learn the secret of the origin of things. In other words, one learns not only how things came into existence but also where to find them and how to make them reappear when they disappear.

What "Knowing the Myths" Means

Australian totemic myths usually consist in a rather monotonous narrative of peregrinations by mythical ancestors or totemic animals. They tell how, in the "Dream Time" (*alcheringa*)—that is, in mythical time— these Supernatural Beings made their appearance on earth and set out on long journeys, stopping now and again to change the landscape or to produce certain animals and plants, and finally vanished underground. But knowledge of these myths is es-

---

15 Cf. *Myths, Dreams and Mysteries,* pp. 30 ff.

sential for the life of the Australians. The myths teach them how to repeat the creative acts of the Supernatural Beings, and hence how to ensure the multiplication of such-and-such an animal or plant.

These myths are told to the neophytes during their initiation. Or rather, they are "performed," that is, re-enacted. "When the youths go through the various initiation ceremonies, [their instructors] perform a series of ceremonies before them; these, though carried out exactly like those of the cult proper—except for certain characteristic particulars—do not aim at the multiplication and growth of the totem in question but are simply intended to show those who are to be raised, or have just been raised, to the rank of men the way to perform these cult rituals."[16]

We see, then, that the "story" narrated by the myth constitutes a "knowledge" which is esoteric, not only because it is secret and is handed on during the course of an initiation but also because the "knowledge" is accompanied by a magico-religious power. For knowing the origin of an object, an animal, a plant, and so on is equivalent to acquiring a magical power over them by which they can be controlled, multiplied, or reproduced at will. Erland Nordenskiöld has reported some particularly suggestive examples from the Cuna Indians. According to their beliefs, the lucky hunter is the one who knows the origin of the game. And if certain animals can be tamed, it is because the magicians know the secret of their creation. Similarly, you can hold redhot iron or grasp a poisonous snake if you know the origin of fire and

snakes. Nordenskiöld writes that "in one Cuna village, Tientiki, there is a fourteen-year-old boy who can step into fire unharmed simply because he knows the charm of the creation of fire. Perez often saw people grasp redhot iron and others tame snakes."[17]

This is a quite widespread belief, not connected with any particular type of culture. In Timor, for example, when a rice field sprouts, someone who knows the mythical traditions concerning rice goes to the spot. "He spends the night there in the plantation hut, reciting the legends that explain how man came to possess rice [origin myth]. . . . Those who do this are not priests."[18] Reciting its origin myth compels the rice to come up as fine and vigorous and thick as it was when *it appeared for the first time*. The officiant does not remind it of how it was created in order to "instruct" it, to teach it how it should behave. He *magically compels it to go back to the beginning,* that is, to repeat its exemplary creation.

The *Kalevala* relates that the old Väinämöinen cut himself badly while building a boat. Then "he began to weave charms in the manner of all magic healers. He chanted the birth of the cause of his wound, but he could not remember the words that told of the beginning of iron, those very words which might heal the gap ripped open by the blue steel blade." Finally, after seeking the help of other magicians, Väinämöinen cried: "I now remember the origin of iron! and he began the tale as follows: Air is the first of mothers. Water is the eldest of brothers, fire the second and

---

16 C. Strehlow, *Aranda Traditions* vol. III, pp. 1–2; L. Lévy-Bruhl, *La mythologie primitive* p. 123. On puberty initiations in Australia, cf. *Birth and Rebirth,* pp. 4 ff.

17 E. Nordenskiöld, "Faiseurs de miracles et voyants chez les Indiens Cuna," *Revista del Instituto de Etnologia* (Tucumán), vol. II (1932), p. 464; Lévy-Bruhl, *La mythologie primitive* p. 118.
18 A. C. Kruyt, quoted by Lévy-Bruhl, *La mythologie primitive,* p. 119.

iron the youngest of the three. Ukko, the great Creator, separated earth from water and drew soil into marine lands, but iron was yet unborn. Then he rubbed his palms together upon his left knee. Thus were born three nature maidens to be the mothers of iron."[19] It should be noted that, in this example, the myth of the origin of iron forms part of the cosmogonic myth and, in a sense, continues it. This is an extremely important and specific characteristic of origin myths, and we shall study it in the next chapter.

The idea that a remedy does not act unless its origin is known is extremely widespread. To quote Erland Nordenskiöld again: "Every magical chant must be preceded by an incantation telling the origin of the remedy used, otherwise it does not act. . . . For the remedy or the healing chant to have its effect, it is necessary to know the origin of the plant, the manner in which the first woman gave birth to it."[20] In the Na-khi ritual chants published by J. F. Rock it is expressly stated: "If one does not relate. . .the origin of the medicine, to slander it is not proper."[21] Or: "Unless its origin is related one should not speak about it."[22]

We shall see in the following chapter that, as in the Väinämöinen myth given above, the origin of remedies is closely connected with the history of the origin of the World. It should be noted, however, that this is only part of a general conception, which may be formulated as follows: *A rite cannot be performed unless its "origin" is known, that is, the myth that tells how it was performed for the first time.* During the funeral service the Na-khi shaman chants:

"Now we will escort the deceased and
    again experience bitterness;
We will again dance and suppress the
    demons.
If it is not told whence the dance
    originated
One must not speak about it.
Unless one know the origin of the dance
One cannot dance."[23]

This is curiously reminiscent of what the Uitoto told Preuss: "Those are the words (myths) of our father, his very words. Thanks to those words we dance, and there would be no dance if he had not given them to us."[24]

In most cases it is not enough to *know* the origin myth, one must *recite* it: this, in a sense, is a proclamation of one's knowledge, *displays* it. But this is not all. He who recites or performs the origin myth is thereby steeped in the sacred atmosphere in which these miraculous events took place. The mythical time of origins is a "strong" time because it was transfigured by the active, creative presence of the Supernatural Beings. By reciting the myths one reconstitutes that fabulous time and hence in some sort becomes "contemporary" with the events described, one is in the presence of the Gods or Heroes. As a summary formula we might say that by "living" the myths one emerges from profane, chronological time and enters a time that is of a different

19 Aili Kolehmainen Johnson, *Kalevala. A Prose translation from the Finnish* (Hancock, Mich., 1950), pp. 53 ff.
20 E. Nordenskiöld, "La conception de l'âme chez les Indiens Cuna de l'Isthme de Panama," *Journal des Américanistes,* N.S., vol. 24 (1932), pp. 5–30, 14.
21 J. F. Rock, *The Na-Khi Nâga Cult and related ceremonies* (Rome, 1952), vol. II, p. 474.
22 *Ibid.,* vol. II, p. 487.

23 J. F. Rock, *Zhi-mä funeral ceremony of the Na-Khi* (Vienna Mödling, 1955), p. 87.
24 K. T. Preuss, *Religion und Mythologie der Uitoto,* vols. I–II (Göttingen, 1921–23), p. 625.

quality, a "sacred" Time at once primordial and indefinitely recoverable. This function of myth, which we have emphasized in our *Myth of the Eternal Return* (especially pp. 35 ff.), will appear more clearly in the course of the following analyses.

Structure and Function of Myths

These few preliminary remarks are enough to indicate certain characteristic qualities of myth. In general it can be said that myth, as experienced by archaic societies, (1) constitutes the History of the acts of the Supernaturals; (2) that this History is considered to be absolutely *true* (because it is concerned with realities) and *sacred* (because it is the work of the Supernaturals); (3) that myth is always related to a "creation," it tells how something came into existence, or how a pattern of behavior, an institution, a manner of working were established; this is why myths constitute the paradigms for all significant human acts; (4) that by knowing the myth one knows the "origin" of things and hence can control and manipulate them at will; this is not an "external," "abstract" knowledge but a knowledge that one "experiences" ritually, either by ceremonially recounting the myth or by performing the ritual for which it is the justification; (5) that in one way or another one "lives" the myth, in the sense that one is seized by the sacred, exalting power of the events recollected or re-enacted.

"Living" a myth, then, implies a genuinely "religious" experience, since it differs from the ordinary experience of everyday life. The "religiousness" of this experience is due to the fact that one re-enacts fabulous, exalting, significant events, one again witnesses the creative deeds of the Supernaturals; one ceases to exist in the every-day world and enters a transfigured, auroral world impregnated with the Supernaturals' presence. What is involved is not a commemoration of mythical events but a reiteration of them. The protagonists of the myth are made present, one becomes their contemporary. This also implies that one is no longer living in chronological time, but in the primordial Time, the Time when the event *first took place*. This is why we can use the term the "strong time" of myth; it is the prodigious, "sacred" time when something *new, strong,* and *significant* was manifested. To reexperience that time, to re-enact it as often as possible, to witness again the spectacle of the divine works, to meet with the Supernaturals and relearn their creative lesson is the desire that runs like a pattern through all the ritual reiterations of myths. In short, myths reveal that the World, man, and life have a supernatural origin and history, and that this history is significant, precious, and exemplary.

I cannot conclude this chapter better than by quoting the classic passages in which Bronislav Malinowski undertook to show the nature and function of myth in primitive societies. "Studied alive, myth...is not an explanation in satisfaction of a scientific interest, but a narrative resurrection of a primeval reality, told in satisfaction of deep religious wants, moral cravings, social submissions, assertions, even practical requirements. Myth fulfills in primitive culture an indispensable function: it expresses, enhances, and codifies belief; it safeguards and enforces morality; it vouches for the efficiency of ritual and contains practical rules for the guidance of man. Myth is thus a vital ingredient of human civilisation; it is not an idle tale, but a hard-worked active force; it is not an intellectual explanation or an artistic imagery, but a pragmatic charter of primitive faith and moral wisdom. . . . These stories. . . are to the natives a statement of a primeval, greater, and more relevant reality, by which the present life, fates and activities of mankind are determined, the knowledge of which supplies man with the motive for ritual and moral actions, as well as with indications as to how to perform them."[25]

[25] B. Malinowski, *Myth in Primitive Psychology* (1926; reprinted in *Magic, Science and Religion* [New York, 1955], pp. 101, 108).

religious organization

ten

from The Sociology of Religion

JOACHIM WACH

Identity of Natural and Religious Grouping

Each society is made up of a variety of smaller and more comprehensive units. Some of these units are "natural," that is, they are composed of members that are related to one another by blood or by marriage. The physiological or biological factor determines the relationship of the members of a family, clan, or tribe. Strong as this tie is, to the sociologist it appears as a basic "minimum" to which various activities may add additional strength and cohesion. Even in very primitive stages of civilization joint activities and interests—provision of food, construction of shelter, production of tools, implements, and weapons, and enterprises like hunting and fighting—integrate the members of a natural group more closely. It does not matter here if these people are actually "related" or if they regard

From *Types of Religious Experience*, by Joachim Wach, pp. 32–33, copyright in the International Copyright Union, and *The Sociology of Religion*, by Joachim Wach, pp. 54–58, 109–12, copyright 1944 by The University of Chicago. Reprinted by permission of The University of Chicago Press.

themselves thus and are thus regarded by others. Among the additional ties which will increase the cohesion of a natural group there is one of particular interest to us here: religion. The religious attitude of a natural group is determined by two factors: (1) a more or less clearly pronounced, characteristic personal (collective or individual) experience of the unknown or the holy and (2) the role of tradition. The first is a basic datum, which can hardly be "explained" and certainly not reduced to influences or environment, climate, or other external factors. The answers to the question why there are variety and heterogeneity in religious experience have not been found yet and most probably never will be.

The second factor is less constant than the first. Though relatively tenacious, religious tradition, even at the level of primitive culture, undergoes change and development. Both factors determine the religious attitude of a natural group, psychologically and with respect to the forms which the characteristic religious experience of its members creates. "Relatives" will tell the same myths, will perform the same simple or complicated rites, and will follow the advice and guidance of the same interpreter of the divine and guardian of tradition. In other words, worship with all it implies is not only an additional bond but very probably the most important nonbiological or physiological tie between people. We will not discuss here the relationship between the material and spiritual interests and activities of men; suffice it to state that religion, religious concepts, and religious rites lend great and perhaps decisive strength to the cohesion of a natural group. The kindred group has been studied by others as a social and economic unit; we will dwell on its religious aspect.

It is not difficult to find examples for the type of group which we characterized as "identical" because it shares the same natural and cultic ties. In ancient Rome the lares of a family or gens, invited its members to common worship. We will speak of an exclusive identical group when the object of its cult and the peculiarities of its form of worship are characteristic exclusively of Group (Family, Clan) A and not shared by other kindred or related units (another family of the same clan, other clans of the same tribe, etc.). Religious myths, dances, sacred bundles, processions, and associations may be shared by members of two tribes. That means that Tribe A and Tribe B are cultic units but not exclusively so. On the other hand, it is possible that one tribe is divided into various groups, with different religious rites. Wherever the division follows tribal lines, there is an identity of social and religious groupings; where it does not, a different principle prevails, and religious allegiance follows spontaneous leadership. We will call this second type of unit a *specifically religious* group.

A specifically religious group would be illustrated by a special cultic group within a larger social or political unit (tribe or nation) or by a religion professed by ethnically or politically disparate adherents. The world religions are good examples of religions made up of different tribes and nations. We shall deal in detail below (chap. v) with this type of group integrated exclusively by religious impulses. At present we shall concern ourselves exclusively with those groups which are simultaneously natural *and* religious. For our purpose we shall subdivide this type of social unit into three categories: groups based on kinship; local groups which may or may not be kindred but are best dealt with in this context; and associations founded on the basis of natural affinity (equality of age, sex, etc.). We shall later examine associations with special purposes when we discuss the stratification of society resulting from the differentiation of society into labor, property, and rank (chap. vi).

It is a mistake to assume that the above classification into natural and specifically religious groups represents a chronological development, although, broadly speaking, religions of universal character appear comparatively late in history. Specifically religious groups are found even in primitive society. However, it is not the "secular" group but rather that in which religious and social ties are identical which is most frequently encountered at less advanced levels of civilization. For example, the family among the Greeks, Romans, Hebrews, Celts, Egyptians, Persians, Indians, Chinese, Japanese, and pre-Columbian high civilizations is both a cultic and a social unit. Greek, Asiatic, ancient American, and Chinese cities were also sociocultic units. Nations in which religious and political loyalties were originally congruent were the ancient Hebrew, Egyptian, Babylonian, Assyrian, Hittite, Persian, Greek, Roman, Chinese, Japanese,

Mexican, and Peruvian. All these were developed by a process of integrating smaller tribal or local units into a "state" (*Reich*). This development, however, in nearly every case involved a transformation of the original sociological setup—a transformation to which a religious development corresponded. The interrelation of these two factors will be discussed more fully later on (chap. vii).

Specifically Religious Organization of Society

A New Principle of Grouping: Specifically Religious Groups

We have hitherto discussed identical types of religious and social organization and have noted that this identity prevails in less complex cultures. Two factors tend to promote a change in this situation: the growing differentiation in the sociological, political, and cultural structure of society and the enrichening of the religious experience of individuals and groups. The beginnings of both processes are clearly discernible in primitive societies. Although the numerical growth of a sociological unit—family, clan, or tribe—does not necessarily alter its religious status, it inevitably leads to divisions and subdivisions for cultic purposes. Age groups which originally aimed to prepare its members for full participation in the rights and duties of manhood and to serve the desires of companionship and fellowship are destined later to be further differentiated. Increasing differences in property, occupation, and rank also favor corresponding variations in religious thought, action, and organization. Finally, the initiative of outstanding leaders in response to momentous events in the life of the people, like wars, plagues, and other *portenta*, greatly influences the religious attitude of the group and its corresponding expression, in spite of the conservative tradition in religious thought which tends to cast this expression in predetermined forms.

This, however, reveals only one side of the picture. We must, as previously indicated, allow not only for changes and developments in the social and political structure of a people, with its effect on traditional religion, but for autonomous religious development as well. It may be questioned whether religious activity can be isolated from other group functions in primitive society, but a careful study of the evidence convinces us that, even in the lesser civilizations, religious experience has its own peculiar dialectic. Moreover, the appearance of individual movements and leaders of primarily religious character indicates that, in spite of the frequent identity and interpenetration of sociopolitical and religious activities, religion maintains a distinct autonomous development.[1]

A new type of grouping appears which, though current throughout the history of civilization, has not always been adequately recognized. The feeling of solidarity developing in these new units is to a certain extent revolutionary.[2] The consciousness of this solidarity will vary; it will in-

[1] Unfortunately, Jakob Wilhelm Hauer's study, *Die Religionen: Ihr Werden, ihr Sinn, ihre Wahrheit* (Berlin: W. Kohlhammer, 1923), Vol. I: *Das religioese Erlebnis auf den unteren Stufen,* which placed decided emphasis on the intensification of the religious experience in his review of the history of religion, has not been completed. It ends with a very understanding discussion of highest types of religious concepts and institutions in the more advanced primitive societies (cf. esp. chap. viii).

[2] The fact is clearly seen and stated by Arthur D. Nock, *Conversion* (London and New York: Oxford University Press, 1933), chaps. i and ii, esp. p. 28 for ancient civilization.

crease and decrease with the development of the new unit. This new form of grouping is characterized by the concept of relationship as spiritual fatherhood and spiritual brotherhood. The new community will differ from the natural groups not only in the type of organization, in rites, and in beliefs but primarily in a new spirit of unity. We have found that it is not so much organic growth which makes for the emergence of this spirit as it is a definite break with the past and with the ties of nature which characterizes its rise. The more pronounced this break, the more definitely can we call the new unit a specifically religious group. Symbols of the break which is consciously experienced even at the level of primitive culture are such concepts as regeneration, rebirth, conversion, and corresponding rites. Those who undergo this experience, either collectively or, more frequently, individually, are stimulated to join in close company. The intimacy of the new religious experience makes for intimacy of the new fellowship. At first it may consist merely in the exchange of the new knowledge between a few; later, of more followers and companions; then it may grow into a lasting association, binding itself to the pursuit of a definite way of life and welding its members into a strongly knit community. The various differences which prevailed in the "old world," now left behind, are meant to be extinguished. They are implicitly or explicitly repudiated, though with the growth of the new community they may reappear. Theoretically there may be agreement that no new differences and distinctions should be allowed to develop, but practically they will emerge, and frequently new groups have frankly and freely postulated and recognized them. Where the difference of sex counts for nought,

another difference, inherited from the world organized according to "natural" ties, will be confirmed: that of age. Of the most important criterion of discrimination—the recognition of religious charisma—we will speak presently. In spite of a minimum of differentiation traceable in almost all cases, the new group is dominated by a spirit of solidarity. The possession of a new experience unites and integrates its members most intimately. But it also sets them apart from the rest of the world which does not, yet, share in it. To make it share is the more or less determined aim of most specifically religious groups. One of the most important differences between them and the identical community which we discussed in the fourth chapter of this book is their potential missionary character. The missionary interest may be principally limited or (potentially) universal. The former we find in groups united by an experience which is thought to be open only to an ethnically, religiously, or otherwise defined minority or majority of people: a religious élite (which, of course, may definitely be far from being a social or political élite). In the first case the "natural" order of things may be partly incorporated into the new religious conception; in the second (religious criterion) a theological explanation for a more or less final dualism of included and excluded is necessary. We will see that the exclusivity of some of the so-called "sectarian" groups is so justified. According to the interpretation of its own nature, significance, and message which a specifically religious group holds, its attitude toward those outside will vary. If it is constitutionally selective, it will discriminate between prospective converts and those who cannot be converted. The first will be treated with care ("potential brother"), the second with indifference or contempt. We shall see that secret and mystery societies and some sects exhibit these two attitudes. If it is (potentially or actually) universal in its aim, the specifically religious group will admit no principal difference in the dealings with members and nonmembers, though actually feelings of superiority toward the latter and double standards will develop easily. *Binnenethik* (ethics valid only within) is, as the history of religion shows very clearly, definitely not limited to natural groups of which they are characteristic.

We shall now turn to the study of different types of specifically religious groups, beginning with more mixed and cruder forms and leading up to the more perfect ones. It is easily understandable that there are two kinds: those whose origin we can trace through historical studies and those whose beginnings are hidden not only from their members but from us as well.

Folk and Universal Religion

GUSTAV MENSCHING

1. Folk Religion*

We distinguish basic structures of religion and religious types within them. We come upon the phenomenon of basic structures when we investigate the historical circumstance that there are some religions which are confined to a single folk and others which have spread among many peoples. There are *folk religions* and *world religions*. The difference thus suggested among historical religions by no means has to do with territorial diffusion alone. Rather it rests upon a deeper structural differentiation of religion itself.

First it must be noted that, in folk religion of every kind, the *folk,* or in nature-religion the tribe, but in any case a vital community, is the carrier

Gustav Mensching, "Folk and Universal Religion," trans. by Louis Schneider, from *Religion, Culture and Society: A Reader in the Sociology of Religion,* ed. by L. Schneider. Copyright © 1964 by John Wiley & Sons, Inc. Reprinted by permission.

* In translating, I have omitted a few references to religious documents, L.S.

of the religion. The individual has not yet discovered himself but has a life quite bound up with that of the collectivity. On this foundation the historically earliest religious communities are of the vital type: family—and house—community, sib and tribe, folk and state. In early religion there are no specific religious communities aside from the vital, given communities of birth. But these vital communities for their part have a sacred stamp and are at the same time religious communities.

The second structural factor in folk religion is that in that religion the "salvation" afforded consists in the condition of positive relationships of the folk community to the divinities that appertain to it. This condition of salvation of the folk community, into which the individual is born, and whose maintenance is the duty of the members of the folk society, is a mystic "life" which binds all together and to separate one's self from which means actual death. "The human being who precedes history or exists outside it leads...a double life. One is the unheeded life whose beginning is actual birth...the other is the true life, which begins with a rite...These two lives are not separate." (C. H. Ratschow, *Magie und Religion,* 1946, p. 43.)

The gods of folk religion are exclusively related to a particular folk and limited to that folk as their province of domination, so to put it. This holds not only for the folk as a whole but also for the vital communities that constitute it: family and sib, tribe and clan also have their proper gods. These gods accordingly lack universality. The idea of one's own gods is thus wholly reconcilable with the view that other peoples have gods proper to them. In the Israelite religion, for example, the claim of the Moabites against that of the Israelite God Jahweh is delimited and recognized. But there prevails between the folk and its divinities a strictly and exclusively binding relationship. Defection to foreign divinities is, thus, repeatedly designated in Israel as seriously sinful. Folk religion is in consequence of this by no means tolerant. But we are confronted by a typically folk-religious intolerance which I designate as inner-religious intolerance; for toward the outside one is tolerant insofar as one does not dispute the existence or right to existence of foreign gods.

The peculiarity of the particular folk involved and the relationship to the folk is substantially more clearly marked out in folk religion than in the universal religions. While the universal religions are in principle supra-national and owe their diffusion and ability to diffuse to this supra-national character, there is naturally and quite directly reflected in the folk religions the special spirit of the folk. This is especially clear (other factors, such as peculiarity of cultus, outlook on the gods, and the like, aside) in what is considered good and bad, in a word in *folk-religious* ethics. In the Teu-

tonic religion, for example, ethical values are related to the weal and woe of the sib, so that the sib is the value standard of good and bad. The same relationship is present in the pre-Mohammedan folk religion of the Arabic tribes. And in Japanese Shinto serious "celestial sins" consist in offense against the interests of the folk community. The "ten commandments" of the Old Testament, also, are explicit folk-law, in which in the fourth commandment the continued existence of the folk is made contingent upon proper conduct toward father and mother and thus upon maintenance of the family. But aside from this relationship of ethic to folk, it may be shown in detail through comparison of the value-tables of different folk religions that, through "preference" of one value over other recognized ethical values, the special spirit of the individual folk religion is determined. As another characteristic of the folk-religious ethic and thereby of the structure of the folk religion itself may be added the circumstance that the recognized ethical values (like the idea of God itself) still neither have nor claim universal validity. The above stressed folk connection of ethics thus means not only that values are related to the welfare and security of the folk but also that they have validity only within the domain of the particular folk. The stranger to folk and sib has no claim to friendly conduct: he is "hostis" (stranger and enemy), and the laws of behavior valid within the folk context are of no effect in relation to him. There is also lacking within the folk religious context the perception of the universality of ethical values and of their *unconditioned* validity—a validity unrestricted by the object of the ethical act or disposition. Good and evil are not yet absolute good and evil, but still the relatively good and evil, that which is valuable or harmful for the welfare and survival of the folk.

As the external circumstance of restriction to a folk points to fundamental structures which determine the character and limits of folk religion, so on the other hand the observation of the external *fate* of the folk religion within the folk world leads to a far more important recognition of essential changes in human existence itself. A glance at the history of religion shows that nearly all the folk religions experienced the fate of being replaced by universal religions. In detail, this happened in different ways. We can distinguish three different ways of replacement of aboriginal folk religion through a universal religion.

One set of folk religions evolved in the course of their history, in their later period, universal tendencies that came out of themselves, although with a maintenance of their folk-detemined limited form and their own folk-religious tradition. This is the case, for example, in India. Universal tendencies indeed emerge early in the Vedas. We already encounter the intuition of the One in the earlier Rigveda. The many folk gods disappear behind the One (whether personally or neutrally conceived) and become simply names for the One. "The singers designate what is merely one by many names—Agni, Mitra, Matarishvan." In the Upanishads the basic structure is already that of universal religion, but the folk-religious *form* has remained. And also in Hinduism, which essentially builds on the Vedic tradition, we deal with pure universal religion (aside from the primitive folk religion of the broad masses, which is also maintained in every universal religion as "folk belief"), but again in the form of folk religion. The folk-religious tradition is not overcome; but it no longer determines essence, although it continues to determine external form. Similarly the *Israelite* religion offers in its evolution the picture of a self-universalizing religion. The real folk religion was founded through Moses on the demonistic foundation that remains clearly visible in the Old Testament in the worship of animals, the dead, ancestors, trees, springs, and stars. Through Moses the individual tribes became a single folk with a conscious and religiously experienced fate under a common God, Jahweh. Jahweh is unequivocally the folk god of Israel.

Through the agency of the great prophets of the eighth century before Christ there begins the universalization of the Israelite religion. But this religion preserves its folk-religious form into the present. The folk religion of *Iran* also won through the prophet Zarathustra a universal character but kept its folk-religious form. In Greece, where every polis had its gods, it was the great tragedians who proclaimed a universal idea of God. Here indeed we have an example of the second form of universalization.

In a second set of folk religions universalization occurs as the folk religion is replaced or complemented by a foreign universal religion. This occurred, for example, in Greece by the agency of the mystery religions coming from abroad, which also came to Rome and appeared beside the Roman folk religion (the latter, for its part, never developed its own universal tendencies). The same process also occurred in Japan: the folk religion of Shintoism was complemented, from 552 A.D. on, by the foreign universal religion of Buddhism.

In a third set of folk religions, there occurred the establishment of a supranational *world religion*. On the ground of Indian folk religion Buddha founded Buddhism. On the ground of the Israelite folk religion and on that of the Arabic folk religion, Christianity and Islam were founded by Jesus and Mohammed respectively. Each of these three world religions came into a peculiar relationship to the field of its own folk-religious origin. The tension between Indian folk-religion and Buddhism led to the overcoming of Buddhism in the Indian field of origin. In the Israelite religious world also the tension, already present in the lifetime of Christianity's founder, between Israelite folk religion and Christianity, was preserved. In contrast to Buddhism in India, Christianity in Palestine never won a victory but remained a foreign religion which neither displaced nor complemented the original religion. But Buddhism, too, was influential in India only perhaps for a millennium. Then it wandered as a foreign religion into the Far East. Only on the ground of the Arabic folk religion did Islam come to replace the aboriginal religion.

In all cases, then, actual folk religion in religious history was replaced by universal religion. That occurred in a later time. The folk religions are early religions. But it is not enough simply to record this historical circumstance. It rests upon a structural change in the mode of existence of men themselves and thus upon *anthropological* presuppositions. There are precise correspondences between the mode of existence of early men and religious structure. Early man, as we may say briefly in connection with important work by G. van der Leeuw (*Der Primitive Mensch und die Religion*, 1937), lives in the unity of an undivided and unexamined life. He does not stand over against the world, but lives in it, and the fullness of powers that animate the world fills him also. In this stage, there is little that separates subject and object, or

indeed object and object. Man is essentially participant in everything. The contours of things in the external world are fluid. In the depths of all phenomena and of man himself there is an ultimate essential identity. In brief, early man is not yet isolated from the elementary unity of life, has not yet fathomed himself as an ego and a self released from community and life-unity. Folk religion corresponds to this stage of human existence, for it is the religion of *unexamined elementary unity*. The various interpretations of the folk-religious stage of belief may be corrected from this perspective. One may characterize the stage of folk religion, with Paul, as a "time of ignorance," which was then overcome through the universal-religious knowledge of one's own religion. In terms of the science of religion it must be said that this theological interpretation does not do justice to historical circumstance. Anthropologically speaking, a universal religion would not have been possible in early times. We shall analyze the structure of universal religion in the next section. It will then be plain that as folk religion corresponded precisely to early human existence, so universal religion, which is a religion of later time, again corresponds to the *transformed* existence of recent man. The emergence of universal religion thus occurred in an historical moment in which it was a human necessity, since, to be sure, folk religion no longer answered man's condition.

But it is not only the flat theological interpretation of folk religion which now becomes corrected. The rationalistic interpretation of the course of religious history is corrected by the above perspective. Historical religions cannot be looked upon as variations, of essentially the same order, of a "natural religion," for there are profound structural differences among religions—differences that are left out of account in the abstraction of a meager "natural religion" as the common religion of man. The historical necessity of the transition from folk to universal religion may be perceived directly from the cognition of anthropological presuppositions.

2. Universal Religion

In the analysis of universal religion, we may also begin with external phenomena which point to profound inner laws and factors. The universality of the religions of which we affirm that they also have an inner structural community is in the first place external: these religions go beyond the boundaries of their religio-historical field of origin or their folk or country and diffuse among many different peoples without regard to race, culture, speech, or other distinctiveness. There is still another observation that points from the external to concealed laws. It is not only in regard to space (diffusion to many lands and peoples) but also in regard to time that the phenomenon of universal religion presents itself to us as a problem. The universal religions emerge in the history of religion at nearly the same time. Rudolf Otto, in another connection and from different viewpoints, first referred to "the law of parallels in the history of religion." Otto speaks of the transition from myth to logos, from mythology to theology, and thinks that this significant step occurred nearly everywhere at the same time among civilized men—between 800 and 500 B.C. In my judgment, the phenomenon Otto had in view can be better described as a transition from the structure of folk religion to that of universal religion. In Greece, this transition took place in the period

between Hesiod and Plato. Pythagoras founded his order in 530 B.C. Confucius died in China about 470 B.C. Lao-tse lived some centuries later, according to recent opinion. This development begins in India in the era of the Upanishads, about 800 B.C., and Buddha was alive in 500 B.C. In Israel also the same period is involved, for the prophets paved the way for the universalization of folk religion in the eighth century B.C. Even in Persia the reform of folk religion by Zarathustra probably falls in these same centuries. These parallels in time are strange. In the same centuries there stirs everywhere among men the longing for a new form of religion. What happened? Clearly, a *fundamental change in human existence* itself set in. But let us first be clear on what the structure of universal religion, which takes account of this altered situation in the human mode of existence, consists of.

The decisively new feature in the structure of universal religion is that in this religion it is no longer the collectivity, as in folk religion, but the *individual* who is the subject of religion. Whereas the individual in folk religion was a member of the overarching community, through which he lived and in whose "sanctity" he participated, in all universal religion we encounter the individual who has become conscious of himself and presents distinctive religious problems.

For this is now the second fundamental factor: no longer is sanctity a given thing, sanctity that one could lose in folk religion in exceptional cases if one got detached from the salvation-community of folk and sib, but *the condition of non-salvation* is the given thing, and indeed a *personal* condition of non-salvation in which the individual finds himself. Salvation is desired, as is contact with divinity or the unity that is no longer given with membership in the great vital communities of sib and folk into which everyone is born. The vital community, indeed, lost its sacred character in later time and became profane. The individual himself perceives himself as detached from the numinous primitive ground of existence. Man did indeed become in growing measure master of the world and its powers as he became subject and the external world increasingly became object. But in his surrender to the world and its goods he lost elemental contact with the numinous world above. Therefore the individual must win anew a soteriological contact which had only to be cultivated and maintained in folk religion. Also on the ground of the individualized universal religion, in a later stage of organization, the effort is made to produce a situation analogous to that of folk religion, insofar as man wins salvation through membership in an objective soteriological organization (the church).

In universal religion *man* is the object of the message of salvation. Thereby a de-nationalization of religious concern takes place. We deal with the need for depth in human existence, flatly, and thus with every man's need. Universal religion is therefore not only externally universal, but has primarily an inner universality, in that it concerns everyone. And therefore in universal religion everywhere a universal offer of salvation is proclaimed over against the existing state of non-salvation. Salvation and man's existence depend on the taking up of this offer.

The universal message encounters a folk-differentiated humanity. The supranational proclamation of universal religion therefore had everywhere to be melted down. Re-minting and minting anew were necessary for all universal religions and were carried out everywhere in East and West. The universal message of salvation is consequently international in content, but in its form it appears in the history of religion in a variety of stampings, according to the spirit of the peoples it conquered. The folk-differentiation of mankind is thus no boundary for the diffusion of a universal religion; for, as the history of religion shows, it is certainly possible for other peoples to appropriate a universal religion which is foreign to them as regards its field of origin. Two thirds of mankind profess a foreign religion. The absolute limit of appropriation lies rather in men themselves, in their religious capacity for understanding or the lack thereof. The great founders of religions have meditated on the fact of their wide-reaching failure or of the downright unbelief which they encountered among men, and adduced an explanation correspondent with the basic character of their message. Buddha construed unbelief in such fashion as to understand it as a sign of immaturity in man's long journey of rebirth. Even the unbeliever will in time attain knowledge when he has attained the necessary stage of maturity. Jesus spoke of the calling to belief by the Father in Heaven, and similarly Mohammed conceived unbelief as the effect of a quite incalculable act of will on the part of the arbitrary Allah. But in any case there are assumed here firm barriers, immovable by men.

A further characteristic of universal religion lies in *the totality of its claim*. The religion of salvation claims the entire personality and existence of man. It is not a matter of modification on the periphery of human life, but of a profound level of existence, from out of which all sectors of human existence receive their new influence.

Folk religion also bound its members totally, for the existence of the secondary individual depended on the community of the folk, whose life was his life. In early religion also, man lives a full and redeemed life only when he lives a "united existence." This redemptive union, however, is given in antecedent folk-solidarity.

In the universal religion of later times there goes forth to the given isolation of the individual the message of salvation. This also aspires to achieve a "united existence," on a new basis, to be sure. But it can do so only if it penetrates to the depth where the disturbance of unity has taken place. Mysticism and prophecy, the two fundamental forms of universal religions, both claim, each in characteristic fashion, the whole man to the very roots of his existence: mysticism as it strives for the elimination of individual being, the merging of the individual in the One; prophecy as it seeks to re-establish the unity-in-belief (of the individual isolated and living remote from God) with the personally conceived savior-deity.

Universal religion, which has in actuality spread among numerous peoples, carries within itself the *tendency to diffusion*. In the pure folk religion, whose divinities are nationally and territorially delimited, there naturally does not exist the object of converting other peoples to one's own religion. On the contrary, the knowledge of one's own gods appears here as a value that puts one at an advantage over other people and that one would therefore rather keep secret than impart. Thus the Romans, for example, called out unknown gods from a besieged city in an act of "evocation" in order to take away divine aid from the besieged. In the folk religion with a universal content the tendency to diffusion is already manifest, as in Judaism, which in the time of Christ had conquered seven per cent of the inhabitants of the Roman Empire. This mission of Judaism broke down in view of the pure religious universalism of Christianity, since the Jewish religion held firm to the specifically folk-religious demand of entrance into the national community of the Jews. On these grounds the substantially universal religion of the Jews could not become a world religion. The same is true of Confucianism, for this too represented specifically Chinese outlooks and claims, side by side with a substantial universality (especially in the realm of ethics). It is thus evident that everywhere that universal contents emerge in a folk religion a tendency to diffusion becomes apparent. But this tendency nevertheless fails: not by reason of historical accident but out of innermost necessity, for on the one hand the universal content has not yet attained the depth in which the universally unredeemed condition of the existential isolation of latter-day man is shown, and on the other this same content, insofar as it is already universal, has not yet transcended its national boundaries and so failed to find understanding among alien peoples.

In the case of genuine world religions, on the other hand, these conditions are fulfilled. They touch upon the unredeemed condition of *man* and transcend the nation. The tendency to diffusion is omnipresent in them and has been everywhere successfully realized, to be sure in differing degrees. The difference in intensity of the desire to missionize is contingent on the essential structure of the universal religion. Mystic religions, which rather incline toward concealment (compare the arcana-discipline in the mystery religions), are less disposed to mission than the prophetic religions. Buddhism as a mystic world religion has nowhere represented a hard Either-Or, as have Islam and Christianity, the prophetic world religions. Buddhism, rather, has considered foreign notions of deity as pre-stages of the Buddhist knowledge of salvation and built them into its own system. But the prophetic religions are strictly exclusive and therefore sought the radical destruction of all alien religions in order to make the prophetic ones all-dominant. Hence Buddhism appears everywhere *beside* other religions. In Japan it came as a universal religion beside genuine Shintoism; in China beside Confucianism and Taoism; and in India, its land of origin, it remained existent, to be sure as a dwindling minority religion, beside Hinduism and Islam.

We return once more to the initially discussed question of *anthropological presuppositions*. It is evident that folk religion corresponded to the mode of existence of early times. This mode of existence was briefly described as that of unexamined unity. After the structure of universal religion (in connection with which it was plain above all that the religious focus is on the isolated individual) was explained, it was easily shown that universal religion corresponds precisely to the change in the mode of human existence that had supervened in the meantime. G. van der Leeuw has shown that in the evolution of mankind there may be clearly recognized the emergence of individual self-consciousness and, at the same time therewith, growing self-differentiation from a world increasingly becoming "object." The general development, the process of "becoming man" (van der Leeuw), amounts to a liberation and an achievement of independence on the part of the individual. But, negatively, this process at the same time involves a threat to man in the depths of his existence through isolation from the metaphysical primitive powers which, without residue, sustained and fulfilled the undiscovered individual within the primitive vital collectivity. The newly discovered ego strives for independence with all its newly awakened powers. All universal religions make answer to this human situation with unmistakable structural unanimity, for, as was shown, they all start from a fundamental break in the depths of human existence and seek in one fashion or another to establish a re-union with the holy. Accordingly, world religion is responsive not, one may say, to a newly recognized need (as an orthodox view of religion would have it) but to a newly arisen need of man awakened to self-consciousness in more recent time. It is from this standpoint that the inner meaning of the circumstance previously mentioned, that folk religions were everywhere replaced by universal religions, is to be understood. Folk religions were not forcibly constrained to their decline. Nor did they disappear before the better or profounder truth of universal religions. They perished because they no longer answered to the newly developed condition of mankind. Of course, universal religion is to this extent the profounder and truer perception as over against folk-religious truth, but its truth would have been valueless in early history insofar as no question had arisen on the part of men to correspond to the answer given by universal religion. This interpretation of the phenomenon of late universal religion also dispenses us from the assumption demanded of us by the orthodox view of religion: that mankind remained in utter darkness and in unqualified, unredeemed error, for millennia, until at last the light of universal truth broke forth. There are no human errors of so fundamental a type. However primitive were the theoretical notions that men had of their gods, in religious substance they were surely oriented in the right direction in the given total situation. It was the gradual change of the total situation which first allowed the ripening of the aspiration toward new truth and deeper knowledge of God which was brought to mankind in the universal message of the world religions.

Part 4

religion
and society

Religion exists because men experience life as *in* the world but not limited *by* it—as somehow pointed beyond the world. The German philosopher and psychiatrist Karl Jaspers characterized man as a "boundary phenomenon," that is, as existing at an "edge," rooted in the here-and-now but related to a Beyond. Functionalist theorists in sociology have pointed to the importance of experiences that bring men to that edge, the breaking points at which the relationship to the Beyond becomes significantly operative. It is as though men have two orientations which, in the conception of biblical religion, may be called two vocations. This implies that the relationship between religion and society is ambiguous. While religion performs positive functions, it is also at least potentially in conflict with many this-worldly societal values and goals.

Religious groups respond in various ways to the ambivalence and conflict of this condition. Religious traditions have various definitions of the meaning of mundane existence and the value of worldly activity. Religious institutions are related variously to the other established structures of society—legal structures, authority structures, and the legitimated forms of ownership and control of resources. The sociologist of religion must analyze religious attitudes toward the world and the institutions that arise from those attitudes, expressing and reinforcing them; he must also analyze the relationship of religious institutions to other institutions of the general society. Because the ways in which man relates to the transcendent and the modes of his participation in religious life are largely determined by the character of his daily life, the sociologist must also study the influence of social change and socially determined needs upon the development of religious attitudes, ideas, and institutions.

There has been much study on the subject of the differential appeal of religious ideas to particular groups in society. Society is divided into subgroups which are often derived ultimately from a differentiation of functions —a division of labor. Such groups, classes, or strata have different opportunities and experiences. Consequently, they see life and its possibilities and problems differently and have different interests. Religious ideas appeal differently to such groups. In *The Sociology of Religion* and *The Protestant Ethic and the Spirit of Capitalism,* Max Weber showed how certain classes, occupational groups, and other status groups are drawn to world views that conform in some way to the needs, aspirations, and values that arise from their concrete experience. Weber showed how the acceptance of a religious outlook is at least in part historically and socially conditioned. Talcott Parsons, who followed Weber and sought to understand how various factors within the social system shape nonempirical ideas which form the world view of a particular society, theorized that ideas with an affinity to special interests have a greater appeal and are accepted. That is, while nonempirical ideas comprising a religious world view are supraempirical in the sense that they cannot be experimentally demonstrated, as can ideas that comprise a scientific theory, they are nevertheless congruent in significant ways with the concrete life experiences of different groups. Because groups have different life experiences, they are attracted to different religious ideas and ideals. For example, the religious interest in salvation arises naturally from and is influenced by worldly needs, although as Norman Cohn has observed, it may indeed be inherent in the human condition. The promise of redemption speaks directly to the oppressed and the underprivileged, providing them with a cognitive framework within which to understand the conditions of their lives.

The emergence of the bourgeois class in Europe and the relation of this class to religious ideas and institutions offers an excellent example of the important role played by social and economic interests in the complex matter of religious motivation. Max Weber studied the relationship of the interests of the rising capitalist class to religious ideas and the independent causal implications of such ideas, once they were accepted by a significant section of society. H. Richard Niebuhr in his classic work, *The Social Sources of Denominationalism,* demonstrated the crucial role of economic and social factors both in shaping the outlooks of emerging Protestant sects and in affecting their transition from sect to denomination—their routinization and accommodation to society. We include here a selection from the recently translated work of Bernard Groethuysen, *The Bourgeois,* which analyzes the conflicts between the emerging French bourgeoisie and the traditional positions of the Catholic Church. Using original sources, Groethuysen showed the tremendous disarticulation between the Church and the "new men," and the misunderstandings that arose between them because of their differing views of the value of man's "earthly vocation." The "enlightened" bourgeois demanded a system of beliefs that would both conform to his Enlightenment ideas and legitimate his capitalist function.

Stratification played a major role in determining the religious affinity of Blacks in the United States. E. F. Frazier described the vital, dynamic, and simple faith of the slaves and their earliest free descendants in the South. He also showed how the attainment of economic success and some measure of social status affected religious life. Middle-class Blacks tended to reject the older religious style of their fathers, characterized by emotional expression, and to seek a more restrained and presumably decorous religious service appropriate to their new status.

The relationship between religious ideas and strategic groups within society is also evident in the history of social movements for which religion has served as an ideology of transition. Movements for change in society are based upon a definition of the meaning of life and an ideal view of human community, both of which have been provided by religion in the past. Religious ideas have often formed the ideational framework and justification for programs of practical reform. An example is the role of Puritanism as an ideology of transition for the emerging middle class in England during the seventeenth and eighteenth centuries. In his book *Religion and the Rise of Capitalism,* R. H. Tawney demonstrated that Puritanism was influential in shaping a new order in English life, and was in turn shaped by the new order. Tawney formulated a thesis to describe the relationship of religion to particular class interests, in this case to a class that in fact carried out a social revolution in English life.

The deeper problem of the relation of the church to the world—the question of how much a specific religious institution accommodates to the demands of mundane existence and the secular sphere or withdraws from that sphere— is indeed a central problem in the sociological study of religion. It received its classic formulation in the work of Ernst Troeltsch, whose definition of the church and the sect as sociological types characterized by specific kinds of responses to the world has been the foundation of sociological research in this area. We include this definition from Troeltsch's monumental work, and point out that many examples of both responses can be isolated and discussed in terms of the elements of withdrawal or accommodation they represent. Two significant historical studies of the church–sect problem are those of H. Richard Niebuhr, *Christ and Culture,* and Franklin H. Littell, *The Origins of Sectarian Protestantism.* Niebuhr's work describes the identification of church and world, while Littell's study depicts the radical withdrawal of churches from the world.

Troeltsch discussed a third stance toward the world and institutional religion: the mystical response. Mysticism arises particularly when the established forms of church life fail to meet the spiritual needs of men, because of either secularization or institutional rigidity. At such times individuals withdraw and cultivate an individual interior relationship to the divine. The mystical response may become a ground for the formation of a group of persons related by their common subjective religious experience, for which no adequate established or official forms of expression are available.

The hasidic movement within Judaism is an example of mystical response. Hasidism became a mass movement, shared by multitudes of Jews who found themselves dissatisfied with the official rabbinic structure and its forms of piety, and who therefore sought a more personal, dynamic kind of religious experience outside the established patterns of Judaism. Hasidism represents "something like a rebellion of religious energy against petrified religious values. . . ."[1] It was a burst of creativity that injected mystical enthusiasm into

---

1 Gershom G. Scholem, *Major Trends in Jewish Mysticism* (New York: Schocken Books, Inc., 1954), p. 238.

the traditional forms of the Jewish law, revitalizing the entire traditional framework of Jewish religious life. Our brief selection by Martin Buber on Hasidism describes the historical and sociological conditions influencing its origin and rise.

religion and social stratification

eleven

The Church and the Social Classes

BERNARD GROETHUYSEN

As men like Bossuet portrayed it, the world was divided into two dis-tinct groups: the great and the poor. The great, to whom God had communicated "a spark of his power";[1] the poor, who were "the good friends of Jesus." Each had its own titles of nobility; the great were graced with the "splendors of power," the poor, with the "splendors of poverty, according to the teachings of the Gospels."[2] The great and the poor, two characters in a divine epic, which would lose something very essential were they to disappear from the scene. Warring and yet complementary, each must seek out the other, and exist, in a way, only for the other. And in order to play a part on the stage of

the world, a man must be clearly seen belonging to one camp or the other. The important thing, then, was not whether he drew down upon himself anathemas or praise; he was in his place in the great Christian tragedy in which both God and the devil, sinner and saint, played their parts.

But what of those who, living in a condition of pleasant mediocrity, were neither one nor the other, neither saints nor sinners, neither poor Lazarus nor the wicked rich man, who experienced neither the splendors of power nor the wretchedness of poverty? Background figures, they did nothing to explain the significance of the drama performed here below. It seemed, then, that their lot was to live on the sidelines of the great Christian tragedy, whose principal roles remained reserved for the powerful and the poor, each marked with the royal seal of divinity. Living in easy circumstances and outside the great conflicts dividing the universe, they represented nothing save ordinariness.

Reading Bossuet's sermons, one might almost be tempted to believe that the Church had forgotten the bourgeois, so small did his place ap-

---

[1] Bossuet, "Sermon on Final Impenitence."
[2] Bossuet, "Panegyric in Honor of St. Francis of Assisi."

From *The Bourgeois* by Bernard Groethuysen. Translated by Mary Ilford. Copyright © 1968 by Holt, Rinehart and Winston, Inc. Reprinted by permission of Holt, Rinehart and Winston, Inc.

pear in a world where the roles were distributed among those who lived in splendor and those who lived in want, both able to claim a special relationship to God. He appeared rather as a gatecrasher in a world formed without him, where he had no *raison d'être*. In vain does one search for his titles in the records of Christian tradition; legend seems silent on this score. Where had he originated, then, and who was he? The God of the Christians, in creating the world seemed not to have foreseen that one day the bourgeois would demand his place in it.

Yet, in the modern age, how could the Church still disregard this citizen? It could not abandon this upright man, conscious of his worth,. to the secular world. As formerly it had been able to bestow a religious character upon those who, rich or beggars, had filled the stage of the world, so now it had to seek to interpret in its own manner the social phenomenon represented in modern times by the bourgeoisie. It had to be able to explain to the bourgeois why God had created him, and it had to assign functions to him on this earth. But how could the Church go about taking hold of this bourgeois with his altogether secular roots? How could it integrate into religious traditions the spirit and mode of the bourgeoisie, in order to be able to hallow it? What, in this order which linked heaven and earth and whose origins were traceable back to God himself, could be the spiritual significance of the bourgeois?

"Yes, my brothers," says Massillon, addressing kings and descendants of illustrious families, "it is not accident that has caused you to be born great and powerful. God, from the beginning of time, had destined this temporal glory for you, marked with the seal of his splendor, and separated from the crowd by the luster of titles and human honors."[3] There were thus transcendent reasons for titles of nobility, and, when a man was born great, he was of divine right. "I do not have to tell you," Bossuet says, "that it is God who grants the great births, the great marriages, children, posterity.... Let us be in no doubt, Christians; God in his eternal counsel has prepared the first families which are the source of nations, and in all nations the dominant qualities which were to make for their greatness."[4] But if Providence was concerned with illustrious families, the ordinary bourgeois could not expect it to attach any particular importance to his fate and that of his descendants. Hence it was hard for him to see how the divine wisdom had been thinking, since the beginning of time, especially of him.

While the bourgeois could not link their birth and particular destiny with an eternal counsel, the same might be said of the poor, who had even less reason than those who lived in decent circumstances to imagine that God took any great interest in their family affairs. Nevertheless, assuming that God, in creating a particular poor man, had no intention of establishing a genealogy for him, and was not concerned with his marriage or with the birth or number of his children or other details of his private life, it was nevertheless a fact—we are speaking the language of men like Bossuet— that in causing the poor to be born in their multitudes, he had prescribed their path for them, dooming them from the beginning of time to be in want and to remain so always.

A man was *born* poor; he was poor by birthright. One might almost say that poverty was a title of nobility

---

[3] Massillon, "Sermon on the Respect which the Great Owe to Religion."
[4] Bossuet, "Funeral Oration for Maria Theresa of Austria."

which the deity granted to the poor, not to this poor man in particular, but to the mass of the disinherited. They, too, had their traditions to cite; they had their ancestry. If the power of the great was regarded as "deriving from the splendor of the first of Masters," the poor had the honor to "represent the God-Man . . . to be the living expression of the Word made flesh."[5] "On the foreheads of the great," says a contemporary preacher, "Jesus imprints some feature of his majesty and of his glory in order to invite us to respect them." But in the poor, "he imprints the seal of his cross and of his sufferings; he paints himself wholly, he breathes, he lives in his poor, to induce us to love them."[6] Thus the poor should be regarded as "portraits of Jesus Christ. The Divine Saviour lived on earth as they live today."[7] "The poor are the figure of Jesus Christ, poor and humiliated for us," says Nicole. "They are wholly clothed in the livery of Jesus Christ, and they represent him to us in the condition which should be most agreeable to us."[8] That, also, is why a poor man should inspire us with "something like religious reverence; he is the most worthy and most sacred object which the face of the earth can offer us. . . . Is not a poor man truly crucified in our midst? . . . Yes, a poor man is another Christ, Son of God."[9]

Thus the great and the small each had titles to display. But where, by contrast, were those of the bourgeois? God had not communicated to him a portion of his power, and the bourgeois life resembled not a whit the life led by the Son of God on earth. He was a commoner in the Christian world, a man of low birth. And that, too, was why it was less easy for him to recognize God's hand in what happened to him here below. Poverty was a destiny, and all the afflictions suffered by the poor were in the order of things; the poor man could see in them the hand of Divine Providence. He could "make a virtue of this necessity" and bless God "for refusing him that which is the loss and cause of damnation of many, and which might have been his."[10]

The great, of course, did not have the resignation of the poor and, trusting in their own strength, they appeared very sure of themselves, to the point that, while recognizing that it was to God that they owed their power, they often seemed to forget Divine Providence. At the same time, they were in a better position than others to realize "the fickleness of human affairs." "You live here at court," says Bossuet, "and without going much farther into the condition of your affairs, I should like to believe that your state was a peaceful one; but you have not so easily forgotten the tempests which so often agitate this sea as to trust yourselves altogether to this lull."[11] "The passion, the god of the great, is success," says Massillon.[12] "Success, deceitful in all else, is at least sincere in this, that it does not hide its deceits from us; on the contrary, it displays them openly

5 Collet, *Traité des Devoirs des gens du Monde et surtout des Chefs de Famille* (1793), pp. 282ff.

6 Abbé Poulle, "Sermon on Almsgiving," *Sermons* (1781), I.

7 Collet, *Traité des Devoirs*, p. 281.

8 Nicole, *Essais de Morale* (ed. 1753), VI, fourth treatise, para.

9 Lamourette, *Considérations sur l'Esprit et les Devoirs de la Vie religieuse* (1785), pp. 102ff.

10 Huodry, *La Bibliothèque des Prédicateurs*, VII, 203.

11 Bossuet, "Sermon on the Love of Pleasures."

12 Massillon, "Sermon on the Obstacles to Truth in the Hearts of the Great."

and, in addition to its usual fickleness, it is pleased from time to time to astonish the world by terrible shocks, as though to recall all its force to the memory of men, and for fear that they might ever forget its inconstancy, its malignity, its eccentricity." It was at these moments that the Church awaited the great; it was then that, understanding that "success tricks us even when it is generous to us," they would realize that the power which it appeared to give was but "a great name by which it dazzles our ailing eyes," and, turning their gaze away from this pagan divinity, they ceased to be "captives subjected to the painful vicissitudes of its hard and malicious power"[13] and become Christians once more.

As for the bourgeois, his more regulated, more unified life seemed to provide fewer chinks through which the mysterious power either of blind fortune or of an infinitely wise God might penetrate. Acting by virtue of certain well-established maxims by which he abided, he was easily disposed to believe that it was he who had fashioned his life. He worked and he saved, he calculated and he measured, he reasoned and he looked ahead, and, establishing order everywhere and leaving nothing to accident, he was able, in his search for solid foundations for his life in the moral as in the economic sphere, to set aside the forces of mystery. He thus attained —and that was what he always had in view—to an honest happiness, unknown to either great or poor, a happiness which did not rule out the vicissitudes of fortune, but reduced and eliminated them as far as possible. Feeling himself master of his fate and conscious of deserving the decent ease which he enjoyed and

which sufficed for him, he was less accessible than the mighty, however sinful they might be, to certain sentiments which are familiar to the Christian soul and which lead it back to God.

"The felicity of the worldly is made up of so many pieces that there will always be one lacking"; "its joys are soon transformed into utter bitterness."[14] The soul could then more easily divest itself of "exterior things" and begin to be "closer to itself."[15] "Vanity of vanities, all is vanity,"[16] said Bossuet to the great of his time, quoting Ecclesiastes, and the great sometimes understood him, and were converted.

The great were bored. "Yes, my brothers, tedium, which one would have expected to be the lot of the populace, has taken refuge, it seems, only among the great; it is like their shadow that follows them everywhere. Pleasures which are nearly all exhausted for them offer them no more than a dull uniformity which benumbs or wearies; however much they diversify them, they merely diversify their tedium." Massillon shows us that the whole life of the great was "but an arduous defense against boredom. . . . Surround yourselves with every entertainment; there will always be spread over them, arising from the depths of your souls, a bitterness which will poison them; refine all pleasures, subtilize them, prove them in a crucible; the only result of all these transformations will be tedium." That, says Massillon again, is precisely what should bring the great closer to God. "The great are less excusable

13 Bossuet, "Sermon on Ambition."

14 Bossuet, "Sermon on the Love of Pleasures."
15 Bossuet, "Sermon on the Profession of Madame de la Vallière."
16 Bossuet, "Funeral Oration for Henrietta of England."

and more unfortunate in not attaching themselves to you, my God, because they realize better and more often the emptiness of everything that is not you."[17]

The bourgeois was not bored, or he was bored differently. He did not experience, or he experienced less, the great tedium which might lead to God, just as he knew nothing of the affliction which naturally caused the poor man to aspire to a brighter future. The great alone, says Massillon again, "experience the distress of a soul delivered over to itself, in which all the resources of the senses and pleasures leave only a frightful emptiness, and to which the whole world, with all the accumulation of glory and smoke which surrounds it, becomes vain if God is not with it."[18] The bourgeois, enjoying fewer pleasures, did not experience the great weariness which sometimes turned men away from the world and led their souls back to God. It would be an error, too, to say too much to them about the afflictions of this world. Equally removed from the tedium of the rich and the bitterness of the poor, they had not sufficiently exhausted what life could offer them, nor had they suffered enough to embrace a life of piety.

At the same time, the bourgeois was not ambitious in the same way as the great, and it was therefore harder for him to see the nothingness of the things of this world. "Ambition, that insatiable desire to lift oneself on the very ruins of others, that worm that pricks the heart and never leaves it alone, that passion which is the mainspring of intrigues and all the agitations of the courts, which forms revolutions in states and daily displays fresh spectacles to the universe—this passion which dares everything and for which no price is too high, is a vice even more pernicious to empires than sloth itself."[19] But from "infinite pretensions"[20] might sometimes emerge pretensions to the infinite. The powerful and sublime God of Bossuet did not have to fear those who exalted themselves. He always had the last word so long as death was on his side. "Nothing can resist death. . . . It confounds and reduces to dust the proudest monarchs as well as the lowest of their subjects."[21] The great were better witnesses to the power of God than the humble, and their inordinate ambitions served divine glory. Sometimes they realized this and, turning aside from the "great drama of the world," took an interest in "the affair of eternity."[22]

"At court, far from regarding ambition as a sin, people regard it as a virtue," says Père Bourdaloue; "or if it passes for a vice, then it is regarded as the vice of great souls, and the vices of great souls are preferred to the virtues of the simple and the small."[23] Ambition, says Bourdaloue again, "is the great malady of our age." There is no condition "where ambition does not reign; it passes even for a virtue, for nobility of sentiment, for greatness of soul."[24] The bourgeois themselves may not have been exempt from ambition. But their ambitions lacked tragic grandeur, and the God of Bossuet would not deign

---

[17] Massillon, "On the Affliction of the Great who Abandon God."
[18] Ibid.
[19] Massillon, "Sermon on the Temptations of the Great."
[20] Bossuet, "Sermon on Final Impenitence."
[21] Bossuet, "Address to the Daughters of the Visitation on Death."
[22] Ibid.
[23] Cf. Feugere, Bourdaloue, p. 373.
[24] Bourdaloue, Oeuvres, ed. Didot, II, 100.

to enter into competition with the *Bourgeois Gentilhomme* and would not overturn politics to show him his almighty power.

But if the respectable citizen did not have the ambitions of the nobleman, neither did he have the resignation or modesty distinctive of the poor. The latter, of course, had no particular awareness of the vanity of things which they had never known, and the reverberations of collapsing empires did not disturb them. On the other hand, they possessed by nature the Christian virtues which others might acquire only at great cost to themselves. A contemporary writer lists these characteristics of the poor: "Simple manners, hearts without conceit, minds without ambition, their cares confined to the necessaries of life; thus they are entirely prepared by their station to receive a Gospel which preaches only humility, detachment, contempt of human splendors; which gives great ideas only of the future life, and inspires respect and desire only for the possessions of eternity."[25] The bourgeois, for his part, possessed neither of the inordinate ambition of the great nor of the patience of the poor, would seem to have to remain ignorant both of the sins of those who exalted themselves and of the merits of those who humbled themselves.

Bossuet, speaking of his world, complains that the "license of great fortunes exceeds all bounds." This, he says, leads to "those prevailing sins which are not satisfied to be tolerated, or even excused, but which seek even to be applauded." The great liked to show greatness even in their sins. "How many have we not seen who like to play the great through their

license in crime; who think they are exalting themselves far above all human things by contempt of the law, to whom modesty itself seems unworthy of them because it is a kind of fear!" The great are thus "bold and arrogant sinners," and Bossuet, following St. Augustine, contrasts them with the poor who commit only "servile and timid sins; when a poor man steals, he hides; when he is discovered, he trembles."[26]

The great, when they sinned, sinned wholeheartedly; they sinned in style, sinned well, so to speak. The same could not, I think, be said of the bourgeois. His sins were less definite, less tangible. Being an upright citizen, he was an amateur in sin, and the Church sometimes was very embarrassed in the presence of this man who, sinner though he was, seemed to elude its anathemas, adducing always his rectitude. In this respect, again, he was distinguished from the poor who, if they tended to hide, as Bossuet claimed, generally committed only well-defined sins, which everyone could agree to condemn roundly. Thus it was only the bourgeois who was bad at sinning and who, by assuming the attitude and manners of an upright citizen, seemed to diminish the idea of sin.

Thus the bourgeois, in more than one respect, appeared to elude the Church. The noble could cut a figure in a world where God, to demonstrate his almighty power, must find powerful men to cast down; he felt at home when he listened to the sermons of men like Bossuet and Massillon. But in one sense it might be said that the Church had done even more for the poor than for the great. For the Church, in a way, had created the poor man. The poor man was every-

---

25 *La Religion Chretienne meditee dans le veritable Esprit de ses Maximes* (1763), pp. 64 ff.

26 Bossuet, "Sermon on Final Impenitence."

where at home in the Christian legend, and could understand his lot only in the context of the ideology of the Church.

There remained the bourgeois, somehow out of place in the Christian universe. "Blood, education, the story of their ancestors sow the seeds of a natural tradition of virtue in the hearts of the great and of princes," says Massillon. "The populace, rough and untutored from birth, find within themselves, for the sublime duties of the faith, only the weight and the baseness of a nature given over to itself. . . . Born in the senses and in the slime of the earth, the poor man has difficulty in rising above himself." But did the bourgeois have seeds of virtue in his heart, or did he not? He was not of that "high birth" which might have prepared him, "so to speak, for the noble and heroic sentiments demanded by the faith." Massillon says again, "A pure blood rises more easily." The bourgeois, in this sense, was not pure-blooded. Was he then to be "rough and untutored"

through "defective birth?"[27] It was a suggestion which he would have taken very much amiss.

So the Church had to find a new language in which to talk to him. It had to create a new ideology in which the idea of the bourgeois would have its due place; it had to trace of him a picture which could be set beside that of the great and of the poor, so that he might feel himself at home in this Christian world of symbols and allegories. Or to put it another way, the Church had to confer titles on this being of secular origins, so that he too might claim a relationship with God and find in religion the substantiation of his claims and the justification of the role which he regarded himself as destined to play in this world. But would it be able to hallow the bourgeois, to raise the bourgeoisie to the dignity of a religious symbol?

_____

27 Massillon, Sermon on the Respect which the Great Owe to Religion."

Negro Religion in the City

E. FRANKLIN FRAZIER

The Migration to Cities

The migrations of Negroes to cities, especially to northern cities, produced a crisis in the life of the Negro similar in many respects to the crisis created by the Civil War and Emancipation. Immediately following Emancipation, Negroes drifted into the cities of the South in larger numbers proportion-

Reprinted by permission of Schocken Books Inc. from *The Negro Church in America* by E. Franklin Frazier. Copyright © 1963 by The University of Liverpool.

ately than the whites. Then, after a decade or so, there was an almost imperceptible drift of the Negroes to hundreds of southern cities until the First World War when the mass migrations of Negroes to northern cities was set in motion. Until the First World War about nine-tenths of the Negroes were still in the South and about four-fifths of those in the South lived in rural areas. The War created an unprecedented demand on the part of northern industries for workers, especially large numbers of unskilled workers. The War had cut off the immigration of workers from Europe and many immigrant workers returned to Europe in order to fight for their homelands. The mass movement of Negroes from the South was stimulated also by floods and the ravages of the boll weevil as well as the oppression which Negroes had suffered. As the result of the mass movements from the South large Negro communities were created in the metropolitan areas of the North. Although the movements slowed down after the War, Negroes continued to migrate to the cities of the North and during the Second World War southern Negroes were attracted by the war industries to the cities of the West. Negroes have continued to move into southern cities as well as into the cities of the North and West, with the result that nearly two-thirds of the Negroes in the country as a whole live under urban conditions.

The movement of Negroes to cities, we have said, created a crisis similar to that resulting from Emancipation. It was a crisis in that it uprooted the masses of Negroes from their customary way of life, destroying the social organization which represented both an accommodation to conditions in the rural South and an accommodation to their segregated and inferior status in southern society. In the city environment the family of the masses of Negroes from rural areas, which lacked an institutional basis and was held together only by co-operation in making a living or by sympathies and sentiments generated by living together in the same household, was unable to stand the shock of the disintegrating forces in urban life. Often men who went ahead to the cities with firm resolve to send for their wives and children acquired new interests and never sent for their families. Even when families migrated to the cities, they often disintegrated when they no longer had the support of friends

and neighbours and the institutions which had held together families in the rural South. As a result there were many footloose men and homeless women in the cities who had broken all family ties. Moreover, since the women in families were required to work as well as the men, the children were no longer subject to family discipline. The disorganization of the Negro family in the city was reflected in the large numbers of women who had been deserted by their husbands, by the increased numbers of unmarried mothers, and by the high rate of juvenile delinquency among Negroes.

In the cold impersonal environment of the city, the institutions and associations which had provided security and support for the Negro in the rural environment could not be resurrected. The mutual aid or "sickness and burial" societies could no longer provide security during the two major crises which the Negroes feared most. In fact, in the crowded slums of northern cities, neighbourliness and friendship no longer had any meaning. The Negro could not find even the warmth and sympathy of the secret fraternal organizations which had added colour and ornament to a drab existence in the South.

The most important crisis in the life of the Negro migrant was produced by the absence of the church which had been the centre of his social life and a refuge from a hostile white world. The Negro church, as we have seen, was not only the organization that had created cohesion among the slaves but it was also the basis of organized life among the Negroes who were free before the Civil War and among the freedmen following Emancipation. Moreover, it had set the pattern for organized social life among Negroes. We are interested in discovering how the breakdown of the traditional social organization of Negro life in the city resulted in the transformation of the Negro church and changed the religious behaviour of Negroes.

Negro Cults in the City

The cults which have developed among Negroes represent something new in the religious life of Negroes. They are sometimes not differentiated from the traditional religious groups which meet in abandoned stores and houses because the cults often meet in the same type of buildings. In most of the "storefront" churches the Negro maintains his traditional beliefs and conceptions of God and the world and himself. On the other hand, in the new cults which flourish in the cities, Negroes have abandoned their traditional notions about God and the world and, what is of crucial importance, their conceptions of themselves. An attempt has been made to classify the different types of cults from the standpoint of such features as faith healing or holiness or whether they claim an Islamic origin,[1] but there is much overlapping. Moreover, while all these cults represent "New Gods of the City,"[2] there is an important difference between those which seek to restore a purer form of Christianity or sanctification and holiness and those which tend to be secular in outlook and represent primarily a complete transformation of the Negro as a race. Of course, in some of those cults in which the Negro escapes from his racial identity, there may be faith

---

[1] See the classification in Raymond J. Jones, *A Comparative Study of Religious Cult Behavior Among Negroes with Reference to Emotional Conditioning Factors,* Master's Thesis (Howard University, Washington, D.C., 1939), pp. 3–6.

[2] See Drake and Cayton, *Black Metropolis,* pp. 641–46.

healing and sanctification but these are subordinate to the main orientation of the cults.

.   .   .

The Religion of the New Middle Class

We have already seen in the last chapter how the Negro church and Negro religion have been affected by the new class structure which is emerging among Negroes in cities, especially in the North. Here we are interested in the religious outlook of the new Negro middle class which has become important among Negroes during the past twenty years or so. It is this class whose outward appearance and standards of behaviour approximate most nearly the norms of the white American society. Moreover, Negroes who have achieved middle-class status participate more largely than any other element in American life. It is for this reason that we shall focus attention upon the new middle class in studying the changes in the religious life of Negroes as they are related to the assimilation of Negroes into American society.

The growing importance of the new middle class in the Negro community is due to the continual differentiation of the population along occupational lines. Therefore, the new middle class is composed almost entirely of those persons who derive their incomes from services rendered as white-collar workers and as professional men and women. Despite the dreams of Negro leaders, fostered by the National Negro Business League at the turn of the century, that Negroes would organize big industries and large financial undertakings, Negroes have not become captains of industry nor even managers of large corporations. So-called "Negro" business continues to consist mainly of small retail stores catering to the personal needs of

Negroes. There are a small number of insurance companies, small banks, and newspapers which constitute their larger business enterprises. The owners and managers of these enterprises constitute the upper layer of the middle class while the increasing number of Negroes in skilled occupations constitute its lowest stratum. For reasons which have been indicated, in the North and West about 25 per cent of the Negro population is able to maintain middle-class standards while in the South only about 12 per cent are in this position.

The new Negro middle class is a new phenomenon in the Negro community because it has a different economic base and a different social heritage from the relatively small middle class which had become differentiated from the masses of Negroes by the first decade of this century.[3] This older middle class was an "aristocratic" *élite* in a sense because its social status and preeminence were based upon white ancestry and family and its behaviour was modelled after the genteel tradition of the Old South. The upper layer derived their incomes from land but the majority of the members of the "*élite*" were employed in a large variety of occupations including positions as trusted retainers in white families. The new middle class has a different occupational basis and occupation is one of the important factors in determining status.

Since the opening of the century there had been a faith among middle-class Negroes in "Negro" business as a means of solving their social as well as economic problems. This faith was somewhat as follows: as Negroes became businessmen they would ac-

cumulate capital and give employment to Negroes and once Negroes possessed wealth, white men would respect them and accord them equality. The new middle class has accepted without the critical attitude which experience should have given them, the faith in "Negro" business as a way to social and economic salvation.

Since the emergence of the new middle class involves the rise of the more ambitious and energetic elements among the masses of Negroes to middle-class status, this new class does not possess the genteel tradition of the older middle class. This new class is largely without social roots except the traditions of the Negro folk represented in the Spirituals. But as these Negroes rise to middle-class status they reject the folk heritage and seek to slough off any reminders of their folk inheritance. However, since their rise to the middle-class status has enabled them to marry into families with the genteel tradition of the old middle class, there is often a confusion of "aristocratic" and folk values. It is for this reason that many middle-class Negroes exhibit in their manners and behaviour the characteristics of both a peasant and a gentleman. Among this new class there is much confusion as to standards of behaviour and beliefs. There is a constant striving to acquire money in order to engage in conspicuous consumption which provides the outward signs of status and conformity to white American standards. They all possess the same goal, which is acceptance into the white community and they all profess, at least, a desire to be integrated into the white community.

Integration for the majority of middle-class Negroes means the loss of racial identity or an escape from the lowly status of Negroes and the contempt of whites. With integration they began to remove as much as possible

---

[3] E. Franklin Frazier, "The Negro Middle Class and Desegregation," *Social Problems*, Vol. IV (April 1957), pp. 291–301.

from the names of their various organizations anything that would identify them as Negroes. This even extended to their church organizations. The Colored Methodist Episcopal Church became the "Christian" Methodist Episcopal Church. It is significant, however, that when the middle-class leaders in the African Methodist Episcopal Church attempted to take "African" out of the name and substitute the word "American," there was a revolt on the part of the masses who demanded that "African" be retained. This incident is indicative of the general attitude of the middle class towards the African background of the Negro. While there is some outward profession of pride in African independence and identification with Africa, the middle class rejects identification with Africa and wants above all to be accepted as "just Americans." It was the new middle class which was rising to importance in the 1920s that was most bitterly opposed to the Garvey Movement which had as its goal the identification of Negroes with Africa and African interests.[4] Middle-class Negroes seize upon identification with Africa only as a means of compensating for their feeling of inferiority and improving their status in the eyes of American whites.

Despite the fact that middle-class Negroes conform to the standards of whites and accept without question the values of American society, they are still rejected by the white world. They feel this rejection more keenly than lower-class Negroes who participate less in the white man's world and conform to the standards of their separate world. Moreover, because of their position, middle-class Negroes have an ambivalent attitude towards their identification as Negroes. On the one hand, they resent the slightest aspersion upon Negroes. When placed in competition with whites they have feelings of inadequacy and when they find themselves in close association with whites they have feelings of insecurity though they may clamour for integration into the white world.[5] They are status seekers in a double sense; they strive to keep up with the expectations of their class in the Negro community and they seek or hope to gain status in the white world. In order to maintain high standards of consumption often both husband and wife work but they constantly complain of the "rat race" to maintain life as they would live it. They live frustrated lives despite their efforts to compensate for their feelings of inferiority and insecurity. They have little time for leisure and the enjoyment of what they call the "cultural" things of life. As a matter of fact, they have little appreciation of music or art and they read very little since reading has not become a tradition in the new middle class.

Their ambiguous position in American society together with their recent rise to middle-class status are reflected in the religious behaviour and attitudes of middle-class Negroes. There is first a tendency for middle-class Negroes to sever their affiliation with the Baptist and Methodist churches and join the Presbyterian, Congregational, and Episcopal churches. The middle-class Negroes who continue their affiliation with the Baptist and Methodist churches choose those churches with intelligent ministers and a relatively large middle-class membership. As a consequence there is a solid core of the Negro middle class that continues to be affiliated with the Negro church. However, middle-class

---

[4] See Frazier, *The Negro in the United States,* pp. 528–31.

[5] E. Franklin Frazier, *Black Bourgeoisie* (Glencoe, Ill., 1957), pp. 216 ff.

Negroes continue their affiliation with the Negro church for a number of reasons. Their families may have been associated with the churches and the churches which they have known since childhood provide a satisfying form of religious worship. Although many middle-class Negroes continue to be affiliated with the church, the church is no longer the centre of social life for them as for the lower class. They are members of professional and business associations and Greek letter fraternal organizations, though "social" clubs constitute the vast majority of these other forms of organized social activities. Some are thus able to satisfy their striving for status outside the church. But for others it is necessary to leave the Baptist and Methodist churches and join the Presbyterian, Congregational, and Episcopal churches in order to satisfy the desire for status.

The striving for status and the searching for a means to escape from a frustrated existence is especially marked among the middle-class Negroes who cannot find a satisfactory life within the regular Negro church organization. This probably accounts for the fact that during the past two decades middle-class Negroes have been joining the Catholic church.[6] Sometimes they send their children to Catholic schools where they will receive a discipline not provided in the public schools for Negroes. Very often after joining the Catholic church with the expectation that they will

escape from their status as Negroes, they find that they are still defined as Negroes by whites. Some middle-class Negroes in their seeking to find escape from the Negro identification have gone from the Catholic church to the Christian Science church and then to the Bahaist church. Moreover, there is a tendency among middle-class Negroes to be attracted to Moral Rearmament, hoping that they would find a group in which they could lose completely their identification as Negroes and escape from their feelings of inferiority and insecurity. A small intellectual fringe among middle-class Negroes have affiliated with the Unitarian church. But some of them may still attend more or less surreptitiously the Methodist and Baptist churches on Friday nights.

This type of dual church affiliation is more characteristic of Negro professional men who affiliate with churches mainly for social and professional reasons. Some professional Negroes affiliate with a church which their friends or middle-class Negroes attend, and at the same time affiliate with churches attended by the lower class who are their clients. They are representative of the growing number of middle-class Negroes who have a purely secular outlook on the world. Some of them express contempt for religion and do not attend church though they may pretend to have some church affiliation. Since they have neither an intellectual heritage nor a social philosophy except a crude opportunism which enables them to get by in the white man's world, they may turn to all forms of superstition. This is because they are still haunted by the fears and beliefs which are a part of their folk heritage. They are often interested in "spiritual" and "psychic" phenomena. Very often the real religious feelings and faith of

---

6 The recent increase during the past twenty years in the number, which remains relatively small, of lower-class Negroes in the Catholic church has been due to aid provided them during the *Depression years* and the better educational facilities, as compared with the public schools, provided them by the Catholic church.

middle-class Negroes are expressed in their obsession with poker and other forms of gambling.[7]

The religious behaviour and outlook of the middle-class Negroes is a reflection of their ambiguous position as Negroes rise to middle-class status and become increasingly integrated into the American community. To the extent that they are becoming really assimilated into American society, they are being beset by the religious dilemmas and doubts of the white middle-class Americans. On the other hand, for the masses of Negroes, the Negro church continues to be a refuge, though increasingly less of a refuge, in a hostile white world.

---

[7] See *Black Bourgeoisie,* pp. 209 ff.

religion as the ideology
of social transition

twelve

The Triumph of the Economic Virtues

R. H. TAWNEY

"One beam in a dark place," wrote one who knew the travail of the spirit, "hath exceeding much refreshment in it. Blessed be His name for shining upon so dark a heart as mine."[1] While the revelation of God to the individual soul is the center of all religion, the essence of Puritan theology was that it made it, not only the center, but the whole circumference and substance, dismissing as dross and vanity all else but this secret and solitary communion. Grace alone can save, and this grace is the direct gift of God, unmediated by any earthly institution. The elect cannot by any act of their own evoke it; but they can prepare their hearts to receive it, and cherish it when received. They will prepare them best, if they empty them of all that may disturb the

---

[1] Carlyle, *Cromwell's Letters and Speeches,* Letter ii.

From *Religion and the Rise of Capitalism* by R. H. Tawney, copyright, 1926, by Harcourt Brace Jovanovich, Inc.; renewed, 1954, by R. H. Tawney. Reprinted by permission of the publishers.

intentness of their lonely vigil. Like an engineer, who, to canalize the rush of the oncoming tide, dams all channels save that through which it is to pour, like a painter who makes light visible by plunging all that is not light in gloom, the Puritan attunes his heart to the voice from Heaven by an immense effort of concentration and abnegation. To win all, he renounces all. When earthly props have been cast down, the soul stands erect in the presence of God. Infinity is attained by a process of subtraction.

To a vision thus absorbed in a single intense experience, not only religious and ecclesiastical systems, but the entire world of human relations, the whole fabric of social institutions, witnessing in all the wealth of their idealism and their greed to the infinite creativeness of man, reveal themselves in a new and wintry light. The fire of the spirit burns brightly on the hearth; but through the windows of his soul the Puritan, unless a poet or a saint, looks on a landscape touched by no breath of spring. What he sees is a forbidding and frost-bound wilderness, rolling its snow-clad leagues towards the grave—a wilderness to be subdued with aching limbs beneath solitary stars. Through it he must take his way, alone. No aid can avail him: no preacher, for only the elect can apprehend with the spirit the word of God; no Church, for to the visible Church even reprobates belong; no sacrament, for sacraments are ordained to increase the glory of God, not to minister spiritual nourishment to man; hardly God himself, for Christ died for the elect, and it may well be that the majesty of the Creator is revealed by the eternal damnation of all but a remnant of the created.[2]

His life is that of a soldier in hostile territory. He suffers in spirit the perils which the first settlers in America endured in body, the sea behind, the untamed desert in front, a cloud of inhuman enemies on either hand. Where Catholic and Anglican had caught a glimpse of the invisible, hovering like a consecration over the gross world of sense, and touching its muddy vesture with the unearthly gleam of a divine, yet familiar, beauty, the Puritan mourned for a lost Paradise and a creation sunk in sin. Where they had seen society as a mystical body, compact of members varying in order and degree, but dignified by participation in the common life of Christendom, he saw a bleak antithesis between the spirit which quickened and an alien, indifferent or hostile world. Where they had reverenced the decent order whereby past was knit to present, and man to man, and man to God, through fellowship in works of charity, in festival and fast, in the prayers and ceremonies of the Church, he turned with horror from the filthy rags of human righteousness. Where they, in short, had found comfort in a sacrament, he started back from a snare set to entrap his soul.

We receive but what we give,
And in our life alone does Nature live.

Too often, contemning the external order as unspiritual, he made it, and ultimately himself, less spiritual by reason of his contempt.

Those who seek God in isolation from their fellowmen, unless trebly armed for the perils of the quest, are apt to find, not God, but a devil, whose countenance bears an embarrassing resemblance to their own. The moral self-sufficiency of the Puritan nerved his will, but it corroded his sense of social solidarity. For, if each individual destiny hangs on a private transaction between himself and his Maker, what room is left for human intervention? A servant of Jehovah more than of Christ, he revered God as a Judge rather than loved him as a Father, and was moved less by compassion for his erring brethren than by impatient indignation at the blindness of vessels of wrath who "sinned their mercies." A spiritual aristocrat, who sacrificed fraternity to liberty, he drew from his idealization of personal responsibility a theory of individual rights, which, secularized and generalized, was to be among the most potent explosives that the world has known. He drew from it also a scale of ethical values, in which the traditional scheme of Christian virtues was almost exactly reversed, and which, since he was above all things practical, he carried as a dynamic into the routine of business and political life.

For, since conduct and action, though availing nothing to attain the free gift of salvation, are a proof that the gift has been accorded, what is rejected as a means is resumed as a

---

2 See on these points Max Weber, *Die Protestantische Ethik und der Geist des Kapitalismus*, p. 94, whose main conclusions I paraphrase.

consequence, and the Puritan flings himself into practical activities with the dæmonic energy of one who, all doubts allayed, is conscious that he is a sealed and chosen vessel. Once engaged in affairs, he brings to them both the qualities and limitations of his creed in all their remorseless logic. Called by God to labor in his vineyard, he has within himself a principle at once of energy and of order, which makes him irresistible both in war and in the struggles of commerce. Convinced that character is all and circumstances nothing, he sees in the poverty of those who fall by the way, not a misfortune to be pitied and relieved, but a moral failing to be condemned, and in riches, not an object of suspicion—though like other gifts they may be abused—but the blessing which rewards the triumph of energy and will. Tempered by self-examination, self-discipline, self-control, he is the practical ascetic, whose victories are won not in the cloister, but on the battlefield, in the counting-house, and in the market.

This temper, of course with infinite varieties of quality and emphasis, found its social organ in those middle and commercial classes who were the citadel of the Puritan spirit, and whom, "ennobled by their own industry and virtue,"[3] Milton described as the standard-bearers of progress and enlightenment. We are so accustomed to think of England as *par excellence* the pioneer of economic progress, that we are apt to forget how recently that rôle has been assumed. In the Middle Ages it belonged to the Italians, in the sixteenth century to the Netherland dominions of the Spanish Empire, in the seventeenth to the United Provinces and, above all, to the Dutch.

---

[3] Milton, *A Defence of the People of England* (1962 ed.), p. xvii.

The England of Shakespeare and Bacon was still largely medieval in its economic organization and social outlook, more interested in maintaining customary standards of consumption than in accumulating capital for future production, with an aristocracy contemptuous of the economic virtues, a peasantry farming for subsistence amid the organized confusion of the open-field village, and a small, if growing, body of jealously conservative craftsmen. In such a society Puritanism worked like the yeast which sets the whole mass fermenting. It went through its slack and loosely knit texture like a troop of Cromwell's Ironsides through the disorderly cavalry of Rupert. Where, as in Ireland, the elements were so alien that assimilation was out of the question, the result was a wound that festered for three centuries. In England the effect was that at once of an irritant and of a tonic. Puritanism had its own standards of social conduct, derived partly from the obvious interests of the commercial classes, partly from its conception of the nature of God and the destiny of man. These standards were in sharp antithesis, both to the considerable surviving elements of feudalism in English society, and to the policy of the authoritarian State, with its ideal of an ordered and graded society, whose different members were to be maintained in their traditional status by the pressure and protection of a paternal monarchy. Sapping the former by its influence and overthrowing the latter by direct attack, Puritanism became a potent force in preparing the way for the commercial civilization which finally triumphed at the Revolution.

The complaint that religious radicalism, which aimed at upsetting the government of the Church, went hand in hand with an economic radicalism, which resented the restraints on individual self-interest imposed in the name of religion or of social policy, was being made by the stricter school of religious opinion quite early in the reign of Elizabeth.[4] Seventeenth-century writers repeated the charge that the Puritan conscience lost its delicacy where matters of business were concerned, and some of them were sufficiently struck by the phenomenon to attempt an historical explanation of it. The example on which they usually seized—the symbol of a supposed general disposition to laxity—was the indulgence shown by Puritan divines in the particular matter of moderate interest. It was the effect, so the picturesque story ran,[5] of the Marian persecution. The refugees who fled the continent could not start business in a foreign country. If, driven by necessity, they invested their capital and lived on the proceeds, who could quarrel with so venial a lapse in so good a cause? Subsequent writers embellished the picture. The redistribution of property at the time of the Dissolution, and the expansion of trade in the middle of the century, had led, one of them argued, to a great increase in the volume of credit transactions. The opprobrium which attached to loans at interest—"a sly and forbid practice"—not only among Romanists and Anglicans, but among

honest Puritans, played into the hands of the less scrupulous members of "the faction." Disappointed in politics, they took to money-lending, and, without venturing to justify usury in theory, defended it in practice. "Without the scandal of a recantation, they contrived an expedient, by maintaining that, though usury for the name were stark naught, yet for widows, orphans and other impotents (therein principally comprising the saints under persecution) it was very tolerable, because profitable, and in a manner necessary." Naturally, Calvin's doctrine as to the legitimacy of moderate interest was hailed by these hypocrites with a shout of glee. "It took with the brethren like polygamy with the Turks, recommended by the example of divers zealous ministers, who themselves desired to pass for orphans of the first rank."[6] Nor was it only as the apologist of moderate interest that Puritanism was alleged to reveal the cloven hoof. Puritans themselves complained of a mercilessness in driving hard bargains, and of a harshness to the poor, which contrasted unfavorably with the practice of followers of the unreformed religion. "The Papists," wrote a Puritan in 1653, "may rise up against many of this generation. It is a sad thing that they should be more forward upon a bad principle than a Christian upon a good one."[7]

Such, in all ages, is history as seen by the political pamphleteer. The

---

[4] See, e.g., Thos. Wilson, *A Discourse upon Usury,* Preface, 1925 ed., p. 178: "There bee two sorts of men that are always to bee looked upon very narroly, the one is the dissembling gospeller, and the other is the wilfull and indurate papiste. The first under colour of religion overthroweth all religion, and bearing good men in hande that he loveth playnesse, useth covertelie all deceypte that maye bee, touching thys sinne of usurie, none doe more openly offende in thys behalfe than do these countergeite professours of thys pure religion."
[5] Fenton, *A Treatise of Usurie,* 1612, pp. 60–61.

[6] *Brief Survey of the Growth of Usury in England,* 1673.
[7] S. Richardson, *The Cause of the Poor Pleaded,* 1653, Thomason Tracts, E. 703 (9), p. 14. For other references, see note 19 below. For extortionate prices, see Thomason Tracts, E. 309 (6), *The Worth of a Penny, or a Caution to keep Money,* 1647. I am indebted for this and subsequent references to the Thomason Tracts to Miss P. James.

real story was less dramatic, but more significant. From the very beginning, Calvinism had comprised two elements, which Calvin himself had fused, but which contained the seeds of future discord. It had at once given a whole-hearted *imprimatur* to the life of business enterprise, which most earlier moralists had regarded with suspicion, and had laid upon it the restraining hand of an inquisitorial discipline. At Geneva, where Calvinism was the creed of a small and homogeneous city, the second aspect had predominated; in the many-sided life of England, where there were numerous conflicting interests to balance it, and where it was long politically weak, the first. Then, in the late sixteenth and early seventeenth centuries, had come the wave of commercial and financial expansion—companies, colonies, capitalism in textiles, capitalism in mining, capitalism in finance—on the crest of which the English commercial classes, in Calvin's day still held in leading-strings by conservative statesmen, had climbed to a position of dignity and affluence.

Naturally, as the Puritan movement came to its own, these two elements flew apart. The collectivist, half-communistic aspect, which had never been acclimatized in England, quietly dropped out of notice, to crop up once more, and for the last time, to the disgust and terror of merchant and landowner, in the popular agitation under the Commonwealth. The individualism congenial to the world of business became the distinctive characteristic of a Puritanism which had arrived, and which, in becoming a political force, was at once secularized and committed to a career of compromise. Its note was not the attempt to establish on earth a "Kingdom of Christ," but an ideal of personal character and conduct, to

be realized by the punctual discharge both of public and private duties. Its theory had been discipline; its practical result was liberty.

Given the social and political conditions of England, the transformation was inevitable. The incompatibility of Presbyterianism with the stratified arrangement of English society had been remarked by Hooker.[8] If the City Fathers of Geneva had thrown off by the beginning of the seventeenth century the religious collectivism of Calvin's régime, it was not to be expected that the landowners and *bourgeoisie* of an aristocratic and increasingly commercial nation, however much Calvinist theology might appeal to them, would view with favor the social doctrines implied in Calvinist discipline. In the reign of the first two Stuarts, both economic interests and political theory pulled them hard in the opposite direction. "Merchants' doings," the man of business in Wilson's *Discourse upon Usury* had observed, "must not thus be overthwarted by preachers and others that cannot skill of their dealings."[9] Behind the elaborate facade of Tudor State control, which has attracted the attention of historians, an individualist movement had been steadily developing, which found expression in opposition of the traditional policy of stereotyping economic relations by checking enclosure, controlling food supplies and prices, interfering with the money-market, and regulating the conditions of the wage contract and of apprenticeship. In the first forty years of the seventeenth century, on grounds both of expediency and of principle, the com-

---

[8] Hooker, Preface to *The Laws of Ecclesiastical Polity*, Everyman ed., 1907, vol. i, p. 128.
[9] Wilson, *A Discourse upon Usury*, p. 250.

mercial and propertied classes were becoming increasingly restive under the whole system, at once ambitious and inefficient, of economic paternalism. It was in the same sections of the community that both religious and economic dissatisfaction were most acute. Puritanism, with its idealization of the spiritual energies which found expression in the activities of business and industry, drew the isolated rivulets of discontent together, and swept them forward with the dignity and momentum of a religious and a social philosophy.

For it was not merely as the exponent of certain tenets as to theology and church government, but as the champion of interests and opinions embracing every side of the life of society, that the Puritan movement came into collision with the Crown. In reality, as is the case with most heroic ideologies, the social and religious aspects of Puritanism were not disentangled; they presented themselves, both to supporters and opponents, as different facets of a single scheme. "All that crossed the views of the needy courtiers, the proud encroaching priests, the thievish projectors, the lewd nobility and gentry ... whoever could endure a sermon, modest habit or conversation, or anything good—all these were Puritans."[10] The clash was not one of theories—a systematic and theoretical individualism did not develop till after the Restoration—but of contradictory economic interests and incompatible conceptions of social expediency.

The economic policy haltingly pursued by the Government of Charles I bore some resemblance to the system of which a more uncompromising version was developed between 1661 and 1685 by Colbert in France. It was one which favored an artificial and State-promoted capitalism—a capitalism resting on the grant of privileges and concessions to company promoters who would pay for them, and accompanied by an elaborate system of State control, which again, if partly inspired by a genuine solicitude for the public interest, was too often smeared with an odious trail of finance. It found its characteristic expression in the grant of patents, in the revival of the royal monopoly of exchange business, against which the City had fought under Elizabeth, in attempts to enforce by administrative action compliance with the elaborate and impracticable code controlling the textile trades and to put down speculation in foodstuffs, and in raids on enclosing landlords, on employers who paid in truck or evaded the rates fixed by assessment, and on justices who were negligent in the administration of the Poor Laws. Such measures were combined with occasional plunges into even more grandiose schemes for the establishment of county granaries, for taking certain industries into the hands of the Crown, and even for the virtual nationalization of the cloth manufacture.[11]

"The very genius of that nation of people," wrote Strafford to Laud of the Puritans, "leads them always to oppose, as well civilly as ecclesiastically, all that ever authority ordains for them."[12] Against this whole attempt to convert economic activity into an instrument of profit for the Government and its hangers-on—against, no less, the spasmodic attempts of the State to protect peasants against landlords,

---

10 *Memoirs of the Life of Colonel Hutchinson, written by his Widow Lucy,* Everyman ed., 1908, pp. 64–65.

11 See the references given in note 13.
12 *The Earl of Strafforde's Letters and Despatches,* by William Knowler, D.D., 1739, vol. ii, p. 138.

craftsmen against merchants, and consumers against middlemen—the interests which it thwarted and curbed revolted with increasing pertinacity. Questions of taxation, on which attention has usually been concentrated, were in reality merely one element in a quarrel which had its deeper cause in the collision of incompatible social philosophies. The Puritan tradesman had seen his business ruined by a monopoly granted to a needy courtier, and cursed Laud and his Popish soap. The Puritan goldsmith or financier had found his trade as a bullion-broker hampered by the re-establishment of the ancient office of Royal Exchanger, and secured a resolution from the House of Commons, declaring that the patent vesting it in Lord Holland and the proclamation forbidding the exchanging of gold and silver by unauthorized persons were a grievance. The Puritan money-lender had been punished by the Court of High Commission, and railed at the interference of bishops in temporal affairs. The Puritan clothier, who had suffered many things at the hands of interfering busy-bodies despatched from Whitehall to teach him his business, averted discreet eyes when the Wiltshire workmen threw a more than usually obnoxious Royal Commissioner into the Avon, and, when the Civil War came, rallied to the Parliament. The Puritan country gentleman had been harried by Depopulation Commisions, and took his revenge with the meeting of the Long Parliament. The Puritan merchant had seen the Crown both squeeze money out of his company, and threaten its monopoly by encouraging interlopers to infringe its charter. The Puritan member of Parliament had invested in colonial enterprises, and had ideas as to commercial policy which were not those of the Government. Confident in their own energy and acumen, proud of their success, and regarding with profound distrust the interference both of Church and of State with matters of business and property rights, the commercial classes, in spite of their attachment to a militant mercantilism in matters of trade, were even before the Civil War, more than half converted to the administrative nihilism which was to be the rule of social policy in the century following it. Their demand was the one which is usual in such circumstances. It was that business affairs should be left to be settled by business men, unhampered by the intrusions of an antiquated morality or by misconceived arguments of public policy.[13]

_____

[13] No attempt has been made in the text to do more than refer to the points on which the economic interests and outlook of the commercial and propertied classes brought them into collision with the monarchy, and only the most obvious sources of information are mentioned here. For patents and monopolies, including the hated soap monopoly, see G. Unwin, *The Gilds and Companies of London*, 1908, chap. xvii, and W. Hdye Price, *The English Patents of Monopoly*, 1906, chap. xi, and *passim*. For the control of exchange business, *Cambium Regis, or the Office of his Majesties Exchange Royall, declaring and justifying his Majesties Right and the Convenience thereof*, 1628, and Ruding, *Annals of the Coinage*, 1819, vol. iv, pp. 201–10. For the punishment of speculation by the Star Chamber, and for projects of public granaries, Camden Society, N.S., vol. xxxix, 1886, *Reports of Cases in the Courts of Star Chamber and High Commission*, ed. S. R. Gardiner, pp. 43 seqq., 82 seqq., and N.S.B. Gras, *The Evolution of the English Corn Market*, 1915, pp. 246–50. For the control of the textile industry and the reaction against it, H. Heaton, *The Yorkshire Woollen and Worsted Industries*, 1920, chaps. iv, vii; Kate E. Barford, *The West of England Cloth Industry: A seventeenth-century Experiment in State Control*, in the *Wiltshire Archaeological and Natural History*

The separation of economic from ethical interests, which was the note of all this movement, was in sharp opposition to religious tradition, and it did not establish itself without a struggle. Even in the very capital of European commerce and finance, an embittered controversy was occasioned by the refusal to admit usurers to communion or to confer degrees upon them: it was only after a storm of pamphleteering, in which the theological faculty of the University of Utrecht performed prodigies of zeal and ingenuity, that the States of Holland and West Friesland closed the agitation by declaring that the Church had no concern with questions of banking.[14] In the French Calvinist Churches, the decline of discipline had caused lamentations a generation earlier.[15] In America, the theocracy of Massachusetts, merciless alike to religious liberty and to economic license, was about to be undermined by the rise of new States like Rhode Island and Pennsylvania, whose tolerant, individualist and utilitarian temper was destined to find its greatest representative in the golden common sense of Benjamin Franklin.[16] "The sin of our too great fondness for trade, to the neglecting of our more valuable interests," wrote a Scottish divine in 1709, when Glasgow was on the eve of a triumphant outburst of commercial enterprise, "I humbly think will be written upon our judgment. . . . I am sure the Lord is remarkably frowning upon our trade . . . since it was put in the room of religion."[17]

In England, the growing disposition to apply exclusively economic standards to social relations evoked from Puritan writers and divines vigorous protests against usurious interest, extortionate prices and the oppression of tenants by landlords. The faithful, it was urged, had interpreted only too literally the doctrine that the sinner was saved, not by works, but by faith. Usury, "in time of Popery an odious thing,"[18] had become a scandal. Professors, by their covetousness,

Magazine, Dec., 1924, pp. 531–42; R. R. Reid, *The King's Council in the North,* 1921, pt. iv, chap. ii; *Victoria County History, Suffolk,* vol. ii, pp. 263–68. For the intervention of the Privy Council to raise the wages of textile workers and to protect craftsmen, Tawney, *The Assessment of Wages in England by the Justices of the Peace,* in the *Vierteljahrschrift für Sozial- und Wirthschaftzgeschichte,* Bd. xi, 1913, pp. 307–37, 533–64; Leonard, *The Early History of English Poor Relief,* pp. 160–63; *Victoria County History, Suffolk,* vol. ii., pp. 268–69; and Unwin, *Industrial Organization in the Sixteenth and Seventeenth Centuries,* 1904, pp. 142–47. For the Depopulation Commissions, Tawney, *The Agrarian Problem in the Sixteenth Century,* pp. 376, 391. For the squeezing of money from the East India Company and the infringement of its Charter, Shafa'at Ahmad Khan, *The East India Trade in the XVIIth Century,* 1923, pp. 69–73. For the colonial interests of Puritan members, A. P. Newton, *The Colonising Activities of the English Puritans,* 1914, and C. E. Wade, *John Pym,* 1912.

14 E. Laspeyres, *Geschichte der Volkswirthschaftlichen Anschauungen der Niederländer und ihrer Literatur zur Zeit der Republik,* 1863, pp. 256–70. An idea of the points at issue can be gathered from the exhaustive (and unreadable) work of Salmasius, *De Modo Usurarum,* 1639.

15 John Quick, *Synodicon* in *Gallia Reformata,* 1692, vol. i, p. 99.
16 For the change of sentiment in America, see Troeltsch, *Protestantism and Progress,* pp. 117–27; for Franklin, *Memoirs of the Life and Writings of Benjamin Franklin,* and Sombart, *The Quintessence of Capitalism,* 1915, pp. 116–21.
17 Rev. Robert Woodrow (quoted by Sombart, *op. cit.,* p. 149).
18 John Cooke, *Unum Necessarium or the Poore Man's Case* (1648), which contains a plea for the regulation of prices and the establishment of *Monts de Piété.*

caused the enemies of the reformed religion to blaspheme.[19] The exactions of the forestaller and regrater were never so monstrous or so immune from interference. The hearts of the rich were never so hard, nor the necessities of the poor so neglected. "The poor able to work are suffered to beg; the impotent, aged and sick are not sufficiently provided for, but almost starved with the allowance of 3*d*. and 4*d*. a piece a week. . . . These are the last times indeed. Men generally are all for themselves. And some would set up such, having a form of religion, without the power of it."[20]

These utterances came, however, from that part of the Puritan mind which looked backward. That which looked forward found in the rapidly growing spirit of economic enterprise something not uncongenial to its own temper, and went out to welcome it

as an ally. What in Calvin had been a qualified concession to practical exigencies appeared in some of his later followers as a frank idealization of the life of the trader, as the service of God and the training-ground of the soul. Discarding the suspicion of economic motives, which had been as characteristic of the reformers as of medieval theologians, Puritanism in its later phases added a halo of ethical sanctification to the appeal of economic expediency, and offered a moral creed, in which the duties of religion and the calls of business ended their long estrangement in an unanticipated reconciliation. Its spokesmen pointed out, it is true, the peril to the soul involved in a single-minded concentration on economic interests. The enemy, however, was not riches, but the bad habits sometimes associated with them, and its warnings against an excessive preoccupation with the pursuit of gain wore more and more the air of after-thoughts, appended to teaching the main tendency and emphasis of which were little affected by these incidental qualifications. It insisted, in short, that money-making, if not free from spiritual dangers, was not a danger and nothing else, but that it could be, and ought to be, carried on for the greater glory of God.

The conception to which it appealed to bridge the gulf sprang from the very heart of Puritan theology. It was that expressed in the characteristic and oft-used phrase, "a Calling."[21] The rational order of the universe is the work of God, and its plan requires that the individual should labor

19 For the scandal caused to the Protestant religion by its alleged condonation of covetousness, see T. Watson, *A Plea for Alms,* 1658 (Thomason Tracts, E. 2125), pp. 21, 33–34: "The Church of Rome layes upon us this aspersion that we are against good workes. . . I am sorry that any who go for honest men should be brought into the indightment; I mean that any professors should be impeached as guilty of this sinne of covetousnesse and unmercifulnesse . . . I tell you these devout misers are the reproach of Christianity. . . I may say of penurious votaries, they have the wings of profession by which they seem to fly to heaven, but the feet of beasts, walking on the earth and even licking the dust. . .Oh, take heed, that, seeing your religion will not destroy your covetousnesse, at last your covetousnesse does not destroy your religion." See also Sir Balthazar Gerbier, *A New Year's Result in favour of the Poore,* 1651 (Thomason Tracts, E. 651 [14], p. 4: "If the Papists did rely as much on faith as the reformed professors of the Gospel (according to our English tenets) doe, or that the reformed professors did so much practice charity as the Papists doe?"

20 S. Richardson, *The Cause of the Poor Pleaded,* pp. 7–8, 10.

21 The first person to emphasize the way in which the idea of a "calling" was used as an argument for the economic virtues was Weber, to whose conclusions I am largely indebted for the following paragraphs.

for God's glory. There is a spiritual calling, and a temporal calling. It is the first duty of the Christian to know and believe in God; it is by faith that he will be saved. But faith is not a mere profession, such as that of Talkative of Prating Row, whose "religion is to make a noise." The only genuine faith is the faith which produces works. "At the day of Doom men shall be judged according to their fruits. It will not be said then, Did you believe? but, Were you doers or talkers only?"[22] The second duty of the Christian is to labor in the affairs of practical life, and this second duty is subordinate only to the first. "God," wrote a Puritan divine, "doth call every man and woman ... to serve him in some peculiar employment in this world, both for their own and the common good. ... The Great Governour of the world hath appointed to every man his proper post and province, and let him be never so active out of his sphere, he will be at a great loss, if he do not keep his own vineyard and mind his own business."[23]

From this reiterated insistence on secular obligations as imposed by the divine will, it follows that, not withdrawal from the world, but the conscientious discharge of the duties of business, is among the loftiest of religious and moral virtues. "The begging friars and such monks as live only to themselves and to their formal devotion, but do employ themselves in no one thing to further their own subsistence or the good of mankind ... yet have the confidence to boast of this their course as a state of perfection; which in very deed, as to the worthiness of it, falls short of the poorest cobbler, for his is a calling of God, and theirs is none."[24] The idea was not a new one. Luther had advanced it as a weapon against monasticism. But for Luther, with his patriarchal outlook on economic affairs, the calling means normally that state of life in which the individual has been set by Heaven, and against which it is impiety to rebel. On the lips of Puritan divines, it is not an invitation to resignation, but the bugle-call which summons the elect to the long battle which will end only with their death. "The world is all before them." They are to hammer out their salvation, not merely *in vocatione*, but *per vocationem*. The calling is not a condition in which the individual is born, but a strenuous and exacting enterprise, to be undertaken, indeed, under the guidance of Providence, but to be chosen by each man for himself, with a deep sense of his solemn responsibilities. "God hath given to man reason for this use, that he should first consider, then choose, then put in execution; and it is a preposterous and brutish thing to fix or fall upon any weighty business, such as a calling or condition of life, without a careful pondering it in the balance of sound reason."[25]

Laborare est orare. By the Puritan moralist the ancient maxim is repeated with a new and intenser significance. The labor which he idealizes is not simply a requirement imposed by nature or a punishment for the sin of Adam. It is itself a kind of ascetic discipline, more rigorous than that demanded of any order of mendicants—a discipline imposed by the will of God, and to be undergone, not in solitude, but in the punctual discharge of secular duties. It is not

---

[22] Bunyan, *The Pilgrim's Progress.*
[23] Richard Steele, *The Tradesman's Calling, being a Discourse concerning the Nature, Necessity, Choice, etc., of a Calling in general,* 1684, pp. 1, 4.

[24] *Ibid.,* pp. 21–22.
[25] *Ibid.,* p. 35.

merely an economic means, to be laid aside when physical needs have been satisfied. It is a spiritual end, for in it alone can the soul find health, and it must be continued as an ethical duty long after it has ceased to be a material necessity. Work thus conceived stands at the very opposite pole from "good works," as they were understood, or misunderstood, by Protestants. They, it was thought, had been a series of single transactions, performed as compensation for particular sins, or out of anxiety to acquire merit. What is required of the Puritan is not individual meritorious acts, but a holy life—a system in which every element is grouped round a central idea, the service of God, from which all disturbing irrelevancies have been pruned, and to which all minor interests are subordinated.

His conception of that life was expressed in the words "Be wholly taken up in diligent business of your lawful callings, when you are not exercised in the more immediate service of God."[26] In order to deepen his spiritual life, the Christian must be prepared to narrow it. He "is blind in no man's cause, but best sighted in his own. He confines himself to the circle of his own affairs and thrusts not his fingers in needless fires. . . . He sees the falseness of it [the world] and therefore learns to trust himself ever, others so far as not to be damaged by their disappointment."[27] There must be no idle leisure: "those that are prodigal of their time despise their own souls."[28] Religion must be active, not merely contemplative. Contemplation is, indeed, a kind of self-

indulgence. "To neglect this [i.e., bodily employment and mental labor] and say, 'I will pray and meditate,' is as if your servant should refuse your greatest work, and tye himself to some lesser, easie part. . . . God hath commanded you some way or other to labour for your daily bread."[29] The rich are no more excused from work than the poor, though they may rightly use their riches to select some occupation specially serviceable to others. Covetousness is a danger to the soul, but it is not so grave a danger as sloth. "The standing pool is prone to putrefaction; and it were better to beat down the body and to keep in subjection by a laborious calling, than through luxury to become a cast-away."[30] So far from poverty being meritorious, it is a duty to choose the more profitable occupation. "If God show you a way in which you may lawfully get more than in another way (without wrong to your soul or to any other), if you refuse this, and choose the less gainful way, you cross one of the ends of your Calling, and you refuse to be God's steward." Luxury, unrestrained pleasure, personal extravagance, can have no place in a Christian's conduct, for "every penny which is laid out . . . must be done as by God's own appointment." Even excessive devotion to friends and relations is to be avoided. "It is an irrational act, and therefore not fit for a rational creature, to love any one farther than reason will allow us. . . . It very often taketh up men's minds so as to hinder their love to God."[31] The Christian life, in short, must be systematic and

---

[26] Baxter, *Christian Directory*, 1678 ed., vol. i, p. 336*b*.

[27] Thomas Adams (quoted in Weber, *Die Protestantische Ethik und der Geist des Kapitalismus,* p. 96n.).

[28] Matthew Henry, *The Worth of the Soul* (quoted *ibid.,* p. 168n.).

[29] Baxter, *Christian Directory*, vol. i, p. 111*a*.

[30] Seele, *The Tradesman's Calling*, p. 20.

[31] Baxter, *Christian Directory*, vol. i, pp. 378*b*, 108*b*; vol. iv, p. 253*a*.

organized, the work of an iron will and a cool intelligence. Those who have read Mill's account of his father must have been struck by the extent to which Utilitarianism was not merely a political doctrine, but a moral attitude. Some of the links in the Utilitarian coat of mail were forged, it may be suggested, by the Puritan divines of the seventeenth century.

The practical application of these generalities to business is set out in the numerous works composed to expound the rules of Christian conduct in the varied relations of life. If one may judge by their titles—*Navigation Spiritualized, Husbandry Spiritualized, The Religious Weaver*[32]—there must have been a considerable demand for books conducive to professional edification. A characteristic specimen is *The Tradesman's Calling*,[33] by Richard Steele. The author, after being deprived of a country living under the Act of Uniformity, spent

his declining years as a minister of a congregation at Armourers Hall in London and may be presumed to have understood the spiritual requirements of the City in his day, when the heroic age of Puritanism was almost over and enthusiasm was no longer a virtue. No one who was writing a treatise on economic ethics today would address himself primarily to the independent shopkeeper, as the figure most representative of the business community, and Steele's book throws a flood of light on the problems and outlook of the *bourgeoisie,* in an age before the center of economic gravity had shifted from the substantial tradesman to the exporting merchant, the industrial capitalist and the financier.

Like Baxter, he is acquainted with the teaching of earlier authorities as to equity in bargaining. He is doubtful, however, of its practical utility. Obvious frauds in matters of quality and weight are to be avoided: an honest tradesman ought not to corner the market, or "accumulate two or three callings merely to increase his riches," or oppress the poor; nor should he seek more than "a reasonable proportion of gain," or "lie on the catch to make [his] markets of others' straits." But Steele rejects as useless in practice the various objective standards of a reasonable profit—cost of production, standard of life, customary prices—which had been suggested in earlier ages, and concludes that the individual must judge for himself. "Here, as in many other cases, an upright conscience must be the clerk of the market."

In reality, however, the characteristic of *The Tradesman's Calling,* as of the age in which it was written, is not the relics of medieval doctrine which linger embalmed in its guileless pages, but the robust common sense, which carries the author lightly over traditional scruples on a tide of genial, if

---

[32] *Navigation Spiritualized: or a New Compass for Seamen, consisting of xxxii Points:*

of {*Pleasant Observations Profitable Applications and Serious Reflections.*

All concluded with so many spiritual poems. Whereunto is now added,

i. *A sober conversation of the sin of drunkenness.*
ii. *The Harlot's face in the scripture-glass, etc.*

Being an essay towards their much desired Reformation from the horrible and detestable sins of Drunkenness, Swearing, Uncleanness, Forgetfulness of Mercies, Violation of Promises, and Atheistical Contempt of Death. 1682.

The author of this cheerful work was a Devonshire minister, John Flavell, who also wrote *Husbandry Spiritualized, or the Heavenly Use of Earthly Things,* 1669. In him, as in Steele, the Chadband touch is unmistakable. *The Religious Weaver,* apparently by one Fawcett, I have not been able to trace.

[33] Steele, *The Tradesman's Calling.*

Philistine, optimism. For his main thesis is a comfortable one—that there is no necessary conflict between religion and business. "Prudence and Piety were always very good friends. . . . You may gain enough of both worlds if you would mind each in its place." His object is to show how that agreeable result may be produced by dedicating business—with due reservations—to the service of God, and he has naturally little to say on the moral casuistry of economic conduct, because he is permeated by the idea that trade itself is a kind of religion. A tradesman's first duty is to get a full insight into his calling, and to use his brains to improve it. "He that hath lent you talents hath also said, 'Occupy till I come!' Your strength is a talent, your parts are talents, and so is your time. How is it that ye stand all the day idle? . . . Your trade is your proper province. . . . Your own vineyard you should keep. . . . Your fancies, your understandings, your memories . . . are all to be laid out therein." So far from their being an inevitable collision between the requirements of business and the claims of religion, they walk hand in hand. By a fortunate dispensation, the virtues enjoined on Christians—diligence, moderation, sobriety, thrift—are the very qualities most conducive to commercial success. The foundation of all is prudence; and prudence is merely another name for the "godly wisdom [which] comes in and puts due bounds" to his expenses, "and teaches the tradesman to live rather somewhat below than at all above his income." Industry comes next, and industry is at once expedient and meritorious. It will keep the tradesman from "frequent and needless frequenting of taverns," and pin him to his shop, "where you may most confidently expect the presence and blessing of God."

If virtue is advantageous, vice is ruinous. Bad company, speculation, gambling, politics, and "a preposterous zeal" in religion—it is these things which are the ruin of tradesmen. Not, indeed, that religion is to be neglected. On the contrary, it "is to be exercised in the frequent use of holy ejaculations." What is deprecated is merely the unbusinesslike habit of "neglecting a man's necessary affairs upon pretence of religious worship." But these faults, common and uncommon alike, are precisely those to be avoided by the sincere Christian, who must not, indeed, deceive or oppress his neighbor, but need not fly to the other extreme, be righteous overmuch, or refuse to "take the advantage which the Providence of God puts into his hands." By a kind of happy, preestablished harmony, such as a later age discovered between the needs of society and the self-interest of the individual, success in business is in itself almost a sign of spiritual grace, for it is proof that a man has labored faithfully in his vocation, and that "God has blessed his trade." "Nothing will pass in any man's account except it be done in the way of his calling. . . . Next to the saving his soul, [the tradesman's] care and business is to serve God in his calling, and to drive it as far as it will go."

When duty was so profitable, might not profit-making be a duty? Thus argued the honest pupils of Mr. Gripeman, the schoolmaster of Lovegain, a market-town in the county of Coveting in the north.[34] The inference was illogical, but how attractive! When the Rev. David Jones was so indiscreet as to preach at St. Mary Woolnoth in Lombard Street a sermon against usury on the text "The Pharisees who were covetous heard all

_____
[34] Bunyan, *The Pilgrim's Progress.*

these things and they derided Christ," his career in London was brought to an abrupt conclusion.

The springs of economic conduct lie in regions rarely penetrated by moralists, and to suggest a direct reaction of theory on practice would be paradoxical. But, if the circumstances which determine that certain kinds of conduct shall be profitable are economic, those which decide that they shall be the object of general approval are primarily moral and intellectual. For conventions to be adopted with wholehearted enthusiasm, to be not merely tolerated, but applauded, to become the habit of a nation and the admiration of its philosophers, the second condition must be present as well as the first. The insistence among men of pecuniary motives, the strength of economic egotism, the appetite for gain—these are the commonplaces of every age and need no emphasis. What is significant is the change of standards which converted a natural frailty into a resounding virtue. After all, it appears, a man can serve two masters, for—so happily is the world disposed —he may be paid by one, while he works for the other. Between the old-fashioned denunciation of uncharitable covetousness and the new-fashioned applause of economic enterprise, a bridge is thrown by the argument which urges that enterprise itself is the discharge of a duty imposed by God. . . .

the relationship of religion
to the world

thirteen

from The Social Teaching of the Christian Churches

ERNST TROELTSCH

The essence of the Church is its objective institutional character. The individual is born into it, and through infant baptism he comes under its miraculous influence. The priesthood and the hierarchy, which hold the keys to the tradition of the Church, to sacramental grace and ecclesiastical jurisdiction, represent the objective treasury of grace, even when the individual priest may happen to be unworthy; this Divine treasure only needs to be set always upon the lampstand and made effective through the sacraments, and it will inevitably do its work by virtue of the miraculous power which the Church contains. The Church means the eternal existence of the God-Man; it is the extension of the Incarnation, the objective organization of miraculous power, from which, by means of the Divine Providential government of the world, subjective results will appear quite naturally. From this point

From *The Social Teaching of the Christian Churches,* by Ernst Troeltsch, published by George Allen & Unwin Ltd. Used by permission.

of view compromise with the world, and the connection with the preparatory stages and dispositions which it contained, was possible; for in spite of all individual inadequacy the institution remains holy and Divine, and it contains the promise of its capacity to overcome the world by means of the miraculous power which dwells within it. Universalism, however, also only becomes possible on the basis of this compromise; it means an actual domination of the institution as such, and a believing confidence in its invincible power of inward influence. Personal effort and service, however fully they may be emphasized, even when they go to the limits of extreme legalism, are still only secondary; the main thing is the objective possession of grace and its universally recognized dominion; to everything else these words apply: *et cetera adjicientur vobis.* The one vitally important thing is that every individual should come within the range of the influence of these saving energies of grace; hence the Church is forced to dominate Society, compelling all the members of Society to come under its sphere and influence; but, on the other hand, her stability is entirely unaffected by the fact of the extent to which her influence over all individuals is actually attained. The Church is the great educator of the nations, and like all educators she knows how to allow for various degrees of capacity and maturity, and how to attain her end only by a process of adaptation and compromise.

Compared with this institutional principle of an objective organism, however, the sect is a voluntary community whose members join it of their own free will. The very life of the sect, therefore, depends on actual personal service and co-operation; as an independent member each individual has his part within the fellowship; the bond of union has not been indirectly imparted through the common possession of Divine grace, but it is directly realized in the personal relationships of life. An individual is not born into a sect; he enters it on the basis of conscious conversion; infant baptism, which, indeed, was only introduced at a later date, is almost always a stumbling-block. In the sect spiritual progress does not depend upon the objective impartation of Grace through the Sacrament, but upon individual personal effort; sooner or later, therefore, the sect always criticizes the sacramental idea. This does not mean that the spirit of fellowship is weakened by individualism; indeed, it is strengthened, since each individual proves that he is entitled to membership by the very fact of his services to the fellowship. It is, however, naturally a somewhat limited form of fellowship, and the expenditure of so much effort in the maintenance and exercise of this particular kind of fellowship produces a certain indifference towards other forms of fellowship which are based upon secular interests; on the other hand, all secular interests are drawn into the narrow framework of the sect and tested by its standards, in so far as the sect is able to assimilate these interests at all. Whatever cannot be related to the group of interests controlled by the sect, and by the Scriptural ideal, is rejected and avoided. The sect, therefore, does not educate nations in the mass, but it gathers a select group of the elect, and places it in sharp opposition to the world. In so far as the sect-type maintains Christian universalism at all, like the Gospel, the only form it knows is that of eschatology; this is the reason why it always finally revives the eschatology of the Bible. That also naturally explains the greater tendency of the sect towards "ascetic" life and thought, even though the original ideal of the New Testament had not pointed in that direction. The final activity of the group and of the individual consists precisely in the practical austerity of a purely religious attitude towards life which is not affected by cultural influences. That is, however, a different kind of asceticism, and this is the reason for that difference between it and the asceticism of the Church-type which has already been stated. It is not the heroic special achievement of a special class, restricted by its very nature to particular instances, nor the mortification of the senses in order to further the higher religious life; it is simply detachment from the world, the reduction of wordly pleasure to a minimum and the highest possible development of fellowship in love; all this is interpreted in the old Scriptural sense. Since the sect-type is rooted in the teaching of Jesus, its asceticism also is that of primitive Christianity and of the Sermon on the Mount, not that of the Church and of the contemplative life; it is narrower and more scrupulous than that of Jesus, but, literally understood, it is still the continuation of the attitude of Jesus towards the world. The concentration on personal effort, and the sociological connection with a practical ideal, makes an extremely exacting claim on individual effort, and avoidance of all other forms of human association. The asceticism of the sect is not an attempt to popularize and universalize an ideal which the Church had prescribed only for special classes and in special circumstances. The Church ideal of asceticism can never be conceived as a universal ethic; it is essentially unique and heroic. The ascetic ideal of the sect, on the contrary, is, as a matter of course, an ideal which is possible to all, and appointed for all, which, according to its conception, united the fellowship instead of dividing it and according to its content is also capable of a general realization in so far as the circle of the elect is concerned.

Thus, in reality we are faced with two different sociological types. This is true in spite of the fact (which is quite immaterial) that incidentally in actual practice they may often impinge upon one another. If objections are raised to the terms "Church" and "Sect," and if all sociological groups which are based on and inspired by monotheistic, universalized, religious motives are described (in a terminology which is in itself quite appropriate[1]) as "Churches," we would then have to make the distinction between institutional churches and voluntary churches. It does not really matter which expression is used. The all-important point is this: that both types are a logical result of the Gospel, and only conjointly do they exhaust the whole range of its sociological in-

fluence, and thus also indirectly of its social results, which are always connected with the religious organization.

In reality, the Church does not represent a mere deterioration of the Gospel, however much that may appear to be the case when we contrast its hierarchical organization and its sacramental system with the teaching of Jesus. For wherever the Gospel is conceived as primarily a free gift, as pure grace, and wherever it is offered to us in the picture which faith creates of Christ as a Divine institution, wherever the inner freedom of the Spirit, contrasted with all human effort and organization, is felt to be the spirit of Jesus, and wherever His splendid indifference towards secular matters is felt, in the sense of a spiritual and inner independence while these secular things are used outwardly, there the institution of the Church may be regarded as a natural continuation and transformation of the Gospel. At the same time, with its unlimited universalism, it still contains the fundamental impulse of the evangelic message; the only difference is that whereas the Gospel had left all questions of possible realization to the miraculous coming of the Kingdom of God, a Church which had to work in a world which was not going to pass away had to organize and arrange matters for itself, and in so doing it was forced into a position of compromise.

On the other hand, the essence of the sect does not consist merely in a one-sided emphasis upon certain vital elements of the Church-type, but it is itself a direct continuation of the idea of the Gospel. Only within it is there a full recognition of the value of radical individualism and of the idea of love; it is the sect alone which instinctively builds up its ideal of fellowship from this point of view, and

---

1 See my treatise: *Religion und Kirche, Preuss. Jahrb., 1895.* It would be an interesting subject of inquiry to find out to what extent the monotheistic universal religions (non-Christian) contain similar differences. It may well be supposed that similar phenomena occur within Islam.

this is the very reason why it attains such a strong subjective and inward unity, instead of merely external membership in an institution. For the same reason the sect also maintains the original radicalism of the Christian ideal and its hostility towards the world, and it retains the fundamental demand for personal service, which indeed it is also able to regard as a work of grace: in the idea of grace, however, the sect emphasizes the subjective realization and the effects of grace, and not the objective assurance of its presence. The sect does not live on the miracles of the past, nor on the miraculous nature of the institution, but on the constantly renewed miracle of the Presence of Christ, and on the subjective reality of the individual mastery of life.

The starting-point of the Church is the Apostolic Message of the Exalted Christ, and faith in Christ the Redeemer, into which the Gospel has developed; this constitutes its objective treasure, which it makes still more objective in its sacramental-sacerdotal institution. To this extent the Church can trace its descent from Paulinism, which contained the germ of the sacramental idea, which, however, also contained some very unecclesiastical elements in its pneumatic enthusiasm, and in its urgent demand for the personal holiness of the "new creature."

The sect, on the contrary, starts from the teaching and the example of Jesus, from the subjective work of the apostles and the pattern of their life of poverty, and unites the religious individualism preached by the Gospel with the religious fellowship, in which the office of the ministry is not based upon ecclesiastical ordination and tradition, but upon religious service and power, and which therefore can also devolve entirely upon laymen.

The Church administers the sacraments without reference to the personal worthiness of the priests; the sect distrusts the ecclesiastical sacraments, and either permits them to be administered by laymen, or makes them dependent upon the personal character of the celebrant, or even discards them altogether. The individualism of the sect urges it towards the direct intercourse of the individual with God; frequently, therefore, it replaces the ecclesiastical doctrine of the sacraments by the Primitive Christian doctrine of the Spirit and by "enthusiasm." The Church has its priests and its sacraments; it dominates the world and is therefore also dominated by the world. The sect is lay Christianity, independent of the world, and is therefore inclined towards asceticism and mysticism. Both these tendencies are based upon fundamental impulses of the Gospel. The Gospel contains the idea of an objective possession of salvation in the knowledge and revelation of God, and in developing this idea it becomes the Church. It contains, however, also the idea of an absolute personal religion and of an absolute personal fellowship, and in following out this idea it becomes a sect. The teaching of Jesus, which cherishes the expectation of the End of the Age and the Coming of the Kingdom of God, which gathers into one body all who are resolute in their determination to confess Christ before men and to leave the world to its fate, tends to develop the sect-type. The apostolic faith which looks back to a miracle of redemption and to the Person of Jesus, and which lives in the powers of its heavenly Lord: this faith which leans upon something achieved and objective, in which it unites the faithful and allows them to rest, tends to develop the Church-type. Thus the New Testament helps to develop both the Church and the sect; it has done so from the beginning, but the Church had the start, and its great world mission. Only when the objectification of the Church had been developed to its fullest extent* did the sectarian tendency assert itself and react against this excessive objectification. Further, just as the objectification of the Church was achieved in connection

_____
* *I.e.* under Hildebrand—Translator's note.

with the feudal society of the Early Middle Ages, the reappearance of the tendency to form sects was connected with the social transformation, and the new developments of city-civilization in the central period of the Middle Ages and in its period of decline—with the growth of individualism and the gathering of masses of people in the towns themselves—and with the reflex effect of this city formation upon the rural population and the aristocracy.

The Fall of the Church

FRANKLIN LITTELL

Our descriptive survey has revealed the concept of the church as the essence of main-line Anabaptism (Anabaptism used now without quotation marks). The centrality of the church view must be grasped in the "concrete" and historical sense as well as in terms of the teaching of the Anabaptist leaders. That is to say, in contrast to many groups in history and in contemporary Christianity the Anabaptists actually meant what they said. The separation between verbalization and action which has been so marked in contemporary church groups can mislead us in our approach to the Anabaptist movement: the Anabaptists meant just what they said, and their teaching is unimportant apart from the direct attempt to give it embodiment in actual groups living in history.

Reprinted with permission of The Macmillan Company from *The Origins of Sectarian Protestantism* by Franklin H. Littell. Copyright © 1964, 1958, 1952 by Franklin H. Littell.

In the Anabaptist church view two notes stand out from the rest:

1. The church must be a voluntary association, taking its spirit and discipline from those who intentionally belong to its fellowship.
2. The church must follow the guide lines of the New Testament as to confession of faith and organizational pattern.

In the history of Christianity there have been some who said that the Bible was ambiguous as to doctrine and organization. The traditional orthodox view has been that it gives clear indications on doctrine but is ambiguous as to organizational pattern. The Anabaptists maintained that the New Testament was clear both as to the content of the Christian faith and the organizational procedures in the true Christian Community.

Anabaptism: A Form of Christian Primitivism

With the exception of Münster and the Hutterite colonies, the Church of the Restitution did not become coterminous with the political community. The Anabaptist congregations were gathered as minorities within a tolerating or persecuting society. However, in terms of theory and typology the point needs to be made; for under toleration, a voluntary church may differ very little from a state church in its social outlook.[1] Continental Mennonitism has remained a voluntary association but has lost the "primitivist" marks of the New Testament community. The ethic, the attitude to the world on the part of Anabaptists, has often been called a new monasticism. A major aspect of its formulation has been nonconformity to dominant social practices. Frequently we are confronted in Anabaptism with a radical attempt to realize in the concrete the ethic of the Sermon on the Mount. But the Anabaptists went further than this: they repudiated not only accepted social standards, but a whole history of accommodation by established Christianity. The whole membership of the "True Church" was pledged to relive in studied fashion the life of the New Testament community (*Urgemeinde*) in all of its phases. *The Anabaptists proper were those in the "Left Wing" who gathered and disciplined a "True Church" (rechte Kirche) upon the apostolic pattern.*[2] We return to the definition proposed in the Introduction.

There is something deeper than mere Biblicism in this social program. It is part of an outlook on life which can best be described under the concept of primitivism. If we inquire as to the goal of these Anabaptist groups we are driven first not forwards but backwards. Their objective was

not to introduce something new but to restore something old. "Restitution" was their slogan, a Restitution grounded in the New Testament. And surrounding their groups was a certain atmosphere, an atmosphere whose precipitation point was a certain vision of the Early Church. In the early period of the movement, before institutional and theological discipline had given ideological coherence to certain groups, and especially before persecution and the necessary defensive organization had weeded out the "centrifugal" tendencies, the single thread running through the Left Wing was this dream of the Early Church. This is the thread which ties together the *Spiritualisten* and *Täufer,* Swiss Brethren and Polish Brethren, Schwenckfelders and Hutterites, Mennonites and the followers of Sebastian Franck and Adam Pastor. The final pattern was to be the Restitution of the Early Church, and following on that Restitution the triumph of the Kingdom on earth.

Religious Primitivism as a Pattern of Thought

The mood of these groups was essentially determined by an attitude of religious primitivism, and as such is but a special manifestation of a widespread and recurrent aspect of "civilized man's misgivings about his performances, about his prospects— and about himself."[3] The concept is

---

[1] See my *The Free Church* (Boston: Starr King Press, 1957), Ch. 4.

[2] They were opposed to all forms of what George Huntston Williams has recently classified under the term, "magisterial Protestantism": *GHW/M,* p. 21.

[3] Arthur O. Lovejoy, *et. al., A Documentary History of Primitivism and Related Ideas . . . in Antiquity* (Baltimore: Johns Hopkins Press, 1935), p. ix. Lovejoy also made representative studies of primitivism in the Church Fathers; see his "The Communism of St. Ambrose," III *Journal of the History of Ideas* (1942) 4:458–68, and " 'Nature' as Norm in Tertullian," reprinted in *Essays in the History of Ideas* (Baltimore: Johns Hopkins Press, 1948), pp. 308–38. For the use of primitivist motifs in the Middle Ages, see George

both cultural and chronological. It is Christian and it is classical. For the Anabaptists and other Left Wingers it involves a philosophy of history: an Eden in the past, a partial Restitution in the present (wiping out the scandal of the fallen period), a divine restoration in the future. Various ingredients of this attitude are discernible in previous movements.

In classical antiquity the Cynics and Stoics believed in a Golden Age without war, slavery, and property. Jews and Christians looked back to Eden as a garden devoid of strife and exploitation between both men and animals. The theory of a "Fall" runs throughout them all. In the early Fathers classical and Christian themes are sometimes fused. The classical-Christian ideal of the communism of the Golden Age was picked up again by Sebastian Franck and through him transmitted to various leaders in the Left Wing.[4]

This might seem at first to be a purely speculative discussion about the past, until we recall that the use of the primitive as a norm involves not only myths but manifestoes. Primitivism is a fertile source of ethical concern, as well as a familiar device in historiography. The projection of Eden into the future was the work of

apocalyptic Judaism, from which the concept passed into Christian eschatology. In the time of the Reformation and pre-Reformation groups there were variant forms of primitivism; frequently this centered in a type of Adam-mysticism which glorified the simple, unlettered, and unspoiled man. In argument, the appeal is made to the plain man's judgment, unspoiled by institutions and less corroded by speculation than the scholar's. Those who work with their hands (craftsmen) or close to the soil (peasants) are presumed to be more receptive in spirit; their minds have not been addled by the folly of the wise and learned.[5] The type of the primitive hero is sought in some contemporary primitive situation.

The exaltation of "primitive" cultures is another form which flourished in the sixteenth century in connection with discovery of primitive people in the New World. Various Humanistic circles spread the tales of simple living and savage nobility.. On the one hand there was a high idealization of the simple life and the man of nature; and on the other there was "what is even more significant . . . not the discovery that savages can be noble, but that civilized people can become good savages and can be regenerated by a natural life."[6] Secular and religious primitivism sometimes fused, in that the primitive man was regarded as fertile soil for the primitive gospel. Bartholome de las Casas gave wide currency to this theme in his "History of the Indies," and established a Uto-

---

Boas, *Essays on Primitivism and Related Ideas in the Middle Ages* (Baltimore: Johns Hopkins Press, 1948).

[4] According to Hans von Schubert, Sebastian Franck drew upon a source which defended theft on the ground that all things are common "as the Greek philosophers say." Von Schubert suspected Seneca's Epistle 90 was the source, and also showed the influence of Seneca's primitivism upon Erasmus, Colet, and More. Von Schubert, "Der Kommunismus der Wiedertäufer in Münster und seine Quellen," X *Sitzungsberichte der Heidelberger Akad. der Wiss. Phil.-Hist. Klasse* (1919) 11:46–47.

[5] Konrad Burdach, *Reformation, Renaissance, Humanismus* (Berlin and Leipzig: Paetel Brothers, 1926), 2nd ed., pp. 174f.

[6] Antonio Pastor, *The Idea of Robinson Crusoe* (Watford, Herts., England: Gongõra Press, 1930), p. 302.

pian colony to implement it.[7] A group of Anabaptists at Zürich announced that they were going "to the red Indians over the sea" when their evangel was greeted with hostility and persecution at the hands of civilized men.[8] Such an attitude is a mixture of admiration for virtue in the primitive age, repudiation of "civilized" religion and religious practices, naivete as to the possibilities for the primitive gospel among primitive people.

The man of the Reformation epoch was thus profoundly uneasy about the manner of his social life and the pattern of his own formal thinking and worship. He thought that his own age was "decadent"; a threefold Fall (*triplex discessio*) had occurred—in national affairs, in the church, in the age.[9] The historians of the Renaissance and Reformation frequently rejected the historiography of Orosius, which had been dominant and which projected a pattern of progressive Christian development. The thinking man of the period was conscious of a renewal to come, a new birth of spiritual vigor following the long decline. A new periodization was introduced, with a Fall both political and religious in imperial Rome, with a Restitution of old virtue in the present. This became the framework of much of the historical thinking of the Renaissance and Reformation.[10]

Sources of Sixteenth-Century Primitivism

Among the radical thinkers there was a frame of mind remarkably parallel to classical primitivism, and reflecting in good part the melancholy of the age. When we consider the detailed structure of Anabaptist life we find many evidences: their normative view of the Early Church, the historical expectancy implied in use of "Fall" and "Restitution." With independents like Franck and Schwenckfeld it is not so difficult to trace the effect of certain pre-Reformation ideas. But with the more Biblically centered groups, who rarely cited any non-Biblical authority, it is a speculative if not futile effort. We may, however, mark certain centers of ideology which affected their intellectual climate and, largely in indirect fashion, their ideas.

Before persecution destroyed the educated leadership of the Anabaptists, the men at the head of the movement were university trained. Among the South Germans and Hutterites there were several converted priests and pastors, highly educated. Other leaders—notably Hans Denck and Leonhard Bouwens—were trained in the literary circles which everywhere marked the spread of Humanistic learning. In Westphalia and the Valley of the Yssel, the schools of the

---

[7] Benj. Bissell, *The American Indian in English Literature of the Eighteenth Century* (New Haven: Yale University Press, 1925), pp. 17–19; Gilbert Chinard, *L'Exoticisme Amèricain dans la Litterature Française au XVIᵉ Siècle* (Paris: Libraire Hachette et Cie, 1911), p. xvi.

[8] *Egli,* #691, p. 307. When a group escaped from Zürich prison, March, 1526, some suggested going to "den roten Juden" over the sea. Correll corrected the date (given by Egli as April, 1525) and the phrase by reference to the material in the Zürich canton archives. It should read "Inden" instead of "Juden," and Correll considers the report to cover a serious suggestion. Correspondence of 5/4/44.

[9] Rudolf Stadelmann, *Vom Geist des ausgehenden Mittelalters* (Halle: Max Niemeyer, 1929), p. 223.

[10] Wallace K. Ferguson, "Humanist Views of the Renaissance," XLV *American Historical Review* (October, 1939) 1: reprint, pp. 3f.

Brethren of the Common Life supplied a number of the most able leaders.[11] To point up the discussion we may take two great leaders: Erasmus and Zwingli.

Desiderius Erasmus (1466–1536)[12] was educated by the Brethren at Gouda, Deventer, and s'Hertogenbosch. He was permanently influenced by their regard for simple living and simple Biblical truth. From Wessel Gansfort, Alexander Hegius, and Rudolph Agricola he learned concern for apostolic Christianity and its manner of life. Pacifism and tolerance were articles of faith. He knew the English Humanists (Colet, More, Warham), worked in Venice with Aldus Manutius (the friend and fellow student of Pico), and corresponded with all the leaders of thought of his day. The Anabaptists admired him greatly for his ethical insight and accent upon sincere and uncompromising New Testament truth. In his writings the return to Gospel simplicity was the way to rejuvenate the faith and the church. But Erasmus, who also influenced the Reformers more than any other single author, was the despair of both Roman Catholic and Protestant parties. If he would not accept Roman Catholic preferment by denouncing the Reformation, he would not declare for the Reformers either.

He did not believe in the rancorous partisanship which characterized both sides. He believed change should be reasonable and enlightened. His last days were embittered by von Hutten's attacks and the accompanying break with Zwingli, and he died with one faithful disciple by his side: his executor, Bonifacius Amerbach.[13]

Ulrich Zwingli (1484–1531)[14] was educated in the Latin School, then at Bern under Lupulus. Following two years at Vienna under Conrad Celtes and Cuspinian, he returned to Basel where Wytenbach taught him the Bible. He also became acquainted with Pico's work and corresponded with Erasmus. At Einsiedeln, as a young priest, he read the Church Fathers—Jerome, Origen, Ambrose—and also Stapulensis and "Dionysius." He copied out the Pauline letters from Erasmus' New Testament, and was moved to the attitude which permanently marked his churchmanship: "Back to Christ!" He never broke, however, with the cultural and political life of the Swiss city-states; but the radicals (Grebel, Manz, Blaurock, Reublin) who left him and went beyond him were following the logic of his message.

The direction of Humanism[15] was

11 Albert Hyma, *The Christian Renaissance* (New York and London: Century Co., 1925). See also C. Ullmann, *Reformers before the Reformation* (Edinburgh: T. & T. Clark, 1855), two volumes translated.

12 On Erasmus, see Albert J. Hyma, *The Youth of Erasmus* (Ann Arbor: University of Michigan Press, 1930); Paul Mestwerdt, *Die Anfänge des Erasmus* (Leipzig: Rudolph Haupt, 1917); R. Stähelin in *Real.-3* (1898) V, 434–44; K. Vos and Neff in *ML* (1913) I, 599–600; Neff and Bender in *ME* (1956) II, 239–40. For a statement on his relation to Anabaptism, see Karl Rembert, *Die 'Wiedertäufer' im Herzogtum Jülich* (Berlin: R. Gaertners Verlag, 1899), p. 194.

13 Th. Burckhardt-Biedermann, *Bonifacius Amerbach und die Reformation* (Basel: R. Reich, 1894), "Good God! What unchristian strife has sprung from books when simple Love alone is 'Christian'!" (p. 37). Erasmus was often cited by Denck, Campanus, Thomas von Imbroich, Menno Simons, Adam Pastor, Dirck Philipsz.

14 On Zwingli, see I:57–59.

15 On Humanism, see article by Emil Händiges in *ME* (1956) II, 841–43. The Dutch Mennonites have been more ready to claim Humanist affiliations than have other wings; according to John Horsch, however, this did not extend even among the Waterlanders to freedom on doctrine. See "Is Dr. Kühler's Conception of Early Dutch Anabaptism Historically Sound?"

away from speculation and dogma to pious ignorance (*pia ignorantia*), away from ecclesiasticism to the simple ethic of the Synoptics (*Nachfolge Christi*), away from the hierarchy to the elemental lay brotherhood of the disciples' democratic band. There was, furthermore, a certain attitude to the origins which is most significant: just as return to classical forms was the purifying principle for their beloved Latin, so a return to the life of the Early Church would revitalize the corrupted faith.

Because primitivism is not essentially a theory of origins but really a device for passing judgment on contemporary society, it is closely linked with views of the future. Eden is also Utopia. The imagery of the lost Paradise reverberates through the apocalyptic visions of the book of Revelation. In the Left Wing, primitivism leads straight into eschatology. The man who above all represented this com-bination in the age preceding the Reformation, whose thought has influenced the underground of Christian dissent ever since, was Joachim of Fiore (c. 1145–1202).

The Abbot Joachim has been significant in one way or another for the radicals of pre-Reformation and Reformation thought from the time when the Fraticelli appropriated the Eternal Gospel in their fight against papacy.[16] Joachim's periodization of history was especially relevant, with seven ages culminating in the *Restitutio ecclesiae*. His followers were far more radical than he, and marked the turning point in history by his own person or that of Saint Francis. Joachim taught that through the prophet of the last times justice and peace were to be re-established in all of the Roman provinces. The prophet was to be a spiritual Constantine, freeing the church from the trammels with which the imperial Constantine had bound her. For with Constantine all heathen had streamed into the church, polluting and compromising her. The Fall of the church which followed the time of the apostles would soon be ended, however; the recovery of the church in the present would precede the last things. Whereas in the middle period salvation was linked to the institutions and sacraments, in the Age of the Spirit these lost their meaning. As Simeon took in his arms the child Jesus, so should

VII *MQR* (1933) 2:97–126. Robert Kreider ends his study. "Anabaptism and Humanism: An Inquiry into the Relationship of Humanism to the Evangelical Anabaptists," XXIV *MQR* (1950) 2:123–41, with the sentence: "The Humanist was a scholar, the Anabaptist a disciple." However, it has been concluded: "In a wider respect the aim of the Reformation can be interpreted as the final break of the medieval synthesis between Christianity and Hellenism; and, on the other hand, an authoritative humanist scholar today ascribes to Huguenot France and Protestant Germany 'the break through to Hellenism.' Indeed, the cry 'Ad Fontes' indicates a parallel move in the Reformation and in Humanism..." Franz Hildebrandt, *Melanchthon: Alien or Ally?* (Cambridge, Eng.: University Press, 1946), p. 3. The truth would seem to be that direct influence on Anabaptism by Humanism cannot be established; certainly the Anabaptists did not have an emancipated view of Biblical truth. Nevertheless, like the Humanists the Anabaptists had a certain attitude to the origins and to the authority of primary sources.

16 Ernst Benz, *Ecclesia Spiritualis* (Stuttgart: W. Kohlhammer, 1934); Herbert Grundmann, *Studien über Joachim von Floris* (Leipzig and Berlin: B. G. Teubner, 1927); Decima L. Douie, *The Nature and Effect of the Heresy of the Fraticelli* (Manchester, Eng.: University Press, 1932). On Joachim's interpretation of history as an attempt to establish independence of the medieval Corpus Christianum, see Jakob Taubes, *Abendländische Eschatologie* (Berlin: A. Francke, 1947), p. 81.

the Curia act to fulfill the *ordo spiritualis* (the "withering away" of the Church).[17] The Great Church was near to death (following the Fall) and would be renewed by a reappropriation of the relationships in an earlier and more vigorous period (*institutio fidei Christianae*—"the people of faith were of one heart and soul," as in Acts).[18] At the end of time there is a secret unfolding, a revelation of that which was hidden in the historical process: that the oppressed, the humble, the anonymous are those who carry history.[19] At the end of time the absurd, dark, obscure passages of Scripture will be revealed as the greatest mysteries.[20] As the Living Word is encased in human and literal forms, so hidden within the outward church is the inner church, slowly revealing itself.

The history of this church leads from the apostles through the martyrs, the hermits and monks of the Greek Church to the Benedictine monasticism of the Western Church; to the Canons Regular and their effort to make the poor life of humility and submission binding upon all clergy; to the Cistercian reform; to the Cluniac monasticism; and expresses itself conclusively in the Franciscan reform movement.[21]

When the old institutional forms opposed and hindered the coming of the New Age, then the old church was recognized as cast in the image of the Anti-Christ: its efforts to hinder the revival of apostolic Christianity were the proof of its diabolical character.[22] The moving power toward the New Age was to be martyrdom, the

willingness to suffer without stint for the Gospel without glosses.[23] Binding this whole structure of thought and historical interpretation together, and illuminating it vividly, was the sense of world mission, of ultimate triumph at hand.[24]

In the radical groups of the Reformation these ideas constantly occur. One of several types, Anabaptism was primitivist and eschatological. The norm is the past, the hope for the future is the Restitution of the Early Church. There is on the one hand an attitude which is conservative, even reactionary; on the other there is a revolutionary spirit which can burst the most secure of ecclesiastical or social forms. The idea of Restitution represents a studied effort to reverse the verdict of history, to shed the accumulated power and intellectual sophistication which seem to corrode and obscure the pure and inspired faith of the founders of the church. In the Anabaptist "Restitution" there was the same agitated historical mood of expectancy which we find in Joachimitism and in the Early Church itself: a keen sense that the end and final reckoning are close at hand, and conjoined with this a vigorous missionary outlook which embraced the whole world in its sweep. Above all, the True Church was a suffering church whose changing patterns were ever cast in the shadow of the Man Upon the Cross.

These were the main elements which went into the intellectual atmosphere of the radical Reformation; they form the backdrop for the emergence of a new type of religious primitivism. This primitivism, in its Anabaptist type, involves a view of the church and its place in history which explo-

---

17 Benz, p. 22.
18 *Ibid.,* p. 27.
19 *Ibid.,* p. 36.
20 *Ibid.,* p. 37.
21 *Ibid.,* p. 310.
22 *Ibid.,* pp. 313, 362f.

---

23 *Ibid.,* p. 357.
24 *Ibid.,* p. 66.

sively combines both reactionary and radical features. In its determined Restitution of the type and style of the Early Church, Anabaptism in fact introduced quite new elements in Christian history. Although the heroic period of the faith is taken as normative, the forerunners of the Free Church way departed radically from patterns of "magisterial Protestantism" which had obtained for more than a millennium.

As we move on to consider the relation of primitivism to Anabaptism, and to study the various factors which make Anabaptism a clear type of church life, we do well to introduce certain distinctions to avoid serious error. The attitudes we were just now considering formed an intellectual climate for the various groups of the time, bound together the Left Wing especially, and are to be considered along with records of their actual group experience. It is not enough to review only what was taught, what ideas circulated among individuals and groups, although this is common practice. Our discussion must deal with "concrete" groups which found a certain place in Christian history. The view of the church which the Anabaptists championed will be tested repeatedly by the actual experience of the groups, and by their encounter both with establishments and with other types of radical protest.

In total perspective, the evidence from classical primitivism and from Humanism and Joachimitism has only relative value. In spite of suggestive eddies to mark the crosscurrents, and a few instances of streaming together, the evidence as a whole is circumstantial. It gives us a good deal of help in understanding the general climate in which Anabaptism emerged, but we shall find few quotations or other evidence of direct influence.

This is the case also with the Florentine rediscovery of antiquity, which contributed so much to the shaping of Reformation as well as Renaissance. The attitude to sources and origins, which has been noted, finds expression in the attitude to the Early Church and the Bible as well as to classical texts. An argument from analogy can even be entered that Anabaptism, with its emphasis upon the hidden truth behind objective evidences, is indebted to the revival of Neo-Platonic thought. But conclusive evidence is lacking. While doubtless the Zürich Anabaptists such as Grebel were familiar with the classical ideal, the prevalence of religious primitivism in Anabaptism is due more to the fact that Christianity is a historical religion with a sacred book in which all reforms seek their inspiration and confirmation. Since the norm provided by the book was itself diverse, it was in turn selectively applied in the light of the real problems of the age.

We may return to our original concerns: to discover what it was certain groups hoped to be, and to what extent they were successful. We shall draw mainly upon their own testimony—now generally available in usable form—in elaborating their church view. In judging to what extent the Anabaptists succeeded, we shall consider the problems they faced both from without (persecution) and from within (centrifugal factors, both doctrinal and organizational). And we shall speak from a footing in Free Church life, which is the eternal memorial to those who championed voluntary religious association and vigorous congregational life at a time when Christianity was for most simply the religious aspect of a civilization, indeed frequently little more than the tool of government. It is only from such vantage that Anabaptism can be truly understood and its importance properly assessed.

The Fall of the Church

The idea of a general Fall of man has been adapted by Christian reforming groups to the history of the church. There are two falls: man fell and the church fell. The whole idea of the recovery of New Testament Christianity is tied up with the thought that at some point in Christian history the pattern was lost.

A very prevalent contemporary opinion is revealed in the approach taken by Hobhouse in the 1909 Bampton Lectures:

Long ago I came to believe that the great change in the relation between the Church and the World which began with the conversion of Constantine is not only the decisive turning-point in Church History, but is also the key to many of the practical difficulties of the present day; and the Church of the future is destined more and more to return to a condition of things somewhat like that which prevailed in the Ante-Nicene Church; that is to say, that instead of pretending to be coextensive with the world, it will accept a position involving a more conscious antagonism with the world, and will, in return, regain in some measure its former coherence.[25]

We see here the familiar teaching of a "Fall," coupled with the hope of an eventual Restitution.

It is not surprising to find that in recent years a book on *The Fall of Christianity* written by the head of the Dutch pacifist organization is being distributed in quantity by the American office of the Fellowship of Reconciliation.[26] The Constantine myth is an essential part of the discussion: "When he was converted to Christianity (in 312), and when he exalted this faith into the State religion (in 324), Christianity began to turn toward the State for support, and became reconciled to war and the soldier's calling."[27] For Heering this is the turning point of Christian history, and the pivot of every discussion of its organization, ethics, and morals.

The idea of the fall of the church with Constantine is far-flung among the Free Churches, however, and is not limited to nonresistant or pacifist elements. A recent book on *The Claims of the Free Churches* states boldly: "When the Church was persecuted by the Empire she was pure in motive and morals: but under the patronage of Constantine it became the fashion for the Roman nobility and obsequious pagans to enter the Church: and pagans they remained within her membership."[28] Nor is the idea limited to Free Churches. In his address at the Extraordinary Synod of the Evangelical Church in Germany, June 27, 1956, in Berlin, General Superintendent Günter Jacob of Cottbus proclaimed:

Aware spirits characterize the situation of Christianity in contemporary Europe by the fact that the end of the Constantinian epoch has arrived.

The Constantinian fusion marked the departure from this genuine way of the Church of Jesus Christ, a way in the world which according to the view of the New Testament will be a way of suffering before the hostility and opposition of the world.

---

25 Walter Hobhouse, *The Church and the World in Idea and in History* (London: Macmillan & Co., 1910), pp. ix–x.
26 G. J. Heering, *The Fall of Christianity* (New York: Fellowship Publica-

tions, 1943). First published in Dutch, 1928.
27 *Ibid.*, p. 33.
28 Henry Townsend, *The Claims of the Free Churches* (London: Hodder & Stoughton, 1949), p. 45.

With the end of illusions about the Constantinian epoch and a return to the early Christian witness we no longer have the right to claim privileges and a monopoly for support of the Gospel from the State.[29]

Whether it appears in its traditional setting in "sectarian Protestantism," or on occasion within the assembly halls of declining establishments, the pattern of thinking involved is well known. What is not familiar is the fact that this is Anabaptist thinking. The Anabaptists were among the first to ground the church in a total and systematic application of primitivist historiography.

Elements in the Idea of the Fall

When we break down the various ideational associations into their constituent parts we find several different themes customarily linked together: glorification of the first three centuries (the "Golden Age" of the faith), a lamentation for the decline in association with the Empire (the "Fall" of the church), a vigorous sense of new beginnings (the "Restitution"). The latter theme will be treated in the next chapter, in a discussion of the constitutive elements in the church view. We shall consider now the attitude to the Early Church and its subsequent decline.

In true primitivist fashion, the Anabaptists considered the earliest times the "Age of Heroes." True, there had been before the sixteenth century a conscious glorification of the life of the Master and His Disciples, buoyed up by a general feeling that the men of the first centuries were spiritual giants after a fashion not equaled by later generations. The imitation of Christ (*Nachfolge Christi*) was a familiar medieval theme, of special importance to the Brethren of the Common Life—whose house at Deventer instituted the practice of community in deliberate imitation of the church at Jerusalem.[30] There were other anticipations, notably among the radical Franciscans and the Hussites. But a well-defined primitivist periodization of Christian history —with the "True Church" beginning to relive in careful fashion the life of the early heroes—was a major Anabaptist contribution.

When we review the cardinal points in Anabaptist thinking about New Testament times and the primitive church, the parallels with the classical "Golden Age" immediately become apparent. There were certain personal virtues and social practices which characterized the good society in both schemes of thought, and we may consider them briefly.

Pacifism was a cardinal principle in the classical Golden Age.[31] In the Anabaptist vision of the Early Church, the witness to peace was accented. For them, pacifism was narrowed to the testimony of the nonresistant martyrs; the atmosphere was eschatological rather than Utopian, the pattern of behavior one of discipleship rather than social strategy. As the early Christians had won the Roman Empire by suffering, so should the martyrdom of the followers of Christ in the later age lead on to the final triumph.

The Anabaptist repudiation of violence was especially related to the

---

[29] Günter Jacob, "Der Raum für das Evangelium in Ost und West," in *Bericht über die ausserordentliche Synode der evangelischen Kirche in Deutschland, 1956* (Hannover-Herrenhausen: Evang. Kirchenkanzlei, 1956), pp. 17–29.

[30] Albert Hyma, *The Christian Renaissance*, p. 61.

[31] Lovejoy, *et. al., A Documentary History*, pp. 32f; 61f.

integrity of life and witness of the believing community. Above all it was wrong to compel religious submission and use force in matters of conscience, for in the years of first faith and strength the Gospel had been spread only by means approved in the New Testament. Just as David, the man of war, was not permitted to build the temple, and even as Solomon built it without either hammer or axe, so the church of Christ was first created in the principle and spirit of voluntary association and without force or compulsion.[32] The law goes out from Zion and the Word of God from Jerusalem, and a people is gathered without force and without weapons.

Communism also characterized the classical Golden Age, and one of the marks of the Fall was dehumanization through the advent of private property.[33] Viewing the Early Church, Leonhard Schiemer wrote that the "Communion of Saints" was most clearly seen in the second, fourth and fifth chapters of Acts, and the true disciples should live as Christians did in that glorious time of the faith.[34] "One Christian should buy nothing from the other, but give freely (read Acts 2.3.4., whether the Christians at Jerusalem didn't have all things common!)."[35]

They were real Christians then, and the people of God most plainly seen! The Hutterites wrote to the Moravian Lords (c. 1546) that their communism was modeled on that of the Early Church.[36] The Holy Spirit visited the Jerusalem community, and they were a people of power of soul. The actual Anabaptist practice differed in various congregations according to the time and place; but the insistence upon community (whether communism of consumption only, or of production also) remained constant.

Sometimes a more general historical understanding entered the picture. Thus Peter Ridemann taught in his "Rechenschaft" that everything was created common in the beginning (I Moses 1:26–29), and private property entered by sin;[37] presumably the Early Church was returning to the life of Eden by practicing communism, and the Church of the Restitution should do likewise. On the other hand, Ulrich Stadler showed a strong historical sense in his treatment of the subject, pointing out that only the church at Jerusalem had communism whereas at the other centers Christians were left alone in their own houses. In his opinion, communism was the only way for the Hutterite Brethren because they were driven together with no other place to go and no other life to lead.[38] Over against these historical observations and interpretations, however, we may place dozens of normative statements concerning the first age of the church: communism was generally considered authoritative simply because it was the style of life of

32 *Z*, p. 298.

33 Lovejoy, *et al., A Documentary History,* p. 53. See also George Boas, *Essays on Primitivism,* pp. 103, 119.

34 "Ein Epistl an die gmain zu Rottenburg geschrieben, darinnen hübsche erklärungen der 12 haupt stück unsers christlichen glaubens begriffen sein," *WtQ 1938,* p. 56.

35 Spitalmeier's court testimony, Nürnberg; #70 (Dec., 1527), in *WtQ1934,* p. 64.

36 *Beck,* pp. 169–73.

37 Rideman, Peter, *Account of Our Religion, Doctrine and Faith...*(London: Hodder & Stoughton/Plough Publishing House, 1950), pp. 88f.

38 "Eine liebe unterrichtung Ulrichen Stadlers, diener des worts, der sünd halben und des ausschluss, wie er darinen stehe, auch gemainschaft der zeitlichen güeter halben. Wider die, so des Herrnwerk pand und strick schelten, mit warhaftiger zeugnus heiliger geschrift, wie hernach volget," in *WtQ1938,* pp. 215–27, 225.

the heroes of the faith in the normative period. Give all to the poor (Matt. 19:21)! Consider the widow, who gave *all she had!* As in other matters, there is an apocalyptic quality in the teaching: as time is telescoped between their congregations and the "Age of Heroes," so it is shortened between them and the end of history. Some felt the end was already begun in themselves; their community was not only a recapitulation of past virtue but a foretaste of the Kingdom of God. When asked their trade and location and station in life in court actions many replied, "No master!" (*kein vorsteer*), for in the New Age only Christ was Master. We have here an attitude as radical in social consequences as it was primitivist in religious type. The Anabaptists counted themselves members of an economy in which all were equal and all were to share according to need.

A vigorous simplicity was the mark of the man whom the world could not victimize: his wants were well controlled, his tastes directed to the truly essential.[39] Like the classical hero, the man of spiritual power in the Early Church was also cut loose

from personal display and absurd convention. This type of man appeared again in the sixteenth century. By a vigorous enforcement of spiritual discipline (including use of the Ban), unethical and immoral practices were avoided—not to mention frivolous clothes and strong language. A congregation of spiritual athletes was trained, committed to the simple life. In his testimony before the court, Julius Lober said: "Luther and the other Christian teachers do not preach nor teach baptism as it was taught at the time of the apostles.... Saith further, that Luther and others promote no true Christian order (in it), that they suffer and permit whoredom, avarice, usury, blasphemy and other depravity in the community, which the apostles did not bear so far, but had the ban among them."[40] The enforcement of heroic virtue by the group raised up a man of superior type and enabled him to perform wonderful deeds: he was able to fulfill the testimony of suffering and on occasion to perform miracles.

A certain attitude to art (technology) might be linked to this vigorously cultivated simplicity.[41] The agriculturalist, close to Mother Nature, was thought to be more wise than he whose spirit was corroded by the artifices of civilization. The man who worked with his hands and produced in co-operation with nature had keener insight than the usurer or trader. The craftsman was said to learn more by his handiwork in the spirit of humility than ever the scribe with his multitude of books. Hans Hut and his disciples

---

[39] Lovejoy, *et. al., A Documentary History,* pp. 96, 119f, 140f. George Boas, *Essays on Primitivism,* pp. 43, 111, 122, 212–13. See Boas on the monks' use of New Testament texts: "Such texts give us a verbal picture of the Christian who is ascetic, poor in worldly goods, free even when enslaved by a terrestrial master, careless of the future, wise without learning. It is not to be wondered that such a person was confused with the pagan Sage of the 'ethical period' nor that the monastic life was described as 'the life of philosophy' " (p. 107). On the other hand, medieval Christian primitivism also had its anti-intellectual expressions; Gregory the Great spoke contemptuously of those "who revere more the talents of the learned than the simple life of the innocent" (p. 122). For specialized aspects of determined simplicity, see articles by John C. Wenger on "Dress," in *ME* (1956) II, 99–104; by

Bender, on Footwashing, *ME* (1956) II, 347–51; on "Alcohol," *ME* (1955) I, 36–40.

[40] Given May 12, 1531; printed in *WtQ1934,* #267, pp. 243–47, 244.

[41] Lovejoy, *et al., A Documentary History,* p. 112. Boas, George, *op. cit.,* pp. 30, 127–28, 187.

preached the *euangelion aller creatur,* pointing out that Jesus made clear to the common man by his trade the great wisdom to which the theologians were blind.[42] The radicals never tired of pointing out that the men who knew Jesus were simple, unlettered, anonymous. They asserted that the poor and depressed and naively literal were those who carried the Gospel.[43] The unsophisticated were said to believe that Jesus meant just what He had said, without any glosses. Only those schooled in the wisdom of this world could write the commentaries and marginal notes which corrupted and rendered null and void the simple Gospel truth. In the great time of the faith, so the radicals claimed, neither doctrine nor church life were bound and corrupted by "forms," by dangerous inflections, by subtle compromises.

When we speculate on how such marked parallels could exist between classical primitivism and Anabaptist thought, since it is difficult to prove direct classical influence upon the radicals (who rarely cited any book but the Bible), we may remember their debt to Erasmus, Zwingli, Oecolampadius, and especially Sebastian Franck. And, although the best-educated leadership was martyred during the first years, the early leaders —Grebel, Hübmaier, Denck, Hetzer— were men of marked accomplishment in the university world, a world inspired by the new Humanistic studies. The devotion which the Renaissance directed toward the origins and the eager quest of the religious for the origins of the faith were related phenomena. It was not a detailed program or body of specific content which carried over, but a certain attitude and method in reference to antiquity.[44] This attitude and method, when related to distinctly Christian concerns, became the hallmarks of Anabaptist thought.

After the Golden Age, a Fall

In Anabaptist portrayal of history, after the "Age of Heroes" life declines and a definite "Fall" occurs. This is an old theme, but it was given special content by the radicals. In secular primitivism the Fall marks a turning point in society and social relationships. The Fall has a cultural aspect. There is also a chronological aspect, revealed in a definite periodization of history and the hope of an eventual restoration. There is almost always a detailed theory of "Fall" in primitivist thought.[45]

It is incumbent upon the servants of the Lord to teach, to instruct and to warn

---

42 Hans Hut, "Vom geheimnus der tauf, baide des zaichens und des wesens, ein anfang eines rechten warhaftigen Christlichen lebens; Joan:5," printed in *WtQ1938,* pp. 14–27, 17: "He teaches the Gospel to the gardener by the trees, to the fisher by the catching of fish, to the carpenter by the building, to the goldsmith by the testing of gold...the women by the leaven...." See also Hans Schlaffer, "Ein kurzer bericht und leer eines recht christlichen lebens," *ibid.,* pp. 14–27, 17. In Sebastian Franck's writing, Nature was extolled as Life and Being, and art was condemned as appearance and sham; he favored the peasants, and liked the fable of the town and country mouse. Arnold Reimann, *Sebastian Franck als Geschichtsphilosoph* (Berlin: Alfred Unger, 1921), p. 97.

43 *Infra,* p. 150.

44 Paul Mestwerdt, *Die Anfänge des Erasmus,* pp. 32, 43. The normative use of the Early Church probably came to the Anabaptists largely from Zwingli; Walther Köhler, "Ulrich Zwingli und die Reformation in der Schweiz," in Julius von Pflugk-Harttung, *Im Morgenrot der Reformation* (Hersfeld: Vertriebsanstalt christl. Kunstwerk, 1912), pp. 669–715, 675.

45 Lovejoy, *et al., A Documentary History,* p. 19. George Boas, *Essays on Primitivism,* p. 21.

to that end [*i.e., spiritual pilgrimage, martyrdom*] with all patience and neither spoil nor condemn, as we have a model in Paul. Decay had scarcely any power to hold those [who were] free, unencumbered, resigned. In the beginning they were living in the Lord. But now, because prosperity is sought, they nestle comfortably back into the world. And consequently they don't see themselves leaving the world; yes, they would far rather live than die.[46]

Lydia Müller has noted the fascination which the Eusebian history of the power and triumph of the Early Church had for the Anabaptists.[47] Here they saw the record of earth-shaking power in apparent weakness, dynamic expansion under martyrdom, triumph out of persecution. Here was the way of the church from Christ to Constantine "in a certain sense . . . a peerless Passionway. The Eusebian church-history is the history of the Church under the Cross. The Imperial-church and later the papal-church were no longer martyr-churches. So after Constantine [it was] above all the communities of heretics who took over and furthered the traditions of the true and precisely for that reason persecuted community of Christ."[48]

The growth and victory of the Early Church against incredible odds was a mysterious thing, a sign of the secret workings of God. *But more mysterious still was the fact that in the very hour of her apparent triumph and well-being, the church fell into disgrace.* The Anabaptists were led to conclude that only a little remnant (*ein klaines heuflen*) has gone the right way since creation.[49] The "True Church" and a territorial church or state church were two different things.

[46] "Eine liebe unterrichtung Ulrichen Stadlers. . . ," *WtQ1938*, p. 226.
[47] *WtQ1938*, p. xxi.

[48] Ethelbert Stauffer, "Märtyrertheologie und Täuferbewegung," LIIZKG (1933) 545–98, 549. Translated in large part by Friedmann, XIXMQR (1945) 3:179–214.
[49] Hans Schlaffer, *WtQ1938*, p. 84.

The Christ of Culture

H. RICHARD NIEBUHR

Accommodation to Culture in Gnosticism and Abelard

In every culture to which the Gospel comes there are men who hail Jesus as the Messiah of their society, the fulfiller of its hopes and aspirations, the perfecter of its true faith, the source of its holiest spirit. In the Christian community they seem to

Pp. 83–101 *Christ and Culture* by H. Richard Niebuhr. Copyright, 1951, by Harper & Row, Publishers, Inc. By permission of Harper & Row, Publishers, Inc.

stand in direct opposition to the radicals, who reject the social institutions for Christ's sake; but they are far removed from those "cultured among the despisers" of Christian faith who reject Christ for the sake of their civilization. These men are Christians not only in the sense that they count themselves believers in the Lord but also in the sense that they seek to maintain community with all other believers. Yet they seem equally at home in the community of culture. They feel no great tension between church and world, the social laws and the Gospel, the workings of divine grace and human effort, the ethics of salvation and the ethics of social conservation or progress. On the one hand they interpret culture through Christ, regarding those elements in it as most important which are most accordant with his work and person; on the other hand they understand Christ through culture, selecting from his teaching and action as well as from the Christian doctrine about him such points as seem to agree with what is best in civilization. So they harmonize Christ and culture, not without excision, of course, from New Testament and social custom, of stubbornly discordant features. They do not necessarily seek Christian sanction for the whole of prevailing culture, but only for what they regard as real in the actual; in the case of Christ they try to disentangle the rational abiding from the historical and accidental. Though their fundamental interest may be this-worldly, they do not reject other-worldliness; but seek to understand the transcendent realm as continuous in time or character with the present life. Hence the great work of Christ may be conceived as the training of men in their present social existence for the better life to come; often he is regarded as the great educator, sometimes as the great philosopher or reformer. Just as the gulf between the worlds is bridged, so other differences between Christ and culture that seem like chasms to radical Christians and anti-Christians are easily passed over by these men. Sometimes they are ignored, sometimes filled in with convenient material derived from historical excavations or demolitions of old thought-structures. Such Christians have been described psychologically by F. W. Newman and William James as constituting the company of the "once-born" and the "healthy-minded." Sociologically they may be interpreted as nonrevolutionaries who find no need for positing "cracks in time"—fall and incarnation and judgment and resurrection. In modern history this type is well-known, since for generations it has been dominant in a large section of Protestantism. Inadequately defined by the use of such terms as "liberal" and "liberalism," it is more aptly named Culture-Protestantism;[1] but appearances of the type have not been confined to the modern world nor to the churches of the Reformation.

There were movements of this sort in the earliest days of Christianity, as it arose in the midst of Jewish society, was carried into the Graeco-Roman world by Paul and other missionaries, and became involved in the complex interactions of the many cultural ingredients that bubbled in the Mediterranean melting pot. Among Jewish Christians doubtless all the variations appeared that we find among ancient and modern Gentile Christians as they wrestle with the Christ-culture problem. Paul's conflict with the Judaizers and later references to Nazarenes and Ebionites indicate that there were groups or movements which were more Jewish than Christian, or which, it might be better to say, sought to maintain loyalty to Jesus Christ without abandoning any important part of current Jewish tradition or giving up the special Messianic hopes of the chosen people.[2] Jesus was for them not only the promised Messiah but the Messiah of the promise, as this was understood in their society.

[1] Karl Barth, I believe, invented the term. See especially his *Protestantische Theologie im 19. Jahrhundert,* 1947, chap. iii.

[2] On Jewish Christianity see H. Lietzmann, *The Beginnings of the Christian Church,* pp. 235 ff.; J. Weiss, *History of Primitive Christianity,* Vol. II, pp. 707 ff.

In early Gentile Christianity many modifications of the Christ-culture theme combined more or less positive concern for culture with fundamental loyalty to Jesus. Radical Christians of a later time have been inclined to relegate them all to the undifferentiated limbo of compromise or apostate Christianity; but there were great differences among them. The extreme attitude, which interprets Christ wholly in cultural terms and tends to eliminate all sense of tension between him and social belief of custom, was represented in the Hellenistic world by the Christian Gnostics. These men—Basilides, Valentinus, the author of *Pistis Sophia,* and their like—are heretics in the eyes of the main body of the church as well as of radical Christians. But they seem to have thought of themselves as loyal believers. They "started from Christian ideas, they were attempting to formulate a Christian theory of God and man; the contest between Catholics and Gnostics was a struggle between persons who felt themselves to be Christians, not between Christians and heathens."[3]

Prof. Burkitt has argued persuasively that in the thought of such Gnostics "the figure of Jesus is essential, and without Jesus the systems would drop to pieces," that what they sought to do was to reconcile the gospel with the science and philosophy of their time. As nineteenth-century defenders of the faith tried to state the doctrine of Jesus Christ in terms of evolution, so these men undertook to interpret it in the light of the fascinating ideas that had been suggested to enlightened minds by Ptolemaian astronomy and by the psychology of the day with its

catchwords *soma-sema,* its theory that the body was the soul's tomb.[4] Nothing is as evanescent in history as the pansophic theories that flourish among the illuminati of all times under the bright sunlight of the latest scientific discoveries; and nothing can be more easily dismissed by later periods as mere speculation. But we may well believe that the Gnostics were no more inclined to fantasy than are those folk in our day who find in psychiatry the key to the understanding of Christ, or in nuclear fission the answer to the problems of eschatology. They sought to disentangle the gospel from its involvement with barbaric and outmoded Jewish notions about God and history; to raise Christianity from the level of belief to that of intelligent knowledge, and so to increase its attractiveness and its power.[5] Emancipated as they were from the crude forms of polytheism and idolatry, and cognizant of profound spiritual depths of being, they set forth a doctrine according to which Jesus Christ was a cosmic savior of souls, imprisoned and confounded in the fallen, material world, the revealer of the true, redeeming wisdom, the restorer of right knowledge about the abyss of being and about the ascent as well as the descent of man.[6] This is the most obvious element in the effort of the Gnostics to accommodate Christianity to the culture of their day: their "scientific" and "philo-

---

[3] F. C. Burkitt, *Church and Gnosis,* 1932, p. 8; cf. also *Cambridge Ancient History,* Vol. XII, pp. 467 ff.; A. C. McGiffert, *History of Christian Thought,* Vol. I, pp. 45 ff.

---

[4] Burkitt, *Church and Gnosis,* pp. 29–35; 48, 51; 57 f.; 87–91.

[5] Albert Ehrhard, *Die Kirche der Maertyrer,* 1932, p .130.

[6] Cf. Burkitt, *Church and Gnosis,* pp. 89 f. The thought of the Gnostics will seem less strange and foreign to those modern students of theology who have become acquainted with the ideas of Nicolai Berdyaev, who calls himself a Christian Gnostic. See especially his *Freedom and the Spirit,* 1935.

sophic" interpretation of the person and work of Christ. What is less obvious is that this attempt entailed his naturalization in the whole civilization. Christianity so interpreted became a religious and philosophic system, regarded doubtless as the best and the only true one, yet one among many. As a religion dealing with the soul it laid no imperious claim on man's total life. Jesus Christ was spiritual savior, not the Lord of life; his Father was not the source of all things nor their Governor. For the church, the new people, there was substituted an association of the enlightened who could live in culture as those who sought a destiny beyond it but were not in strife with it. Participation in the life of culture was now a matter of indifference; it involved no great problems. A Gnostic had no reason for refusing to pay homage to Caesar or to participate in war; though perhaps he had no compelling reason, apart from social pressure, for yielding to the mores and the laws. If he was too enlightened to take seriously the popular and official worship of idols, he was also too enlightened to make an issue out of its rejection; and martyrdom he scorned.[7] In the Gnostic version, knowledge of Jesus Christ was an individual and spiritual matter, which had its place in the life of culture as the very pinnacle of human achievement. It was something that advanced souls could attain; and it was the advanced, the religious, attainment of such souls. Doubtless it was connected with ethics—sometimes with very rigoristic conduct of life, sometimes with indulgence and even license; but the ethics was grounded not upon Christ's commandment nor upon the loyalty of the believer to the new community. It was rather the ethics of individual aspiration after a destiny highly exalted above the material and the social world, and at the same time an ethics of individual adjustment to this indifferent world. From the point of view of the culture problem, the effort of the Gnostic to reconcile Christ with the science and philosophy of his day was not an end but a means. What he accomplished for himself—wittingly and designedly or unwittingly—as the corollary of this effort, was the easing of all tensions between the new faith and the old world. How much of the gospel he retained is another question, though it must be pointed out that the Gnostic was selective in his attitude toward culture as well as toward Christ. He rejected, for himself at least, what seemed ignoble in it, and cultivated what appeared to be most religious and most Christian.[8]

The movement represented by Gnosticism has been one of the most powerful in Christian history, despite the fact that its extreme representatives have been condemned by the church. At its center is the tendency to interpret Christianity as a religion rather than as church, or to interpret church as religious association rather than as new society. It sees in Jesus Christ not only a revealer of religious truth but a god, the object of religious worship; but not the Lord of all life, and not the son of

---

[7] Irenaeus, *Against Heretics,* IV, xxxiii, 9; cf. Ehrhard, *Die Kirche der Maertyrer,* pp. 162, 170 f.

[8] Another kind of cultural Christianity in the early period is represented by Lactantius and those theologians and statesmen who, at the time of the Constantinian settlement, sought to amalgamate Romanism and the new faith. It has been excellently described by Cochrane in his *Christianity and Classical Culture,* Pt. II, especially chapter V.

the Father who is the present Creator and Governor of all things. It is too easy to say that Gnosticism retains the religion and drops the ethics of Christianity; the acceptance of the terms "religion" and "ethics" as characteristics of Christianity is itself an acceptance of the cultural point of view, of a pluralistic conception of life in which activity can be added to activity. The difficulty involved appears partly in the fact, evident in the case of the Gnostics, that when what is called religion is separated from ethics it becomes something very different from what it is in the church: it is now a metaphysics, a "Gnosis," a mystery cult rather than a faith governing all life.

The problems raised by Gnosticism regarding the relations of Christ to religion and of religion to culture became more rather than less acute with the development of so-called Christian civilization. There can be no doubt that medieval society was intensely religious, and that its religion was Christianity; yet the question whether Christ was the Lord of this culture is not answered by reference to the pre-eminence of the religious institution in it, nor even by reference to the pre-eminence of Christ in that institution. In this religious society the same problems about Christ and culture appeared that perplexed Christians in pagan Rome, and similarly divergent efforts at solution resulted. If some varieties of monasticism and some of the medieval sects followed Tertullian, then in an Abélard we may discern the attempt to answer the question somewhat as the Christian Gnostics answered it in the second century. Though the content of Abélard's thought is very different from that of the Gnostics, in spirit he is much akin to them. He seems to quarrel only

with the church's way of stating its belief; since this prevents Jews and other non-Christians, especially those who revere and follow the Greek philosophers, from accepting something with which in their hearts they agree.[9] But in stating the faith, its beliefs about God and Christ and its demands on conduct, he reduces it to what conforms with the best in culture. It becomes a philosophic knowledge about reality, and an ethics for the improvement of life. The moral theory of the atonement is offered as an alternative not only to a doctrine that is difficult for Christians as Christians but to the whole conception of a once-and-for-all act of redemption. Jesus Christ has become for Abélard the great moral teacher who "in all that he did in the flesh ... had the intention of our instruction,"[10] doing in a higher degree what Socrates and Plato had done before him. Of the philosophers he says that "in their care for the state and its citizens, ... in life and doctrine, they give evidence of an evangelic and apostolic perfection and come little or nothing short of the Christian religion. They are, in fact, joined to us by this common zeal for moral achievement."[11] Such a remark is revelatory not only of a broad and charitable spirit toward non-Christians, but, more significantly, of a peculiar understanding of the gospel, markedly different surely from that of radical Christians. Abélard's ethics reveals the same attitude. One seeks in vain in his *Scito te Ipsum* for a recognition of the hard demand which the Sermon on the Mount

---

[9] Cf. J. R. McCallum, *Abélard's Christian Theology*, 1948, p. 90.

[10] *Ibid.*, p. 84.

[11] *Ibid.*, p. 62; cf. Maurice De Wulf, *History of Medieval Philosophy*, 1925, Vol. I, pp. 161–66.

makes on the Christian. What is offered here is kindly and liberal guidance for good people who want to do right and for their spiritual directors.[12] All conflict between Christ and culture is gone; the tension that exists between church and world is really due, in the estimation of an Abélard, to the church's misunderstanding of Christ.

"Culture-Protestantism" and A. Ritschl

In medieval culture Abélard was a relatively lonely figure; but since the 18th century his followers have been numerous, and what was heresy became the new orthodoxy. A thousand variations of the Christ-of-culture theme have been formulated by great and little thinkers in the Western world, by leaders of society and of the church, by theologians and philosophers. It appears in rationalistic and romantic, in conservative and liberal versions; Lutherans, Calvinists, sectarians, and Roman Catholics produce their own forms. From the point of view of our problem, the catchwords "rationalism," "liberalism," "fundamentalism," etc., are not highly significant. They indicate what lines of division there are within a cultural society, but obscure the fundamental unity that obtains among men who interpret Christ as a hero of manifold culture.

Among these many men and movements one may name a John Locke for whom *The Reasonableness of Christianity* commended itself to all who not only used their reason but used it in the "reasonable" manner characteristic of an English culture that found the middle way between all extremes. Leibnitz belongs here; and fundamentally Kant, with his translation of the gospel into a *Religion Within the Limits of Reason,* for in this case also the word "reason" means the particular exercise of man's analytical and synthetic intellectual power characteristic of the best culture of the time. Thomas Jefferson is one of the group. "I am a Christian," he declared, "in the only sense in which he [Jesus Christ] wished any one to be," but he made that declaration after he had carefully excerpted from the New Testament the sayings of Jesus which commended themselves to him. Though Jesus' doctrines, in the sage of Monticello's judgment, have not only come down to us in mutilated and corrupted form but were defective in their original pronouncement, yet "notwithstanding these disadvantages, a system of morals is presented to us, which, if filled up in the style and spirit of the rich fragments he left us, would be the most perfect and sublime that has ever been taught by man." Christ did two things: "1. He corrected the Deism of the Jews, confirming them in their belief in one only God, and giving them juster notions of his attributess and government. 2. His moral doctrines relating to kindred and friends, were more pure and perfect than those of the most correct of the philosophers, and greatly more so than those of the Jews; and they went far beyond both in inculcating universal philanthropy, not only to kindred and friends, to neighbors and countrymen, but to all mankind, gathering all into one family, under the bonds of charity, peace, common wants and common aids."[13] The phi-

[12] J. R. McCallum, *Abailard's Ethics,* 1935.

[13] From a letter to Dr. Benjamin Rush, Apr. 21, 1803; in P. S. Foner, *Basic Writings of Thomas Jefferson,* pp. 660–62. Cf.

losophers, statesmen, reformers, poets, and novelists who acclaim Christ with Jefferson all repeat the same theme; Jesus Christ is the great enlightener, the great teacher, the one who directs all men in culture to the attainment of wisdom, moral perfection, and peace. Sometimes he is hailed as the great utilitarian, sometimes as the great idealist, sometimes as the man of reason, sometimes as the man of sentiment. But whatever the categories are by means of which he is understood, the things for which he stands are fundamentally the same— a peaceful, co-operative society achieved by moral training.

Many of the leading theologians of the church in the nineteenth century joined the movement. The Schleiermacher of the *Speeches on Religion* participated in it, though he does not so evidently represent it in his writing of *The Christian Faith*. The former, youthful utterance is characteristically directed to "the cultured among the despisers of religion." Though the word "culture" here means the specialized attainment of the most self-consciously intellectual and aesthetic group in society, yet it is also indicated that Schleiermacher is directing himself, like the Gnostics and Abélard before him, to the representatives of culture in the broad sense. Like them also he believes that what they find offensive is not Christ but the church with its teachings and ceremonies; and again he conforms to the general pattern by dealing with Christ in terms of religion. For Christ is in this presentation less the Jesus Christ of the New Testament than the principle of mediation between finite and infinite. Christ belongs in culture, be-

cause culture itself, without "sense and taste for the infinite," without a "holy music" accompanying all its work, becomes sterile and corrupt. This Christ of religion does not call upon men to leave homes and kindred for his sake; he enters into their homes and all their associations as the gracious presence which adds an aura of infinite meaning to all temporal tasks.[14]

Karl Barth, in a brilliant appreciation and critique, emphasizes the duality and unity of Schleiermacher's two interests: he was determined to be both a Christo-centric theologian and a modern man, participating fully in the work of culture, in the development of science, the maintenance of the state, the cultivation of art, the ennoblement of family life, the advancement of philosophy. And he carried out this double task without a sense of tension, without the feeling that he served two masters. Perhaps Barth sees Schleiermacher as too much of one piece; but certainly in the *Speeches on Religion,* as well as in his writings on ethics, he is a clearcut representative of those who accommodate Christ to culture while selecting from culture what conforms most readily to Christ.[15]

As the nineteenth century moved on from Kant, Jefferson, and Schleier-

---

also Thomas Jefferson, *The Life and Morals of Jesus of Nazareth,* extracted textually from the Gospels.

[14] *On Religion.* Translated by John Oman, 1893; cf. pp. 246, 249, 178 *et passim.*
[15] K. Barth, *Die Protestantische Theologie im 19. Jahrhundert,* 1947, pp. 387 ff.; cf. also K. Barth "Schleiermacher" in his *Die Theologie und die Kirche,* 1928, pp. 136 ff.; Richard B. Brandt, *The Philosophy of Schleiermacher,* 1941, pp. 166 ff. The unity of Christian and philosophical ethics is asserted most unambiguously by Schleiermacher in his essay "On the Philosophical Treatment of the Idea of Virtue," in *Saemmtliche Werke* (Reimer), Pt. III, Vol. II, pp. 350 ff.

macher to Hegel, Emerson, and Ritschl, from the religion within the limits of reason to the religion of humanity, the Christ-of-culture theme was sounded over and over again in many variations, was denounced by cultural opponents of Christ and by radical Christians, and merged into other answers that sought to maintain the distinction between Christ and civilization while yet maintaining loyalty to both. Today we are inclined to regard the whole period as the time of cultural Protestantism; though even as we do so we make our criticism of its tendencies with the aid of such nineteenth century theologians as Kierkegaard and F. D. Maurice. The movement toward the identification of Christ with culture doubtless reached its climax in the latter half of the century; and the most representative theologian of that time, Albrecht Ritschl, may be taken as the best modern illustration of the Christ-of-culture type. Unlike Jefferson and Kant, Ritschl stays close to the New Testament Jesus Christ. Indeed, he is partly responsible for the intense concentration of modern scholarship on the study of the Gospels and the history of the early church. He retains a much larger share of the creed of the church than do the cultured lovers of Christ and despisers of the church. He counts himself a member of the Christian community; and believes that only in its context can one speak significantly about sin and salvation. Yet he also takes seriously his responsibility in the community of culture, and stands at the opposite extreme from his contemporary Tolstoy in his attitude toward science and state, economic life and technology.

Ritschl's theology had two foundation stones: not revelation and reason, but Christ and culture. He resolutely rejected the idea that we could or should begin our Christian self-criticism by seeking out some ultimate truth of reason, self-evident to all; or by accepting the dogmatic pronouncement of some religious institution; or by looking into our own experience for some persuasive feeling or sense of reality. "Theology," he wrote, "which ought to set forth the authentic content of Christian religion in positive form, needs to draw its content from the New Testament and from no other source."[16] The Protestant dogma of the authority of Scriptures verifies but does not constitute the ground for this necessity; the church is not the foundation of Christ, but Christ is the founder of the church. "The Person of its Founder is . . . the key to the Christian view of the world, and the standard of Christians' self-judgment and moral effort," as well as the standard which shows how such specifically religious acts as prayer should be carried on.[17] Thus Ritschl begins his theological task resolutely as a member of the Christian community, which has no other beginning than Jesus Christ as set forth in the New Testament.

In fact, however he had another starting point in the community of culture, which has as its principle the will of man to gain mastery over nature. As a modern man and as a Kantian, Ritschl understands the human situation fundamentally in terms of man's conflict with nature. Popular thought celebrates as the greatest human achievement the victories of applied science and technology over natural forces. Doubtless Ritschl was also impressed by these

---

[16] A. Ritschl, *Rechtfertigung und Versoehnung*, 3d ed., 1889, Vol. II, p. 18.
[17] A. Ritschl, *The Christian Doctrine of Justification and Reconciliation: The Positive Development of the Doctrine*, 1900, p. 202.

conquests; but what concerned him more as a moral thinker and as a Kantian was the effort of the ethical reason to impress on human nature itself the internal law of the conscience; to direct individual and social life toward the ideal goal of virtuous existence in a society of free yet interdependent virtuous persons. In the ethical realm man faces a double problem: he needs not only to subdue his own nature, but also to overcome the despair which arises from his understanding of the indifference of the external natural world to his own lofty interests. What Ritschl accepts as given is "man's self-distinction from nature and his endeavours to maintain himself against it or over it."[18] Man must regard personal life; whether in himself or another, as an end in itself. All the work of culture has its source in the conflict with nature, and its goal in the victory of personal, moral existence; in the achievement, to use Kantian terms, of the kingdom of ends—or, in the New Testament phrase, of the kingdom of God.

With these two starting points Ritschl might have become a Christian of the median sort, who sought to combine two distinct principles by accepting polar tensions or grades of existence or otherwise. There may be, here and there in his writings, indications of tendencies toward such solutions. But on the whole he found no problem. The difficulties other Christians encountered seemed to him to be due to erroneous interpretations of God, of Christ, and of the Christian life; they were due, for instance, to the use of metaphysical ideas rather than of those critical methods that enabled men to understand the true doctrine of God and the true meaning of forgiveness. In his own views there

were dualities, to be sure, but no real conflicts save between culture and nature. Christianity itself needed to be regarded as an ellipse with two foci, rather than as a circle with one center. One focus was justification or the forgiveness of sins; the other, ethical striving for the attainment of the perfect society of persons. But there was no conflict between these ideas; for forgiveness meant the divine companionship that enabled the sinner after every defeat to arise again and resume his work at the ethical task. There was the duality of the church and the cultural community; but here also Ritschl found no conflict, and attacked most sharply monastic and pietistic practices in separating the church from the world.[19] If the Christian church was the community in which everything was referred to Jesus Christ, it was also the true form of ethical society, in which members of different nations are combined together in mutual love and for the sake of achieving the universal kingdom of God.[20] There is the duality of Christian calling and Christian vocation, but only medieval Catholicism finds conflict here. The Christian can exercise his calling to seek the kingdom of God if, motivated by love of neighbor, he carries on his work in the moral communities of family and economic, national, and political life. Indeed "family, private property, personal independence and honor (in obedience to authority)" are goods that are essential to moral health and the formation of character. Only by engagement in civic work for the sake of the common good, by faithfulness in one's social calling, is

---

18 *Ibid.,* p. 219; cf. 222 ff.

19 Cf. his *Geschichte des Pietismus,* 3 vols. 1880–1886.

20 *Unterricht in der christlichen Religion,* 1895, p. 5; *Justification and Reconciliation,* pp. 133 ff.

it possible to be true to the example of Christ.[21] There is duality in Ritschl's thought between the work of God and the work of man; but it is not of such a sort that the strictures of anti-Christian exponents of culture regarding Christian reliance on God rather than on personal effort are in any sense validated. For God and man have in common the task of realizing the kingdom; and God works within the human community through Christ and through conscience, rather than on it from without. There is duality, finally, in Christ himself; for he is both priest and prophet, he belongs both to the sacramental and praying community of those who depend on grace, and to the cultural community which through ethical striving in many institutions labors for the victory of free men over nature. But there is no conflict and no tension here either; for the priest mediates forgiveness in order that the prophet's ideal may be realized, and the founder of the Christian community is at the same time the moral hero who marks a great advance in the history of culture.[22]

It is largely by means of the idea of the kingdom of God that Ritschl achieved the complete reconciliation of Christianity and culture. When we attend to the meaning he attaches to that term, we become aware of the extent to which he has interpreted Jesus as a Christ of culture, in both senses: as the guide of men in all their labor to realize and conserve their values, and as the Christ who is understood by means of nineteenth-century cultural ideas. "The Christian idea of the Kingdom of God," writes Ritschl, "denotes the association of mankind—an association both extensively and intensively the most comprehensive possible—through the reciprocal moral action of its members, action which transcends all merely natural and particular considerations.[23] If Jesus' eschatological hope in the manifestation of God is lacking here, so also is his noneschatological faith in the present rule of the transcendent Lord of heaven and earth. All the references are to man and to man's work; the word "God" seems to be an intrusion, as perhaps those later Ritschlians recognized who substituted the phrase "brotherhood of man" for "kingdom of God." This statement of the end of human striving in cultural work is, moreover, wholly in line with the thought of the nineteenth century. As we have noted, the conception of the kingdom of God Ritschl ascribes to Jesus Christ is practically the same as Kant's idea of the kingdom of ends; it is closely related to Jefferson's hope for a mankind gathered into one family "under the bonds of charity, peace, common wants and common aids"; in its political aspects it is Tennyson's "Parliament of Man and Federation of the World"; it is the synthesis of the great values esteemed by democratic culture: the freedom and intrinsic worth of individuals, social cooperation, and universal peace.

Yet it must be said, in fairness to Ritschl, that if he interpreted Christ through culture he also selected from culture those elements which were most compatible with Christ. Many other movements were present in the flourishing civilization of the late nineteenth century besides the highly ethical Kantian idealism that was for Ritschl the key to culture. He

21 *Unterricht in der christlichen Religion*, pp. 53 f.; cf. *Justification and Reconciliation*, pp. 661 ff.

22 *Justification and Reconciliation*, chap. VI.

23 *Ibid.*, p. 284.

did not find or seek as some did, to establish contact between Jesus Christ and the capitalistic or the nationalistic or the materialistic tendencies of the time. If he used Christianity as a means to an end, he chose an end more compatible with Christianity than were many other goals of the contemporary culture. If he selected among the attributes of the God of Jesus Christ the one quality of love at the expense of his attributes of power and of justice, still the resultant theology, though a caricature, was recognizably Christian. Moreover, Ritschl sought to do justice to the fact that Christ accomplished some things for men which they could never accomplish for themselves in culture, even by imitation of the historic example. He mediated and mediates the forgiveness of sin; and he brings to light the immortality that no human labor and wisdom can achieve. Man's lordship over the world has its limits; he is limited by his own corporeal nature, and by the multitude of natural forces he cannot tame, "and the multitude of hindrances which he has to tolerate from those on whose support he is reckoning." Though he "identifies himself with the advancing forces of human civilization," he cannot hope to conquer by his labor the system of nature that opposes him. In this situation, religion and Jesus Christ, as a teacher of high religion— assure man that he stands close to the supramundane God, and give him the certainty that he is destined for a supramundane goal.[24] Of course this also sounds more like the gospel according to St. Immanuel than according to St. Matthew or St. Paul.

It is not necessary to develop in further detail Ritschl's solution of the problem of Christ and culture; to

---

[24] *Ibid.*, pp. 609 ff.

show how loyalty to Jesus leads to active participations in every cultural work, and to care for the conservation of all the great institutions. The general outlines are familiar to most modern Christians, especially to Protestants, whether or not they have ever heard of Ritschl, not to speak of having read his works. Partly because of his influence, but even more because he was a representative man who made explicit ideas that were widespread and deeply rooted in the world before the Wars, his understanding of Christ and culture has been reproduced in essence by scores of leading theologians and churchmen. Walter Rauschenbusch's social gospel presents the same general interpretation of Christ and the gospel, though with greater moral force and less theological depth. Harnack in Germany, Garvie in England, Shailer Mathews and D. C. Macintosh in America, Ragaz in Switzerland, and many others, each in his own way, find in Jesus the great exponent of man's religious and ethical culture. Popular theology condenses the whole of Christian thought into the formula: The Fatherhood of God and the Brotherhood of Man.

Back of all these Christologies and doctrines of salvation is a common notion that is part of the generally accepted and unquestioned climate of opinion. It is the idea that the human situation is fundamentally characterized by man's conflict with nature. Man the moral being, the intellectual spirit, confronts impersonal natural forces, mostly outside himself but partly within him. When the issue in life is so conceived, it is almost inevitable that Jesus Christ should be approached and understood as a great leader of the spiritual, cultural cause, of man's struggle to subdue nature, and of his aspirations to transcend it. That man's fundamental situation is not one of conflict with nature but with God, and that Jesus Christ stands at the center of that conflict as victim and mediator— this thought, characteristic of the church as a whole, culture-theology never seems to entertain. In its view, those Christians who so understand the human dilemma and its solution are obscurantists in man's cultural life and perverters of the gospel of the kingdom.

the mystical response

fourteen

from The Origin and Meaning of Hasidism

MARTIN BUBER

Hasidism, like early Christianity, has at times been described as a result of the *am-haaretz,* that is, the uneducated "country people," the strata of the people who do not occupy themselves with the study of the teaching. By this was meant that the essential impulse of the Hasidic movement was the rebellion of the "ignorant" mass, in many ways treated with contempt by the religious tradition, against this scale of values in which the scholar, the man devoted to the knowledge of the Torah, occupied the highest rung. The true aim of the movement is thereby understood as one toward the revolution of values, toward a new order of rank in which it is not the man who "knows" the Torah, but the man who lives in it, who realizes it in the simple unity of life that stands in the highest place; and the simple unity is, in fact, more often found in the *am-haaretz* than in the *lamdan,* the thoroughly learned. The root of this striving for a revolu-

Reprinted from *The Origin and Meaning of Hasidism* by Martin Buber, copyright 1960, by permission of the publisher, Horizon Press, New York.

tion of values was seen to lie in the change of the social structure in East European Jewry since it took place in just that time when Hasidism came into the world.

The kernel of truth in this conception is unmistakable. One cannot understand the enormous influence that Hasidism exercised on the masses of the people if one does not recognize the "democratic" strain in it, the tendency native to it to set in place of the existing "aristocracy" of spiritual possession the equal right of all to draw near to the absolute Being. Inequality might rule in all matters of external life: in the innermost realm, in the relation to God it may not penetrate. From this standpoint it is easier to bear the reality of the distinction between the privileged and the unprivileged since the worst special privilege has been done away with. Certainly such a transformation can only take place in the history of religions when it has been preceded by convulsions in the inner core of the community; but the essential question is how great is the share of the social factor in this general process.

Since the significance of the social factor in the history of the spirit was discovered, one has naturally been inclined to give it undue weight. The main task here, in contrast, as in every genuine inquiry, is the demarcation of the spheres. But the limits of the power of the social factor can nowhere else be so clearly designated as in the history of religion. It determines that new contents of teaching and of life forms, new dogmas and myths, new symbols and rituals shall at a certain time outgrow others and find entrance into the life of the people—their extent and their reverberation depend on the social factor; but not the content itself. The belief that religious forms arise ever again out of social "relationships" is an error capable of impoverishing the world of the spirit. These relationships influence the sphere within which the forms hold force: only under certain social conditions can the new prepare its way. But the new itself arises from the contacts and conflicts in the heart of religion itself. The economic development supplies here only the fertilizing forces; the spirit supplies the forces of the seed.

This holds particularly for that sphere of religious life within which Hasidism is one of the great historic manifestations. One is accustomed to call this sphere mysticism; but for the sake of clarity it must be pointed out that what is in question here is not speculations detached from human experience, speculations, perhaps, about the relation between God and the world by means of divine emanations, but a teaching that is grounded in human experience and that is solely concerned with the happenings between man and God. To be sure, this teaching makes use of those speculations and it may be that it will always continue to use them, as Hasidism does; but only in order to bind them ever again to human existence and the personal task of man, in order to authenticate them in exis-

tence and task. Mysticism in this sense points to the sphere of the person and builds on it, even though in its extreme forms it proclaims as its final goal the dissolution of the person, his merging into divine being. This is not to be understood, however, as if one had to concern oneself with this mysticism just in its isolation, because it is "personal." The mystic enters the room of his mystical experience, which is destined to become the foundation of his teaching, not from a neutral world-space but from the life-space of a concrete religion in which he is at home and to which he ever again returns home; indeed, even his experience itself is in no small measure stamped by the traditions and ordinances of this religion. Even if he seems to renounce the dogmas of his religion, he remains bound with its vitality. Mysticism is a historical phenomenon. It comes forward most strongly where it becomes a "movement," that is, where the teaching and the manner of teaching of the mystic takes effect outside the circle of his disciples, seizes the people, gives it example and model and calls forth profound transformations in the faith and the soul of the people.

If we ask now about the character of the historical situation in which the spark of mystical existence leaps over into the people, then we find for the most part that it is a time of a more or less public inner crisis of the religion. If the validity and reality of faith of the traditional contents and structures of a religion are shaken, whether because of an increasing degeneration or because of an extraordinary event, if, therefore, the response of this religion to the problematic of human existence, the existence of the individual and the existence of the people, becomes questionable, then mysticism not infrequently rises up against the spreading doubt, against the breaking out of despair. It remolds the basic motif of mystical speculation into life motifs, not merely in the presentations of the teaching, but above all in life itself, on the soil of the religious context from which it arose, and thus leads this religion to a fullness of new life-force. It strengthens the shaken structures, it dispenses new content to the statements that have become questionable and makes them worthy of belief, it pours a new meaning into the forms emptied of their meaning and renews them from within, it restores to religion its binding power. The fact that the people accept mysticism to such an extent is conditioned by social motives, by social changes, by social strivings, but what mysticism gives to the people is not understandable from the standpoint of the soil; the life-force that it presents to religion has its source in the inner religious dynamic itself, the formative sap in it ascends from those root beds in which the substance of faith decomposes and renews itself.

So it is with Hasidism.

Part 5

religion
and conflict:
ambiguities
and dilemmas

While religious ideals are ultimately concerned with conditions of peace and harmony, religious approval of conflict and of particular conflicts is not uncommon. Moreover, the relationship of religion and life is, as we have seen, often conducive to conflict. In this chapter, which deals with the problems discussed in Chapters five and six of *The Sociology of Religion,* we attempt to focus on certain key questions concerning religion and conflict. We also point out instances when religion performs a negative rather than a positive function within the life of societies. The text showed how elements of dilemma lurk within the process of institutionalization itself, and how these elements become significant in the history of religion. It isolated five dilemmas, characteristic of the internal life of religious institutions, that may seriously affect the relationship of such institutions to the general society within which they exist. The selections that follow concentrate on the latter aspect of the problem. We deal with the special problems inherent in the existence of an institution related to transcendence but situated within the everyday world.

Religious institutions come to maturity in relation to specific social contexts and cultural values. Social structures and cultural values change in the course of time; they may become increasingly inappropriate to new conditions and may impose hardships that are experienced as unjust. If the dominant religion in a society has successfully accommodated to that society, it has probably come to approve and sanctify the established values, and although these values may become less and less appropriate to changing conditions, they remain a significant aspect of the concrete understanding and interpretation of the religious outlook. Religious leaders consequently may be either unwilling or unable to face and solve the problem of change and reinterpretation. Relative and increasingly obsolete formulations become confused with universal truth. In such cases the established religion becomes part of the general establishment in the sense that it sanctifies the existing social order and justifies the special interests seeking its perpetuation, while providing either no support for or actual opposition to those who seek change. In such cases religion performs a dysfunction to society, standing as an obstacle to the kind of reform that would in the long run increase the viability of society and improve the welfare of its members. Max Weber discusses such problems in the selection on caste in Hinduism. For Hindus the established sacralized social structure is the embodiment of religious values, but to many non-Hindus that view is tantamount to sanctifying an unjust social system. Weber shows that the Hindu concept of salvation, and the belief in a rationally and ethically determined universe in which each man's fate is set by necessity, can deter any change in the Indian caste system. The doctrine of Karma has functioned concretely to preserve existing social structures and to inhibit any effort for change.

Gunnar Myrdal, in his vast and comprehensive study of the social, political, and economic problems of developing countries in South Asia, has explored the contemporary relationship of traditional religion to established society in that part of the world. Myrdal finds that religion is a major force in shaping the attitudes, aspirations, and horizons of people in these countries, but he charges that as religion exists at present it seriously inhibits the kinds of change necessary for the socioeconomic development advocated by most of the governments in the region and so desperately needed to alleviate extreme conditions of poverty. Myrdal says, "Religion should be studied for what it really is: a ritualized and stratified complex of highly emotional beliefs and valuations that give the sanction of sacredness, taboo, and immutability to inherited institutional arrangements, modes of living, and attitudes."[1] Myrdal in effect affirms in the South Asian case the Marxist indictment of religion, pointing to the negative functions of religion as an opiate dulling the sense of the need for change, the possibility of executing it, and its authentic desirability for the suffering masses.

Another example of religion legitimating unjust, outmoded ideas, values, and social conditions is American Protestantism during the latter half of the nineteenth century. During this period, according to church historian Sidney Mead, Protestantism in the United States abdicated it prophetic function and tended to identify completely with the prevailing American value system. It embraced individualism and unrestricted capitalistic competition—"free enterprise"—even when social evils involving clear violation of Christian moral standards were committed in the name of these values. The converging of religious and cultural values tends to "relativize the absolute by absolutizing the relative" and thereby to undermine the transcendence of moral values. Thus the prophetic function is abandoned and lost and with it the spiritual substance of a religious tradition. In America, the identification of religion and culture not only impoverished religion but also contributed to the development of a sense of national self-righteousness and superiority that smacked of idolatry in terms of transcendent biblical faith. Such accommodation tends to father protest, and American Protestants in the late nineteenth and early twentieth centuries protested. The Social Gospel movement arose, with important and serious Protestant thinkers and leaders attempting to face the new oppressive conditions of developing industrialism, to understand them and the dynamic of their development, and to judge them in the light of a truly

---

[1] Gunnar Myrdal, *Asian Drama* (New York: Pantheon Books, Inc., 1968), Vol. I, p. 103.

prophetic Christian ethic. Thus did the dynamic, characteristic of Christian history despite the many instances of dysfunctional accommodation, reassert itself. We offer here, however, a discussion of the process and condition of that accommodation as a striking example of negative function.

A final dilemma confronting religion in society is the problem of instrumentalism. It is accepted that one of the obvious functions of religion is to be a force for practical good in this world. However, the relationship to the divine is seen by all profoundly religious men as a good in itself—indeed, as the ultimate good, as an end, not a means. If religion is consciously manipulated for the sake of ends, practical and mundane, which are in truth its byproducts, then a threat to the substance of faith arises. The benefits of religious faith for the individual's psychological well-being and for community solidarity are derivative; when they become central goals of religious activities and institutions, then a significant transformation and corruption of religious life has taken place. In fact, the derivative functions themselves are undermined. As a former Archbishop of Canterbury said, "The man who says his prayers may sleep better at night, but not if that is why he says them." Instrumentalism can lead to the secularizing of religion and the withering away of its interior substance. Religion is inherently non-manipulative and nonulitilarian and instrumentalism will destroy it. Louis Schneider's discussion of the problems involved illustrates the strains and tensions that are a constant element in the life of institutional religion.

the sanctification of an unjust
social order

fifteen

The Religious Promise of Caste

MAX WEBER

...Hinduism is unusually tolerant of doctrine (mata) while placing greatest emphasis on ritual duties (dharma). Nevertheless, Hinduism has certain dogmas—to be discussed presently—if by dogma one means credal truths whose denial is considered heretical and places the group if not the individual outside the Hindu community.

Hinduism recognizes first of all a number of official systems of doctrine. We shall discuss them briefly later in a survey of the salvation religions of the intellectual strata. Here we are interested only in the fact that heterodox doctrines do exist. Two are particularly mentioned in the literature: the philosophy of the materialists and that of the Bauddhas (Buddhists).

What, specifically, makes Buddhism heterodox? Certainly not the rejection of Brahmanical authority

Reprinted with permission of The Macmillan Company from *The Religion of India* by Max Weber, trans. and ed. by Hans H. Gerth and Don Martindale. Copyright 1958 by The Free Press, a Corporation.

since this is found also among Hindu castes. The admission of all castes to salvation is also found among the Hindus. The recruitment by Buddhism of monks from all castes might have turned it into a ritually impure sect-caste. The rejection of the Vedas and Hindu ritual as without value for salvation, however, was a greater gravamen. The Buddhists established their own *dharma* which in parts was more severe than that of the Brahmans. And they are reproached not only for their ritualistic casteless-ness but also for their heretical teaching, regardless of whether this was the true reason for denying them recognition as Hindus.

What was the heresy of the Buddhists and what does it have in common with the heresy of the materialists in opposition to the teaching of the orthodox schools? The Buddhists, like the materialists, denied the existence of the soul, at least, as a unity of the "I." (For the time being we use the term "soul" in a quite provisional and undifferentiated way, hence without regard to the fact that Hindu philosophy developed several metaphysical conceptions of the nature of the soul.) The denial of the belief in a soul had for the

Buddhists—and, indeed, at the decisive point to be mentioned presently —an almost purely theoretical significance. Yet the decisive (theoretical) impulse (for the development of the heresy) was apparently located here. For Hindu philosophy and all that one can designate as "religion" of the Hindu beyond pure ritualism depends on the belief in the soul.

All Hindus accept two basic principles: the *samsara* belief in the transmigration of souls and the related *karman* doctrine of compensation. These alone are the truly "dogmatic" doctrines of all Hinduism, and in their very interrelatedness they represent the unique Hindu theodicy of the existing social, that is to say, caste system.

The belief in the transmigration of souls (*samsara*) grew directly out of universally diffused representations of the fate of the spirit after death. It appears elsewhere in the world, for example, in Hellenic antiquity. In India the fauna and an existence of different colored races may have facilitated the origin of the idea. It is quite probable that the "army of monkeys" which, according to the *Ramayana,* appeared in South India, was in fact an army of dark Dravidians. Rightly or wrongly it appears that apes and men were thought to be all and that this idea suggested South India, the seat of black peoples, who looked like apes to the Aryans.

Originally, the departed soul was as little viewed as "immortal" in India as elsewhere. The death sacrifice was intended to put the souls at rest and allay their envy and wrath against the fortunate living. The residence of the "fathers" remained problematical. According to the Brahmanas they faced death by starvation without sacrifice. Sacrifice, therefore, was considered to be the

primary merit. Occasionally, also, one wished the gods a long life and increasingly the assumption appears that the existence of neither gods nor men is eternal in the next world.[1]

When the Brahmans began to speculate about their fate, there gradually appeared the teaching of a "second death" leading the dying spirit or god into another existence. The idea that this existence was also on earth was joined to the concept of "animal souls" which probably existed in India as elsewhere. With this the basic elements of the teaching were given.

The connecting of the doctrine of transmigration of souls with that of compensation for good and evil deeds in the form of a more or less honorable rebirth is not exclusively Indian, but is found elsewhere, for example, among the Hellenes. However, two principles are characteristic of Brahman rationalism which determined the pervasive significance of the doctrinal turn: (1) it was believed that each single ethically relevant act has inevitable consequences for the fate of the actor, hence that no consequence can be lost; the doctrine of *karma;* (2) the idea of compensation was linked to the individual's social fate in the societal organization and thereby to the caste order. All (ritual or ethical) merits and faults of the individual formed a sort of ledger of accounts; the balance irrefutably determined the fate of the soul at rebirth, and this in exact proportion to the surplus of one or other side of the ledger.

In India, belief in destiny, astrology, and horoscope-casting were

---

[1] See S. Boyer, *Journal Asiatique* (1901), Serie 18. Concerning "repeated deaths" see especially H. Oldenberg, *Die Lehre der Upanishaden und die Anfänge des Buddhismus* (Göttingen, 1915).

widely diffused for a long time. On closer inspection it seems that the horoscope might well indicate man's fate, but that *karma* determined the good or evil significance of the constellation for the individual. There could be no "eternal" reward or punishment for the individual; such, indeed, would be entirely out of proportion to finite doings. One can stay in heaven or hell only for a finite period.

In general, both heaven and hell play a secondary role in Indian thought. Originally, heaven for the Hindus was probably only a Brahman and warrior heaven. Moreover, hell could be avoided by the blackest sinner through the most convenient purely ritualistic means—the speaking of a certain formula in the hour of death, even when this was spoken by others (even unknowingly and by the enemy).

There was however no sort of ritual means and in general no (inner-worldly) deed which would allow one to escape rebirth and second death. The universal representation that sickness, infirmity, poverty—in short all that was feared in life—resulted from one's own conscious or unconscious, magically relevant failings was here elaborated into the view that man's fate was his own doing. Appearances all too clearly contributed the idea that ethical compensation comes to each life here and now. The idea of metempsychosis had been developed; close at hand was the conception that merits and failings of past lives determine present life and those of the present life determine one's fate in future lives on earth. This conception was evidently developed by the Brahmans at first as an esoteric doctrine. That man was bound in an endless sequence of ever new lives and deaths and he determines his own fate solely by his deeds—this was the most consistent form of the *karma* doctrine.

To be sure, the sources, particularly inscriptions on monuments, indicate that this was not always consistently maintained. The traditional death sacrifice insofar as it aimed at influencing the dead contradicted this. As in Christendom we find prayers, sacrifices, donations, and construction of buildings in order to raise the merits and improve the future fate of one's ancestors. However, such residues of different conceptions did not alter the fact that the individual was continuously and primarily concerned with the question of how to improve his fate of rebirth. The inscription indeed shows this. One brings sacrifices and establishes foundations to be reborn into similarly good or better circumstances; for example, to be born again with the same wife or same children; princes wish to reappear in the future in a similar respectable position on earth. And here is to be found the decisive interrelation with the caste order.

The very caste situation of the individual is not accidental. In India the idea of the "accident of birth" so critical of society is almost completely absent. The idea of "accident of birth" is common to traditionalistic Confucians and occidental social reformists. The Indian views the individual as born into the caste merited by conduct in a prior life. The individual Hindu is actually believed to have used or failed to use "foresight" in the choice of his caste, though not of his "parents" as the German joke has it. An orthodox Hindu confronted with the deplorable situation of a member of an impure caste would only think that he has a great many sins to redeem from his prior existence. (Blunt, in the Census Report of 1911, reports an expression of distinguished Hindus to this effect, with reference to the Chamar.) The reverse of this is that a member of an impure caste thinks primarily of how to better his future social opportunities at rebirth by leading an exemplary life according to caste ritual. In this life there is no escape from the caste, at least, no way to move up in the caste order. The inescapable on-rolling *karma* causality is in harmony with the eternity of the world, of life, and, above all, the caste order.

No true Hindu doctrine knows of a "last day." Widely diffused doctrines maintain that there are epochs in which the world, like the Germanic *Götterdämmerung,* returns to chaos, but only to begin another cycle. The gods are as little immortal as men. Indeed, some teachings maintain that a god such as Indra, for example, is but a name for changing and exchangeable personalities. An especially virtuous man may, indeed, be reborn as a god such as Indra. The fact that the devout individual Hindu usually did not realize the grandiose presuppositions of *karma* doctrine as a whole is irrelevant for their practical effect which is our concern.

Karma doctrine transformed the world into a strictly rational, ethically-determined cosmos; it represents the most consistent theodicy ever produced by history. The devout Hindu was accursed to remain in a structure which made sense only in this intellectual context; its consequences burdened his conduct. The *Communist Manifesto* concludes with the phrase "they (the proletariat) have nothing to lose but their chains, they have a world to win." The same holds for the pious Hindu of low castes. He too can "win the world," even the heavenly world; he can become a Kashtriya, a Brahman, he can gain Heaven and become a god—only not in this life, but in the life of the future after rebirth into the same world pattern.

Order and rank of the castes is eternal (according to doctrine) as the course of the stars and the difference between animal species and the human race. To overthrow them would be senseless. Rebirth can drag man down into the life of a "worm in the intestine of a dog," but, according to his conduct, it might raise and place him into the womb of a queen and Brahman's daughter. Absolute prerequisites, however, were strict fulfillment of caste obligations in this present life, the shunning of ritually sacrilegious yearning for renouncing caste. The commandment "let every man abide in the same calling"—eschatologically motivated in early Christendom—and lasting devotion to one's calling were anchored in the Hindu promise of rebirth and more firmly than in any other "organicist" social ethic. For Hinduism did not join occupational stability to teachings of the moral nature of the person's vocational stability and humble modesty, as do patriarchal forms of Christendom, but to the individual's very personal interest in salvation.

Hinduism is characterized by a dread of the magical evil of innovation. Even today the Indian jute peasant can hardly be moved to fertilize the land because it is "against custom."[2] In addition to this Hinduism places its supreme premium upon caste loyalty. The salvation doctrine of Hinduism promises rebirth as a king, noble, etc., according to present caste rank to the artisan who in his work abides by prescribed traditions, never demands overpay,

---

[2] V. Delden, *Die Indische Jute-Industrie* (1915), p. 179.

never deceives as to quality. In the often cited principle of classical teaching: "It is better to fulfill one's (caste) duty even without reward than someone else's no matter how excellently, for therein always lies danger." The neglect of one's caste duties out of high pretensions unfailingly is disadvantageous in the present or future life.

It is difficult to imagine more traditionalistic ideas of professional virtues than those of Hinduism. Estranged castes might stand beside one another with bitter hatred—for the idea that everybody had "deserved" his own fate, did not make the good fortune of the privileged more enjoyable to the underprivileged. So long as the *karma* doctrine was unshaken, revolutionary ideas or progressivism were inconceivable. The lowest castes, furthermore, had the most to win through ritual correctness and were least tempted to innovations. Hinduism's particularly strong traditionalism finds its explanation also in the great promises which indeed were at stake for the lowly caste whenever the members deviated from their caste.

It was impossible to shatter traditionalism, based on caste ritualism anchored in *karma* doctrine, by rationalizing the economy. In this eternal caste world, the very gods in truth, constituted a mere caste—to be sure, superior to the Brahmans, but as we shall see later—inferior to the sorcerers who through asceticism were provided with magical power. Anyone who wished to emancipate himself from this world and the inescapable cycle of recurrent births and deaths had to leave it altogether —to set out for that unreal realm to which Hindu "salvation" leads. More will be said later about this Indian concept of salvation. We must first consider a different problem.

Developmental Conditions of the Caste System

Peculiar to Hinduism is the combination of *karma* theodicy—to be found elsewhere—with the caste structure. Granted this the question is: from whence is this caste order, found nowhere or only incipiently elsewhere, and why, of all things, in India?

In view of the numerous disagreements among even the most distinguished Indologists and the reservation that accordingly only guesses are possible, some previous observations may be developed further. Obviously, mere occupational stratification per se could not give birth to such sharp segregations. The origin of the castes in liturgical organization is neither demonstrable nor probable. The great number of originally ethnic castes, moreover, indicates that occupational differentiation alone is not a sufficient explanation however great its contribution may have been. That ethnic factors alongside status and economic factors were important for the formation of castes is beyond doubt.

The attempt has been made more or less radically to simply equate caste stratification with racial differences. The eldest term for "status," (*varna*) means "color." Tradition often distinguishes the castes by typical skin color: Brahmans, white; Kshatriyas, red; Vaishyas, yellow, Shudras, black. Anthropometric researches, especially those of Risley, have yielded typical degrees of anthropometric differences by caste. Hence correlation has been established. However, one should not assume that the caste order could be explained as a product of "race psychology"—by mysterious tendencies inherent in the "blood" or the "Indian soul." Nor can one assume that caste is the expression of antagonism of different racial types or produced by a "racial repulsion" inherent "in the blood," or of differential "gifts" and fitness for the various caste occupations inherent "in the blood."

Such notions also creep into the discussion of the North American Negro problems. With reference to the alleged "natural" antipathy of races it has been rightly pointed out that several million mixed bloods represent a sufficient refutation of this alleged "natural" strangeness. Indian blood is at least as strange if not more so, yet, every Yankee seeks to trace Indian blood in his pedigree. If the chieftain's daughter Pocohontas were responsible for the existence of all those Americans who wish to stem from her, she must have had as many children as August the Strong.

At best we can say that race or, better, the juxtaposition of racial differences and—this is sociologically decisive—of externally striking different racial types has been quite important for the development of the caste order in India.[3] But one must see this in proper causal interrelation.

Only the antagonism of the *Arya* and the *Dasyu* appears in the ancient Vedic period. The name *Arya* remains as a term for the distinguished, the "gentleman." The *Dasyu* was the dark colored enemy of the invading conqueror; his civilization, presumably at least, was on the same plane. The *Dasyu* had castles and a political organization. Like all peoples from China to Ireland the Aryan tribes then lived through their epic period of charioteering, castle-dwelling knights. This knighthood is technically called *Maghavan,* dispensers of gifts. The knights were named by singers and wizards dependent upon their gifts, praising the donator, deriding and attempting magically to damage the stingy. Among the Aryans these singers and wizards played a powerful and in time apparently increasingly important role. "We and the Maghavan," "our Maghavan" were phrases by which the sorcerers affixed themselves to the knights. Their magic was thought to contribute a great deal to victory. In the period of the Brahmanas and epics magic mounted in importance to unheard-of proportions.

Originally, the transition between the warrior and priestly (Rishi) gentes was free. In the epics, however, the king Visvamitha had to practice asceticism for thousands of years until the gods, in fear of his magical powers, endowed him with Brahman quality. The prayer of the Brahman procured victory for the king. Like a tower the Brahman overshadowed the king. He was not only a ritualistic "superman," but his power equalled that of the gods, and a king without a Brahman is simply said to be "without guidance" for guidance by the *purohita* was self-understood. Reality often contradicted these claims. In areas conquered by the knights during the early Middle Ages—of pre-Buddhistic times—the present-day Bihar, the knightly community (Kshatriya) did not think of recognizing the Brahmans as their peers.

At first the great patrimonial Hindu kingdoms used the Brahmans in support of their legitimation interest. Then the Islamic conquest smashed the politico-military power

---

[3] As late as the twelfth century the ethnic boundary between Arians and Dravids at the Intraviti is expressed in the different languages of the inscriptions. The administration retained the division. Yet, a place for people who "came from everywhere," hence represented an ethnic mixture was granted for a temple, *Epigraphia Indica,* Vol. IX, p. 313.

of the Kshatriya but sustained the Brahmans as an instrument of social control. The pretensions of the Brahmans in classical literature and the law books were then stereotyped.

There were a number of reasons for the channelization of priestly power into the caste system. Ethnic antagonism takes form with respect to contrasts of external bearing and way of life of various social groups. The most striking contrasts in external appearance simply happens to be different skin color. Although the conquerors replenished their insufficient supply of women by taking women from among the conquered, color differences still prevented a fusion in the manner of the Normans and Anglo-Saxons.

Distinguished families the world over make it their honor to admit only their peers for courting their daughters while the sons are left to their own devices in satisfying their sexual needs. Here and not in mythical "race instinct" or unknown differences of "racial traits" we reach the point at which color differences matter. Intermarriage with despised subjects never attained full social recognition. The mixture, at least from a sexual union, of upper-class daughters with sons of the lower stratum remained socially scorned. This stable barrier was reenforced by magical dread. It led to the elevation of the importance of birthright, of clan charisma, in all areas of life.

We noted that under the sway of animistic beliefs positions are usually linked to the possession of magical charisma, particularly power positions of a sacerdotal and secular nature. But the artisan's craft in India soon tended to become clan charismatic, finally it became "hereditary." This phenomena—found elsewhere—nowhere appears so strongly as in India. This was the nucleus of the caste formation for those positions and professions. In conjunction with a number of external circumstances this led to the formation of true castes. Charismatic sibs and phratries occupied the conquered land, settled in villages, reduced the conquered to rent-payers or village artisans, agricultural or industrial workers, referred them to the outskirts and *Wurthen,* or into special helot and craftsman villages.

Soon, however, workers from industrial pariah tribes settled outside the villages. The conquerors retained the "right to the land" in a manner similar to the Spartans, as the right to assign a rent-yielding landlot (*kleros*).

In order to understand the process of caste formation one should constantly keep in mind the external resemblance of the situation of the Indian village artisan and of conquered tribes to the place of the helots in the Spartan state regardless of how great the difference was in other respects. The village-dwelling sibs of the conquerors and the conquered stood opposite one another as collectivities. Personal slavery lost importance in view of the fact that the subject (Shudra) indeed was a servant, but in principle, not a servant of a single individual, but of the community of the "twice-born."

The conqueror found some presumably quite considerable industrial development among the conquered people. These industries and the sale of products, however, did not develop into local specializations centered around the market and city, but, in reverse, transformed the economy from one of self-sufficient households to production for sale by way of interlocal and interethnic professional specialization. We know the equivalent in primitive form, for example, from von der Steinen's description of Brazil and other studies. The individual tribe, tribal division, or village as a special group engages in tribal industry for markets, producing a special export product, selling the accumulated surplus products of their domestic industry. This may be facilitated by the near location of raw materials, rivers and other means of communication, by the accidental acquisition of a skill and its subsequent hereditary and secret transmission. The trained specialists turn into journeymen and settle as guest workers temporarily, finally permanently in foreign communities. Such interethnic division of labor appears in very different continents and areas. Of course, considerable vestiges are to be found also in antiquity and the medieval Occident.

The continued predominance of interethnic specialization in India was due to the weak development of cities and urban markets. For centuries the markets were represented by princely castles and peasant villages. In their villages, the conquerors preserved their sib cohesion even after they became completely rusticated. This was due to the "racial" antagonisms which provided effective support for clan charisma.

In its initial stages patrimonial fiscalism reinforced this development. Fiscal authorities found it convenient, on the one hand, to have dealings with only a single responsible taxpayer; on the other, to hold the full village associates jointly responsible for tax payments. Fiscal authorities turned first to the old conqueror villages, accepting a guarantee of the tax payment through the joint liability of all full village associates and leaving distribution and disposition over ploughland to their discretion. It is probable though not ascertainable that subject tribes engaging in special industrial activities had to pay

tributes in lump sums—this would have stabilized the traditional structure of crafts.

All cities were fortresses of the realm. Guest workers settled in and around them and were placed liturgically, hence usually hereditarily, under a princely supervisor. The artisans consisted of bondsmen restricted to special occupations, leagues of guest workers sharing joint tax liability, or industrial tribes. The fiscal interest of the patrimonial administration in license fees and excise taxes led, indeed, as noted, to a sort of urban market policy similar to that of the Occident. The development of urban industries, particularly urban price work, stimulated the emergence of merchant and craft guilds and finally of guild confederations. These, however, comprised only small islands surrounded by an ocean of village artisan cotters, of tribal industries, of guest trades. By and large, industrial specialization was bound to the developing guest peoples. In the cities, however, racial and ethnic strangeness of guest artisans led to the segregation of the groups from one another and prevented the multitude of craftsmen from organizing in the manner of the occidental *popolo*. And, finally, nowhere did the fraternization of the citizens per se produce a highly developed military force in the manner of the *polis* of antiquity and the city of the south European medieval Occident. Instead, princely overlords directly stepped into the place of the knights, and they were religiously pacifistic due to the politically neutral character of Indian salvation religions.

With the overthrow of the guilds by the princes, incipient urban developments of occidental stamp were destroyed. Allying themselves with the Brahmans, the patrimonial princes, in accord with the continental nature of India, relied upon the rural organizations as sources for armies and taxes. In rural areas, however, division of labor by guest peoples and old village artisan cotters remained the main line of development. The cities brought only an increase in the number of trades and the establishment of rich merchant and price workers' guilds. In accordance with the *jajmani* principle, the Brahmans and village artisans established a quota regulation of subsistence opportunities and the hereditary appropriation of patronage. Once again the universally accepted principle of clan charisma supported developments. The princely grants of interlocal trade monopolies led in the same direction, for these too were unusually granted to marginal trading peoples. Sib and village exogamy, endogamy of guest tribes, the permanent, mutual segregation of guest peoples sanctioned by ritual and worship, never shattered by religious fraternities of autonomous citizenries ruling the country—all these gave the Brahmans the opportunity to stereotype religiously the given order in terms of ritualistic regulation.

The Brahmans' interest was to sustain their power position which grew out of their ancient monopoly of magical qualities, the means of coercion, and the requisite training and education. Princely prerogatives supplied the Brahmans with the means to suppress the heterodox salvation religions of the urban citizenry, the aspirations of the distinguished merchant and craft guilds. The guilds had often restrained or newly established non-Brahmanical tribal or professional priests who claimed Brahman rank. The Brahmans defined the autonomy of these associations as usurpation and suppressed them.

The importance of these urban developments is indicated in the very means used by the contemporary anti-Brahmanical, genteel bourgeois castes. First, they aim at abolishing participation in the official temple cult and at restricting themselves to the house-cult. This gives the individual opportunity to choose an agreeable Brahman, thereby, a powerful coercive weapon of the princes and Brahmans (hence a sort of "interdict"), the closing of the temple is voided. A second, more radical means of revolt against Brahmanical authority is to train priests from members of one's own caste and employ them in place of Brahmans. A third consists in the anti-Brahmanical tendency to settle caste affairs, including ritualistic ones, through the *panchayats,* or finally, to settle them in modern caste meetings instead of turning to a *pandit* or a *math* (monastery) for their solutions.

The development of a stratum of magicians into a charismatic estate is, indeed, not peculiar to India. Inscriptions from Hellenic antiquity (Milet) occasionally report a guild of holy dancers as an estate in power. However, there was no room on the soil of *polis* fraternization for the mutual and general religious and ritualistic estrangement of guest artisans and tribes.

Purely professional, hence freely recruited traders and craftsmen occurred only spottily in India and remained dependent on conformism with the ritualistic usages prevalent among the multitude. Such conformism was supported by ritualistic closure guaranteed to vocational associations, the legitimate monopolization of their subsistence opportunities. As in the Occident, patrimonial bureaucracy did not at first hinder, but rather promoted, the closure of trades and guilds. In the first place, the administration's policy was merely to substitute some interlocal association for purely local monopolies of the city economy. The second stage of occidental princely politics, however, namely, the alliance of the princes with capital in order to increase their power against the outside, was out of the question in India because of its continental character and the value of the land tax which could be raised *ad libidum*.

At the time of guild power the princes were financially quite dependent on them. However, the unmilitary urban stratum was in no position to resist princely power once the prince tired of what seemed to him an outrageous dependency and when he financed the costs of administration by substitution of tax liturgies for capitalistic tax farming. With the aid of the Brahmans, princely patrimonialism successfully mastered the guild citizenry which was at times powerful. Brahmanical theory served in an unequalled manner to tame the subjects religiously. Finally, the invasion and domination of foreign conquerors benefited the power monopoly of the Brahmans. The foreign conquerors divested the most important competitors of the Brahmans of all power because it conceived them to be politically dangerous. Thus the knighthood and the residue of urban guilds were reduced.

The power of the Brahmans, on the other hand, grew during the time of the conquerors. After a period of fanatical iconoclasm and Islamic propaganda, the conqueror resigned himself to accept the continued existence of Hindu culture. Indeed, priestly power under foreign domination always serves as a refuge for the conquered and as a tool of domestication for the foreign overlords.

With the increasing stabilization of economic conditions the ritually segregated guest and pariah tribes were more and more integrated into the expanding caste order which thus became the dominant system. For a thousand years, from the second century of our era to the beginning of Islamic rule, we find the caste system in an irresistible and ever-continued expansion, slowed down through the propaganda of Islamism. As a closed system, the caste order is a product of consistent Brahmanical thought and could never have come to power without the intensive influence of the Brahmans as house priests, respondents, father confessors, advisors in all life situations, and princely officials whose writing skill brought them into increasing demand with the rise of bureaucratic administration.

Ancient Indian conditions, however, provided the structural elements for the caste system: the interethnic specialization of labor, the development of innumerable guest and pariah peoples, the organization of village crafts on the basis of hereditary artisan cotters, the monopoly of internal trade by guest trades, the small extent of urban development, and the flow of occupational specialization into the channels of hereditary status segregation and monopolization of patronage. Likewise the secondary beginnings of liturgical and fiscal organization of occupations by the princes, and their strong interest in legitimacy and domestication of the subjects encouraged an alliance with the Brahmans and the joint preservation and stabilization by prince and Brahman of the established sacred order of Indian society.

All factors important for the development of the caste system operated singly elsewhere in the world. Only in India, however, did they operate conjointly under special Indian conditions: the conditions of a conquered territory within ineffable, sharp, "racial" antagonisms made socially visible by skin color. More strongly than anywhere else, magical as well as social rejection of communion with strangers was called forth. This helped preserve the charisma of distinguished sibs and established insurmountable barriers between strange ethnic subject tribes, guest and pariah peoples and their overlords even after definitive integration of guest and pariah peoples into the local economic community.

Individual acceptance for apprenticeship, participation in market deals, or citizenship—all these phenomena of the West either failed to develop in the first place or were crushed under the weight first of ethnic, later of caste fetters.

We repeat, however: this well-integrated, unique social system could not have originated or at least could not have conquered and lasted without the pervasive and all-powerful influence of the Brahmans. It must have existed as a finished idea long before it conquered even the greater part of North India. The combination of caste legitimacy with *karma* doctrine, thus with the specific Brahmanical theodicy—in its way a stroke of genius—plainly is the construction of rational ethical thought and not the product of any economic "conditions." Only the wedding of this thought product with the empirical social order through the promise of rebirth gave this order the irresistible power over thought and hope of members and furnished the fixed scheme for the religious and social integration of the various professional groups and pariah peoples.

Where the connection between the theodicy and social order is lacking, indeed—as in the case of Indian Islam—the caste order can be assimilated externally but it remains a *caput mortuum,* fit to stabilize status difference, to represent economic interests through the borrowed *panchayat,* and, above all, to adapt men to the constraint of the social environment; but it is devoid of the "spirit" which nourishes this order on its native soil. On Islamic ground this order could not have emerged; nor does it exert marked influence over the "vocational ethic" similar to that of the Hindu professional castes. The Census Reports[4] plainly show that the Islamic castes lack some of the most important characteristics of the Hindu caste system, especially ritualistic defilement through commensalism with non-members—even though commensalism and social intercourse among different social strata may be avoided and rather rigidly so, as is often the case, after all, in Western society. Ritual defilement, however, must be lacking; the religious equality before Allah of all who profess the prophet precludes it. Endogamy, to be sure, exists but with far less intensity. Properly understood, the so-called Islamic castes are essentially status groups and not castes. Furthermore, the specific anchoring of the vocational ethic in caste is lacking; missing, too, is the authority of the Brahman.

The prestige of the Brahmans which was behind the developing caste system is in part purely magical and in part cultural—deriving from the fact that as a stratum the Brahmans represented a special quality and distinct cultivation. We have still to examine the peculiarity of Brahmanical education and its underlying conditions.

There is a further reason for examining the peculiarities of Brah-

---

4 See the Census Report for Bengal (1911), Part I, para. 958, p. 495.

manical education. The caste system and *karma* doctrine place the individual within a clear circle of duties and offer him a well-rounded, metaphysically-satisfying conception of the world. However certain and unambiguous this ethically rational world order might present itself, the individual, once he raised the question of the "meaning" of his life in this compensatory mechanism, could experience it as dreadful.

The world and its cosmic social order was eternal and individual life but one of a series of the lives of the same soul. Such lives recur *ad infinitum:* therefore, any one in the last analysis is a matter of complete indifference. The Indian representation of life and the world prefers the image of an eternally rolling "wheel" of rebirths—which by the way, as Oldenberg has observed, also is to be found occasionally in Hellenic philosophy.

It is no accident that India has produced no historiography to speak of. The interest in historically unique forms of political and social relations was far too weak for a man contemplating life and its passage. It is sometimes maintained that alleged Indian "passivity" derives from a climatically determined "enervation."

This belief is completely unfounded. India has been permanently involved in a state of ferocious warfare and unbridled lust of relentless conquest as no land on earth. However, to any thoughtful and reflective person, life destined to eternal repetition could readily appear completely senseless and unbearable.

It is important to realize that it was not primarily the dread of ever-new life on this earth which is after all so beautiful. Rather it was dread of the ever-new and ineluctable death. Ever and again the soul was enmeshed in the business of living and the heart enchained to things and, above all, to dear ones. Ever again it must be senselessly torn from them through rebirth to be entangled in unknown relations to face the same fate. Such repeated death was truly dreadful. One can hardly fail to feel this and to be moved by the pathos when reading between the lines of the inscriptions the preachings of Buddha and other redeemers.

All salvation religions of Hinduism are addressed to one common question: how can man escape from the wheel of rebirth and thereby ever new death? How is salvation possible from eternally new death and therefore salvation from life?

The Role of Religion

GUNNAR MYRDAL

Understood in this realistic and comprehensive sense, religion usually acts as a tremendous force for social

Myrdal, Gunnar, *Asian Drama: An Inquiry into the Poverty of Nations.* © 1968 by The Twentieth Century Fund, New York.

inertia. The writer knows of no instance in present-day South Asia where religion has induced social change. Least of all does it foster realization of the modernization ideals—though, of course, appeals to religious principles on the "higher" level can be used for, as well as against, those ideals, while cruder religious conceptions can be exploited to incite people to resistance or to demonstrations, riots, and lynchings. From a planning point of view, this inertia related to religion, like other obstacles, must be overcome by policies for inducing changes, formulated in a plan for development. But the religiously sanctioned beliefs and valuations not only act as obstacles among the people to getting the plan accepted and effectuated but also as inhibitions in the planners themselves insofar as they share them, or are afraid to counteract them.

Among the masses, these traditional beliefs that with their related valuations have religious sanction are normally irrational, for they are superstitious and imply a mystical rather than a logical way of thinking. Religious conceptions to that degree irrational have not commonly been held in the West for centuries. To a considerably lesser extent, irrational beliefs sanctioned by religion are also present among the educated class, including its intellectual elite. Even Islam and Buddhism, which at the rarefied "higher" level are so rational and free from iconism and magic, have, in the forms in which they actually influence life and social relations, become demonological and permeated by taboos, magic, and mysticism. In particular, social and economic stratification is accorded the sanction of religion. The attitudes, institutions, and modes of living and working that make up and are reflected in this stratification do constitute very real inhibitions and obstacles to planning and the execution of plans. Considerable differences exist among the countries of the region, but in general the inherited stratification implies low social and spatial mobility, little free competition in its wider sense, and great inequalities. This system of social relations is the product of history and is strongly supported by custom in traditional society; religious beliefs and valuations furnish the emotional support. It is evidence of the stability and strength of this social and economic stratification that it is not commonly challenged by the underprivileged and exploited lower strata but is generally considered by them to be natural and right—a fate ordained by the gods and the whole paraphernalia of supernatural forces. It is this feeling, for instance, that restrains the untouchables in India from pressing into the temples and using the wells of the higher castes.

In India, K. M. Panikkar was one of many enlightened Hindus who have tried to strip institutions such as caste and the subordinate status of women of their religious protection by stressing that Hinduism, as expressed by the scriptures since ancient times, does not sanction them; he concluded that "every kind of custom however poisonous, came to be tolerated and received sanction under the cover of [Hindu] religion."[1] Primary among the modernization ideals is the quest for rationality; hence efforts to realize these ideals conflict with religion, not necessarily or even ordinarily on the "higher" level, but religion as it exists among the people. Even aside from the factor of inertia, implying that the social and economic *status quo* has religious sanction, the permeation of religion, as it is commonly experienced, by irrational views and illogical thinking is inimical to the spread of the modernization ideals and to their realization by planning for development and the effectuating of plans.

An important problem for research is whether, to what extent, and how

---

[1] K. M. Panikkar, *Hindu Society at Cross Roads,* Asia Publishing House, Bombay, 1955, p. 40.

fast, secularization is diminishing the force of this source of social inertia and irrationality, as a result of the spread of the modernization ideals and of planning and other social and economic changes. Probably, secularization varies in amount and speed both for different social groups and for the several countries in South Asia.[2] It should be noted that from the point of view of the modernization ideals what is needed is merely the eradication of the ballast of irrational beliefs and related valuations. As pointed out in Section 2, no religion on the "higher" level need be in conflict with the modernization ideals. But as religion is part and parcel of the whole complex of people's beliefs and valuations, their modes of living and working, and their institutions, it needs to be reformed in order to break down inhibitions and obstacles to development.[3]

---

[2] W. Norman Brown asserts that secularization all over the Indian peninsula had proceeded fast even in British times and that "With both Hindus and Muslims religion and magic are contracting into narrower and more sharply defined boundaries...Within the cities Brahmans are called upon less frequently for prayers and ceremonies in times of illness and misfortune. Brahmans add that in the cities witchcraft has come to hold fewer terrors for the populace, magicians are less patronized, and their own antidotes are less in demand. Muslims say that charm workers have fewer customers...urban temples and shrines seemed less frequented than in 1922 or 1928 or 1935." The observations he records are, however, qualified by the statement that they all refer to cities and towns: "There is no reason to think that any great change has taken place in the villages." (*The United States and India and Pakistan,* Oxford University Press, Oxford, 1955, pp. 50–51.) An eminent Indian sociologist, M. N. Srinivas, states in the same vein: "Indians are still, by and large, a religious people, but large areas of life are becoming secularised," Contrary to Brown, he holds, however, that "pilgrimages have become more popular than ever before," and that the "demand for the services of the Brahmin priest is increasing among castes which hitherto did not resort to him." (M. N. Srinivas, "Changing Attitudes in India Today," *Yojana,* October 1, 1961, pp. 27–28.) As he attributes the former change to the development of communications and the latter to the "Sanskritization," meaning the imitating in lower castes of the rituals, customs, and way of life of the Brahmans, there need not be a contradiction implied. The general question whether, how fast, and with what differences for the several countries and social and economic strata a secularization is taking place in South Asia, has not been made an object of scientific research. An example of the type of generalizing judgment that needs to be tested by empirical research, and that in this case relates broadly to "ancient civilizations," is an article by A. Vanistendael, "Thinking about Asia," in *World Justice,* Vol. I (1959–1960), No. 1, September, 1959, p. 73:

"There are the ancient rites and old customs, to be sure, but these are mere gestures and customs. The political leaders and the intellectuals no longer believe in the absolute secret value of these rites and traditions. Do the young ones still believe in them with all the strength which is necessary for a favorable evolution? Again, I very much doubt it. The intellectuals whom I met are certainly very much permeated with Western ideas. Do they still consider themselves as Orientals differing from us in other ways over and above the opposition existing between them and us as whites, as Europeans, as Americans? Have they not become a rather sceptical group, a group of agnostics, who are forced to follow the current of customs and traditions, of social pressures the importance whereof is very rapidly increasing?"

[3] "The fight against such customs leads directly to the reform of religion. It is significant that every movement for religious reform in free society has been against traditionalism. The breakdown of religious *tabus,* priestly influence and of social practices having a religious sanction has been the noticeable characteristic of the establishment of liberal political institutions on a traditional society. Even in Islamic societies, there has been a notable trend against such institutions as polygamy, seclusion of women and similar customs. The purifying

In India, from the beginning of the nineteenth century a series of religious reformers tried to modernize Hinduism.[4] They were under obvious Western influence and can indeed be regarded as harbingers of the spread of the modernization ideals. Their immediate appeal was to the intellectual elite; their message did not directly reach the masses. And, like other reformers in the same line, they evoked reaction. Gandhi himself was in this great line of religious reformers. By being sympathetic to a purified version of the old beliefs and, in particular, by identifying his message with Indian nationalism in the struggle for independence and coordinating these beliefs with his policy lines in this struggle, he appealed also to strata other than the intellectual elite.

Although recognizing that their basic approach was determined by Western influences, these reformers were able to find support for their ideals in the Hindu scripture from the ancient time of the Vedas; this indeed, became their chief message.[5] They could also point to an ancient ideological lineage of reformers including Buddha. The present-day social reformers in India who, like Panikkar, attach interest to religion, follow this method of attempting to show that pure Hinduism in its original form did not sanction the popular prejudices and social arrangements they now want to change. Occasionally they express themselves as if the Hindu religion had no connection with attitudes, customs, and institutions, and maintain that they are out to reform not religion but society;[6]

---

of religion and the revival of the great religions of the East have gone side by side with the development of liberal ideas in society." (K. M. Panikkar, *Afro-Asian States and Their Problems,* Allen & Unwin Ltd., London, 1959, pp. 94–95.)

4 K. M. Panikkar, *Asia and Western Dominance,* Allen & Unwin Ltd., London, 1955, pp. 321 ff. *et passim.*

5 "As a religion Brahmo Samaj was based firmly on the Vedanta of genuine Hindu tradition, but its outlook on life was neither Christian nor Hindu, but European, and derived its inspiration from the intellectual movements of the eighteenth century.

"Thus it may be said that as early as 1820 India had come into the direct current of European thought and had begun to participate in the ideal. Its social message was Westernization, to purge Hinduism of the customs and superstitions with which it was overlaid, to raise the status of women, to bridge the yawning gulf between popular and higher Hinduism, to fight relentlessly against caste, social taboo, polygamy and other well entrenched abuses. To the educated Hindu, who felt unsettled in mind by the attack of the missionaries, the Brahmo Samaj provided the way out." (K. M. Panikkar, *Asia and Western Dominance,* p. 321.)

"This seemed all the more the right path since the Vedas gave no authority to the usages and superstitions that had come to be accepted by the masses as Hinduism. There was no sanction in the Vedas for caste, for the prohibition of the marriage of widows, for untouchability, for the taboo on food and the other characteristics of popular Hinduism which had been seized upon by the missionaries in their campaign and were being widely rejected by Hindu intellegentsia." (*Ibid.,* p. 323.)

"Ram Mohan Roy and his followers, petitioning for the abolition of *Suttee,* for education in English, for greater freedom for women, though they quote from Hindu scriptures in justification of their reforms, are really thinking in terms of Rousseau, watered down to meet Indian conditions. European inspiration of the Asian reform movements of the first half of the nineteenth century cannot be denied." (*Ibid.,* p. 484.)

6 This was Gandhi's position. "Caste has nothing to do with religion," he said. "It is harmful both to spiritual and national growth." Later Panikkar made himself the principal protagonist for this view:

"The major difficulty of Hinduism which had made it a wild jungle growth of widely varying customs, usages and superstitions was lack of a machinery of reform and unification. The institutions of Hinduism,

this may be good tactics, but it is bad sociology. Religion as a social fact cannot be identified with, and has, indeed, very little relation to, the religion on the "higher" level that they want to preserve.

A remarkable situation has gradually come about in South Asia. First, practically no one is attacking religion.[7] Even the Communists do not take a stand against religion in any of the South Asian countries. In spite of its obvious relevance for all those who want to modernize South Asian society, Marx's declaration that religion is the opium of the people is never quoted. What is insisted on in India and constantly preached by those intellectual leaders who support the modernization ideals is that religion should be relegated to private life; it should not influence those in public life. While occasionally a bow is made to religion in the abstract as a force for creating good citizens— which from their point of view must be contrary to truth, if popular reli-

which in a large measure got identified with the religion itself, were the results of certain historical factors. They were upheld by law and not by religion. Vivekananda put the point well when he wrote: 'Beginning from Buddha down to Ram Mohan Roy, everyone made the mistake of holding caste to be a religious institution... But in spite of all the ravings of the priests, caste is simply a crystallized social institution, which after doing its service is now filling the atmosphere of India with stench.' " (*Ibid.*, p. 327.)

"Among the more enlightened Hindus themselves, at one time this view gained wide acceptance. Most of the reform movements of the last century were, it would be remembered, directed orthodox Hinduism. They proceeded on the assumption that what was necessary was a purification of the Hindu Religion. The Brahmo Samaj, the Arya Samaj and other similar movements, which were started with the laudable object of reforming Hindu society confused the main issue and organised themselves on the basis of a reform of religion. This basic misconception had two very significant results. It aroused the dormant powers of the Hindu religion which called forth from its ancient armoury all its weapons to defend its institutions, right or wrong. Practices which had authority neither in religion nor in tradition, came to be regarded as fundamental. Even the self-immolation of widows, which was never widely prevalent and which certainly had no sanction in religion found its defenders at one time. Secondly, it made even the internal reorganisation of Hindu society difficult as reformers came to be identified with the thought and practice of other religions." (Panikkar, *Hindu Society at Cross Roads*, p. 1.)

"It is a religion giving sustenance to every aspect of human life, and the modification of laws or the abolition of customs will no more adversely affect the religion of Hinduism than the discarding of old and dirty clothes and wearing of clean and new ones affect a man." (*Ibid.*, p. 88.)

"The attack on religion has definitely failed now. Even the most ardent workers in the mission field do not have any longer the hope of converting India to Christianity. Equally decisive has been the failure of movements from inside which aimed at a large-scale reform of religious ideas. Hindu religion has emerged triumphant from the struggle and today does not feel her supremacy challenged from any side. But the problem of the Hindu social organisation has remained materially unchanged except that it has now come to be recognised that its solution does not lie through the machinery of religion. It is the Hindu society that has to be basically reorganised and not Hindu religion." (*Ibid.*, p. 2.)

[7] Nehru was almost alone in publicly admitting agnosticism, though he did not make an issue of it. He had stated in his autobiography, however: "The spectacle of what is called religion, or at any rate organized religion, in India and elsewhere, has filled me with horror." (*An Autobiography*, p. 374.) In his last will and testament he wrote: "I wish to declare with all earnestness that I do not want any religious ceremonies performed for me after my death. I do not believe in any such ceremonies and to submit to them, even as a matter of form, would be hypocrisy and an attempt to delude ourselves and others." (*Indian and Foreign Review*, June 15, 1964, p. 4.) On this point his will was not respected.

gion is meant—the secular character of the state, public institutions, education, politics, and business is constantly stressed. Any division of people according to religious creed is branded as "communalism" and put on a par with "casteism, provincialism, and linguism" as a danger to national consolidation. This position cannot be shared, of course, by the leaders of the communal political parties; yet even they mostly play down the religious issue publicly and use it in an almost underhanded way. The official views, which are a legacy of the liberation movement, do not prevent all political parties, including the Communist Party, from exploiting religious communalism for their own purposes in elections, despite public condemnation of such maneuvers.

The situation is, of course, different in Pakistan, because it was created as an independent state for the Moslems; its Islamic character at first was, however, played down by the military regime that took power in autumn 1958. In Ceylon, the dominant Singhalese group identifies itself openly with Buddhism, while the Tamil minority stresses its Hinduism. In Indonesia, one of the five guiding principles is "belief in God," which to the Moslem majority implies that Indonesia is basically an Islamic country, though this is not much stressed. In Burma, Buddhism was by gradual steps made the state religion; nevertheless, as in all the other countries, religious freedom is an accepted principle. In both Indonesia and Burma there has been what may be called a religious revival. In Indonesia, though not in Burma, this is a reversal of earlier tendencies toward religious skepticism among the intellectuals.

Secondly, there are now very few organized attempts at religious refor-

mation in any South Asian country. In India, there is a definite retreat from the nineteenth century movements to purify Hinduism; a hands-off attitude is observed by the intellectual elite, who do not even carry forward Gandhi's criticism of the filth in the temples and of all the superstitions connected with popular religion.[8] To the progressive rationalists among the intellectual elite in India who are working for modernization, avoidance of any interference with religion, even in its most irrational manifestations, and the relegation of it to private life is the way to achieve progress: let sleeping dogs lie.

These tactics undoubtedly have some pragmatic basis. Important legislative reforms—for instance in regard to family legislation—are being carried out, and support for them is found in the "higher" forms of religion now prevalent among the intellectual elite, while silence is preserved about the fact that popular religion is different. The hope is that through these and other reforms, and through education, religious reformation will take place without a frontal attack. In fact, this ideological and political process started under British rule.[9] There are, however, the urgent

---

[8] Gandhi was in many ways more courageous than later popular leaders; he also upbraided the people for disorderliness and laziness.

[9] "The unifying doctrine was the Vedanta, but the abstract conceptions of this philosophical approach could only appeal to the elite. Popular Hinduism continued in the old way, sectarian, devotional and based on daily rituals. But it also underwent extraordinary changes. The gnarled branches of this ancient tree either fell away by themselves or were chopped off by legislative action promoted by the reformers. Child marriage, which many Hindu communities considered as an essential part of their religion, was abolished by law through the insistence of popular agitation. The remarriage of widows was

problems of whether "communalism" can be eradicated; whether the reform legislation will be observed in practice; whether, more generally, people will change in the way development requires; and whether all these changes will happen rapidly enough, without a deliberate reformation of popular religion that would drive out superstitious beliefs and elevate in their place the cherished rites, philosophical thoughts, and general moral precepts accepted by most of the intellectuals. But there may well be no basis for a reformation of religion, in which case a choice of this alternative to the present tactical policy of the intellectual elite in India could bring about a violent reaction that would spell disaster for all the efforts toward modernization and development.

By characterizing popular religion as a force of inertia and irrationality that sanctifies the whole system of life and work, attitudes and institutions, we are, in fact, stressing an important aspect of underdevelop-

ment, namely, the resistance of that system to planned, induced changes along the lines of the modernization ideals. This wider definition of popular religion by the social scientist is defensible on the ground that any narrower definition is arbitrary and does violence to reality.

It should be noted, however, that not all elements of that system are necessarily irrational from the point of view of the modernization ideals. Some beliefs and practices undoubtedly represent a pragmatic accommodation to actual conditions and are in accord with rational considerations in planning. For example, the ritual washing of the body observed by some castes in India and by groups in other South Asian countries can certainly be a health-protecting custom. It can also be a basis for attempting to educate people to more hygienic habits. Likewise, the vegetarian diet, observed by many in the higher and middle castes in India, particularly in the South, and increasingly by some lower castes, has a justification in terms of planning in a country as poor as India where climate makes the preservation of animal food so difficult and where vegetable crops can be grown that are high in protein and vitamins and cheaper than animal food. Often the positive valuations attached to various elements of the inherited culture in the broad sense of the word are irrelevant from the point of view of the modernization ideals.[10] This is

---

permitted. Social disabilities based on caste vanished by themselves, and the occupational basis of caste-communities was weakened. Temples were thrown open to the untouchables, and in the most orthodox province of Madras, Hindu religious endowments were placed under the control of public bodies. The movement for the regeneration of the depressed classes assumed a national character, and their participation in social and political life became a major factor in the last days of British rule. Popular Hinduism had a more vigorous life than it ever had in the immediately preceding times, but it had in the course of a hundred years changed its character and temper, though it had kept much of its form." (Panikkar, *Asia and Western Dominance,* p. 326.) This account may have an element of truth, though it displays exaggerated optimism on every single point.

---

[10] This is, essentially, what Kingsley Davis means in the following passage:

"First, from any standpoint as fundamental as that which we are pursuing, much of so-called cultural change is irrelevant, because it has little to do with the kinds of national requirements just described. Important social changes may occur while countless cultural elements

true of dress, for instance. An old custom is often based on utilitarian considerations that justify it from a modernization point of view. We now realize that this is true of many of the inherited customs in the construction of buildings.

Other traditional attitudes related to religious beliefs and valuations are not inimical to rational planning in the present stage of development in South Asian countries. Thus, as long as there is so great a scarcity of trained doctors and nurses prepared to serve in the villages, the popular emotional attachment to indigenous systems of medicine is harmless, or even advantageous, especially if public policy is directed to improving the training of the practitioners of these ancient arts of medicine. Furthermore, it has been found that the use of modern medicines and, in particular, inoculation, does not arouse much resistance, for the masses rapidly incorporate the new medications into their old magical way of thinking about illnesses and their cure.

Relatively innocuous too is the belief in astrology and horoscopes, often entertained even by intellectuals. In all South Asian countries one meets politicians, businessmen, doctors, engineers, and experts of every kind who are rational and effective in their particular vocation but hold such beliefs and conduct their private affairs accordingly. And it is never made a public issue. Even when politicians are occasionally moved to arrange public events in accordance with the advice of astrologers, this usually does not greatly upset rational planning. Among the lower strata these beliefs are cruder and probably more important in their life and work, though not too consequential. Nevertheless, a considerable increase in general well-being, productivity, and savings would result if people in all strata spent less money on weddings, funerals, and other social events, to which custom and tradition, usually with some religious sanction, commit them.[11] Un-

---

remain stable. For instance, neither the Russian language nor the Russian tea-drinking habit changes much despite the whole Communist revolution in Russia. Conversely, cultural changes may occur with no significant national or social consequences. Whether women wear skirts or pants, whether they believe in one god or three, smoke pipes or cigarettes, or prefer cubistic to representational art, it is hardly of significance to a nation. Only when such cultural traits take on some kind of national significance may their change become relevant. Then they are important for what they mean not in economic or technological context, but in a ritual or emotional context in which case it is the national or international context that makes them important, not the traits themselves. For this reason, when we approach the subject of change from the standpoint of a systematic discipline—political science, sociology, or economics—we are not faced with the encyclopedic task of talking about the endless variety of 'cultural change.' Our interest lies specifically in *social* change, and with criteria of relevance plainly in view." (Kingsley Davis, *Identification of Fundamental Social Changes which Condition Inter-Nation Relations*, 1958, roneod.)

---

11 "Still greater effort is involved when a change in what may be called social mores is required. An instance is the reduction of expenditure on social events or religious ceremonies. It this were achieved on a large scale, a substantial contribution to capital formation might be made in many rural areas. It is obvious that such an advance depends entirely on educative effort in the widest sense of the term. There have been isolated cases of success in this type of effort in India. For example, among one large semi-aboriginal tribe the alcohol-drink habit was almost eradicated in one area through the efforts of an indigenous social and religious leader. For

necessary family expenditure for social—or, rather, status—purposes is paralleled by extravagance in official functions in all South Asian countries.

As a whole, however, this combination of attitudes, institutions, and customary modes of living and working, sanctioned by popular religion, creates a tremendous weight of social and political inertia, which planning for development must try to lift. And the irrational elements in people's thinking about themselves and society erect a wall of confusion that makes the very idea of planning difficult to disseminate rapidly and effectively. After all the diligent efforts to popularize the Indian development plans, one wonders how much has taken hold in the minds of villagers and slum dwellers, and how this thinking in terms of planning, if transmitted, has been molded by the transference. Among the educated and the intellectuals the irrationality inherent in traditional thinking undoubtedly contributes to the relative lack of interest in facts and straight reasoning from facts that has been commonly observed as a regional characteristic.

A most important general problem for investigation is whether whatever attitudes, institutions, and modes of living and working should prove to be peculiarly South Asian are primarily a function of South Asian poverty and low levels of living including poor educational facilities. For instance, the survival-mindedness of the people, their unresponsiveness to opportunities for betterment, and their scorn of manual labor, especially work for an employer, may result, directly or indirectly, from long ages of hopeless poverty. The fact that they are not very different, at least in the type, from those that prevailed in pre-industrial Europe, and that were widely discussed in the Mercantilist literature, rather supports this view.[12] The inegalitarian social stratification, in particular, may partly be a result of stagnation in poverty. We shall comment on these behavioral peculiarities in other parts of the book. The intensity and stale forms they have acquired in South Asia may be due to the much lower economic levels that have long been the rule in most of the South Asian countries and to the absence until independence of a functioning and self-reforming national community.

In any case, it is completely contrary to scientific principles to follow the easy, speculative approach of explaining the peculiarities in attitudes, institutions, and modes of living and working by reference to broad concepts of Hinduism, Buddhism, or Islam, or to personality or cultural traits such as abstention, spiritualism, lack of materialism, and other allegedly "Asian values." And it is not accidental that these broad generalizations can so easily be shown to

---

sustained progress over a wide area, however, the emergence of local leadership alone cannot be depended upon. Success can be achieved only by a national movement conducted on a moral or spiritual plane such as to attract and inspire local leadership everywhere. A beginning in many directions in this wider field can be made only by a wide national movement which may or may not be directly sponsored by the State. Obviously, political, social and religious leaders would all have to come together in such efforts." (D. R. Gadgil, *Economic Policy and Development, A Collection of Writings,* Gokhale Institute of Politics and Economics, Sangam Press Ltd., Poona, 1955, p. 148.)

12 Chap. 21, Sec. 3.

be unrealistic. It should rather be an hypothesis for further study that people in this region are not inherently different from people elsewhere, but that they live and have lived for a long time under conditions very different from those in the Western world, and that this has left its mark upon their bodies and minds.[13] Reli-

gion has, then, become the emotional container of this whole way of life and work and by its sanction has rendered it rigid and resistant to change.

---

[13] "Europe and Asia are divided chiefly by time. Between them lie barriers still more effective than oceans—the Industrial Revolution, the growth of modern science, and the evolution of modern parliamentary government. The antithesis of East and West refers ultimately to the consciousness of different stages of political and economic development; it distinguishes a world which, for the most part, has yet to undergo them." John M. Steadman, "The Myths of Asia," *The American Scholar* (Spring 1961), p. 175.

the sanctification of a particular culture's values as ultimate

sixteen

from The Lively Experiment

SIDNEY MEAD

In brief, Christianity was made relevant to the public welfare at the expense of cherishing unresolved theoretical difficulties. And so long as these remain unsolved, discussions of the sects' relation to the general welfare are likely to remain ambiguous. For example, the common fervency of the insistence upon the dogma of "real, but indirect connection," which, I take it, has usually meant what Tocqueville noted, that the religious denominations in common inculcate the same basic moral standards which are the foundation of the Republic. This it is that makes their work relevant to the general welfare of the democracy. And this amounts to tacit acceptance of the rationalists' view of the matter.

Meanwhile the whole grand dream of American destiny, under God, instrumented through the democratic way while its tangled roots drew

From pp. 141–55 in *The Lively Experiment* by Sidney E. Mead. Copyright © 1963 by Sidney E. Mead. Reprinted by permission of Harper & Row, Publishers, Inc.

nourishment from many different soils in past centuries, was nevertheless profoundly religious in origins and conception. Hence the democratic faith had always a positive and apparently independently legitimate place in the religious affections of the people. This the free churches, in order to make themselves relevant, have always been under pressures to accept on faith and to sanctify.

Grant all this, plus the prevalence of a fuzzy and amorphous intellectual structure in the religious groups, and the way is left open for the uncritical adoption of whatever standards do actually prevail in the society. Hence, as noted, the American denominations have successively lent themselves to the sanctification of current existing expressions of the American way of life.

John Herman Randall, Jr., by taking a more theoretical route as befits a philosopher, arrives at the similar conclusion that "Protestantism left the way open for the assimilation of any pattern of values that might seem good in the light of men's actual social experience . . . [and] has thus tended to become largely an emotional force in support of the reigning secular social ideals." However, it is not quite fair to conclude, as he does, that Protestantism has offered "*no* opposition to any ideal deeply felt" and "no independent guidance and wisdom," although the denominations have always exhibited a surprising lack of ability to launch a cogent criticism of their culture. During the period we are discussing such criticism was almost nonexistent. "The most significant feature of the New Theology" of the period, as W. S. Hudson makes clear, "was its lack of normative content," which made it "compatible with every conceivable social attitude."[1] It is not to be wondered at that businessmen, who during the great depression looked to their churches for guidance, complained that they received back only the echoes of their own voices.

But whatever historical explanations are accepted as most plausible, there remains the general agreement that at the time Protestantism in America achieved its greatest dominance of the culture, it had also achieved an almost complete ideological and emotional identification with the burgeoning bourgeois society and its free-enterprise system. This gives point to Henry May's thesis that "in 1876 Protestantism presented a massive, almost unbroken front in its defense of the social status quo."[2]

Furthermore, Protestants, in effect, looked at the new world they had created, were proud of its creator, and, like Jehovah before them, pronounced it very good. A widespread complacency, a smug self-satisfaction with things as they were (or as they were supposed to be), settled upon them as soot settles on Chicago. This complacency, while a bit incredible to the mid-twentieth century, is not too difficult to understand historically. To do so, it is necessary to keep in mind the almost universal prevalence of a providential view of history— which itself is no mean evidence for the cultural dominance of the denominations. Late in 1864 Horace Bushnell proclaimed:

We associate God and religion with all that we are fighting for. . . . Our cause, we love to think, is especially God's and so we are connecting all most sacred impressions with our government itself, weaving in a woof of holy feeling among all the fibres of our constitutional polity and government. . . . The whole shaping of the fabric is Providential. God, God is in it, everywhere. . . every drum-beat is a hymn, the cannon thunder God, the electric silence, darting victory along the wires, is the inaudible greeting of God's favoring work and purpose.[3]

Granted this sentiment, it was natural that the outcome of the Civil War should suggest to those of the North that "the sword of victory had been wielded by the arm of Providence." At the same time many in the South tended humbly to submit "to the inscrutable ways of the

---

[1] Hudson, *The Great Tradition of the Churches* (New York: Harper & Brothers, 1953), p. 161.

[2] May, *Protestant Churches and Industrial America* (New York: Harper & Brothers, 1949), p. 91. Cf. Paul Tillich's comment that the churches which "replaced the one Church" after the Reformation "were supported either by the state or by the dominant group in society—the former predominantly in Europe, the latter especially in America. In both situations, the Churches largely surrendered their critical freedom. They tended to become

agencies of either the state or the ruling classes." His "The World Situation," in Henry P. Van Dusen, ed., *The Christian Answer* (New York: Charles Scribner's Sons, 1945), p. 38.

[3] Horace Bushnell, *Popular Government by Divine Right* (Hartford: L. E. Hunt, 1864), pp. 15, 12, 15.

same Power."[4] So the young South Carolinian interviewed by John Trowbridge had concluded, "I think it was in the decrees of God Almighty that slavery was to be abolished in this way, and I don't murmur."[5]

However, the ways of Providence were not to all as inscrutable as to Abraham Lincoln, who, after plumbing the awful depths of the war's events, spoke of the altogether righteous judgment on both North and South of the Almighty who has His own purposes in history—purposes which might not fully coincide with the desires of either side. Lincoln concluded in humility that it behooved finite men to proceed "with malice toward none, with charity for all."

There was little of such humility in the heart and hardly a hint of such somber mystery tingeing the thought of the Rev. Henry Ward Beecher—that magnificent weathervane of respectable opinion. When in May, 1863, he addressed the anniversary meeting of the American Home Missionary Society in Chicago, he exulted, "see how wonderfully... God, in his good providence, is preparing us for the work." For "while the South is draining itself dry of its resources...the Northern States are growing rich by war." "And what does it mean but this—that God is storing us with that wealth by which we are to be prepared to meet the exigencies which war shall bring upon us?"

And what exigencies are to be brought upon us? Beecher expressed no doubts:

We are to have the charge of this continent. The South has been proved, and has been found wanting. She is not worthy to bear rule. She has lost the scepter in our national government; she is to lose the scepter in the States themselves; and this continent is to be from this time forth governed by Northern men, with Northern ideas, and with a Northern gospel.

The reasons were clear to Beecher: "this continent is to be cared for by the North simply because the North has been true to the cause of Christ in...a sufficient measure to secure her own safety;...and the nation is to be given to us because we have the bosom by which to nourish it."[6]

Instructed by such religious leaders, it is not to be wondered at if the final victory was widely interpreted as a vindication of the righteousness of the cause of the victors. And this in turn easily merged with a vindication of what the victorious North was rapidly becoming—an industrialized civilization under business control. For, to quote a college textbook, "the Northern victory meant that certain forces and interests, long held in check by the combination of the agricultural South and West, could now have free and full play.... Finance and industrial capitalism could move forward to completion without effective opposition."[7]

4 Herman E. Kittredge, *Ingersolls a Biographical Appreciation* (New York: Dresden Publishing Co., 1911), p. 288.

5 Quoted by Edmund Wilson in *New Yorker,* XXX (April 3, 1954), 115, in a review of Frederick Law Olmsted, *Cotton Kingdom; a Traveller's Observations on Cotton and Slavery in the American Slave States.* Based on three former volumes of journeys and investigations, Arthur M. Schlesinger, ed. (New York: Alfred A. Knopf, 1953).

6 Henry Ward Beecher, "Home Missions and Our Country's Future," in *Home Missionary,* XXXVI (September, 1863), 112.

7 Avery Craven and Walter Johnson, *The United States: Experiment in Democracy* (Boston: Ginn & Co., 1947), pp. 417–18.

the sanctification of a particular culture's values as ultimate   **183**

From here it was but another short step to the enshrinement of the political instrument which, in the hands of Providence, had guided the Union to victory over slavery and disunion. By 1865 a writer in the Methodist *New York Christian Advocate* had already proclaimed that "we find the political parties of the day so made out, that it may...be determined on which side an orderly and intelligent Protestant will be found, and on which the profane, the dissolute and the Romanist."[8] The Republican party, said Henry Wilson, contained "more of moral and intellectual worth than was ever embodied in any political organization in any land.... [It was] created by no man...[but] brought into being by Almighty God himself." This, of course, meant enshrinement of what the party became soon after Lincoln's death, when "it allied itself with the forces of corporate industry, which represented a greater investment of capital and, consequently, a greater concentration of power in politics and economic life than the slaveholders had ever dreamed of possessing."[9]

But if Americans were idealistic, they were also pragmatic. If it appears that they too simply saw the smiles of beneficent Providence in the trinity of Northernism, business, and the Republican party, it must also be remembered that the system appeared to work—to produce tangible fruits in the great and obvious material prosperity that o'erspread the land like a flood and promised, eventually at least, to saturate all levels of society. Thousands of inventions, garnered up and universally applied by free and daring enterprisers, revolutionized transportation, communication, agriculture, and industry, while the prevailing system seemingly distributed the benefits more widely and equitably than any had before it.[10] It was these tangible results that provided the most convincing argument for "the American way of life" and tended to dampen all critical, as well as carping, voices in whatever realm as "un-American." Further, as time passed, a rather definite and complete ideological structure—constituting an explanation and defense—was compounded out of conservative *laissez-faire* economic theory, the common-sense phi-

---

[8] As quoted in Ralph E. Morrow, "Northern Methodism in the South During Reconstruction," in *Mississippi Valley Historical Review,* XLI (September, 1954), 213.

[9] As quoted in Craven, *The United States,* pp. 430, 422.

[10] Cf. Arthur M. Schlesinger, Jr., *Political and Social Growth of the American Peoples, 1865–1940,* 3d ed. (New York: The Macmillan Co., 1941), p. v: "Yet the record as a whole sums up a people who, despite the ills to which mankind is prey, managed to fashion a way of life and a system of government which at every period of American history served as a beacon light for struggling humanity everywhere."

Robert Baird in *The Christian Retrospect and Register: a Summary of the Scientific, Moral, and Religious Progress of the First Half of the XIXth Century,* 3d ed. (New York: M. W. Dodd, 1851) held that no one will deny that "in all that relates to their MATERIAL INTERESTS our race has...made great progress since the commencement of the XIXth century" and that "the latter half of the century will show still greater progress, we are far from being disposed, either to deny, or to doubt." Further, "that there has also been a great progress in all that has a bearing on the MORAL AND RELIGIOUS INTERESTS of Humanity, during the same era, is a position which none can question." But, he added, the authors "are pained to be compelled to admit" that "the progress in the moral and Religious Interests of our race, during the period... has not equalled that of their Material Interests."

losophy of the schools, and the orthodox theology of the churches.

The foundation of the whole structure was the idea of progress. It was belief in progress that made tolerable the very rapid changes to which people were being subjected, as well as some of the less desirable aspects of what was happening. The idea of progress was compounded of the Christian doctrine of Providence and the scientific idea of evolution and was summed up in the slick phrase popularized by John Fiske and Lyman Abbott: "Evolution is God's way of doing things." So, for example, it could be proclaimed as late as 1928 that "the fact of human progress is seen to be part of the inevitable evolutionary process; and religious faith seeks in the cosmos which produced us and which carries us along the evidence of the activities of God."[11]

To those standing on such a teleological escalator, change held no terrors. Undesirable features of the passing scene might be endured with patience bred of the knowledge that they would inevitably be transcended, since, as Henry Ward Beecher assured a Yale audience, "man is made to start and not to stop; to go on, and on, and up, and onward...and ending in the glorious liberty of the sons of God."[12] Meanwhile, as John Bascom had said, "death is of little moment, if it plays into a higher life. The insects that feed the bird meet their destination. The savages that are trodden out of a stronger race are in the line of progress." And "we—we as interpreters—are not to

bring higher and impossible motives and feelings into a lower field."[13]

That such sentiments were not restricted to well-placed leaders is suggested by the lyrics of popular gospel songs that common people sang in their churches:

He leadeth me; O blessed thought!
O words with heavenly comfort fraught!
Whate'er I do, where'er I be,
Still 'tis God's hand that leadeth me.

And when bleak failure seemed to encompass them and cankerous despair threatened to eat away their souls, they sang,

We wonder why the test
When we try to do our best.
But we'll understand it better by and by.

The understanding on all levels was aided by the articulation of a constellation of basic doctrines which gave plausibility to the idea of progress by explaining its practical workings in human society. One of the most complete statements of these doctrines was achieved by Andrew Carnegie in his article called "Wealth," which appeared in the June, 1889, issue of the *North American Review*. It was described by the editor as one of the finest articles he had ever published.

Carnegie eschewed airy speculation and proposed to speak of "the foundations upon which society is based" and of the laws upon which "civilization itself depends"—the laws which "are the highest results of human experience" and "the soil in which society so far has produced the best fruit." He added as an anathema, "Objections to the foundations upon which society is based are not in order."

---

[11] Gerald Birney Smith, *Current Christian Thinking* (Chicago: The University of Chicago Press, 1928), p. 189.
[12] As quoted in Hudson, *The Great Tradition*, p. 175.

---

[13] John Bascom, "The Natural Theology of Social Science. IV. Labor and Capital," in *Bibliotheca Sacra*, XXV (October, 1869), 660.

First was the familiar law of the sacredness of property or the right of every individual to have and to hold and be protected by the government in the possession of whatever property he could get.

Second were the twin laws of competition and the accumulation of wealth. The competition is for property, and these laws explain the way in which property gets distributed in a society. All men enter into the competition. But men differ in inherent aptitudes or talents in relationship to it. Some men are gifted with a talent of organization and management which invariably secures for them "enormous rewards, no matter where or under what laws or conditions." Ergo, "it is a law, as certain as any of the others named, that men possessed of this peculiar talent for affairs, under the free play of economic forces, must, of necessity, soon be in receipt of more revenue than can be judiciously expended upon themselves." In brief, "it is inevitable that their income must exceed their expenditures, and that they must accumulate wealth." The wealthy man Carnegie regarded as the victim of circumstances over which he had no control.

Carnegie was realist enough to recognize that society pays a great price for the law of competition which indeed "may be sometimes hard for the individual." Nevertheless, since this law has produced "our wonderful material development, . . . it is best for the race, because it insures the survival of the fittest in every department." This suggests a rather clear and universal, not to say comforting, criterion for judging who are the "fittest" in every area of the society.[14]

The Rt. Rev. William Lawrence of Massachusetts propounded his ecclesiastical version of the agnostic's sentiments in an article published in January, 1901.[15] Sensing "a certain distrust on the part of our people as to the effect of material prosperity on their morality," he suggested that it would be well to "revise our inferences from history, experience, and the Bible" and shed that "subtle hypocrisy which has beset the Christian through the ages, bemoaning the deceitfulness of riches and, at the same time, working with all his might to earn a competence, and a fortune if he can." Having rid himself of such false inferences and hypocrisy, man may now recognize two great guiding principles for his life. The first is that it is "his divine mission" to "conquer Nature, open up her resources, and harness them to his service." The second is that "in the long run, it is only to the man of morality that wealth comes" for "Godliness is in league with riches." This being the case, the good Bishop added, "we return with an easier mind and clearer conscience to the problem of our twenty-five billion dollars in a decade," confident that "material prosperity is in the long run favorable to morality."

Third was the law or rule of stewardship, which followed upon the views of the sacredness of property and the laws of competition and accumulation. In brief, the use and disposition of the property, as well as its mere possession, are sacred to the man who accumulates it. God gave it to him by endowing him with certain talents, and he is responsible for it *to God* alone, and certainly not to the lesser fit in the community.

"We start," said Carnegie, "with

14 Kennedy, *op. cit.*, pp. 1–2.

15 *Ibid.*, pp. 68–76.

a condition of affairs under which the best interests of the race are promoted, but which inevitably gives wealth to the few." And "thus far... the situation can be surveyed and pronounced good." Therefore, the "only question with which we have to deal," he continued, is "What is the proper mode of administering wealth after the laws upon which civilization is founded have thrown it into the hands of the few?" There were, he thought, but three possibilities. The few might leave it to their families, they might bequeath it for public purposes, or they might administer it during their lives. He rules out the first two as irresponsible, even coming to the radical conclusion that the state might well confiscate through inheritance taxes at least half of fortunes so left.

The true duty of "the man of Wealth" is to live modestly and unostentatiously, "provide moderately for the legitimate wants of those dependent upon him," and, beyond that,

to consider all surplus revenues which come to him simply as trust funds, which he is . . . strictly bound as a matter of duty to administer in the manner which, in his judgment, is best calculated to produce the most beneficial results for the community . . . thus becoming the mere agent and trustee for his poorer brethren, bringing to their service his superior wisdom, experience, and ability to administer, doing for them better than they would or could do for themselves.

The main rule to be followed is to help those who will help themselves and to eschew the indiscriminate charity which presents "one of the most serious obstacles to the improvement of our race," by encouraging "the slothful, the drunken, the unworthy." To this we shall return in the next essay.

Here it is necessary to note only that such stewardship was taken seriously by many wealthy men of the day and produced in them an honest and consecrated devotion to their sacred duties which only the sneering souls of the mean in mind could belittle. In 1856 John P. Crozer was awed to note that "wealth flows in from all sources." This, he added, made him feel "as often before, in making up my yearly accounts, oppressed with the responsibility of my stewardship. I am, indeed, perplexed how I shall use, as I ought to, the great and increasing stores of wealth which God has bestowed upon me." "I love to make money almost as well as a miser," he wrote a year later, and added, "I love to give it away for charitable purposes." But he realized, as he searched his soul, "I...must set a guard over myself, lest the good designed be lost in the luxury of giving." For

excuses are so easily framed, and the heart of man so deceitful, that one can easily reason himself into the belief that, all things considered, he has done pretty well. I find such a process of reasoning in my own mind; but calm reflection tells me that I have not done well. I am a very unprofitable servant to so good a Master; and as he has made me the steward of a large estate, it becomes me "to lend it to the Lord" freely of my substance.

Still troubled, he prayed with real humility, "O my lord, if it is thy righteous pleasure, direct me clearly and decisively to some path of duty and of usefulness, apart from the absorbing influence of wealth and worldly mindedness."[16]

Later, of course, when such devoted stewards were harassed by the

16 John P. Crozer, *Standard,* XV (May 7, 1868), 4, col. 4.

rise of the unfit and strikes rocked their companies, this paternalistic conception of stewardship would show another face, as when George F. Baer, president of the Philadelphia and Reading Railway, wrote in 1902 to an inquirer:

I beg of you not to be discouraged. The rights and interests of the laboring man will be protected and cared for—not by the labor agitators, but by the Christian men to whom God in His infinite wisdom has given the control of the property interests of the country, and upon the successful management of which so much depends.[17]

Meanwhile, as intimated previously, Protestantism—at least · in the respectable churches—effused a benign sanctity over all. The older people's churches were rapidly becoming middle class, at least in mentality and leadership. As A. M. Schlesinger, Sr., says, even the Baptists "abandoned their contempt for wealth," as God gave gold in abundance to some of their more worthy members.[18] In 1866 a writer in the *Christian Advocate* was pleased to note that "by virtue of the habits which religion inculcates and cherishes, our Church members have as a body risen in the social scale, and thus become socially removed from the great body out of which most of them originally gathered." And he added with a hint of smugness, "this tendency of

things is natural and universal, and in its results unavoidable; perhaps we might add, also, not undesirable."[19]

At the same time, American scholars, many of them ministers turned professors, worked out, as Henry May says, "a school of political economy which might well be labeled clerical *laissez faire*." The ideological amalgamation of which we have spoken is best and most clearly illustrated here. Said the Rev. John McVicker of Columbia: "That science and religion eventually teach the same lesson, is a necessary consequence of the unity of truth, but it is seldom that this union is so satisfactorily displayed as in the researches of Political Economy."[20]

Americans, in spite of the long century of relative peace and stability in the world following 1814 and their almost complete freedom from embroilment in European affairs, were never complete isolationists in spirit. From this they were saved by the strong sense of destiny under God which pervaded their thinking from the beginning. By 1825 Francis Wayland, Jr., had already proclaimed sentiments that should have raised eyebrows in Europe: "What nation will be second in the new order of things, is yet to be decided; but the providence of God has already announced, that, if true to ourselves, we shall be inevitably first."[21]

The keynote of the American idea of destiny was struck by John Winthrop in his address "Written on

[17] Caroline Augusta Lloyd, *Henry Demarest Lloyd, 1847–1903, a Biography* by Caro Lloyd with an introduction by Charles Edward Russell (New York: G. P. Putnam's, 1912), II, 190.

[18] Arthur M. Schlesinger, *The Rise of the City, 1878–1898,* "A History of American Life Series," X (New York: The Macmillan Co., 1933), p. 331.

[19] As quoted in May, *Protestant Churches and Industrial America,* p. 62.

[20] *Ibid.,* p. 14.

[21] Francis Wayland, *The Duties of an American Citizens Two Discourses, Delivered in the First Baptist Meeting House in Boston, on Thursday, April 7, 1825* (Boston: James Loring, 1825), p. 29.

Boarde the Arrabella" in 1630. He said: as

for the worke wee haue in hand, it is by a mutuall consent through a speciall over-ruleing providence, and a more than an ordinary approbation of the Churches of Christ to seeke out a place of Cohabitation and Consorteshipp vnder a due forme of Government both ciull and ecclesiasticall.

If we are faithful to our covenant with him, Winthrop continued,

Wee shall finde that the god of Israell is among vs...when hee shall make vs a prayse and glory, that men shall say of succeeding plantacions: the Lord make it like that of New England: for wee must Consider that wee shall be as a Citty vpon a Hill, the eies of all people are vpon vs.[22]

Thenceforth throughout American history this strong sense of particular calling, of destiny under God, has remained a constant part of the ideological structure of the nation. In the Discourse quoted above, Francis Wayland, Jr., echoed Winthrop when he wrote, "Our power resides in the force of our example. It is by exhibiting to other nations the practical excellence of a government of law, that they will learn its nature and advantages, and will in due time achieve their own emancipation."[23] Already, he thought, "our country has given to the world the first ocular demonstration, not only of the practicability, but also of the unrivalled superiority of a popular form of government."[24]

---

[22] John Winthrop, "A Modell of Christian Charity," in Perry G. E. Miller and Thomas H. Johnson, eds., *The Puritans* (New York: American Book Co., 1938), pp. 197, 197–99.
[23] Wayland, *The Duties...*, pp. 35–36.
[24] *Ibid.*, p. 27.

William R. Williams in 1846 more obviously wove the strands of evangelical Christianity into those of American destiny. "Our Heavenly Father has made us a national epistle to other lands," he wrote.

See that you read a full and impressive comment to all lands, of the power of Christian principle, and of the expansive and self-sustaining energies of the gospel, when left unfettered by national endowments, and secular alliances. The evangelical character of our land is to tell upon the plans and destinies of other nations.[25]

Clothed in various languages in various times and places, the theme of American destiny has remained the same, although God, like Alice's Cheshire Cat, has sometimes threatened gradually to disappear altogether or, at most, to remain only as a disembodied and sentimental smile.

It was the idea of destiny which added "the inducements of philanthropy to those of patriotism" in the American mind and broadened the idea of progress and its laws to include all of humanity. America's destiny came to be seen as her call to spread the amazing benefits of the American democratic faith and its free-enterprise system throughout the world, gradually transforming the world into its own image.

The idea of destiny tempered Bishop Lawrence's belief that "Godliness is in league with riches." The call for today, he argued, is for

the uplift of character...and every means of culture;...and, above all, the deepening of the religious faith of the people; the rekindling of the spirit, that, clothed

---

[25] Winfred E. Garrison, *The March of Faith: the Story of Religion in America since 1865* (New York: Harper & Brothers, 1933), p. 174.

with her material forces, the great personality of this nation may fulfill her divine destiny.[26]

When Lawrence wrote this in 1901 the United States, fresh from its venture in imperialistic war, was already beginning to be impressed by the meaning and possibilities of her physical power. The idea had been hatched that the power as well as the wealth was given by divine appointment to be used.

Josiah Strong, erstwhile Congregational pastor in Cheyenne, Wyoming, and at the time secretary of that denomination's Home Missionary Society, sounded the Christian version of this view in his very popular book *Our Country* published in 1885.[27]

Strong argued that the Anglo-Saxon race—and in the United States all immigrants soon become Anglo-Saxon—is the bearer of two closely related ideas, Civil Liberty and "pure *spiritual* Christianity." Ergo, "the Anglo-Saxon...is divinely commissioned to be, in a peculiar sense, his brother's keeper." And when we add to this the equally obvious fact of his "rapidly increasing strength in modern times...does it not look as if God were not only preparing in our Anglo-Saxon civilization the die with which to stamp the peoples of the earth, but as if we were also massing behind that die the mighty power with which to press it?"

Citing the Americans as "the noblest; for we are 'The heirs of all the ages in the foremost files of time,' " he explained that God, with infinite wisdom and skill, was training them "for an hour sure to come"—the hour of the "final competition of races." He had no qualms about the outcome: "Can anyone doubt that the result of this competition of races will be the 'survival of the fittest'?" Standing firmly on the evolutionary escalator, he proclaimed the present knowledge that the "inferior tribes were only precursors of a superior race, voices in the wilderness crying; 'Prepare ye the way of the Lord!' "

So this influential Congregational leader admired God's "two hands"— with one of which He was "preparing in our civilization the die with which to stamp the nations" while with the other He was "preparing mankind to receive our impress."

With such well-nigh infallible religious guides abroad in the land, it is small wonder that a mere junior Senator, Albert J. Beveridge, of Indiana, was prepared to defend annexation of the Philippines on January 9, 1900, with the words:

We will not renounce our part in the mission of the race, trustee, under God, of the civilization of the world.... He has made us...the master organizers of the world to establish system where chaos reigns.... He has made us adepts in government that we may administer government among savage and senile peoples. ...And of all our race, He has marked the American people as His chosen Nation to finally lead in the regeneration of the world. This is the divine mission of America, and it holds for us all the profit, all the glory, all the happiness possible to man. We are trustees of the world's progress, guardians of its righteous peace. The judgment of the Master is upon us: "Ye have been faithful over a few things; I will make you ruler over many things."[28]

---

[26] Hudson, *The Great Tradition,* p. 161.

[27] Alfred North Whitehead, *Science and the Modern World,* "Lowell Lectures, 1925" (Harmondsworth, Middlesex, Eng., Penguin Books, Ltd., 1938), p. 240.

[28] As quoted in John R. Bodo, *The Protestant Clergy and Public Issues, 1812–1848* (Princeton: Princeton University Press, 1954), p. 241; from "Christ, a Home Missionary," in *Missionary Enterprise* (Boston, 1845), p. 93.

Finally, "exhibiting a nugget of gold, he cried: 'I picked this up on the ground in one of these islands. There are thousands of others lying about.' "

A Christian note of profounder depth was struck, however, by Senator George F. Hoar, who rose merely to say: "The Devil taketh him up into an extremely high mountain and showeth him all the kingdoms of the world and the glory of them and saith unto him, 'All these things will be thine if thou wilt fall down and worship me.' "[29]

We have noted then that the bulk of American Protestantism achieved during this period a working ideological harmony with the modes of the modern industrialized civilization, the free-enterprise system, and the burgeoning imperialism. Professor W. S. Hudson, treating the more purely theological aspects of this development in a most discerning book on *The Great Tradition of the American Churches,* makes good his claim that "the New Theology was essentially a culture religion."[30] The doctrines of the "gospel of wealth" in the context of the idea of destiny under God gave a satisfactory explanation of the facts of human life as experienced in the United States. It should never be forgotten that at this time the observational order coincided in high degree with the conceptual order and that such coincidence defines social stability.

This it was that created an atmosphere in which those actually in control—the only people that really mattered—could live at ease in the vast expanding new Zion. This was Edith Wharton's "age of innocence," Henry S. Canby's "age of confidence"; and its flower was a host of middle-class "fathers" of the type pictured by Clarence Day. Perhaps its outstanding characteristic was complacency, based on the feeling that God was in His heaven and all was right with the world. Surveying the period in retrospect, we may agree with Whitehead that "the prosperous middle classes, who ruled the nineteenth century, placed an excessive value upon placidity of existence." With Whitehead, we can affirm that this is hardly a sufficient basis for an enduring culture.[31]

Looking backward today from a world which promises to be very different from that Utopia which Edward Bellamy anticipated in 1888, it seems obvious enough that the outward harmony was achieved by overlooking certain incongruous elements in the situation that had troubled only such gloomy and lonesome prophets as Nathaniel Hawthorne, Herman Melville, Walt Whitman, and Henry Adams. The world that seemed so fine and stable to Carnegie and Bishop Lawrence, to Crozer and Henry Ward Beecher, to Josiah Strong and Russell Conwell—to all the "fathers" of Day's type—was about to explode. The period of cultural triumph of the denominations merged—not with a whimper, but with a bang—into the period of upheaval and crisis.

[29] Kennedy, *op. cit.,* p. 76.

[30] The following quotations are from chap. 14, "The Anglo-Saxon and the World's Future," in Josiah Strong, *Our Country, Its Possible Future and Its Present Crisis,* with an introduction by Austin Philips, rev. ed. based on the census of 1890 (New York: Baker & Taylor Co., for the American Home Missionary Society, 1891).

[31] As quoted in Sullivan, *op. cit.,* I. 47–48.

the dilemma of instrumentalism

seventeen

from **Sociological Approach to Religion**

Some Aspects of American and Japanese Practical Religion

Glock has made an interesting classification of forms of deprivation that underlie religious movements.[1] Economic deprivation has to do with such things as disadvantage involved in differential income distribution within a society; social deprivation with status or prestige disadvantages; organismic deprivation with poor physical and mental health (here the reader may be reminded of integrative functions of religion); ethical and psychic deprivation with felt disappointments in relation to problems of meaning, philosophically (psychic deprivation) and in terms of operative organization of one's life (ethical deprivation). Practical religion certainly

needs to be understood in the light of these modes of deprivation, with particular reference to organismic, economic and (to some extent) social deprivation. Practical religion, as it moves toward extreme popular form, tends precisely to *extreme* man-centeredness[2] in its preoccupation with (physical and mental) health and "success."

A stream of inspirational religious literature has long been flowing from the presses in the United States. Much of this literature has significance for its movement in the direction of making practical "use" of religion for cherished worldly or everyday ends.[3] The question of the *precise* extent to which the literature reflects or reinforces popular religious impulses cannot be answered. But it can be noted that the literature constitutes a kind of focussing of significant elements in such cultist or

---

[1] Charles Y. Glock, "The Role of Deprivation in the Origin and Evolution of Religious Groups," in Robert E. Lee and Martin E. Marty, eds., *Religion and Social Conflict,* New York: Oxford University Press, 1964, pp. 24–36.

Louis Schneider, *Sociological Approach to Religion* (New York: John Wiley & Sons, Inc., 1970), pp. 134–53. Copyright © 1970 by John Wiley & Sons, Inc.

[2] See the next section of this [selection].

[3] The writer now has various reservations about the analysis of the literature presented in Louis Schneider and Sanford M. Dornbusch, *Popular Religion: Inspirational Books in America,* but he remains persuaded that the literature merits study as a cultural phenomenon.

192 religion and conflict: ambiguities and dilemmas

sectarian phenomena, more especially, as New Thought.[4] It can also be noted that the literature has enjoyed appreciable prosperity. Its practical bias is clear, both in that it has concern for the every day preoccupations of ordinary men and women and in that it points to, advocates and has undoubtedly to some extent been adhered to in, "practical" conduct not in strict conformity with what certain ideal, formal Christian prescriptions might be conceived to lay down. There is a kind of religion that the literature captures and expresses and that we may here conveniently tap precisely by way of the literature itself.

The literature features a special religious strain, which has not been culturally trivial and which it is certainly important not to miss. Possibly this strain is doomed in the very long run, but it has unquestionably existed and it clearly reaches into the present. It is perhaps hardly needful to say that to "make fun" of the literature in any way would be inept, if for no other reason than for the reason that it shows signs of aspiration beyond its own limitations and it would be sheer inaccuracy to miss this. But the literature is *sometimes* so extreme in its assertions that a description can easily give the quite unintended impression of caricature.

It has been noted that the literature has been prosperous. Joshua Liebman's *Peace of Mind* had sold over a million copies by 1956. Books by Emmet Fox, who writes with a strong emphasis that "proper" mental attitudes generate "proper" conditions of the emotions or the body, and even of the external world, have done extremely well. Fox's *Sermon on the Mount* alone has, to date, sold over 600,000 copies. Norman Vincent Peale's *The Power of Positive Thinking* (originally, 1952), perhaps the catchiest title one can refer to in the long listing one could make of books of this type, has sold over two and a half million copies;[5] and Hackett reports that with Peale's ninth book, *Stay Alive All Your Life,* his book sales had gone beyond the four million mark.[6] We assume that all this (even in a time of generally high book sales) is not without important social and psychological correlates, although we cannot assess these with the accuracy we would like.

What is more significant for present purposes in the literature may be summed up by saying that the contemporary or near-contemporary writers of it tend to show strong organismic (or integrative) and economic preoccupations, in particular, and that this is accompanied by a very powerful instrumental bias. It is so well known that the writers are concerned to point to ways to obtain "peace of mind" and emotional health that it hardly seems needful to give the point considerable documentation. The works of Peale, Fox,

---

[4] See Charles S. Braden, *Spirits in Rebellion,* Dallas: Southern Methodist University Press, 1963; and for a literate, revealing older treatment, Horatio W. Dresser, *Handbook of the New Thought,* New York: Putnam's, 1917. New Thought has a powerful "positive thinking" component.

[5] See Alice P. Hackett, *Seventy Years of Best Sellers, 1895–1965,* N.Y.: R. R. Bowker Co., 1967, *passim.* It is possibly indicative of new trends that while, among Peale's recent books *Stay Alive All Your Life* made the nonfiction best seller list for 1957 (being third on the list of ten highest-selling non-fiction items for that year), his books since that year, through 1966, have not done so. It should be said that the description of the literature given in these pages is based mainly on information extending through the late 1950's.

[6] *Ibid.,* p. 114.

and Liebman, among numerous others, make the point utterly clear, as did the work of other writers in the same vein in earlier years. The physical health preoccupation of the literature, which is also very marked, may be allowed to be adequately exemplified by the title of Glenn Clark's book, *How to Find Health through Prayer*.[7] Clark may be cited again in connection with economic concerns to give some slight sense of the depth in time, or long history, of this kind of literature, although Clark is far from being one of the most unrestrained advocates of the notion that a man's religion will bring him worldly prosperity. Clark inquires what would happen if we should "ask, seek, and knock for spiritual ideas, and not for material things." His answer is that "a veritable downpour of ideas," nearly "a hurricane or blizzard of ideas, if you please" would come down upon us; and "as soon as these ideas struck the atmosphere of this earth they would —many of them, at least—be converted into good round hard practical dollars."[8]

The instrumental bias goes along with the preoccupations noted. "Practical needs," "results," the formula "it works"—all these receive emphasis. And there is stress that there is close affinity between religion on the one hand and science and technology on the other. Sometimes this presumed affinity is asserted in highly dramatic fashion. In what is actually a rather restrained statement, taking the literature in more recent years as a whole, Peale and the psychiatrist Smiley Blanton argue that the church is "a scientific laboratory dedicated to the reshaping of men's daily lives" and that "its great principles are formulas and techniques designed to meet every human need."[9] Peale and Blanton go on to say that the New Testament is a textbook of laws, "spiritual laws as specific as the laws of physics and chemistry." Further, they aver that the church encourages people to have faith "but does not give them specific techniques for attaining it," and that it urges the practice of love but affords "no detailed methodology" for its practice in daily life.

The entire language of science, technique, methodology is not a matter of accidental metaphors in this literature. Its writers are on the whole far too insistently and single-mindedly concerned to employ religious resources, or what they regard as such, instrumentally and "rationally" for the deliberate achievement of health, wealth and happiness for the accidental metaphor notion to be persuasive. The practical and eudae-

---

[7] New York: Harper and Brothers, 1940.

[8] *The Soul's Sincere Desire,* Boston: Little, Brown, 1925, pp. 37–38. Clark's reference to "good round hard practical dollars" may serve to set off a long-time strain of association in popular American thought between business and religion. A half century before Clark wrote, the *Congregationalist* for June 21, 1876, had commented that "men who have tried it have confidently declared that there is no sleeping partner in any business who can begin to compare with the Almighty." (As quoted by Henry F. May, *Protestant Churches and Industrial America,* New York: Harper and Bros., 1949, p. 51). And a generation after Clark, Peale strongly encourages the notion of the affinity of business and religion, as in the assertion (in its context very significant) that "it is well to study prayer from an

efficiency point of view." *The Power of Positive Thinking,* New York: Prentice-Hall, 1952, p. 53. This, however, also already adumbrates the matter of instrumental use.

[9] See Peale and Blanton's *The Art of Real Happiness,* New York: Prentice-Hall, 1950, pp. 12–13.

monistic and at the same time "scientific-technical" orientation of the literature could be virtually endlessly illustrated. A generation before Peale's most successful writing Clark could say that " a man who learns and practices the laws of prayer correctly should be able to play golf better, do business better, work better, love better, serve better." Clark could also recommend that one "pray if possible out of loyalty to God, for the joy of it, not for practical results," and this strikes quite a different note, but again he could aver that "the trouble with most of our praying, as with our breathing, is that it is too negative," and the suggestion of "technique" that this may convey is reinforced by the advocacy of "scientific" prayer.[10] The above is not intended to suggest that the inspirational religious literature contains *nothing but* the elements that have been presented. Nevertheless, when all significant reservations have been made, the biases indicated remain powerful, and this is what is crucial.

In a very different part of the world, religious phenomena have emerged that show striking resemblances to the kind of religion involved in the literature just reviewed. We turn to Japan's so-called "new religions." Drummond writes that the popular designation of the new Japanese religions is "religions of personal advantage." That is, he amplifies, "they are seen as essentially spiritual techniques to get what one wants out of life." Such material on the new religions as is available in Western languages would seem to give good warrant to such a characterization. Drummond indicates that the characterization is apt enough, but he adds that "it applies almost equally to the whole of the popular side of the Japanese religious tradition, including both Buddhism and Shinto." "Empirical Christianity," too, Drummond avers, has at different times and places shown much of the bias toward being a "religion of personal advantage."[11] This is correct and it is important. It is also important to recognize the presence of other than purely "crass" and materialistic impulses in these religions themselves. After all qualifications, however, a distinctive picture emerges.[12]

---

10 *The Soul's Sincere Desire,* pp. 12, 17, 34, 49.

11 Richard H. Drummond, "Japan's 'New Religious' and the Christian Community," *The Christian Century,* 81, Dec. 9, 1964, pp. 1521–23.

12 Maurice Bairy sees in the success of the new religions in Japan a confused but genuine popular striving to attain to personal experience and individual contact with the divine. If not with entire clarity, then dimly but again genuinely one may discern in the new religions an element of awakening of both a sense of personal identity and of conscience. This does not prevent Bairy from writing with respect to P L Kyodan, the new religion he came to know best, that "prayer for earthly goods is the true essence of this religion" and that the religion belongs among those naturalistic faiths in which "prayer serves to avert misfortune and to attain good fortune in this earthly world." Bairy later avers that this religion "does not rise above the realm of a magical religion with prayers for earthly goods." It is clear that he would take this as a fair characterization of the new religions in general. Maurice A. Bairy, *Japans Neue Religionen in der Nachkriegszeit,* Bonn: L. Röhrscheid Verlag, 1959, pp. 68–69, 110, 111. One may note more recently numerous similar characterizations, as by McFarland, who remarks that "anticipation of concrete results—which is fairly common among all religions, particulary at the folk or mass level—has been especially prominent throughout the religious history of Japan. It is now one of the most conspicuous characteristics of the New Religions." It is of interest that McFarland employs Yinger's term, "bridging" sects, to suggest that the new religions "have at least the poten-

The new religions are "popular," if indeed one wishes to distinguish popular from practical on the ground that the former is more extreme. But even popular religion is *not* altogether lacking in "spiritual" elements. *Nor* must more "spiritual" religious complexes lack *all* of the elements of practical or popular religion. Tentatively, we may specify popular religion in this fashion: It exhibits a relatively *very heavy* stress on this-worldly goods, especially on the line of physical and emotional health and economic prosperity. It has a considerable "technological" or magical-instrumental component. Its concerns on the lines of metaphysics, cosmology, eschatology and the like are likely to be lacking in intellectual profundity and to appear exceedingly simple. It has widespread appeal. We cannot attend in detail to all of these things in the case of the new Japanese religions, but the following statement may help to clarify our specification.

According to Thomsen, some of the so-called new religions in Japan are actually not so new, in that they began in the nineteenth century, while others that came into formal being in the aftermath of World War II hark back to earlier Shinto and Buddhist beginnings.[13] The new religions numbered 171 in 1963, of which approximately a third were registered under Buddhism, a larger number under Shinto, while some thirty were listed as "miscellaneous." These religions claimed one of every five Japanese as a member when Thomsen wrote.[14] They are obviously of some importance on the Japanese scene. The new religions are evidently easy to enter, comprehend and follow. They are optimistic. If it is well attested that they are this-worldly and strongly preoccupied with organismic and economic ends, it would also seem that a case can be made for the view that "for a large number of the adherents of the New Religions, religion is nothing more than a tool utilized for the purpose of attaining completely selfish aims."[15]

It is a constant emphasis of one of the religions, known as Seicho no Ie, with a membership of about a million and a half when Offner and van Straehlen wrote, that such a thing as sickness does not exist. "It is merely a dream, a figment of the imagination. Thinking on sickness, aches and pains results in the body experiencing them." Indeed, for this religion "health or sickness, wealth or poverty depends upon the thoughts which pass through our minds;" and phenomenal existence itself is shadow, the mind's mere reflection. Offner and van Straehlen quote from Taniguchi, the founder of this religion, drawing from his "Revise Fate through the Power of Thought." It is impossible not to think of Western inspirational analogues to this title. (The mentalism suggested, to-

tiality of helping to carry their members over into a new life." See H. Neill Mc-Farland, *The Rush Hour of the Gods,* New York: Macmillan, 1967, pp. 78–79, 229. We need not deny the bridging function, any more than we need to deny the less crass elements Bairy finds.

13 But Drummond, "Japan's 'New Religious'," p. 1521, suggests that while this is true the emergence of the new religions as "highly significant sociological phenomena" has been subsequent to the second World War.

14 Harry Thomsen, *The New Religions of Japan,* Rutland: C. E. Tuttle Co., 1963, pp. 15–17.

15 Clark B. Offner and Henry van Straehlen, *Modern Japanese Religions,* New York: Twayne Publishers, 1963, p. 273. Cf. also Ichiro Hori, *Folk Religion in Japan,* Chicago: University of Chicago Press, 1968, ch. 6, which deals with the new religions and old shamanic tendencies.

gether with emphasis on thinking positively, is definitely not confined to this particular one among the new religions.) Referring to Seicho no Ie again, Offner and van Straehlen write: "One must make his mind receptive and repeat over and over again such thoughts as 'God fills the universe. Everything in the universe loves me. There is nothing that is hostile to me.' "[16] Physical as well as mental health is a great concern. Taniguchi, for one, averred that cancer, too, is an embodiment of a mental condition.

Very pertinent to the new religions is Sōka Gakkai, a much discussed movement that already claimed a membership amounting to some ten percent of the population of Japan a few years ago. It is especially interesting that Offner and van Straehlen[17] observe that, although this huge organization receives much criticism from both Buddhist and non-Budhist sources, it is simply an "outward and unashamed expression of an attitude which views religion as a means to attain present, immediate benefits which is implicit in the teaching and propaganda of many other New Religions as well." We once more put our stress on religion as an instrumentality or means here and may profitably turn to some further material on Sōka Gakkai.

Sōka Gakkai is not itself, technically, a religion. But it has regarded itself as the "advertising arm" of Nichiren Shoshū and therefore as affiliated with the latter, whose religious affinities are in turn with the Nichiren religious complex and go back to the thirteenth century. A figure in the founding of Sōka Gakkai, who may be referred to here simply as Makiguchi (born in 1871), held the view that a religion must justify itself by its ability to "work" and bring happiness. Accordingly the loyalty one may have to a religion can be a qualified one, contingent on the receipt of worldly benefits. Toda Jōsei (born in 1900), the second president of Sōka Gakkai, was at one time a Christian but, according to one writer, gave up Christianity "because it did not enable him to pay off his debts."[18] Makiguchi wanted to "apply the scientific method to religion." Science and religion, for him, were both concerned with ultimate truth, but also with how to make men happy in their daily lives, and thereby religion became com-

---

16 *Ibid.,* pp. 163, 164, 204. The resemblance of some of the conceptions of the new religions to elements in Western thought is noted also by these authors, who write of "the metaphysical world of Christian Science, Unity and New Thought" in discussing Seicho no Ie (*ibid.,* p. 127). One cannot help suspecting actual contacts, and McFarland (*The Rush Hour of the Gods,* p. 249) writes of Seicho no Ie that "it is quite possible that its essential message would appeal to many people in this country, as we may assume from the persistence here of various other 'peace of mind' and 'divine science' cults, from some of which indeed Taniguchi initially appropriated some of his initial teachings." Braden explicitly takes Seicho no Ie as a "branch" of New Thought. He writes: "It would not do...to say that Seicho no Ie is identical with any Western New Thought system. It is clearly oriental in many respects.... But the characteristic ideas and techniques of New Thought are there." See *Spirits in Rebellion,* pp. 494, 497.

17 *Ibid.,* p. 108.

18 Robert L. Ramseyer, "The Sōka Gakkai: Militant Religion on the March," in *Studies in Japanese Culture,* ed. R. K. Beardsley, Ann Arbor: The University of Michigan Press, 1965, pp. 141–92, at p. 187. Ramseyer comments (p. 160) that "this element of personal gain is found to some degree in all of the great religions of the world, but only in perversions of them does it achieve the dominance that it is given" in Makiguchi's views. This is clearly in accord with our interpretation, although we might put the matter somewhat differently.

parable to applied science, whose affinity with religion he and other Gakkai leaders have stressed.[19]

Several years ago a Sunday newspaper magazine carried an article on Sōka Gakkai with the interesting title, "Sōka Gakkai Brings 'Absolute Happiness.'"[20] The title is cited here for obvious reasons. But it must also be said that the concerns of the new religions are already in some flux. They may be making some important accommodations in the interest of presenting an appearance of greater "respectability" in the face of higher-status conversion prospects. Indeed, according to Thomsen, Sōka Gakkai, which initially advised followers against consulting doctors, now advises them in case of disease to consult doctors first and come to Sōka Gakkai later; and Tenrikiyo (another of the new religions) has shifted its stress away from faith healing, once a major preoccupation: "Tenrikiyo and a few others have even built hospitals whose doctors more often than not are unbelievers."[21]

Babbie, in a very thoughtful article on Sōka Gakkai, has noted how that organization has mitigated its stress on organismic and economic deprivation and concentrated more on other kinds of deprivation as it has sought to expand its appeal.[22] But we have not sought to sustain any thesis to the effect that popular religion is unchanging. It is of interest, finally, that there appears to be a measure of agreement that the new religions have gotten much support from Japan's lower classes. Thus, Offner and van Straehlen contrast them in this respect with the Christian Church in Japan and observe that they have demonstrated "a definite ability" to reach the lower strata. Thomsen observes that "the vast majority of new religions seem to concentrate on the farmers and workers in the first stage of development." Ramseyer noted that Sōka Gakkai political candidates got strong support from wards with high percentages of very poor people. Morris has emphasized the appeal of the same organization to the lower levels of the working class in the cities.[23] But a definitive study of this matter is not yet available. The statements of individual writers are not always clear nor do all writers seem quite consistent with one another so far as one can tell. Kitagawa asserts that for the most part the new religions draw their followers from the "lower middle" class.[24]

Instrumentalization

Much of religious history has been informed by a tension between a "for God" or (more broadly) "spiritual" principle and a "for man" principle. On the one hand we have a principle that asserts that God's existence is

19 Ramseyer, ibid., pp. 160, 162.
20 New York Times Magazine, July 18, 1965, pp. 8, 9, 36–39.
21 Thomsen, ibid., pp. 23–24.
22 Earl R. Babbie, "The Third Civilization," Review of Religious Research, 7, 1966, pp. 101–21. In the light of our references to Makiguchi, above, it is of interest that Babbie contends with regard to the Gakkai movement (loc. cit., p. 105) that "justification for present activities is found in the life of Nichiren, and Makiguchi has greatly faded into the background as an historical figure for the religion."

23 Offer and van Straehlem, Modern Japanese Religions, p. 269: Thomsen, The New Religions of Japan, p. 17; Ramseyer, "The Sōka Gakkai," p. 179; Ivan Morris. "The Challenge of Sōka Gakkai." Encounter, 26, May, 1966, pp. 78–83, at p. 82.
24 Joseph M. Kitagawa, Religion in Japanese History, New York: Columbia University Press, 1966, p. 333.

for God's "benefit" regardless of men or that concentrates on and advocates exclusively the intrinsic spiritual merit of things spiritual, and on the other hand a principle whereby God's existence, or the spiritual realm, is presumed to be for men's benefit regardless of God or the spiritual. Broadly, men have "wanted" things from their religions, beyond a doubt—health, serenity, wealth, and much else. "Some of the Quietists," Knox notes, "seem to have spent their whole lives under the conviction that they were destined to be lost." This is at least a conviction that men ordinarily want to get away from. They want to be saved. Knox observes, too, that "perhaps we must not quarrel with the eccentric legacy by which a disciple of Père Piny endowed a series of Masses, not for the welfare of her soul, but in thanksgiving to God for having decreed her salvation or damnation, as the case might be." But this features a rather remarkable neutrality about one's self, a kind of heroic devotion to the "for God" principle.

Knox also refers, finally, to "a young priest who asked God in set terms to send him to hell, so that the Divine justice and the Divine glory might be more fully manifested."[25] This takes the "for God" principle to great lengths and exhibits a downright "enthusiastic" abnegation of one's own interest in salvation. It is unusual, to say the least. Ordinarily the two principles are in tension within religion. Conze observed that the message of the Prajnaparamita books in Buddhism was that "perfect wisdom can be attained only by the complete and total extinction of all self-interest" and yet noted that side by side with this "extreme spiritual teaching" there was stress on "the tangible and visible advantages which perfect wisdom confers in this very life here and now."[26] The two principles we refer to are thus clearly suggested, and it may be added that, as the present writer has expressed the matter elsewhere, "either principle alone (insofar as either has ever been adhered to alone) has constantly generated difficulties for the religious or religiously interested, and the blending of the two principles constantly threatens to be unstable."[27]

The blending is threatened in popular religion in the direction of a very powerful "for man" emphasis —and this has been one of the central matters in our conception of this kind of religion. Once more, it is not that it contains no "spirituality," nothing "for God." It is not that generally different, more "spiritual" religious phenomena are quite without "for man" components. One may well doubt whether in utterly extreme form in either direction any "religion" (if that term could still be retained) could endure for any length of time. One of the principles seems constantly to hover in the background even when the other is to the fore, and too strong a movement toward either pole appears to gen-

25 Ronald Knox, *Enthusiasm,* New York: Oxford University Press, 1961, pp. 272, 273.

26 Conze, *Buddhism,* New York: Harper and Row, pp. 84–85.

27 See Robert E. L. Faris, ed., *Handbook of Modern Sociology,* Chicago: Rand McNally, 1964, p. 785. The above paragraph draws on the article by Louis Schneider, "Problems in the Sociology of Religion," in Faris, pp. 770–807, from which these words are quoted, and the article is further drawn upon, with what now appear to be suitable modifications, in what follows.

erate a countermovement to the other.[28]

It is well to recall now our earlier reference to Merton's distinction of manifest and latent functions, in connection with which he raised the question, "What are the effects of the transformation of a previously latent function into a manifest function (involving the problem of the role of knowledge in human behavior and the problems of 'manipulation' of human behavior?)"[29] This is a most pregnant query for the type of religion that is more particularly set out in the inspirational religious literature, as will be indicated. Historically, in a broad, general way, there has undoubtedly been considerable awareness, especially on the part of persons in certain social positions, of various functions of religion. To that extent, as a mere matter of definition, functions of religion have been manifest. But there also has been such a thing as becoming aware of functions previously unsuspected or only dimly known.

Pratt argued very plausibly that in human history after long periods of a kind of "innocent" worship unconscious of human effects, "more reflective worshipers discovered that the cult in its various forms exerted an influence not only upon the gods but upon their own spirits." This suggests an important event of the kind to which Merton's basic query points. Not only did religion "originally" (a dubious though useful word in this context) actually work in certain ways, without the knowledge of worshipers that it did so; but there followed a time when some knowledge of its effects came at least to "more reflective worshipers." Information not previously available became available to some; and causal reinforcement could be added to original effect as men were consciously motivated to engage in religious exercises *because of knowledge of* their social and psychological consequences. Pratt adds that "the leaders of religion" were presumably the first to find out that religion influenced men, and the next stage in the relevant development was for those leaders "to conduct the cult in such fashion as not only to influence the gods but also to affect their fellow worshipers." Pratt also observes that the whole history of religion

---

[28] Alexis de Tocqueville long ago perceived how religion is constrained to blend ingredients of the "material" and the "spiritual," the "selfish," and the "unselfish," that which is "for God" and that which is "for man." Tocqueville wrote: "We shall see that of all the passions which originate in or are fostered by equality, there is one which it renders peculiarly intense, and which it also infuses into the heart of every man; I mean the love of well-being. The taste for well-being is the prominent and indelible feature of democratic times." To this Tocqueville added at once: "It may be believed that a religion which should undertake to destroy so deep-seated a passion would in the end be destroyed by it; and if it attempted to wean men entirely from the contemplation of the good things of this world in order to devote their faculties exclusively to the thought of another, it may be foreseen that the minds of men would at length escape its grasp to plunge into the exclusive enjoyment of present and material pleasures." And finally one kind of "blending" or compromise: "The chief concern of religion is to purify, to regulate, and to restrain the excessive and exclusive taste for well-being that men feel in periods of equality; but it would be an error to attempt to overcome it completely or to eradicate it. Men cannot be cured of the love of riches, but they may be persuaded to enrich themselves by none but honest means." *Democracy in America* (ed. Phillips Bradley), New York: A. A. Knopf, 1945, Vol. 2, p. 26. Tocqueville is close enough to what interests us here.

[29] *Social Theory and Social Structure,* p. 51.

might be written in the light of the process reviewed, in its course "from the naive attempt to influence the deity to the sophisticated and deliberate effort to bring about a psychological effect on the worshiper."[30] It may be added that it is not necessary to confine this kind of "model" strictly to "psychological effect on the worshiper" but that it may be extended to include "social" functions. The two kinds of phenomena are of course closely connected. A death ceremony that allays the sorrow of any individual ("psychological effect") also helps to return him to the circle of the living and enables him to resume his ordinary routines and associations (thereby exercising "integrative" social function).

Where there is awareness of psychological effects and social functions of religion and where those effects and functions are regarded as good or useful, it is not by any means a fantastic notion that some men should seek to "help along" the "natural" workings of religion. If religion brings peace of mind (as it *sometimes* does), for example, why not help it out a bit and use it to bring peace of mind? One may even wish to "talk one's self" into faith because one has pressing emotional difficulties and believes that faith may afford a way out of them, on the line of a kind of desperate "will to believe." The content and tone of the American inspirational literature strongly suggest a process whereby there has come to some persons, at least, an awareness of effects and social functions of religion that are taken to be desirable; whereby, further, these persons have sought to utilize religion instrumentally so that

it becomes something on the order of a set of devices to attain peace of mind, prosperity, and the like; and whereby, finally, these persons have sought to make the instrumentalized religion available to others. There is a kind of reversal of spiritual principle in all this. The principles adhered to in inspirationalism do *not* seem to follow the line suggested by "Seek ye first the kingdom of God and all these things will be added unto you." One interesting question is whether inspirational devices actually "work" or are perhaps selfdefeating, in that the "good things" of this world that religious activity may possibly bring and has sometimes brought come most surely as byproducts and not when they are directly pursued.[31]

But we must not understand what is involved here too crudely and unqualifiedly. If there is indeed something like a movement from latent to manifest functions (which is after

---

30 James B. Pratt, *Eternal Values in Religion,* New York: Macmillan, 1950, p. 27.

31 Also involved here is the question of how much intrinsic "truth" or presumption of religious verity one retains in an inspirational outlook. Pratt comments that "it is interesting to note the fervor with which certain psychological writers extol the value of prayer and in the same breath either state or imply that its value is due entirely to subjective conditions." He continues, observing that "since the subjective value of prayer is chiefly due to the belief that prayer has values which are *not* subjective, it will with most persons evaporate altogether once they learn that it is *all* subjective. Hence if it be true both that the subjective value of prayer is very great and also that it is the only value which prayer possesses, this latter fact should assiduously be kept secret." Pratt concludes his reflections on this line with the remark that if the subjective value of prayer is all the value it has, then "we wise psychologists of religion had better keep the fact to ourselves," on pain of soon having no religion left about which to psychologize. Pratt, *The Religious Consciousness,* p. 336.

all a matter of the emergence or spread of awareness or knowledge), we must, for one thing, specify *for whom* the new awareness or knowledge supervenes. If new knowledge of psychological effects and social functions of religion is employed in a kind of reconstruction of religious activity, *who* does the reconstructing? Is it merely inspirational "leaders" or is it followers also, and in what degree does it occur for members of each category? Instrumentalization need not be "absolute." Thus, there may be some measure of instrumental utilization of religion on a person's part while the same person also adheres to religious ways that have nothing particularly instrumental about them. Granted that there must be an element of the deliberate in instrumetalization there is no suggestion here, say, of a very purposeful, perhaps even cynical, plan on the part of "leaders" to instrumentalize religion and dilute or even destroy the high spirituality of a spotless Christian tradition. Instrumentalization in the sense in which we have been employing the term is a more subtle phenomenon than this.

It should by now be entirely plain that we do not in the case of inspirational religious literature postulate a breakthrough of utter, wholly unprecedented coarseness and concentration on the good things of this world. It will be recalled that we cited Drummond, above, to the effect that empirical (that is, historically actual) Christianity has at various times and places shown considerable tendency toward being a "religion of personal advantage." So much of historical religious activity has in fact been pointed toward "getting" things, so decidedly "for man"—oriented, that instrumentalization as here understood might well often have been superfluous. But if we think of in-

strumentalization as a significant *strain* in various concrete religious manifestations and do not seek to set off the strain in absolute terms, the category would appear to have considerable utility. Possibly instrumentalization is decidedly more important in the American religious situation than in the Japanese. The new religions of Japan clearly rest on a very old folk base of phenomena like popular magic and there is need for caution in imputing to them an instrumentalizing, de-spiritualizing process, considering the large magical and homocentric component that is present in them as it were "naturally." Yet there is the suggestion of instrumentalization that comes to us via the description of the outlook of someone like Makiguchi. It may be proposed that each of the two popular religious manifestations we have touched upon is a "mix" of the naively popular and of instrumentalization, while the Japanese, by comparison with the American case, has a relatively smaller instrumentalization component. Clearly, we should know more about all this. But it is worthwhile, in considering phenomena on the line of instrumentalization, to keep in view a simple paradigm (into which various subtleties and qualifications may be introduced as needed) which involves these elements:

1. Latent functions of religion become manifest.
2. They are then recast as goals.
3. Old ceremonial or other religious activity (such as prayer) becomes new technological device.

(Instrumentalization can be *self*-referring, in accordance with resolve to find for one's self health, wealth, peace of mind, through prayer; or *other*-referring, as in elite machinations to exploit the sincere religious beliefs of a nonelite. Obviously, the "meaning" of the paradigm will differ for these two kinds of cases.)

The above discussion may be allowed to give occasion to a wider consideration of the whole matter of instrumental use of religion. We may note first the bias toward use of religion for what are regarded as desirable psychological results. One of its most distinguished representatives was William James. James cites James H. Leuba's view that "so long as men can *use* their God, they care very little who he is, or even whether he is at all." He quotes Leuba further: "*God is not known, he is used* —sometimes as meat-purveyor, sometimes as moral support, sometimes as friend, sometimes as an object of love. If he proves himself useful, the religious consciousness asks for no more than that." It would seem, too, that "not God, but life, more life, a larger, richer, more satisfying life, is, in the last analysis, the end of religion."[32] James himself did not hesitate in making use of deity or religion. His *Varieties* is in a sense a very "practical" book. He was most alert to the psychotherapeutic potential of religion and was concerned to develop a psychology and philosophy of religion that would exploit that potential. James made the potential itself entirely plain. He had clearly come to think of it as something that could be formulated as a goal for "seekers." Problems of instrumentalization are thus once more suggested, obviously long before Peale wrote and against a background of far greater sophistication. Once again, questions of "amount" and of "blend" arise. In particular, the query always remains whether, given a certain

amount of instrumental emphasis, the "religious" enterprise does not become self-defeating. If religion can at times produce tranquillity, to put the matter bluntly, will a rather deliberate search for tranquillity via a religion relatively unblended with different ("spiritual," "for-God," "unselfish") components have prospects of success?

Instrumental thought has not been lacking with regard to broader social functions of religion. In an interesting essay on the antirevolutionary Joseph de Maistre (1753–1821), Lord Morley once wrote that in the eighteenth century, prior to the French Revolution, men were wont to ask of Christianity whether it was true or not, whereas after the Revolution their question was likely to be whether and how it might contribute to the rebuilding of society. People had come to ask "less how true it was than how strong it was." They had come to be concerned less about Christianity's "unquestioned dogmas" than about "how much social weight it had, or could develop." They inquired "less as to the precise amount and form of belief that would save a soul" than as to the way in which Christianity might specifically "be expected to assist the European community."[33] Whether the before-the-Revolution-after-the-Revolution contrast is overstated or not, there certainly was considerable post-Revolutionary interest in the social functions of religion.[34] Particularly prominent in this connection is the philosopher and sociologist Auguste Comte. In his early work Comte had

---

32 See William James, *The Varieties of Religious Experience,* New York: Modern Library, 1936, p. 497.

33 John Viscount Morley, "The Champion of Social Regress," in *The Works of Lord Morley,* vol. 12, London: Macmillan, 1921, p. 177.

34 See D. G. Charlton, *Secular Religions in France,* 1815–1870, London: Oxford University Press, 1963.

already revealed a considerable understanding of various social aspects of religion. When in his later work he conceived that some kind of religion was indispensable to social order, he unquestionably drew on his knowledge of social functions of religion and tailored a new religion ("the Religion of Humanity") to the "uses" he derived from that knowledge. In a popular book on religion, Comte's follower, the English thinker Frederic Harrison, suggested that Comte had seen "deeply" to the foundations of all religion and had "apprehended what religion *really has to do*."[35] The emphasis is Harrison's own and the suggestion of an instrumental orientation to religion, of thinking in terms of the "uses" to which it must be devoted, is very far from alien to Comte's work.[36]

Comte's outline of the Religion of Humanity is a very detailed affair. We confine ourselves to noting a few pertinent matters. Comte was convinced that man must be subordinated to some larger existence than his own in order to perpetuate his life, which otherwise must be transitory. This larger existence for man is a Great Being, a Grand Etre, roughly a kind of essence of the "best" in deceased humanity. Man is a selfishly inclined creature who must be made more altruistic, and this can be effected through worship of women, which will ultimately be transferred to the Great Being. Religion will perform an indispensable function in "combining" and in "regulating" individuals. A new priesthood will guide mankind religiously. In all this, the Great Being is a species

of invented divine or quasidivine substance or essence, and religion is deliberately enlisted in the performance of important social functions, although it is certainly also supposed to afford "spiritual" satisfactions. An interesting speculative set of questions is suggested by all this. Just *who* was to be enlightened as to what religion "really has to do," to use Harrison's words? How much popular enlightenment was there to be? Would enlightenment on the uses of religion be compatible with authentic belief in and devotion to the Great Being? A number of commentators on Comte have been much concerned with the last of these questions in particular. It is important to note their skepticism about instrumentalization à la Comte. The general tone of these commentators is suggested by the philosopher, Edward Caird:

In Comte's reconstruction of religion there seems to be something artificial and factitious, something "subjective" in the bad sense. It is religion made, so to speak, out of *malice prepense*. "We have derived," he seems to say, "from the experience of our own past and of the past of humanity a clear idea of what religion should be: and we also know from the same experience that, without a religion, we cannot have that fulness of spiritual life of which we are capable. Go to, let us make a religion, as nearly corresponding to the definition of religion as modern science will permit. . . ."[37]

Caird's last sentence, "Go to, let us make a religion. . . ." is exceedingly apt. It fits the Comtean case quite precisely. Another commentator, Hawkins, evidently paraphrasing a much earlier critic of Comte, asks: "What can produce a more profound sense of unreality than the conscious-

35 *The Positive Evolution of Religion,* London: Heinman, 1913, p. 233.

36 See particularly Comte's *System of Positive Polity,* Vol. 4, London: Longmans, Green, 1877.

37 See Caird's *The Social Philosophy and Religion of Comte,* Glasgow: Maclehose and Sons, 1885, pp. 163–64.

ness that we are worshiping a deity who is nothing but our own memory of the dead, who is avowedly a mere doll-providence, made and dressed for us by the priest, and handed to us to be worshiped in order to satisfy our craving for the Infinitely Lovely and Great?"[38] And near the end of his illuminating review of nineteenth-century "secular religions" in France, Charlton comments that "it is surely doubtful whether we can for long feel awe, experience 'the sense of the holy,' in contemplating what we have ourselves invented."[39] In Comte's work there was unquestionably a strain toward instrumentalization within the context of latent-becoming-manifest (for to the eye of Comte much had become manifest that would not have been so to dimmer sociological sight), and it is at least entirely plain that critics of Comte were dubious about the feasibility of an invented, instrumentalized religion or deity or similar entities. It may be suggested that the doubt had some justification.

Comte's particular efforts are of special interest for a number of reasons, not least because they present the speculative religious endeavors of a very gifted (if in a number of respects quite rigid) man. But the problems Comte suggests in this particular context go well beyond him and his followers and the religion he invented. The question of *who* (or what social strata, or other significant portions of a societal community) knows what, of the distribution of knowledge, is important in the sociology of religion beyond what Comte brings up—as is the allied question of whether religion can continue to exer-

cise a variety of social functions when people are merely aware of those functions but have lost faith in the professions and exercises that constitute religion itself. It is worth quoting two pertinent statements, one by a sociologist and the other by a church historian. Ronald Dore writes in his study of a ward in Tokyo, Japan:

For socially useful fictions to be maintained it is, perhaps, necessary that only a small minority should be aware that they are fictions and should keep the knowledge to themselves. It is difficult to imagine a society in which everyone performs rites towards supernatural beings which they (*sic*) believe not to exist *as if* they did exist, solely because they consider that the sentiments which they are thereby inducing *in themselves* are necessary to that society. In ancient China, Mo-tzu, whose rationalistic approach led him to assert that 'to hold that there are no spirits and learn sacrificial ceremonies is like learning the ceremonies of hospitality when there is no guest, or making fishnets when there are no fish,' explicitly attacked the skepticism of the Confucians because, diffused among the common people, it led to an abandonment of moral standards and the disintegration of society in unfilial conduct, wickedness and rebellion. For the common people to hold a skeptical Confucian outlook and yet train their moral responses by performance of the rites he clearly held to be impossible.[40]

This plainly suggests certain difficulties likely to arise if social functions of religion are projected as goals and an effort is made to achieve them by a process of self-manipulation (and also suggests difficulties about manipulating others). We are inevitably reminded of Pratt's view that, since the psychological value of prayer rests on the presumption that it has more than psychological value, prayer is likely to disappear when

[38] Richmond L. Hawkins, *Positivism in the United States,* Cambridge: Harvard University Press, 1938, p. 85.

[39] *Secular Religions in France,* pp. 214–15.

[40] *City Life in Japan,* p. 328.

the persuasion arises that its value is all, or merely, psychological. Félicité de Lammennais (1782–1854), a most significant figure in Catholicism who sought in a parlous time to combine firm adherence to Catholicism with a liberal outlook in social, political and economic matters, lived well over two millennia after Mo-tzu. But the following statement by the church historian Vidler shows that Lammennais held views reminiscent of Mo-tzu:

[Lammennais] pointed out that *les philosophes* admitted that the people needed religion to persuade them to those duties without the performance of which society would not hold together. Indeed their theory was that God and morality had been invented by governments for this very reason. Lammennais naturally made play with this fantasy, and also pressed the point that religion must be believed to be true if it is to provide the required sanction for order and morality. But *les philosophes,* while they admitted the necessity of religion, were engaged in disseminating proofs of its falsehood. They were therefore involved in a hopeless contradiction and they should think again.[41]

This has evident enough implications for our present themes and at this point it is no longer needful to elaborate them. Let us here simply remark some scattered historical instances in which the ancient insight that religion exercises significant social functions is accompanied by the disposition to exploit those functions in some sense and in which we are consequently close to an instrumental orientation toward religion. Dansette quotes Voltaire's cynical comment, "I like my attorney, my tailor, my servants and my wife to believe in God because I can then expect to find myself less often robbed

and less often cuckolded."[42] Dansette also notes that Napoleon held the view that religion must be reckoned along with money, honors, and fear of punishment or death as something close to the springs of human action. The people needed religion, Buonaparte was persuaded, and he was persuaded as well that their religion had to be governmentally controlled. In this conception, religion was an instrumentality of the law. The state had at its disposal the force represented by religion, "which bridled men's instincts and influenced their intentions," and the force represented by the police, which punished where religion did not effectively restrain.[43] Cross reports that Mark Hanna was supposed to have viewed the Supreme Court and the Roman Catholic Church as the sole safeguards against American anarchy, as he remarks that William Howard Taft in a similar spirit averred that Catholicism was "one of the bulwarks against socialism and anarchy in this country, and I welcome its presence here."[44] And Baltzell observes that the railroad baron, James Hill, a Protestant who donated a large sum to establish a Catholic theological seminary, answered a query as to why he did this with the words, "Look at the millions of foreigners pouring into this country for whom the Catholic Church represents the only authority they fear or respect."[45] In these views of

41 Alec R. Vidler, *Prophecy and Papacy,* New York: Scribner's 1954. p. 75.

42 Adrien Dansette, *Religious History of Modern France,* New York: Herder and Herder, 1961, Vol. 1, p. 265.

43 *Ibid.,* p. 142.

44 R. D. Cross, *The Emergence of Liberal Catholicism in America,* Cambridge: Harvard University Press, 1958, p. 35.

45 E. Digby Baltzell, *Philadelphia Gentlemen,* Glencoe: The Free Press, 1958, p. 224.

Hanna's, Taft's and Hill's, we are close indeed to instrumental outlooks on religion. (Of course, the mere *observation* that religion can exercise control functions is in itself "innocent" and does not necessarily imply an instrumental orientation.)

There are three points we would indicate terminally, having to do with relations of religion, magic and instrumentalization; with ambiguities in the term, instrumentalization; with the "future" of instrumentalization.

First, then, we may note what we regard as a fruitful way in which religion, magic and instrumentalization can be conceived to relate to one another, giving a special turn to things already said. There is more than one way in which magic can be defined, or, alternatively, there are various types of magic. The "for God"—"for man" tension, however, obviously suggests that religion and magic may be considered to blend into one another. When the "for God" element in religion recedes into the background and men's own needs are clamorously to the fore and when various manipulative techniques come into play (such as using the name of a spiritually exalted figure to obtain power over that figure for one's own practical purposes), we shall, accordingly, now say that we have to do with magic. Magic as here understood, however, arises in a cultural situation where there is at least some "high-level" comprehension of what a "for God" orientation means. In other words, magic, as we wish to define it, refers to a potentiality in an entire "religiomagical" complex. When the emphasis within the complex moves toward the "for God," nontechnique and nonmanipulative side, there is movement toward "religion" rather than toward "magic." Again, this is not the only possible

way to define magic (or there are other types of magic) and it leaves out phenomena that might in other perspectives be legitimately labeled magical. Thus, it does not pretend to deal with "primitive" magic, or cases where there is no cultural background of a so-called high religion. Instrumentalization (in a *self*-referring sense, as when one seeks to utilize prayer to attain peace of mind) is an enterprise in magic that of course (since it is "magic" in our sense to which we refer) comes within a high-religion cultural context and that very strongly seeks to exploit "religious" resources (such as belief in high, ethically elevated divinities).

Second, we may reaffirm the utility of the term, instrumentalization. But to recognize that utility it is not necessary to overlook the point that the term suggests certain ambiguities. Given the use that has been made of the term here, it is easy—perhaps too easy—to associate it with what may strike many as undesirable phenomena in the field of religion. But this could be a misleading association. One might conceivably argue that there is an element of instrumentalization in giving movements of social reform a religious backing, as it could be contended that ministers and rabbis who publicly support the civil rights movement and engage in certain demonstrations "use" their religion to further reform. No doubt, quite a few who would be content to let pass what might appear to be a hint of the pejorative in the application of the term, instrumentalization, to inspirational religious literature would resist any such hint in relation to the "application" of religion to the uses of enhancement of Negro rights. On the other hand, the men of religion committed to furthering reform and their followers might for their part argue that they were merely "realizing" or "acting out" their religion and that the employment of the term instrumentalization in relation to their activity was completely inept. Once again, to complicate matters, some persons might take the position that it is indeed a "use" of religion to employ it to further reform, that this is a decidely better and more justifiable use than some others, but that it is still a use and therefore subject to criticism in the light of ultimate religious values. We need not go further into the problems hereby suggested. It suffices to suggest them, but they are unavoidable and they are important.

Finally: it may be that a growing skepticism and an increasing secularization—understood in the sense of releasing more and more of the "world" from the presumption that one has to do with the sacred, as when problems of sickness once within the sacred orbit come to be handled in nonreligious and nonmagical ways— it may be that skepticism and secularization will ultimately make some of the religious phenomena touched upon in this chapter effectively obsolete. But as long as something on the order of "religion" continues to exist at all, it will inevitably continue to have psychological effects and social functions of some sort. If these appear desirable to particular persons and groups, the impulse to *make* religion bring them about, to make religion "useful" will presumably be hard to eliminate altogether. Whatever ambiguities the term instrumentalization conceals, the substantial sociological and psychological issues the term suggests, which we have sought to delineate, will remain, and sociologists of religion, if any there be, will be constrained to try to understand them.

Part 6

secularization

It is a common observation that America is a post-Christian society and that religion in the United States is highly secularized. However, the meaning of the term *secularization* is far from clear. In this section we try to explicate the various phenomena subsumed under the general rubric of secularization. We begin with a discussion of the term by the eminent sociologist, Peter Berger, who in his book *The Sacred Canopy* traces the various stages of secularization in the West. He shows how the consequences of secularization have challenged the plausibility of religious beliefs and have penetrated religious structures and attitudes. The Berger selection defines secularization on the levels both of individual consciousness and of institutional patterns.

Modern Western civilization is in a state of crisis. This condition is partly the consequence of the inability of traditional religion to speak to many contemporary men and of the failure of the various religious surrogates, such as faith in science and in progress, to fulfill needs and aspirations formerly met by religion itself. The full impact of this crisis was late in reaching America, but in the 1960s it arrived in dramatic forms. One form that may be symptomatic of the nature of the crisis as a whole is the youth rebellion of the late '60s. Many American young people demonstrated through this phenomenon their serious denial of faith in the all-sufficiency of science, in the adequacy of liberalism and its capacity to change society, in the work ethic and the American occupational structure which is its institutional embodiment, and in many other aspects of American middle-class life. Christopher Dawson seems to have foreseen the approaching crisis many years ago when he wrote that "this spiritual alienation of its own greatest minds is the price that every civilization has to pay when it loses its religious foundations, and is contented with material success. We are only just beginning to understand how intimately and profoundly the vitality of a society is bound up with its religion. . . ."[1] American youth, in challenging the basic structures, orientations, and life style of society, challenged the secular religion. Youth's quest for significance and for significant human community has been the subject of much discussion.

---

[1] Christopher Dawson, *Progress and Religion* (Garden City, N.Y.: Doubleday & Company, Inc., 1961), p. 184.

We present a brief section from *The Making of a Counter Culture,* by Theodore Roszak, which describes the special interest of youth in religion. Roszak finds such interest widespread and encompassing all kinds of phenomena that are in some way extraordinary, mysterious, or sacred. The growth of the Jesus movement, the interest in Eastern religions, and the increasing study of religion by college and university students all testify to the truth of this observation. The quest for new religious substance and sustenance and the experimentation with symbolic form and social organization, offer fascinating contemporary subject matter for the sociological study of religion.

Traditional religion has attempted to respond to the challenges of modernity. During the past one hundred fifty years in the West there have been movements within Protestantism, Catholicism, and Judaism to bring religion into a new and more fruitful relationship with modern science, with technological developments and the intellectual and social situations they tend to create, and with the social and political needs and aspirations of people in our modern technologically-based world. The sociologist of religion is able to observe the continuing dialectic between traditional religion and modernity; he can analyze the effect of secularization on the substance of religion, and the effects of renewed religious life on secular society. In this respect the Second Vatican Council stands as the most significant occurrence in recent religious history. Before Vatican II the Roman Catholic Church was the largest traditional religious body in the world. It stood in a defensive posture before modern trends, although within it small groups of hardy and profoundly religious men sought to work out new ways of confronting the world and to urge the abandonment of long-standing postures of defense. In Vatican II, such tendencies came to fruition. It represents the effort by the largest Christian communion to understand itself anew, to evaluate its positions and modes of life, and to make itself an effective spiritual force in the last half of the twentieth century. Analysis of the council on the historical, sociological, and theological levels not only provides a view of one traditional organization in confrontation with modernity, but also illuminates the basic problems that all religions groups must face when attempting to change and at the same time to preserve the reality of their essential visions. The selections by Thomas F. O'Dea concerning the council concentrate on the strategic elements of strain involved in the relationship of a traditional religion of transcendence to significant secular characteristics of the modern world. They show how the Fathers at the Council initiated the process of "institutional molting" required at this moment of the Church's history. O'Dea's study is an empirical example of how a sociologist can observe the continuing relation of religion and society by studying a strategic event in which the diagnostic issues and the alignment of elements within the religious body become evident.

the meaning of secularization

eighteen

from The Sacred Canopy

PETER BERGER

It is not difficult to put forth a simple definition of secularization for the purpose at hand. By secularization we mean the process by which sectors of society and culture are removed from the domination of religious institutions and symbols. When we speak of society and institutions in modern Western history, of course, secularization manifests itself in the evacuation by the Christian churches of areas previously under their control or influence—as in the separation of church and state, or in the expropriation of church lands, or in the emancipation of education from ecclesiastical authority. When we speak of culture and symbols, however, we imply that secularization is more than a social-structural process. It affects the totality of cultural life and of ideation, and may be observed in the decline of religious contents in the arts, in philosophy, in literature and, most important of all, in the rise of science as an autonomous, thoroughly,

From *The Sacred Canopy* by Peter L. Berger. Copyright © 1967 by Peter L. Berger. Reprinted by permission of Doubleday & Company, Inc.

secular perspective on the world. Moreover, it is implied here that the process of secularization has a subjective side as well. As there is a secularization of society and culture, so is there a secularization of consciousness. Put simply, this means that the modern West has produced an increasing number of individuals who look upon the world and their own lives without the benefit of religious interpretations.

While secularization may be viewed as a global phenomenon of modern societies, it is not uniformly distributed within them. Different groups of the population have been affected by it differently.[1] Thus it has been

---

[1] Probably the largest amount of data on the social differentiation of religious identification has been collected by Gabriel LeBras and those (mainly Catholic sociologists) who have followed his methods. *Cf.* his *Etudes de sociologie religieuse* (Paris, Presses Universitaires de France, 1955). Also, *cf.* Emile Pin, *Pratique religieuse et classes sociales* (Paris, Spes, 1956), and F. A. Isambert, *Christianisme et classe ouvrière* (Tournai, Casterman, 1961). The works of Joseph Fichter, beginning with *Southern Parish* (Chicago, Chicago University Press, 1951), reflect a very similar orientation in American Catholic sociology. The classical work

found that the impact of secularization has tended to be stronger on men than on women, on people in the middle age range than on the very young and the old, in the cities than in the country, on classes directly connected with modern industrial production (particularly the working class) than on those of more traditional occupations (such as artisans or small shopkeepers), on Protestants and Jews than on Catholics, and the like. At least as far as Europe is concerned, it is possible to say with some confidence, on the basis of these data, that church-related religiosity is strongest (and thus, at any rate, social-structural secularization least) on the margins of modern industrial society, both in terms of marginal classes (such as the remnants of old petty bourgeoisies) and marginal individuals (such as those eliminated from the work process).[2]

The situation is different in America, where the churches still occupy a more central symbolic position, but it may be argued that they have succeeded in keeping this position only by becoming highly secularized themselves, so that the European and American cases represent two variations on the same underlying theme of global secularization.[3] What is more, it appears that the same secularizing forces have now become worldwide in the course of westernization and modernization.[4] Most of the available data, to be sure, pertain to the social-structural manifestations of secularization rather than to the secularization of consciousness, but we have enough data to indicate the massive presence of the latter in the contemporary West.[5] We cannot here

---

dealing with this general problematic in the sociology of religion in America is Richard Niebuhr, *The Social Sources of Denominationalism* (New York, Holt, 1929), which has stimulated a number of empirical case studies. For a recent example, cf. N. J. Demerath, *Social Class in American Protestantism* (Chicago, Rand McNally, 1965). The most thorough study of its kind in America is probably Gerhard Lenski, *The Religious Factor* (Garden City, N.Y., Doubleday, 1961).

2 This has been succinctly summarized by Thomas Luckmann: "Dagegen ist aus den Forschungsergebnissen zu entnehmen, dass Kirchlichkeit zu einem Randphaenomen in der modernen Gesellschaft geworden ist. In Europa charakterisiert Kirchlichkeit nur einen geringen Bruchteil der Bevoelkerung, und zwar bezeichnenderweise jenen Teil, der selbst sozusagen am Rand der modernen Gesellschaftsentwicklung steht, so vor allem die Bauern, das Kleinbuergertum, die Ueberbleibsel 'staendischer' Herkunft innerhalb der Mittelschicht, die noch nicht in den Arbeitsprozess Eingeschalteten oder die aus dem Arbeitsprozess schon Ausgeschalteten" (*Das Problem der Religion in der modernen Gesellschaft* [Freiburg, Rombach, 1963], p. 29). Also,

cf. Reinhard Koester, *Die Kirchentreuen* (Stuttgart, Enke, 1959).

3 This point has also been stated very well by Luckmann, *Das Problem der Religion*. For secularization *within* institutional religion in America, cf. Will Herberg, *Protestant—Catholic—Jew* (Garden City, N.Y., Doubleday, 1955), and my *The Noise of Solemn Assemblies* (Garden City, N.Y., Doubleday, 1961).

4 Cf. Daniel Lerner, *The Passing of Traditional Society* (Glencoe, Ill., Free Press, 1958); Robert Bellah (ed), *Religion and Progress in Modern Asia* (New York, Free Press, 1965); Donald Smith (ed.), *South Asian Politics and Religion* (Princeton, Princeton University Press, 1966).

5 While the material accumulated by Catholic sociologists mainly concerns the institutional aspects of secularization (particularly as expressed in the externals of religious practice), a good many data on the subjective correlates of this may also be found there. Cf. Sabino Acquaviva, *L'eclissi del sacro nella cività industriale* (Milan, Edizioni Commusta, 1961), for a summary, as well as Hervé Carrier, *Psycho-sociologie de l'appartenance religieuse* (Rome, Presses de l'Université Grégorienne, 1960). Also, cf. Gordon Allport, *The Individual and His Religion* (New York, Macmillan, 1950); Hans-Otto Woelber, *Religion ohne Entscheidung*

pursue the interesting question of the extent to which there may be, so to speak, asymmetry between these two dimensions of secularization, so that there may not only be secularization of consciousness within the traditional religious institutions but also a continuation of more or less traditional motifs of religious consciousness outside their previous institutional contexts.[6]

If, for heuristic purposes, we were to take an epidemiological viewpoint with regard to secularization, it would be natural to ask what are its "carriers."[7] In other words, what sociocultural processes and groups serve as vehicles or mediators of secularization? Viewed from outside Western civilization (say, by a concerned Hindu traditionalist), the answer is obviously that it is that civilization as a whole in its spread around the world (and it need hardly be emphasized that, from that viewpoint, Communism and modern nationalism are just as much manifestations of Westernization as their "imperialist" predecessors). Viewed from inside Western civilization (say, by a worried Spanish country priest), the original "carrier" of secularization is the modern economic process, that is, the dynamic of industrial capitalism. To be sure, it may be "secondary" effects of this dynamic that constitute the immediate problem (for example, the secularizing contents of modern mass media or the influences of a heterogeneous mass of tourists brought in by modern means of trans-

portation). But it does not take long to trace these "secondary" effects back to their original source in the expanding capitalist-industrial economy. In those parts of the Western world where industrialism has taken socialist forms of organization, closeness to the processes of industrial production and its concomitant styles of life continues to be the principal determinant of secularization.[8] Today, it would seem, it is industrial society in itself that is secularizing, with its divergent ideological legitimations serving merely as modifications of the global secularization process. Thus the anti-religious propaganda and repressive measures of Marxist regimes naturally affect the secularization process (though, perhaps, not always in quite the way intended by their initiators), as do the pro-religious policies of various governments outside the Marxist sphere. It seems likely, however, that both these political-ideological attitudes must reckon with basic societal forces that antedate the particular policies in question and over which governments have only limited control. This state of affairs becomes amusingly evident when we see very similar sociological data for socialist and non-socialist countries (say, with regard to the secularity of working class and the religiosity of the peasants) used by Marxist observers as an occasion to bemoan the limited effectiveness of "scientific atheist" agitation and by Christian observers to lament the failures of evangelism, to the point where one is

---

(Goettingen, Vandenhoeck & Ruprecht, 1959); Rose Goldsen et al., What College Students Think (Princeton, Van Nostrand, 1960).

[6] On the latter possibility, cf. Eberhard Stammler, Protestanten ohne Kirche (Stuttgart, Kreuz, 1960).

[7] The term "carrier" (Traeger) is used here in a Weberian sense.

[8] Cf. Olaf Klohr (ed.), Religion und Atheismus heute (Berlin, Deutscher Verlag der Wissenschaften, 1966). For a nice comparison with recent data from an emphatically non-socialist context, cf. Ramón Bayés, Los ingenieros, la sociedad y la religión (Barcelona, Fontanella, 1965). The comparison would have entertained Veblen!

tempted to suggest that the two groups might get together and comfort each other.

We would regard it as axiomatic that a historical phenomenon of such scope will not be amenable to any monocausal explanations. Thus we have no interest in denigrating any of the various factors that have been suggested as causes of secularization (such as, for example, the pervasive influence of modern science). Nor are we interested, in the present context, in the establishment of a hierarchy of causes. We are interested, however, in the question of the extent to which the Western religious tradition may have carried the seeds of secularization within itself. If this can be maintained, as we think it can, it should be clear from our systematic considerations that the religious factor must *not* be considered as operating in isolation from other factors, but rather as standing in an ongoing dialectical relationship with the "practical" infrastructure of social life. In other words, nothing could be farther from our minds than to propose an "idealist" explanation of secularization. It should also be clear that any demonstration of the secularizing consequences of the Mestern religious tradition tells us nothing about the intentions of those who shaped and carried on this tradition.[9]

The suspicion that there may be an inherent connection between Christianity and the character of the modern Western world is by no means new. At least since Hegel the connection has been repeatedly asserted by historians, philosophers,

theologians, though, of course, their evaluation of this has varied greatly. Thus the modern world could be interpreted as a higher realization of the Christian spirit (as Hegel interpreted it), or Christianity could be regarded as the principal pathogenic factor responsible for the supposedly sorry state of the modern world (as, for instance, by Schopenhauer and Nietzsche). The notion that a peculiar role in the establishment of the modern world was played by Protestantism has, of course, been a matter of widespread discussion among sociologists and historians for the last fifty years or so. It may be useful, though, to briefly summarize this notion here.[10]

If compared with the "fullness" of the Catholic universe, Protestantism appears as a radical truncation, a reduction to "essentials" at the expense of a vast wealth of religious contents. This is especially true of the Calvinist version of Protestantism, but to a considerable degree the same may be said of the Lutheran and even the Anglican Reformations. Our statement, of course, is merely descriptive —we are not interested in whatever theological justifications there may be either for the Catholic *pleroma* or for the evangelical sparseness of Protestantism. If we look at these two religious constellations more careful-

---

9 Both these points, of course, are crucial to an understanding of Weber's work in this area and in the sociology of religion generally.

10 The following summation closely follows Weber, particularly his *The Protestant Ethic and the Spirit of Capitalism*. Also, cf. Ernst Troeltsch, *Die Bedeutung des Protestantismus fuer die Entstehung der modernen Welt* (1911); Karl Holl, "Die Kulturbedeutung der Reformation," in his *Gesammelte Aufsaetze zur Kirchengeschichte*, Vol. 1 (1932). For a linkage of this with the problematic of secularization, cf. Howard Becker, "Saekularisationsprozesse," *Koelner Vierteljahreshefte fuer Soziologie* (1932), 283 ff. and 450 ff.

ly, though, Protestantism may be described in terms of an immense shrinkage in the scope of the sacred in reality, as compared with its Catholic adversary. The sacramental apparatus is reduced to a minimum and, even there, divested of its more numinous qualities. The miracle of the mass disappears altogether. Less routine miracles, if not denied altogether, lose all real significance for the religious life. The immense network of intercession that unites the Catholic in this world with the saints and, indeed, with all departed souls disappears as well. Protestantism ceased praying for the dead. At the risk of some simplification, it can be said that Protestantism divested itself as much as possible from the three most ancient and most powerful concomitants of the sacred—mystery, miracle, and magic. This process has been aptly caught in the phrase "disenchantment of the world."[11] The Protestant believer no longer lives in a world ongoingly penetrated by sacred beings and forces. Reality is polarized between a radically transcendent divinity and a radically "fallen" humanity that, *ipso facto,* is devoid of sacred qualities. Between them lies an altogether "natural" universe, God's creation to be sure, but in itself bereft of numinosity. In other words, the radical transcendence of God confronts a universe of radical immanence, of "closedness" to the sacred. Religiously speaking, the world becomes very lonely indeed.

The Catholic lives in a world in which the sacred is mediated to him through a variety of channels—the sacraments of the church, the intercession of the saints, the recurring eruption of the "supernatural" in

miracles—a vast continuity of being between the seen and the unseen. Protestantism abolished most of these mediations. It broke the continuity, cut the umbilical cord between heaven and earth, and thereby threw man back upon himself in a historically unprecedented manner. Needless to say, this was not its intention. It only denuded the world of divinity in order to emphasize the terrible majesty of the transcendent God and it only threw man into total "fallenness" in order to make him open to the intervention of God's sovereign grace, the only true miracle in the Protestant universe. In doing this, however, it narrowed man's relationship to the sacred to the one exceedingly narrow channel that it called God's word (not to be identified with a fundamentalist conception of the Bible, but rather with the uniquely redemptive action of God's grace—the *sola gratia* of the Lutheran confessions). As long as the plausibility of this conception was maintained, of course, secularization was effectively arrested, even though all its ingredients were already present in the Protestant universe. It needed only the cutting of this one narrow channel of mediation, though, to open the floodgates of secularization. In other words, with nothing remaining "in between" a radically transcendent God and a radically immanent human world *except* this one channel, the sinking of the latter into implausibility left an empirical reality in which, indeed, "God is dead." This reality then became amenable to the systematic, rational penetration, both in thought and in activity, which we associate with modern science and technology. A sky empty of angels becomes open to the intervention of the astronomer and, eventually, of the astronaut. It may be maintained, then, that Protestantism

11 Weber—"Entzauberung der Welt."

served as a historically decisive prelude to secularization, whatever may have been the importance of other factors.

If this interpretation of the historical nexus between Protestantism and secularization is accepted (as it probably is today by a majority of scholarly opinion), then the question inevitably suggests itself as to whether the secularizing potency of Protestantism was a *novum* or whether it rather had its roots in earlier elements of the Biblical tradition. We would contend that the latter answer is the correct one, indeed that the roots of secularization are to be found in the earliest available sources for the religion of ancient Israel. In other words, we would maintain that the "disenchantment of the world" begins in the Old Testament.[12]

In order to appreciate this position one must see ancient Israel in the context of the cultures amid which it sprang up and *against* which it

defined itself.[13] While it would be erroneous to underestimate the considerable differences between these cultures (notably between the two cultural foci of Egypt and Mesopotamia), one common characteristic is the one that has aptly been called cosmological."[14] This means that the human world (that is, everything that we today would call culture and society) is understood as being embedded in a cosmic order that embraces the entire universe. This order not only fails to make the sharp modern differentiation between the human and non-human (or "natural") spheres of empirical reality, but, more importantly, it is an order that posits continuity between the empirical and the supra-empirical, between the world of men and the world of the gods. This continuity, which assumes an ongoing linkage of human events with the sacred forces permeating the universe, is realized (not just reaffirmed but literally re-established) again and again in religious ritual. For example, in the great New Year festival of ancient Mesopotamia the creation of the world is not only represented (as we today might understand it in terms of some sort of symbolism) but once more realized, made a reality, as human life is brought back again to its divine source. Thus everything that happens "here below" on the human plane has its analogue "up above" on the plane of the gods, and everything that happens "now" is linked with the cosmic

---

12 This point is made, quite explicitly, in Weber's *Ancient Judaism,* although the term "secularized" occurs only once (albeit in an interesting place, where Weber discusses the effect of the centralization of the cult in Jerusalem on the religious significance of the clan). But Weber's main interest in the Old Testament was in a related but different question—namely, that of the development of the Jewish economic ethic and its relationship (minimal, he thought) with the origins of modern capitalism. All the same, Weber's work on the Old Testament is of great importance for our present question as well. Biblical scholars have repeatedly pointed out the "desacralizing" and "demythologizing" tendencies of the Old Testament, at least since Wellhausen (who spoke of "denaturalization" in comparing Israel with the surrounding Near Eastern religions). For a very clear statement of this view (though geared to a theological rather than historical purpose), cf. Friedrich Gogarten, *Verhaengnis und Hoffnung der Neuzeit* (1953).

13 *Cf.* Henri Frankfort *et al., The Intellectual Adventure of Ancient Man* (Chicago, University of Chicago Press, 1946), and *Kingship and the Gods* (Chicago, University of Chicago Press, 1948); Eric Voegelin, *Israel and Revelation* (Baton Rouge, Louisiana State University Press, 1956).

14 This term is taken from Voegelin.

events that occurred "in the begin-ning."[15] This continuity between the human microcosm and the divine macrocosm can, of course, be broken, particularly by misdeeds on the part of men. Such misdeeds may be of the sort we today would call "uneth-ical" or "sinful," but they might also be of a quite different kind, such as in the breaking of tabus or in the improper performance of sacred cere-monies. In such cases the cosmic order has been "wronged"—and must again be "righted" by the appropriate ritual and moral acts. For example, dis-obedience to the god-king of Egypt is not only a political or ethical mal-feasance, but a disturbance of the cosmic order of things (expressed as *ma'at* by the Egyptians) that may affect the annual flooding of the Nile as much as the proper functioning of social relations or the safety of the frontiers—its "correction," then, is not only a matter of just punishment of the malfeasant but of the re-establishment of the proper relation-ship between the land of Egypt and the cosmic order on which it rests. To use two terms discussed previously, human affairs are ongoingly nomized by means of cosmization, that is, by being brought back into the cosmic order outside of which there is noth-ing but chaos.[16]

One point that should be strongly emphasized is that this sort of uni-verse is one of great security for the individual. Put negatively, it is a universe furnishing highly effective barriers against anomy. This does not mean at all that nothing terrible could happen to the individual or that he is guaranteed perennial happiness.

It does mean that whatever happens, however terrible, *makes sense* to him by being related to the ultimate mean-ing of things. Only if this point is grasped can one understand the per-sistent attractiveness of the various versions of this worldview to the Israelites, even long after their own religious development had decisively broken with it. Thus, for instance, it would be very misleading to think that the persistent attraction of sacred prostitution (against which the spokesmen of Yahweh thundered for centuries) was a matter of mundane lust. After all, we may assume that there were plenty of *non*-sacred pros-titutes around (to which, it seems, Yahweh's objections were minimal). The attraction rather lay in an alto-gether religious desire, namely in the nostalgia for the continuity between man and the cosmos that was sacra-mentally mediated by sacred sexuality.

It is profoundly significant that the traditions later incorporated in the canon of the Old Testament inter-preted the origins of Israel as a *double* exodus—the patriarchs' exodus from Mesopotamia and the great exodus from Egypt under Moses. This prototypical Israelite exodus was not just a geographical or political move-ment. Rather, it constituted a break with an entire universe. At the heart of the religion of ancient Israel lies the vehement repudiation of both the Egyptian and the Mesopotamian ver-sions of cosmic order, a repudiation that was, of course, extended to the pre-Israelite indigenous culture of Syria-Palestine. The "fleshpots of Egypt," from which Yahweh led Israel into the desert, stood above all for the security of the cosmic order in which Egyptian culture was rooted. Israel defined itself as separation from that cosmic unity that the Memphite Theology (in many ways the *magna*

---

[15] *Cf.* Mircea Eliade, *Cosmos and History* (New York, Harper, 1959).
[16] The term "cosmization" is taken from Eliade.

charta of Egyptian civilization) identified with the divinity Ptah—"for everything came forth from him, nourishment and provisions, the offerings of the gods, and every good thing."[17] This great denial of Israelite religion may be analyzed in terms of three pervasive motifs—transcendentalization, historization, and the rationalization of ethics.[18]

The Old Testament posits a God who stands *outside* the cosmos, which is his creation but which he confronts and does not permeate. It is not very easy to decide at what point in the religious development of ancient Israel there emerged that conception of God which we now associate with Judeo-Christian monotheism. By the eighth century, at the very latest, we find that conception fully developed and radically divergent from the general religious conceptions of the ancient Near East. This God is radically transcendent, not to be identified with any natural or human phenomena. He is not only the creator of the world but the *only* God—if not the only one in existence, at any rate the only one who mattered for Israel. He appears without mates or offspring, unaccompanied by a pantheon of any sort. Furthermore, this God acts historically rather than cosmically, particularly

though not exclusively in the history of Israel, and he is a God of radical ethical demands. But even if we cannot completely identify the earlier Israelite conceptions of its God with the one we find expressed by Amos, Hosea, and Isaiah in the eighth century, there are certain features that it apparently possessed from the earliest times, probably antedating the coming of the Israelite tribes to Palestine. Yahweh, whatever he may have been before his "adoption" by Israel (a process that, of course, Israel viewed as *its* "adoption" by *him*), was for Israel a God from far away. He was not a local or tribal divinity "naturally" connected with Israel, but a God linked to Israel "artificially," that is, historically. This linkage was established by the covenant between Yahweh and Israel, a relationship that entailed very specific obligations for Israel and one that could be abrogated if these obligations were not fulfilled (*that,* indeed, was the terrible message of eighth-century prophecy). Yahweh was consequently a "mobile" God, who could not be tied down either geographically or institutionally—he had *chosen* Palestine as the land of Israel, but he was not tied to it—he had *chosen* Saul and David as kings over Israel, but the monarchy was by no means an institution of divinity in the Egyptian or even the (modified) Mesopotamian sense. This "mobility" of Yahweh was well expressed in the portable character of the ark of the covenant, which was only "accidentally" deposited in this or that sanctuary, but even when it finally came to rest in the temple at Jerusalem the latter could in no way be regarded as Yahweh's necessary habitat (with the tremendously important consequence that Israel survived the destruction of Jersualem first by the Babylonians and then, in a different form, by the Romans). This God demanded sac-

---

17 James Pritchard (ed.), *Ancient Near Eastern Texts* (Princeton, Princeton University Press, 1955), p. 5. For a commentary of this fascinating text, *cf.* John Wilson, *The Burden of Egypt* (Chicago, University of Chicago Press, 1951).

18 The last of these three terms is taken from Weber. The terms "rationalization" and "rationality" are understood in a Weberian sense throughout. For our general view of Israelite religion, *cf.* Edmond Jacob, *Théologie de l'Ancien Testament* (Neuchâtel, Delachaux & Niestlé, 1955); Voegelin, *Israel and Revelation,* Gerhard von Rad, *Theologie des alten Testaments,* Vols. 1–2 (Munich, Kaiser, 1957 and 1960).

rifice, but he was not dependent upon it. And, consequently, he was fundamentally immune to magical manipulation.[19]

The radical transcendentalization of God in the Old Testament can be best seen in precisely those places where elements of extra-Israelite religion are incorporated. A good example is the creation story of Genesis 1, which incorporates a number of cosmogonic elements from Mesopotamian mythology. However interesting these may be for the historian of religion, even a cursory comparison with the Enuma Elish, the great Akkadian creation epic, brings out sharply the transformation of these elements at the hand of the Israelite adaptors. There we find a luxuriant world of gods and their deeds—here the lonely action of the creating God. There the divine forces of creation spring themselves from primeval chaos—here there is nothing before God, whose act of creation is the beginning of all things, with chaos (the *tohu vavohu* of the Genesis text) reduced to mere negativity awaiting the actions of God. Even in the one place of the Genesis account in which there remains the unmistakable trace of a mythological name—the *tehom*, the "deep" over which there was darkness, a Hebrew cognate of the name of the Mesopotamian goddess Tiamat from whose waters the gods were formed—this has been reduced to an abstract metaphysical category. And, significantly, the Genesis account ends with the creation of man as a being highly distinct from all other creatures, that is, in emphatic *dis*continuity not only with God but with the rest of creation. We find here expressed very clearly the fundamental Biblical polarization between the transcendent God and man, with a thoroughly "demythologized" universe between them.[20]

The historization motif is already implied in this polarization. The world, bereft of mythologically conceived divine forces, becomes the arena on the one hand of God's great acts (that is, the arena of *Heilsgeschichte*) and on the other of the activity of highly individuated men (that is, the arena of "profane history"), who populate the pages of the Old Testament to a degree unique in ancient religious literature. Israel's faith was a *historic* one from the earliest sources to their canonical codification.[21] It referred above all to a series of historically specific events— the exodus from Egypt, the establishment of the covenant at Sinai, the taking of the land. Thus the first known "creed" of ancient Israel, the text now contained in Deuteronomy 26:5-9, is nothing but a recital of

---

[19] Most of these points were explicitly made by Weber. Indeed, amazingly little has to be added to Weber's picture of the Israelite conception of God, despite the much wider knowledge of the general Near Eastern context since then. For more recent discussions of the early history of Yahwism, *cf.* Albrecht Alt, *Der Gott der Vaeter* (1929), and Samuel Nyström, *Beduinentum und Jahwismus* (1946).

[20] *Cf.* Hermann Gunkel, *Genesis* (1917), and Gerhard von Rad, *Das erste Buch Mose* (1950). The text of the Enuma Elish may be found in Pritchard, *Ancient Near Eastern Texts*. Also, *cf.* Anne-Marie Esnoul *et al.*, *La naissance du monde* (Paris, Editions du Seuil, 1959).

[21] *Cf.* Artur Weiser, *Glaube und Geschichte im alten Testament* (1931); Edmond Jacob, *La tradition historique en Israël* (1946); C. R. North, *The Old Testament Interpretation of History* (1946). The same understanding of the historicity of the entire Old Testament is elaborated in great detail in the already cited work of von Rad's, *Theologie des alten Testaments,* particularly in Vol. 1. Also, *cf.* Oscar Cullmann, *Christ et le temps* (Neuchâtel, Delachaux & Niestlé, 1947).

historical events, all, of course, attributed to acts of God. It may be said, without too gross exaggeration, that the entire Old Testament—"Torah, prophets, and 'writings' "—is but an immense elaboration of this creed. There are almost no books now contained in the Old Testament that are devoid of historical orientation, either directly or by rootage in the historically oriented cult (the two clear exceptions, Ecclesiastes and Job, are characteristically very late). About one half of the Old Testament corpus is occupied by the "historiographic" works proper—Hexateuch, Kings, and Chronicles, with other purely historical works such as Esther. The orientation of the prophetic books is overwhelmingly historical. The Psalms are rooted in a cult constantly referring to the historic acts of God, as most clearly expressed in the annual cycle of Israelite festivals. The Old Testament revolves around history in a way no other great book of world religion does (not, incidentally, excluding the New Testament).

It may be said that the transcendentalization of God and the concomitant "disenchantment of the world" opened up a "space" for history as the arena of both divine and human actions. The former are performed by a God standing entirely outside the world. The latter presuppose a considerable individuation in the conception of man. Man appears as the historical actor before the face of God (something quite different, by the way, from man as the actor in the face of fate, as in Greek tragedy). Thus individual men are seen less and less as representatives of mythologically conceived collectivities, as was typical of archaic thought, but as distinct and unique individuals, performing important acts as individuals. One may only think here of such highly profiled figures as Moses, David, Elijah, and so forth. This is true even of such figures as may be the result of "demythologizations" of originally semi-divine figures, such as the patriarchs or heroes like Samson (possibly derived from the Canaanite god Shamash). This is not to suggest that the Old Testament meant what the modern West means by "individualism," nor even the conception of the individual attained in Greek philosophy, but that it provided a religious framework for a conception of the individual, his dignity and his freedom of action. There is no need to stress the world-historical importance of this, but it is important to see it in connection with the roots of secularization that interest us here.

The development of a grand theology of history in the prophetic literature of the Old Testament is too well known to require elaboration here. But it is well to see that the same historicity pertains to cult and law in ancient Israel. The two major cultic festivals of the Old Testament constitute historizations of previously mythologically legitimated occasions. The Passover, originally (that is, in its extra-Israelite origins) the feast celebrating divine fertility, becomes the celebration of the exodus. The New Year festival (including Yom Kippur), originally the reenactment of cosmogonic myths, becomes the celebration of Yahweh's kingship over Israel. The same historicity pertains to the lesser festivals. Old Testament law and ethics are also located in a historical framework, in that they always relate to obligations arising for Israel and the individual Israelite from the covenant with Yahweh. In other words, by contrast with the rest of the ancient Near East, law and ethics are not grounded in a timeless cosmic order (as in the Egyptian ma'at), but in the concrete and historically mediated commandments of the "living God." It is in this sense that one must understand the recurrent phrase of condemnation, "Such a thing is not done in Israel." Similar phrases, of course, may be found in other cultures, but here they refer precisely to that law that was, historically, "given to Moses." It is on the basis of these very early presuppositions that the Israelite view of history developed, from the original faith in the election of the people by Yahweh to the monumental theodicies of history and eschatologies of the later prophets.

The motif of ethical rationalization in the Old Testament (in the sense of imposing rationality on life) is closely related to the two other motifs just described.[22] A rationalizing element was present from the beginning, above all because of the anti-magical animus of Yahwism. This element was "carried" by both priestly and prophetic groups. The priestly ethic (as in its monumental expression in Deuteronomy) was rationalizing in its purge from the cult of all magical and orgiastic elements, as well as in its development of religious law (torah) as the fundamental discipline of everyday life. The prophetic ethic was rationalizing in its insistence on the totality of life as service to God, thus imposing a cohesive and, ipso facto, rational structure upon the whole spectrum of everyday activities. The same prophetic ethic provided the peculiar theodicy of history (as especially in Deutero-Isaiah) that allowed Israel to survive the catastrophe of the Babylonian exile, after which, however, one may say that its his-

torical efficacy was "exhausted." The priestly ethic (which, to be sure, was strongly influenced by the prophetic teachings) went on to develop the cultic and legal institutions around which the post-exilic community could be reconstituted under Ezra and Nehemiah. The legal institutions, constituting the peculiar structure of what then became Judaism, finally proved capable of surviving even the end of the cult, following the destruction of the second temple by the Romans. Diaspora Judaism may be regarded as a triumph of rationality, in a specifically juridical sense. Because of its marginal character within the context of Western culture, however, it would be difficult to maintain that diaspora Judaism played an important role in the rationalization processes at the roots of the modern world. It is more plausible to assume that the rationalizing motif achieved efficacy in the formation of the modern West by means of its transmission by Christianity.

Needless to say, it has not been our purpose in the preceding pages to give a thumbnail sketch of Israelite religious history. We have simply tried to give some indications that the "disenchantment of the world," which has created unique nomic problems for the modern West, has roots that greatly antedate the events of the Reformation and the Renaissance that are commonly regarded as its starting points. Equally needless to say, we cannot try here to give an account of the manner in which the secularizing potency of Biblical religion, combined with other factors, came to fruition in the modern West. Only a few comments can be made about this.[23]

---

[22] The following account is closely dependent on Weber. On the relationship of Israelite ethics and Israelite history, cf. Adolphe Lods, Les prophètes d'Israël et les débuts du judaïsme (1935), and Antonin Causse, Du groupe ethnique à la communauté religieuse (1937).

---

[23] In our view of the historical role of Christianity we are, again, heavily dependent on Weber. Our understanding of the

Whatever may have been the religious character of Jesus and his earliest followers, there seems little question but that the form of Christianity that finally became dominant in Europe represents a retrogressive step in terms of the secularizing motifs of Old Testament religion (a descriptive statement to which, of course, no evaluative intent on our part should be attached). While the transcendent character of God is strongly asserted, the very notion of the incarnation and then even more its theoretical development in trinitarian doctrine represent significant modifications in the radicality of the Israelite conception. This point was seen more clearly by the Jewish and Muslim critics of Christianity than by those standing within the Christian camp. Thus there is some justification (again, of course, in a purely descriptive sense) in the classic Muslim view that the essence of the Christian "apostasy" from true monotheism is in the doctrine of *hullul*—"incarnationism," as the idea that anything or anyone could stand beside God, or serve as a mediator between God and man. Perhaps it is not surprising that the central Christian notion of incarnation brought in its wake a multiplicity of other modifications of transcendence, the whole host of angels and saints with which Catholicism populated religious reality, culminating in the glorification of Mary as mediator and co-redeemer. In the measure that the divine transcendence was modified, the world was "re-enchanted" (or, if one wishes,

"re-mythologized"). We would contend, indeed, that Catholicism succeeded in re-establishing a new version of cosmic order in a gigantic synthesis of Biblical religion with extra-Biblical cosmological conceptions. In this view, the crucial Catholic doctrine of the *analogia entis* between God and man, between heaven and earth, constitutes a replication of the mimesis of archaic pre-Biblical religion. Whatever their other important differences may be, we would see both Latin and Greek Catholicism performing essentially the same replication on this level. It is precisely in this sense that the Catholic universe is a secure one for its "inhabitants"—and for this reason of intense attractiveness to this day. It is the same sense that Catholicism may be understood as the continuing presence in the modern world of some of the most ancient religious aspirations of man.

By the same token, Catholicism arrested the process of ethical rationalization. To be sure, Latin Catholicism absorbed a highly rational legalism inherited from Rome, but its pervasive sacramental system provided innumerable "escape hatches" from the sort of total rationalization of life demanded by Old Testament prophecy or, indeed, by rabbinical Judaism. Ethical absolutism of the prophetic variety was more or less safely segregated in the institutions of monasticism, thus kept from "contaminating" the body of Christendom as a whole. Again, the starkness of the Israelite religious conceptions was modified, mellowed, except for those chosen few who chose the ascetic life. On the theoretical level, the Catholic view of natural law may be said to represent a "re-naturalization" of ethics—in a sense, a return to the divine-human continuity of Egyptian *ma'at* from which Israel went out into the desert of Yahweh. On the practical level,

relationship of Christianity to the mythological cosmos on the one hand and to Judaism on the other has been strongly influenced by Rudolf Bultmann. *Cf.* not only his writings on "demythologization," but also his *Theology of the New Testament,* as well as his *Das Urchristentum* (Zurich, Artemis, 1949). Also, *cf.* Gogarten, *Verhaengnis und Hoffnung.*

Catholic piety and morality provided a way of life that made unnecessary any radical rationalization of the world.[24]

But whereas it can be plausibly argued that Christianity, specifically in its victorious Catholic form, reversed or at least arrested the secularizing motifs of transcendentalization and ethical rationalization, this cannot be said of the motif of historization. Latin Christianity in the West, at any rate, remained thoroughly historical in its view of the world. It retained the peculiarly Biblical theodicy of history and, except for those mystical movements that (as everywhere in the orbit of Biblically derived monotheism) always moved on the periphery of heresy, rejected those religious constructions that would despair of this world as the arena of redemption. Catholic Christianity thus carried within it the seeds of the revolutionary impetus, even if this often remained dormant for long periods under the "cosmicizing" effects of the Catholic universe. It erupted again and again in a variety of chiliastic movements, though its release as a force of world-historical dimensions had to await the disintegration of Christendom as a viable plausibility structure for Western man.

There is another central characteristic of Christianity that, again in a most unintended manner, eventually served the process of secularization— the social formation of the Christian church. In terms of the comparative sociology of religion, the Christian church represents a very unusual case of the institutional specialization of religion, that is, of an institution specifically concerned with religion in counterposition with all other institutions of society.[25] Such a development is relatively rare in the history of religion, where the more common state of affairs is a diffusion of religious activities and symbols throughout the institutional fabric, though the Christian case is not unique (for example, in quite a different way, the Buddhist *sangha* represents another case of such institutional specialization). The concentration of religious activities and symbols in *one* institutional sphere, however, *ipso facto* defines the rest of society as "the world," as a profane realm at least relatively removed from the jurisdiction of the sacred. The secularizing potential of this conception could be "contained" as long as Christendom, with its sensitive balance of the sacred and the profane, existed as a social reality. With the disintegration of this reality, however, "the world" could all the more rapidly be secularized in that it had already been defined as a realm outside the jurisdiction of the sacred properly speaking. The logical development of this may be seen in the Lutheran doctrine of the two kingdoms, in which the autonomy of the secular "world" is actually given a *theological* legitimation.[26]

If we look at the great religious constellations derived from the Old Testament, therefore, we find quite differential relationships to the latter's secularizing forces. Judaism appears as an encapsulation of these forces in a highly rationalized but historically ineffective formation, the ineffectiveness to be ascribed both to the extrinsic factor of the fate of the Jews as an

---

[24] Again, our dependence on Weber is obvious here. Also, *cf.* Ernst Troeltsch, *Die Soziallehren der christlichen Kirchen* (1911).

[25] This point has been excellently stated by Luckmann, *Das Problem der Religion.*
[26] *Cf.* Troeltsch, *Die Soziallehren,* as well as the discussion of Lutheranism in Weber's *The Protestant Ethic and the Spirit of Capitalism.*

alien people within Christendom and the intrinsic factor of the conservative impact of Jewish legalism. In this latter respect Islam bears a close resemblance to Judaism, with the obvious difference that it succeeded in imposing its conservatory structures not just within a segregated subculture but over an empire of vast geographical expanse.[27] Catholic Christianity, both Latin and Greek, may be seen as an arresting and retrogressive step in the unfolding of the drama of secularization, although it preserved within it (at least in the Latin West) the secularizing potential, if only by virtue of its preservation of the Old Testament canon (decided upon once and for all in the rejection of the Marcionite heresy). The Protestant Reformation, however, may then be understood as a powerful re-emergence of precisely those secularizing forces that had been "contained" by Catholicism, not only replicating the Old Testament in this, but going decisively beyond it. To what extent the historical coincidence of the impact of Protestantism with that of the Renaissance, with its resurgence of the quite different secularizing forces of classical antiquity, was simply an accident or rather a mutually dependent phenomenon cannot be pursued here. Nor can we try to weigh here the relative effect of Protestantism as against other factors, both "ideal" and "material," in the process of secularization of the last 400 years. All we wanted to indicate was that the question, "Why in the modern West?" asked with respect to the phenomenon of secularization, must be answered at least in part by looking at its roots in the religious tradition of the modern West.

In terms of the general socio-religious processes discussed in the first part of this book, secularization has posited an altogether novel situation for modern man. Probably for the first time in history, the religious legitimations of the world have lost their plausibility not only for a few intellectuals and other marginal individuals but for broad masses of entire societies. This opened up an acute crisis not only for the nomization of the large social institutions but for that of individual biographies. In other words, there has arisen a problem of "meaningfulness" not only for such institutions as the state or of the economy but for the ordinary routines of everyday life. The problem has, of course, been intensely conscious to various theoreticians (philosophers, theologians, psychologists, and so forth), but there is good reason to think that it is also prominent in the minds of ordinary people not normally given to theoretical speculations and interested simply in solving the crises of their own lives. Most importantly, the peculiar Christian theodicy of suffering lost its plausibility and thereby the way was opened for a variety of secularized soteriologies, most of which, however, proved quite incapable of legitimating the sorrows of individual life even when they achieved some plausibility in the legitimation of history. And finally the collapse of the alienated structures of the Christian worldview released movements of critical thought that radically de-alienated and "humanized" social reality (the sociological perspective being one of these movements), an achievement that often enough was bought at the price

27 Cf. Montgomery Watt, *Islam and the Integration of Society* (Evanston, Northwestern University Press, 1961), and Reuben Levy, *The Social Structure of Islam* (Cambridge, Cambridge University Press, 1962). The highly intriguing question of the general relationship of Islam to secularization cannot, of course, be pursued here.

of severe anomy and existential anxiety. What all of this means for contemporary society is the principal question for an empirical sociology of knowledge. Within our present considerations we cannot deal with all this except tangentially. The question, though, that we will turn to next is what the process of secularization has meant for the traditional religious contents and for the institutions that embody them.

the quest of youth
for a new religion

nineteen

from The Making of a Counter Culture

THEODORE ROSZAK

Indeed, we are a post-Christian era—despite the fact that minds far more gifted than Ginsberg's, like that of the late Thomas Merton, have mined the dominant religious tradition for great treasures. But we may have been decidedly wrong in what we long expected to follow the death of the Christian God; namely, a thoroughly secularized, thoroughly positivistic culture, dismal and spiritless in its obsession with technological prowess. That was the world Aldous Huxley foresaw in the 1930s, when he wrote *Brave New World*. But in the 1950s, as Huxley detected the rising spirit of a new generation, his utopian image brightened to the forecast he offers us in *Island,* where a non-violent culture elaborated out of Buddhism and psychedelic drugs prevails. It was as if he had suddenly seen the possibility emerge: what lay beyond the Christian era and the "wasteland" that was its immediate successor might be a

From *The Making of a Counter Culture* by Theodore Roszak. Copyright © 1968, 1969 by Theodore Roszak. Reprinted by permission of Doubleday & Company, Inc.

new, eclectic religious revival. Which is precisely what confronts us now as one of the massive facts of the counter culture. The dissenting young have indeed got religion. Not the brand of religion Billy Graham or William Buckley would like to see the young crusading for—but religion nonetheless. What began with Zen has now rapidly, perhaps too rapidly, proliferated into a phantasmagoria of exotic religiosity.

Who would have predicted it? At least since the Enlightenment, the major thrust of radical thought has always been anti-religious, if not openly, defiantly atheistic—perhaps with the exception of the early Romantics. And even among the Romantics, the most pious tended to become the most politically reactionary; for the rest, the Romantic project was to abstract from religion its essential "feeling" and leave contemptuously behind its traditional formulations. Would-be Western revolutionaries have always been strongly rooted in a militantly skeptical secular tradition. The rejection of the corrupted religious establishment has carried over almost automatically into root-and-branch rejection of all things spiritual. So "mysticism" was to become one of the dirtiest words in the Marxist vocabulary. Since Diderot, the priest has had only one thing the radical wanted: his guts, with which to strangle the last king. Shaw writing in 1921 on the intellectuals of what he called the "infidel half-century" (he was dating from the time of Darwin), summarized the situation thus:

We were intellectually intoxicated with the idea that the world could make itself without design, purpose, skill, or intelligence: in short, without life. . . . We took a perverse pleasure in arguing, without the least suspicion that we were reducing ourselves to absurdity, that all the books in the British Museum library might have been written word for word as they stand on the shelves if no human being had ever been conscious, just as the trees stand in the forest doing wonderful things without consciousness.

The first effect was exhilarating: we had the runaway child's sense of freedom before it gets hungry and lonely and frightened. In this phase we did not desire our God back again. We printed the verses in which William Blake, the most religious of our great poets, called the anthropomorphic idol Nobodaddy, and gibed at him in terms which the printer had to leave us to guess from his blank spaces. We had heard the parson droning that God is not mocked; and it was great fun to mock Him to our hearts' content and not be a penny the worse. (From the preface to *Back to Methusaleh*.[1])

When he wrote these words, Shaw had himself long since abandoned the crusading skepticism of his generation's intelligentsia in favor of a species of Vitalism, convinced that it was destined to become the new religion. Instead, it became only another of the enclaves from which alienated artists, eccentric psychiatrists, and assorted cranks could do no more than

---

[1] By permission of The Society of Authors, for the Bernard Shaw Estate.

snipe at the secularized mainstream culture. Only the debased mysticism of the fascists, as the ideology of an aggressive war machine, has seriously troubled the scientized intellectual consensus of the twentieth century. Even so, the *Schwärmerei* of fascism, as I have remarked, really served as the facade behind which one of the most formidable technocracies of the age was consolidated.

But now, if one scans any of the underground weeklies, one is apt to find their pages swarming with Christ and the prophets, Zen, Sufism, Hinduism, primitive shamanism, theosophy, the Left-Handed Tantra. . . . The Berkeley "wandering priest" Charlie (Brown) Artman, who was in the running for city councilman in 1966 until he was arrested for confessing (quite unabashedly) to possession of narcotics, strikes the right note of eclectic religiosity: a stash of LSD in his Indian-sign necklace, a chatelaine of Hindu temple bells, and the campaign slogan "May the baby Jesus open your mind and shut your mouth." Satanists and Neo-Gnostics, dervishes and self-proclaimed swamis . . . their number grows and the counter culture makes generous place for them. No anti-war demonstration would be complete without a hirsute, be-cowbelled contingent of holy men, bearing joss sticks and intoning the Hare Krishna. An underground weekly like *The Berkeley Barb* gives official Washington a good left-wing slamming on page one, but devotes the center spread to a crazy mandala for the local yogis. And in the back pages, the "Servants of Awareness . . . a unique group of aware people using 136 symbols in their meditation to communicate directly with *Cosmic Awareness* . . ." are sure to take out a four-column ad. The San Francisco *Oracle* gives us photos of stark-naked madonnas with flowers in their hair, suckling their babies...and the effect is not at all pornographic, nor intended to be so.

At the level of our youth, we begin to resemble nothing so much as the cultic hothouse of the Hellenistic period, where every manner of mystery and fakery, ritual and rite, intermingled with marvelous indiscrimination. For the time being, the situation makes it next to impossible for many of us who teach to carry on much in the way of education among the dissenting young, given the fact that our conventional curriculum, even at its best, is grounded in the dominant Western tradition. Their interest, when not involved with the politics of revolution, are apt to be fathoming phenomena too exotic or too subterranean for normal academic handling. If one asks the hip young to identify (a) Milton and (b) Pope, their answers are likely to be: (a) Milton *who?* and (b) *which* Pope? But they may do no mean job of rehearsing their kabbala or *I Ching* (which the very hip get married to these days) or, of course, the *Kamasutra.*

What the counter culture offers us, then, is a remarkable defection from the long-standing tradition of skeptical, secular intellectuality which has served as the prime vehicle for three hundred years of scientific and technical work in the West. Almost overnight (and astonishingly, with no great debate on the point) a significant portion of the younger generation has opted out of that tradition, rather as if to provide an emergency balance to the gross distortions of our technological society, often by occult aberrations just as gross.

adaptation of traditional religion in a secular age

twenty

from The Catholic Crisis

THOMAS F. O'DEA

The Pastoral Constitution on the Church in the Modern World

Writing in 1922, shortly before his death, Ernst Troeltsch felt that the position of Christianity was a precarious one, that its future was unpredictable. Christianity was, he thought, "at a critical moment of its further development." Moreover, if Christianity was to have any future, "very bold and far-reaching changes were necessary, transcending anything that had yet been achieved by any denomination."[1]

The nearly half century that separates Vatican II from Troeltsch's observation saw two important developments in Protestant theology. Again to oversimplify, we may suggest the substance and significance of these developments with the names of Karl Barth and Rudolf Bultmann.

Barth called for a return to the

---

[1] Ernst Troeltsch, *Die Absolutheit des Christentums und die Religionsgeschichte* (2nd ed.) (Tübingen: J. C. B. Mohr, 1912), p. 60.

Copyright © 1968 by Thomas F. O'Dea. Reprinted by permission of Beacon Press.

basic meaning of the Bible as the Word of God, for the abandonment of the *Kulturprotestantismus,* whose sociological and cultural bases had been demolished by the First World War. In contrast to the complacent liberalism of the dominant prewar theology, Barth called European man back to transcendence—to an accounting. The uneasy peace ended in 1939 with a second catastrophe, greater even than the first, and the old world, with Europe as it crown and liberal Protestantism its fairest jewel, vanished forever.

In this situation Bultmann came forward in an attempt to free the New Testament message from those archaic and mythical elements that made it incomprehensible to the men of our day. Several centuries of secularization, of scientific development, of technological revolution, and a half century of total war, had deprived western civilization of its older institutional and cultural substance and had removed it from world dominance. The world itself was being "demythologized": its consensually validated convictions were disappearing. Bultmann tried to demythologize the scripture so it could speak once again to the men of this age.

Were Barth's emphasis upon transcendence and Bultmann's attempts to shear off the culturally specific elements in Christian understanding the beginnings of the "very bold and far-reaching changes" which Troeltsch thought necessary? And does the Second Vatican Council represent the "beginnings of these beginnings" within the historic Church of Rome?

To ask these questions is to suggest the magnitude of what needs must be involved in an *"aggiornamento* in depth." We must not think of the Roman Catholic Church as an unchanging monolith, standing recalcitrant and intransigent across the path of history, which has suddenly as by some intervention from on high become an engine of progress and a force for liberation. The preconciliar Roman Church was not unchanging. Indeed, in many of the matters dealt with by the Council—liturgy, the Bible, attitude toward democratic civil government, and others—alterations of considerable scope had been introduced, often on curial initiative and with curial approval. The preconciliar Church was rather the locus of a struggle in which a new spirit attempted to bring about the renewal of the Church, and in which the forces and structures of that ancient organization were, almost of historical necessity, "rigged" or "loaded" against such renewal. Yet whatever historical accidents attended the decision to call a council, the fact is that the time was fast approaching when Rome had to consider what Troeltsch called "very bold and far-reaching changes."

We have already seen that in the century and a half preceding this Council attempts to advocate *aggiornamento* had been put forward by thoughtful Catholics. Although most of them were suppressed, they did have some degree of influence and did create a kind of officially disavowed sub-rosa tradition. Such semi-rejected traditions, however, are hard to transmit. They do not have at their disposal the resources of the general ecclesiastical community. Consequently there is an element of reinvention in their continual reappearance. What keeps such a tradition alive is much more the continuing need for what it suggests and prescribes than the transmission of its own ideas from one generation to another. Authority could condemn and proscribe, but it could not conjure away the dilemmas to which the proto *aggiornamentists* addressed themselves. Whatever astigmatisms of time and cultural setting— and they were many, of course—may characterize the list we have suggested, from Lamennais and Möhler to Loisy, Tyrrell, and Murri, it becomes more and more clear that they were responding to real existing dimensions of modern civilization, real elements of the human situation as it was experienced by men in the new society which revolution and technology were bringing into the world. The tradition they inaugurated and supplemented never achieved genuine legitimacy. Their ideas had to be either consciously sought or met with by fortuitous accident. Yet from the end of the French Revolution to the close of the Second World War, Catholics invented modernization over and over again. They made repeated attempts at *aggiornamento.* They did not do so because of the institutionalization within the Church of a legitimate opposition party to authoritarian episcopal and ultramontane conservatism. They did so because the meaning of the Catholic faith and the realities of modern life stood in a state of reciprocal challenge in the minds of the educated and intelligently devout. The modern conditions could not be dismissed. They continued to issue their challenge. In fact those elements of modernity which the Church saw as particularly threatening to its traditional institutional and intellectual positions became ever more salient aspects of modern society.

This century and a half came after many previous centuries of change and saw an intensification of it. It was a time of political revolution, of unprecedented technological advance, of social transformation, of scientific development, and of intellectual metamorphosis. It was the time of the German historians—of Ranke, of Harnack, of Troeltsch; of Wellhausen, of Bauer, of Schweitzer. It was the time of the sociologists, from Auguste Comte and Saint-Simon to Emile Durkheim; from Fredinand Toennies and Max Weber to Karl Mannheim. It watched the development of cultural anthropology from Tylor to Boas. It was the era of Marx, Darwin, Freud, and Einstein. It was a time in which both Whig and Liberal England and Revolutionary and bourgeois France passed away, together with Catholic Austria and Spain. Pitt and Gladstone, Robespierre and Bonaparte, Metternich and Thiers— all were gone. The time had witnessed the decline of Europe, torn by two bitter world wars, and the rise of America; the end of czarist Russia and the rise of a new Marxist orthodoxy. It saw the end of empire and the development of the third world.

The third quarter of the twentieth century found a less structured, more insecure, less stable, more open world than man had perhaps ever been in before. It was a world shedding the institutions within whose context it had lived for decades, for centuries, and in some cases for millennia. It was a world being denuded of its illusions and its assurances. It was a world being demythologized. It could be a world come of age, or it could become the scene of frightened and frantic attempts to escape the freedom into which man was emerging. It was a world full of chaos and suffering, and under the threat of nuclear destruction. But it was at the same time a world in which man began to realize that, together with the dissolution of the older contexts of his vanished security and the enormous dangers surrounding him, he was also offered greater promise than at any previous time in his history. Science put within his grasp the instruments for making life truly humane, the tools, material and intellectual, not only for subduing the earth to human designs but also for transforming himself.

To the evolution of this world the Church, officially and in terms of its ordinary teaching, had juxtaposed Gregory XVI, Pius IX, Leo XIII, Pius X, and Pius XII. To this world the Church responded by proclaiming the dogmas of the Immaculate Conception, Papal Infallibility, and the Assumption. To this world the Church had presented the two syllabuses—that of 1864 and that of 1907.

The Church had made a palpably inadequate set of responses, yet to human observation they appear almost inevitable under the circumstances. Small wonder that within its ranks the semioutlawed forces of modernization began to gather momentum once again. The defensive position assumed by the Church, though seemingly inevitable and the predictable consequence of historical conditioning and sociological situation, was becoming obviously less and less tenable. The Church was reaching that point in its development when to remain in its own self-enforced isolation was to lose its catholicity. As Abbot Butler said, "Aggiornamento in depth" became "a pastoral necessity." He wrote,

A species, when no longer adapted to its actual environment, can evolve, or it can perish. The Church cannot perish. But there is a third possibility. Sometimes a species succeeds in taking refuge in a backwater of existence, where—in diminished numbers and with no further relevance except to historians of past evolution—it prolongs an insignificant story. As we look back on the Church before 1962, do we not sometimes seem to be catching a glimpse of what might have become a monumental irrelevance?[2]

It is not easy to understand the multitude of factors that influence such a major restructuring of outlook. The Church's defensive behavior of the previous 150 years is precisely what a sociologist would have predicted had he known all the conditions and been able to look at them with some objectivity. But the interesting question is, Why did that defensiveness give way to a radical shift of attitude at this point in the Church's history? We have argued that the time was fast approaching when the choice was between change and irrelevance. But that it was recognized was a surprise to all. An Anglican historian had written in 1961,

If the full measure be taken of the revolutionary changes that have taken place in the worlds of thought and invention, in political and social structures, and in the conditions of living and working, and if the rootedness of the Churches in the prerevolutionary order or the *ancien regime* be borne in mind, then their survival with so many of their ancient characteristics and appurtenances intact is remarkable, to say the least. They have not survived because they were well-prepared for the turmoil in which they

were to be ineluctably involved, nor because, when it came upon them, they showed ready powers of adaptation to new circumstances and of taking time by the forelock. On the contrary, we have seen how recalcitrant they were to change, how blind or short-sighted in the days of visitation, how disposed to stone or silence or jettison the would-be prophets in their midst, and how lacking in the imaginative compassion and sensitive humanity that might have given them a secure standing in the hearts of peoples when they were deprived of earthly privileges and the active support of governments.[3]

But recognized it somehow was. There were many influences, many changes of conditions. There was, of course, the older liberal Catholic position, quite in the background. There were the slow thaw in theology and biblical studies and the new developments of the postwar years. There were the continuing external conditions, the continuing challenge, the brute facts of reality that could be conjured away neither by the prayers of the pious nor by the regulations of the authoritarians.

Most important was the fact that the "defeats" suffered by the institutional Church did have the end effect of uprooting it. The Church was no longer a part of the traditional culture, no longer integrated into a conservative institutional complex central to civil society. It was now "freed" from that earlier outmoded "incarnation"—freed against its majority will, no doubt, but not less free for that. The greater part of its "vested interests" had been taken away from it by history. It was now free to seek new ways to embody itself in the life of 20th century man. In Europe the Church was no longer part of the

<hr>

2 Abbot Christopher Butler, "The Aggiornamento of Vatican II," in John H. Miller, C.S.C. (ed.), *Vatican II: An Interfaith Appraisal* (Notre Dame, Ind.: University of Notre Dame Press, 1966), p. 7.

<hr>

3 Alec R. Vidler, *The Church in an Age of Revolution* (Baltimore: Penguin Books, Inc., 1961), p. 270.

old order. In the mission regions of the world, the breakup of imperialism put churchmen in touch with the most advanced and at times the most chaotic realities; in America and throughout the entire "oceanic" Church, the Church was functionally a denomination in a pluralist society.

Shortly before his death in 1878, Pope Pius IX, who had fought so valiantly to preserve the Church in the only way he knew how—by defending its concrete form of organization and doctrine—is reported to have said the following: "I hope my successor will be as much attached to the Church as I have been and will have as keen a desire to do good: beyond that, I can see that everything has changed; my system and my policies have had their day, but I am too old to change my course; that will be the task of my successor."[4] Pius IX did not find his true successor until John XXIII, who called the Council in which the great change came to fruition.

A council offered a new kind of arena for the activity of the forces of modernization, at that time working under difficulties and official disapproval. The first significant fact to note in this respect is an obvious but a structurally strategic one. A council is a place of discussion, and discussion means that problems are faced in the discursive mode—not in action but in discourse. They are talked about. Talking about them requires that they be defined in general terms and thought about. By its very structure a council gives genuine leverage to those who are skillful in the intellectual sphere. It gives an advantage to the intellectuals.

From the 19th century on, bishops assumed the role of functionaries—of

bureaucrats. They held an office in a hierarchical structure. Catholic theology considered them "successors to the Apostles," and canon law defined the episcopal office as possessing "ordinary authority," that is, authority in its own right, not authority delegated by the pope. Yet this older version of the bishop's office was embedded in a later developed bureaucratic one. The bishops were line functionaries of a centralized organization with authority coming from the top down. However, after a brief period of being disoriented by their unwonted collegiality, the bishops at Rome came to feel themselves a college once again. The establishment of a context in which problems were to be handled discursively and intellectual problem solving was consequently to become the mode of conduct, and the discovery of their own collegial discursive role by the bishops set the stage for the changes that were to come.

One of the revolutions that had brought about the world so long resisted by the Church was the revolution in communications. The consequences of that transformation of human relationships placed the Second Vatican Council in the closest contact with the outside world. The eyes of the world were literally upon it; the ears of the world heard its discussions. *Urbi et orbi* took on a new literalness.

Furthermore, the outside world was not simply nearer; it had changed too. The great changes we have pointed out before had dissipated much of the old Reformation attitude of anti-pope and anti-Rome—so much so that John XXIII became a trans-confessional and interconfessional symbol. Protestants looked to the Council John had called with vague but real, and indeed often enthusiastic, hopes. Men of no formal faith,

_____
[4] *Ibid.,* p. 153.

aware of the danger and promise of our age, hoped that the oldest and largest Christian body might say something useful to men. Especially in America, perhaps, where a liberal Democrat and a Roman Catholic had just been elected President, and where a successful pluralist society enjoying unprecedented prosperity emphasized good will among its diverse confessions, the Council was greeted with anticipation.

The Second Vatican Council thus became responsible to the world in a quite genuine and immediate sense. In considering the *Pastoral Constitution on the Church in the Modern World* the Council discussed the problem of whether to direct the document to Catholics or to all men. It decided to address itself "without hesitation, not only to the sons of the Church, but to the whole of humanity" (art 1). Thus it followed the precedent set by John XXIII, whose encyclical *Pacem in Terris* was for "all men of good will." Paul VI adopted the same mode of address in his inaugural encyclical *Ecclesiam Suam*. In this the Council and the popes reflect the new position of the Church.

In this Council the Fathers gathered to *discuss,* a fact that was to increase the influence of intellectuals— both among the episcopate and among their advisers—on policy making. In this Council the Fathers soon came to feel their own collegial status and responsibility. As we have indicated, reflection might well suggest to the more thoughtful the bankruptcy which threatened the defensive policies and rigid postures of the past. In this Council the Fathers met within view and within earshot of a world favorably disposed to expect something worthwhile from them, a world which would hold them responsible in a new way. They were, in a sense, on trial.

In this situation the modernizers, who had come into existence with the slow thaw of the antimodernist mentality, came into their own. The context threw the balance in favor of the intellectuals, but conservative theologians were prepared to do scarcely more than repeat the older positions. They had little to offer except further condemnations of the well known sources of threat: communism, atheism, etc. Yet John XXIII had called the Council in the spirit of dialogue, of pastoral concern, of updating the Church, and not of polemic and anathema. The conditions within the Church and the position of the Church in the world—the total context—cried out for something new. In this situation the new theologians —those who, under official discouragement and disapproval, explored the theology of the secular world, of the Church, of history and the Bible —had something to offer. Not surprisingly, they were more and more called upon. It was a great moment of fulfillment for a century and a half of unsuccessful efforts at *aggiornamento* when the progressive theologians emerged as the most influential *periti* at the Council. It meant that the Church would meet the trial it faced, that it would begin the massive task of reorienting itself by rational discussion and fraternal dialogue. The molting of the old Church would begin.

Thus the Council was called and thus it became occupied with *aggiornamento* in depth. Its results record the beginning of such an *aggiornamento,* genuine though in a sense—in relation to the magnitude of the tasks—modest. "The Council marked the decisive beginning of the aggiornamento, it established the renewal, it called us to the ever necessary repentance and return; in other words, it was only the beginning of the beginning."[5] Yet in view of the condition of the Roman Catholic Church in the late 18th and 19th centuries, in view of the historical burdens with which it entered the modern period, a decisive beginning of the beginning represents a tremendous accomplishment. In braving the "terrifying, threatening, unknown future facing the Church,"[6] the Fathers considered the two most fundamental questions concerning ecclesiology. The first, as Pope Paul VI put it, was "What is the Church? This has been the great question of the Council." And the second was "the other theme, which inquires as to how the Church, in its turn, views the world."[7] Paul observes that the conciliar answers to this second "immense question" are marked by "optimism." A "beginning" begun with "optimism" of a genuine "aggiornamento in depth" could indeed point to the "very bold and far-reaching changes" necessary if Christianity in our day is to survive with relevance. It is against the background of these considerations that one should attempt to evaluate the *Pastoral Constitution on the Church in the Modern World*.

We have made this summary examination of the various attempts to reorient the Catholic Church in its relation to evolving modernity in order to discover the points of strain. Obviously, no single phenomenon can be designated as "liberal Catholicism." Rather, a series of efforts have been made around specific issues to change the direction of Catholic policy and

5 Karl Rahner, *The Church After the Council* (New York: Herder and Herder, Inc., 1966), pp. 19 f.

6 *Ibid.,* p. 39.

7 Quoted in *The Sixteen Documents of Vatican II,* with commentary by the Council Fathers, NCWC translation (Boston: Daughters of St. Paul, n.d.), p. 745.

the tenor of Catholic thought and feeling. We must now ask what tendencies expressed themselves again and again, to be generally rejected and condemned by the authorities in the Church. What were the issues involved in the attempts at "proto *aggiornamento*"?

First of all, the thrust of the whole undertaking was to break out of the condition of overinstitutionalization which was characteristic of the Church in that period. This condition involved two different but related aspects. One was an over-development and overrigidity of forms of thought and organization: detailed definitions carried down from previous ages and half-forgotten cultural settings; rigid social forms such as exaggerated differential clerical and lay status; and a high degree of verbalism. The other was an inherited burden of forms of relationship with the world—intellectual and political —evolved in the past and fast losing their suitability. These may be called fundamental ossifying consequences of overinstitutionalization such as are likely to plague any old human organization.

There is a second side of the matter in the Catholic case. The askewness characteristic of the relation of the Church to the world from the late Middle Ages on, an askewness increased greatly by the Reformation and exacerbated into an open warfare on basic principles by the Revolution, introduced a more and more rigid defensiveness into the picture and made creative rethinking extremely difficult—and liable to authoritative rebuke when it did come about. Yet we have seen, in these most unlikely circumstances, significant attempts at creative innovation in Catholic thought and action. They were struggles to escape from the overinstitutionalized condition of such long standing and to confront the new world with a renewed freshness and vigor. They were efforts to emancipate the Catholic faith from the defensive hostility and encumbering bureaucracy of the spirit in which it had become encased.

We may summarize in a series of dichotomies these attempts at breaking out of the awry cage which history had jerry-built for the Church. It must be stressed that we describe here tendencies, not fully developed religious attitudes or theological positions. It must also be recalled that there were not two parties in any simple sense, and that many who would appear liberal on one issue might indeed show up as conservative on others. Yet what becomes visible is a series of new emphases and perspectives which amount to the emergence of an open and liberal view of the implications of modernity for religion.

The *innovators* placed their emphasis upon *experience,* while *those who held the established positions* gave priority to *codified definitions* derived from past experience.

The *innovators* recognized the significance of *emotion* and *feeling,* while *those who maintained the established positions* rested their faith on *assent to intellectual formulas.*

The *innovators* recognized that life was in some basic way a *process,* while *those who held the established positions* saw it as an interaction of *fixed intellectual, cultural, and social forms.*

The *innovators* saw the coming victory of *democracy* and faced the implications that social forms came into being and passed away, while *those who maintained the established positions,* though they might cite Aristotle on generation and corruption, saw the world as a substantial *hierarchical order,* within which particular social and political forms were sacral.

The *innovators* suspected the vast implications of *historical specificity* and the problems they raised for the transmission of lasting truths, while *those who maintained the established positions* appeared to be satisfied with their own earlier *general statements* made in medieval Latin as adequately embodying older ideas and immediately comprehensible to men of "right reason."

The *innovators,* with a new understanding of experience, of emotion, of the historical process, and of the inevitability of change, saw the importance of coming to understand the forces and tendencies that are *immanent* in social life, how they achieve expression, and their relation to what is already evolved and established, while *those who maintained the older positions* saw in their old codified formulas an adequate and timeless embodiment of the *transcendent,* and seemed often to understand transcendence in a manner closer to the rationalism they condemned than to their own admitted philosophical sources.

The *innovators* saw, to one extent or another, that life was *open ended,* while *those who maintained the established positions* seemed to think there really was *nothing new* under the sun.

The *innovators* saw that the Church could not base its propaedeutic to faith upon reason and history and then make its own rules to curtail reason and enclose history, while *those who maintained the established positions* pretended to see no problem in this circularity.

The *innovators* saw the approach of a greater *equality* and a *coming of age* for modern man, while *those who maintained the established positions* saw *submission* of inferior to superior as part of the divinely ordained nature of things and emphasized the religious importance of *obedience.*

The work of the *innovators* suggested that no historically evolved conceptions of being or value could be final and definitive, while *those who maintained the established positions* tended to see both being and value and their human formulations as fixed and complete.

The *innovators* began to appreciate that men act out, in their lives and generations in history, complex and subtle dramas, whose script is original and whose source and consummation are obscure, while *those who maintain the established positions* were prone to see the activity of the layman as having meaning only in its moral aspects, and to see in their own highly conventionalized presentation of the religious experience the only noble human end.

Once again, at the end of the 19th century and the beginning of the 20th, before the fateful assassination at Sarajevo put an end to the 19th century world, this drama of innovation and its repression was to be reenacted within the Church of Rome. The history we have briefly surveyed suggests three areas of conflict and of growth: the philosophical, the historical, and the practical—the social and political. And in these three fields, a new attempt was to be made to bring the encounter between Christianity and modernity to a happy issue for the Catholic Church. This attempt, though the work of a small number of scholars and thinkers, was—at least in proportion to its numbers, and indeed perhaps absolutely—to shake the Roman Church more thoroughly than any of its predecessors. The reaction it called forth would remain intense for half a century, and its effects are still very much with us.

. . .

The Dogmatic Constitution on the Church (De Ecclesia or Lumen Gentium)

The *Dogmatic Constitution on the Church* is one of the great documents of the Council, and it represents the results of a long period of new theological thinking in the Church. The different theological tendencies among the assembled Fathers began to become apparent early in the Council. The differences could already be felt in the discussion of the schema proposed on Sacred Liturgy. They were clearly in the open in the debate on the schema on Revelation. They came out, as might indeed be expected, in the reception the first draft of this Constitution met on the Council floor. Of all the documents of the Council, this Constitution received perhaps the greatest amount of revision, so that the document passed by the Council on November 19, 1964, and again in the solemn session presided over by Pope Paul VI, on November 21, differs drastically from that originally presented for debate on December 1, 1962.

The earlier version resembled in its general treatment the typical theological manual of the interwar period. In the words of one Council Father, it presented the Church more as an institution than as a mystery, or, as another put it, the earlier version dealt too much with external characteristics of the ecclesiastical organization. Its "juridicism" and its great emphasis on hierarchy represented the typical conservative view as that view had developed in the centuries since the Reformation.

The proposed text was subjected to a thorough revision following the debates of the second session in 1963. More changes were introduced in the third session.

Although the document does not

define any new dogmas, it is called a *Dogmatic Constitution,* which means that it is the most solemn form of conciliar document. It is unquestionably one of the most significant accomplishments of the Council. One Protestant commentator has observed that it "is the first full-orbed *conciliar* exposition of the doctrine of the Church in Christian history,"[8] and another has commented that it is "by far the fullest dogmatic statement on the nature of the church that has ever been formulated by any Christian body."[9] The document was formed in vigorous controversy. Yet, despite that fact, it received the approval of 2,134 Fathers out of 2,145 voting on the definitive text (10 voted no, and there was 1 null vote), and, in the solemn session two days later over which Paul VI presided, 2,156 Fathers voted *placet* as against 5 who voted *non placet.*

The Constitution is, of course, a compromise, as must be any such statement drawn up in a long process of argument and debate which reveives the final approval of so large and varied a body. It is, moreover, a compromise that can be read to contrasting effect by men with different religious predispositions and different theological preferences. The conservative can find here much to reinforce traditional positions; the liberal can see a remarkable expression of the newer, more open tendencies in Catholic thinking. Placed in its setting, it will be recognized by the critical scholar

as a compromise that brings forward with a new emphasis the progressive conceptions of the "newer" theologies and brings them forward in ways that ensure their having a genuine effect upon the future life of the Church and future development of theology.

The Constitution represents the fruits of ecclesiastical self-reflection; it is record and formulation of the Church's thinking upon and defining itself. As such a document, brought forth in discussion and debate, it reflects the two overall tendencies which came into contact and conflict in the Council. Thus we may expect to find in it the reflection and record of the basic encounters of modernity and the older theological positions as they pertain to the idea of the Church itself. Six of these encounters to be seen in the Constitution invite consideration as an introduction to our analysis. They are the following:

1. The different and to some extent unharmonized conceptions of the Church found in the document;
2. The contrasting conceptions of the world with their implications for the Church's mission;
3. A new emphasis upon the dignity of the lay state and a new emphasis upon the priesthood of believers together with an older stress upon hierarchy and upon special clerical status as central to the Church's structure;
4. The new idea that all callings, worldly as well as religious, share equally in God's plan, as against the older special recognition of the formally religious and quasimonastic religious roles as central and exemplary;
5. The use of scriptural concepts in preference to the established scholastic vocabulary to describe the content of faith and the equally important reliance at certain junctures upon the scholastic conceptions; and
6. The expression of a genuine and enthusiastic ecumenicity and the endeavor to reconcile it with a reformed

8 Albert C. Outler, "A Response," in Walter M. Abbott, S. J. (gen. ed.) and Joseph Gallagher (trans. ed.), *The Documents of Vatican II* (New York: Guild Press, Inc., America Press, Association Press, 1966), p. 102.

9 George A. Lindbeck, "A Protestant Point of View," in John H. Miller, C.S.C., (ed.), *Vatican II: An Interfaith Appraisal,* p. 219.

version of the older exclusiveness of Catholic claims.

Let us examine each of these briefly.

1. Conceptions of the Church

The Catholic Church historically has seen itself as a sacramental entity mediating between God and man, a continuation of the incarnation of the Son of God, performing his high-priestly and mediating roles. (Journet gives a clear presentation of the Catholic theological understanding of the meaning of the Church.)[10] Its sacraments embody this mediation, especially that of the Holy Eucharist and its propaedeutic, Penance (Confession). The Church gives priority of status to and invests authority in the clergy, who rule, teach, celebrate the Eucharist, and administer the sacraments. It holds up the religious life under formal rules in separated communities as the more complete realization of the counsels of the gospel.

This idea of the Church evolved in a long history that began when Christians realized that the second coming of the Lord was not imminent. It is the consequence of a shift from chiliastic expectation to a more ontological understanding of man's relation to God, a shift to be seen within the canonical scriptures themselves, especially in the Fourth Gospel and the Epistle to the Hebrews. It is a shift whose seeds are already present, in the writings of Paul, alongside expectation of the Lord's return. It is an understanding of the Church generally accepted from the 2d century on, one fundamental to the medieval Church and confirmed and reasserted at Trent. It reached its

apotheosis of formulation at the First Vatican Council in the proclamation of Papal Infallibility.

In the background remained two other conceptions of the Church, both eminently scriptural but long allowed to lapse into secondary significance. It is these that the Constitution revived and gave both dogmatic and practical emphasis. Speaking of this Constitution, Julius Cardinal Doepfner, Archbishop of Munich, declared, "The Church is presented to us as the chosen people of God, with the men of every country and nation called to be her members; as the sign of salvation raised up in the world; as the Mystical Body of Christ, of which Our Lord, as Head, is the principle of life, working out salvation among men."[11]

The middle characterization of Cardinal Doepfner—the Church as the sign of salvation—refers to the classic conservative definition. The third—the Church as the Mystical Body, based upon the conceptions of St Paul—is capable of both a classic vertical interpretation to fit in with the definition presented above and a more historical understanding compatible with the revived synoptic conception. The Council put great emphasis upon the first definition—the Church as the Pilgrim People of God —and, after discussion, placed it in Chapter II, before the treatment of the hierarchical structure and the episcopate. Moreover, it is to be noted that the Council document treats the doctrine of the Mystical Body rather differently from the way the encyclical of Pius XII had treated it.

None of these interpretations of the character of the Church is made primary over or fundamental to the other two in the Constitution. No

---

10 Charles Journet, *The Church of the Word Incarnate* (A. H. C. Downes, trans.) (New York: Sheed & Ward, 1955).

11 *The Sixteen Documents of Vatican II*, p. 662.

doubt all three can be reconciled. Yet it is easier to reconcile the first and third and the second and third than to reconcile in depth the second and first. Between the older classic vertical conception of the Church as a mediating institution that continues the Incarnation and the revived biblical notion of the Pilgrim People there is an important difference of emphasis. The notion of the Mystical Body mediates between this contrast in emphasis, but this whole treatment of the Church opens up an important area of future conflict and discussion. There is here a great openness which calls for future theological development and will present ample occasion for dialogue and controversy.

2. Conceptions of the World

The traditional Catholic understanding of the world was ontological rather than historical. Although, for over a millennium and a half, the biblical ideas of salvation history remained latently present, the dominant emphasis has been upon a two-story, metaphysically conceived reality. It was a world structured vertically in terms of time—*the here below,* and eternity—*the eternal now of the divine life of the Holy Trinity.* The Church mediated between these levels, providing through its sacraments by divine gratuity the Christian equivalent of Plato's path from the Cave to the Sun. This notion of the world and the classic conception of the Church as the sacrament of salvation fitted together with satisfying intellectual and aesthetic elegance. The Constitution introduces a historical notion of the World as the setting for the historical Pilgrim Church. Concomitant with the first and second understandings of the Church discussed above are these two conceptions of the world, one ontological and one historical. Fitting

the two together and exploring in depth the challenge of doing so offers a profound task for Catholic theology.

It is often overlooked by some critics of the Roman Church—often friendly Protestants, in fact—that a satisfying conception of the world, and not just a theological one, demands some putting together of history and ontology, as Professor Fackenheim has pointed out.[12] (In fact, there are those who see scholasticism as an example of unbiblical conceptions that have been brought into Christianity unwarrantedly. At the same time they overlook the ambiguities of neoorthodoxy. These people are behaving in a thoroughly biblical manner: they strain at gnats and swallow camels!)

Related to these conceptions of the Church and the world are different emphases upon the nature of the Church's mission in the world. Is salvation to be seen as a group concern or as an individual matter? The vertical conception of the Church and the two-story metaphysical world gave individual religiosity and individual salvation precedence. The revived historical conceptions of both Church and world give the matter a more sociological tone and therefore more of a group emphasis. Here too, an important area of openness is left over from the Council.

3. The Problems of Hierarchy— Collegiality and the Papacy—Clergy and Laity

The new collegiality represents a drawing back from the long-term trend of papal centralization. The

---

12 Emil L. Fackenheim, *Metaphysics and Historicity* (Milwaukee, Wis.: Marquette University Press, 1961), and "On the Self-Exposure of Faith to the Modern Secular World: Philosophical Reflections in the Light of Jewish Experience," *Daedalus* (Winter 1967), pp. 193–219.

relationship of the episcopal college and the pope, however, is left most ambiguous. A direct quotation from the Constitution will indicate the basic ambiguity:

The order of bishops is the successor to the college of the apostles in teaching authority and pastoral rule, or, rather, in the episcopal order the apostolic body continues without a break. Together with its head, the Roman Pontiff, and never without this Head, the episcopal order is the subject of supreme and full power over the universal Church [art 22].

Here indeed the structural contradiction expressed in the 1917 Code of Canon Law is continued. That code recognizes the bishops as the successors of the apostles with genuine authority. That is, they are ordinaries having authority by virtue of their episcopal office and not by virtue of its being delegated to them by the pope. At the same time, the pope also possesses direct and immediate authority in every diocese of the Church. He is not simply an *episcopus episcoporum* but if need be can exercise direct rule and exert direct jurisdiction in the diocese of every bishop. Although this ambiguity remains, the very establishment of a collegial body is important and tends to tilt the balance away from the centralizing proclivities of the past. Only time will tell how this will work out, and it will no doubt be the occasion of inner conflict.

The Constitution also contains new conceptions of the dignity of the laity and a new insistence upon the priesthood of believers, as well as the older conceptions of the special character of the clerical status. The layman is seen as truly part of the Church, and the action in the world of the lay person as a matter of true vocation involving an "engaging in temporal affairs and ordering them according to the plan of God" (art 31). "The apostolate of the laity is not, therefore, their participation in the apostolate of the hierarchy.... This is why the exercise of a secular profession, of intellectual and manual labor, of administrative, industrial or commercial activities, which are carried out according to God's will are, properly speaking, the apostolate of the laity."[13]

Yet alongside the new emphasis upon the role of the layman and the legitimacy of the secular, the older segregation of clerical and lay status and function remains. The Constitution speaks in a conservative manner of "the distinction which the Lord made between sacred ministers and the rest of the People of God" (art 32). Within the Church itself the laity can participate in the work of the Church properly so-called. This work is seen in quite conservative terms as the "apostolate of the hierarchy" (art 33 et passim). A reading of the document as a whole, however, reveals a considerable change in conception from that characteristic of older papal documents, which saw the laity acting in the world under clerical guidance and leadership. Pius XI, for example, regarded Catholic Action groups as the agencies of the layman's Christian vocation and as organs for "the participation and collaboration of the laity with the Apostolic Hierarchy."[14] Nevertheless, the position of the clergy within the Church remains basically unchanged

---

13 Gregory Baum, O.S.A., *De Ecclesia: The Constitution on the Church* (Glen Rock, N.J.: Paulist Press, Deus Books, 1965), p. 42.

14 Pius XI, "Non Abbiamo Bisogno" (On Catholic Action), in Gerard F. Yates (ed.), *Papal Thought on the State* (New York: Appleton-Century-Crofts, 1958), p. 54.

as far as this document goes. Lay people do

...have a definite role to play in the life of the Church, in liturgy, missionary movements, etc. They may even be called to exercise some functions that properly belong to priests or deacons, such as distributing holy communion in crowded churches. In this context the participation of the laity in the teaching and sanctifying office of Christ assumes its fullest meaning. Laymen may be true Christian teachers, but as teachers of the Gospel they remain dependent on the hierarchy; laymen may exercise an active role in the liturgy but, again, their activity in this area remains dependent on the hierarchy.[15]

However, the document also exhorts,

let sacred pastors recognize and promote the dignity as well as the responsibility of the layman in the Church. Let them willingly make use of his prudent advice. Let them confidently assign duties to him in the service of the Church, allowing him freedom and room for action. Further, let them encourage the layman so that he may undertake tasks on his own initiative. Attentively in Christ, let them consider with fatherly love the projects, suggestions, and desires proposed by the laity. Furthermore, let pastors respectfully acknowledge that just freedom which belongs to everyone in this earthly city [art 37].

The attempt to reconcile the traditional post-Tridentine position of the priest in the vertically conceived Church with the recognition of the priesthood of all believers in the Pilgrim People of God (art 10) reveals the dialectic between past and future characteristic of the Church's present position. Seen in the light of the general setting of the Council and the general overall thrust of its constitu-

tions and declarations, clearly the document has here a most important growing point. Events since the Council have shown vigorous lay action, and the new reality of a public opinion in the Church in America is apparent everywhere. The fact is that relation of the episcopate and the papacy and of the clergy and the laity is undergoing change. The basic changes in modern society are having and will have their effect upon this ancient element of Church organization.

4. Inner-Worldly Vocation as Against the Older Special Calling of the Religious

From what we have said above concerning the recognition of the vocation of the layman in the world and the legitimacy of secular pursuits as the genuinely Christian activity of the layman, it is plain that the Council represents the fruition of an important trend in modern Catholic life. It is a far cry from the older position set down in the Middle Ages by the great canonist Gratian, which recognized, as it were, two species of Christians—clerics and monks as against the laity (seen as inferior in Christian substance and function).[16]

The Constitution recognizes as "evident to everyone that all the faithful of Christ of whatever rank or status are called to the fullness of the Christian life and to the perfection of charity" (art 40). Further, it is stated that "in the various types and duties of life, one and the same holiness is cultivated by all who are moved by the Spirit of God, and who obey the voice of the Father, worshipping God the Father in spirit and in truth" (art

---

15 Baum, *De Ecclesia,* pp. 42–43.

16 Yves M. J. Congar, O.P., *Lay People in the Church* (Donald Attwater, trans.) (Westminster, Md.: The Newman Press, 1957), p. 41.

41). Yet this does not immediately alter in principle the older position.

The holiness of the Church is also fostered in a special way by the observance of the manifold counsels proposed in the gospel by our Lord to His disciples. Outstanding among them is that precious gift of divine grace which the Father gives to some men (cf. Mt. 19:11; 1 Cor. 7:7) so that by virginity, or celibacy, they can more easily devote their entire selves to God alone with undivided heart (cf. 1 Cor. 7:32–34). This total continence embraced on behalf of the kingdom of heaven has always been held in particular honor by the Church as a sign of charity and a stimulus toward it, as well as unique fountain of spiritual fertility in the world [art 42].

Moreover, the "evangelical counsels of chastity dedicated to God, poverty, and obedience are based upon the words and example of the Lord" (art 43). It is held that "the religious state by giving its members greater freedom from earthly cares more adequately manifests to all believers the presence of heavenly goods already possessed here below" (art 44). And through the religious, "the Church truly wishes to give an increasingly clearer revelation of Christ" (art 46).

5. The Use of Scriptural in Preference to Scholastic Categories of Formulation

The effects of renewed scriptural scholarship and the consequence of this scholarship upon the thinking of the more progressive theologians of the Roman Church is evident throughout the Constitution, as it is, indeed, in all the statements of the Council. The utilization of the categories of biblical thought—especially of what might be called "synoptic ideas"—is impressive; probably nothing superior to it is to be found in any Christian statement

from any communion. The scholastic notions of "nature" and "supernature" are not explicitly used at all, either in this document or in any other conciliar document.

Yet in a very important sense the constitution still rests upon and derives from important aspects of scholastic theology. After all, behind this document stand the dogmatic definitions of the ages. Perhaps it is in dealing with the bishops and collegiality in the third chapter, and in the discussion of the Blessed Virgin Mary, that the scriptural scholar will feel least comfortable, whether he be Catholic or Protestant. Nevertheless, the issues of Mariology are subordinated to the conception of the Church to a great extent, and the general treatment is certainly less bothersome to Protestants that the policies of Mariological aggrandizement of the past. In reading this, the Protestant, as Dr. Lindbeck put it, "is happy that the maximalist surge in progress up until 1950 has not been pushed farther."[17]

This section suggests several future problems. There is first of all the problem of relating together the scholastic and the biblical conceptions which we have seen in the definitions of the Church, of the World, and of the various callings of Christians. If in the past ontology did not do away with the importance of history, so now, it should be frequently recalled, the recognition of history will not of itself solve ontological problems. A second level of difficulty concerns what biblical scholarship tends to regard as the likely interpretations of the scripture and the use made of the scripture by theologians in the defense of dogma and tradition. The latter are

---

17 Lindbeck, "A Protestant Point of View," p. 223.

often seen in the light of a scholastic view of the world and understood in relation to scholastic categories. A third set of problems concerns the place of Mariology in the newly emphasized conception of salvation history and the relation of this to the older quasi-independent position the Blessed Virgin seemed to occupy in Catholic thought and popular piety.